BY PETER STARK

*Gallop Toward the Sun: Tecumseh and William Henry
Harrison's Struggle for the Destiny of a Nation*

*Astoria: John Jacob Astor
and Thomas Jefferson's Lost Pacific Empire*

*Young Washington: How Wilderness and War
Forged America's Founding Father*

*The Last Empty Places: A Journey
Through Blank Spots on the American Map*

*At the Mercy of the River: An Exploration of
the Last African Wilderness*

Last Breath: The Limits of Adventure

*Ring of Ice: True Tales of Adventure, Exploration,
and Arctic Life* (editor)

Winter Adventure: A Complete Guide to Winter Sports
(with Steven M. Krauzer)

Driving to Greenland

GALLOP TOWARD THE SUN*

—◆—

* A galloping horse—*Ne-kat-a-cush-e Ka-top-o-lin-to*—being driven westward toward the setting sun. (From Tecumseh Speech to Harrison, August 20, 1810)

GALLOP TOWARD THE SUN

Tecumseh *and* William Henry Harrison's
Struggle *for the* Destiny of a Nation

PETER STARK

RANDOM HOUSE
NEW YORK

Published in the United States by Random House, an imprint and
division of Penguin Random House LLC, New York.

RANDOM HOUSE and the HOUSE colophon are registered trademarks
of Penguin Random House LLC.

Image on page 49 used with permission of the artist, Scott Kiefer

Library of Congress Cataloging-in-Publication Data
Names: Stark, Peter, author
Title: Gallop toward the sun : Tecumseh and William Henry Harrison's struggle for the destiny
of a nation / Peter Stark.
Description: First edition. | New York : Random House, 2023. | Includes bibliographical
references and index.
Identifiers: LCCN 2023004922 (print) | LCCN 2023004923 (ebook) |
ISBN 9780593133613 (hardcover) | ISBN 9780593133620 (ebook)
Subjects: LCSH: Tecumseh's War, 1811–1817. | Tecumseh, Shawnee Chief, 1768–1813. |
Harrison, William Henry, 1773–1841. | Harrison, William Henry, 1773–1841—Relations with
Indians. | Indians of North America—Land tenure. | Indians of North America—Government
relations—1789–1869. | Northwest, Old—History.
Classification: LCC E83.812 .S73 2023 (print) | LCC E83.812 (ebook) |
DDC 977.004/97317—dc23/eng/20230315
LC record available at https://lccn.loc.gov/2023004922
LC ebook record available at https://lccn.loc.gov/2023004923

Printed in Canada on acid-free paper

randomhousebooks.com

9 8 7 6 5 4 3 2 1

First Edition

Book design by Jo Anne Metsch

To Indigenous Nations

Sell a country!? Why not sell the air, the great sea, as well as the earth? Did not the Great Spirit make them all for the use of his children?

—TECUMSEH, Shawnee chief

If it were not for the vicinity of the United States, he would perhaps be the founder of an empire that would rival in glory Mexico or Peru.

—WILLIAM HENRY HARRISON, future U.S. president

CONTENTS

Contents

LIST OF MAPS

AUTHOR'S NOTE

The English-language term for the original inhabitants of the continent now known as North America (itself a European term) has evolved over the last five centuries since permanent European colonists arrived. I have tried to use the current generally accepted terms for Indigenous Americans based in part on guidance from Native scholars.

With this guidance in mind, I've used the preferred terms of "Native," "Native American," and "Indigenous," understanding that they are not perfect terms themselves. "Indigenous" is also inclusive of Native Americans and First Nations in Canada. In historical references, I have tried to use the name of the individual tribal affiliation as much as possible, such as "a Shawnee hunter" rather than "a Native hunter." When referred to as a whole, the name of a tribe or nation is singular—in other words, "the Shawnee" (meaning the Shawnee tribe) not "the Shawnees." In the case of several bands existing within the same tribal group, the plural is used, such as "the Potawatomi tribes."

While these are the general guidelines followed in this book, there are exceptions. The term "Indian" has been widely used in the centuries since European contact by both Natives and non-natives alike. It continues to be used by Natives, especially those of an older generation, and in many institutional names, but is also considered somewhat outdated by some Native scholars.

As author, I've retained the use of "Indian" in some instances where it occurs in a specific historical context, quote, or name. Whatever shortcomings in this book in the use of terms are my responsibility alone, and not the result of any advice or editorial help I've received.

The reader should also note that in quoting historical documents, I've chosen to keep the original (and sometimes archaic) spelling intact where the meaning is obvious. In cases where a word or phrase is unintelligible to a modern reader, I've substituted the modern equivalent.

PROLOGUE

On a hot Wednesday afternoon in August 1810, Shawnee chief Tecumseh and his entourage of forty tribal chiefs swung their birchbark canoes toward the Wabash River's shore. Having paddled for two hundred miles among forests and prairies, they stepped with moccasined feet into a panorama of white gentility—the front lawn of the Indiana Territory's finest home, Grouseland, fronted by a pillared portico designed in the Virginia plantation style.

At this mansion-in-the-wilderness built by territorial governor William Henry Harrison, Tecumseh and his fellow chiefs intended to discuss treaty disputes. The meeting with Harrison, however, would soon escalate into an angry confrontation over contrary visions for North America's future, two diametrically opposed ways of life. In an atmosphere heavy with symbolism, the fate of much of the continent would be left hanging in the balance.

Approaching Grouseland from his canoe, Tecumseh spotted a row of chairs carefully arranged on the grass near the redbrick mansion's portico.

A new rail fence separated the lawn and chairs from the bank of the smooth-flowing river. He hesitated.

Watching from the portico, Harrison noticed Tecumseh pause. He dispatched Joseph Barron, his Shawnee-speaking interpreter, to summon the Native contingent forward. Tecumseh refused, indicating an open grove of walnut trees along the riverbank about one hundred yards from Grouseland's heavy front door. Granting the request, Harrison ordered the chairs and benches moved into the walnut grove.

A council fire was kindled to open the conference. Tecumseh's party—their faces painted red, black, and yellow, their heads plucked bald but for a warrior's topknot adorned with feathers—entered the circle, having left their firearms outside by prior agreement, although they still carried tomahawks, knives, and war clubs tucked into their belts. Twelve U.S. soldiers armed with muskets provided the guard for Governor Harrison and the other U.S. officials gathering near the council fire. Knowing from experience the discomfort of a soldier's uniform in hot weather, Harrison directed the lieutenant in charge to move the troops into the cool shade of a walnut tree.

The territory's judges and officers took their seats in the row of chairs serving as a dais. An armchair for Governor Harrison stood at its center. The warriors sat on the ground in a half circle, but Harrison offered Tecumseh a chair on the dais, alongside the other distinguished guests.

"It is the wish of the Great Father, the President of the United States, that you do so," said Governor Harrison who, many years in the future, would become that "great father" himself—the ninth U.S. president.

Tecumseh, witnesses reported, stood still. He gazed at the governor, briefly. Then he looked up and reached with his arm toward the sky.

"*My father?*" he replied dismissively. "The sun is *my* father—the earth is my mother—and on her bosom I will recline."

The effect was "electrical," reported witnesses. "For some moments, there was a perfect silence."

Although Tecumseh and Harrison had faced off at a distance during the Battle of Fallen Timbers, sixteen years earlier, they'd never spoken. Since that conflict, which had opened the land that is now Ohio to white settlers, each had risen to high command. Now in his early forties, Tecumseh had emerged as the powerful and persuasive leader of a movement unifying tribes across the continent's center—spanning from Lake Superior in the North to the Gulf of Mexico in the South, and from the Appalachians in the East to far out on the Great Plains in the West. Harrison, now in his midthirties, governed the sprawling Indiana Territory—a quarter-million square miles of land east of the Mississippi River. Encompassing an area the size of France, it was inhabited primarily by Indigenous people.

Each man single-mindedly strove to defend or impose his radically different vision on the heart of North America. This clash of competing imaginations had reached a pivotal moment. It could tilt toward Harrison's vision—a second wave of America's founding that rolled unstoppably westward by handing out cheap, abundant land to the small farmer, a step toward a truer democracy by giving the little guy the vote, but coming at the expense of Native American tribes.

Or it could pivot toward Tecumseh's vision—blossoming into a powerful tribal alliance that Tecumseh and his brother the Prophet had promised to their thousands of followers across the continent. Holding the land as one, the tribal confederacy would refuse to cede more territory to the U.S. government. Tecumseh's vision offered the Indigenous leadership its last, best hope to repel a relentless white onslaught bent on engulfing their ancestral lands and tearing up their ancestral cultures by the roots.

Wearing a dress uniform, with his officer's sword dangling at his side, Governor Harrison opened the council with an acknowledgment of Tecumseh's complaints and an offer to make amends. Two great warriors such as Tecumseh and himself, Harrison said, should be able to speak to each other frankly "under a clear sky, and in an open path." He sat down in his armchair as Tecumseh stood.

"*Brother!* I wish you to listen to me well," the Shawnee chief began in a clear strong voice. "I wish to reply to you more explicitly, as I think you do not clearly understand what I before said to you. I shall explain it again."*

He moved gracefully about the council circle in moccasins embroidered with porcupine quills and a fringed shirt and leggings of softened deerskin.

"You have taken our lands from us, and I do not see how we can remain at peace with you if you continue to do so."

As he detailed the tribes' complaints, the men were silent except for occasional sounds of assent from the gathered warriors. He concluded with both a plea and a warning. He asked Harrison to "take pity on all the red people." He warned that if white settlement continued to cross the boundary onto the lands in question, it will "produce great troubles among us." They didn't want war, Tecumseh insisted. But they were prepared to go to war if necessary.

He looked directly at Governor Harrison. "I wish you, Brother, to consider everything I have said is true." Then he sat down on the earth.

Rising from his armchair, Harrison justified his conduct, according to eyewitness accounts. There was "no foundation in fact" for the charges of "bad faith" made against the government. The governor could personally say in the presence of the Great Spirit that his own conduct "had been marked with kindness, and all his acts governed by honor, integrity and fair dealing." He had always been a friend of the red man. Tecumseh's

---

* Nations and tribes of eastern North America often framed their connections with one another in terms of family relationships, such as uncle, brother, or grandfather. These were terms of respect. When the French first arrived in North America, they adopted the role of a "father" who was expected to take care of his "children" by giving gifts and other privileges. A ceremonial term, "father" was then used by tribes to address the British and American powers who claimed North American lands and a patron relationship to the Indigenous people. In his opening words to Harrison, Tecumseh notably dismissed the notion that the U.S. president was his "Great Father."

assertions marked the first time in the governor's life that "his motives had been questioned" by any chief who cared about the truth.

Harrison returned to his chair, and Barron translated the governor's words from English into Shawnee. He had turned to the Miami and Potawatomi leaders to translate into their languages, when Tecumseh, sitting in the council circle, called out in Shawnee: "Tell him . . . HE LIES!"

The warriors began to stir.

Barron hesitated. He didn't want to offend Harrison and his visiting officials. He softened Tecumseh's words when he translated them into English, and delivered them to the officials with an apologetic tone.

But Tecumseh understood some English. Again, he angrily burst out at Barron in Shawnee. "No, no," Tecumseh insisted. "TELL HIM HE LIES."

It's easy today to think that, once the American Revolution was won and the British were ousted, a growing United States would inevitably push westward across the North American continent. All that remained were the details. America had felt a western destiny starting soon after those first landings at Jamestown and Plymouth when colonial adventurers heard the call of bounty and possibility from the vast, unknown lands beyond the Appalachian Mountains. The question became, How far? Where to draw the boundary of the newly created nation—The Ohio Valley? The Mississippi? The Pacific?—or whether to draw one at all. Hundreds of independent tribes and nations, however, stood in the way. Westward expansion was not at all a fait accompli.

Our usual national mythology has long celebrated a heroic westward push by pioneers who braved howling blizzards, ferocious beasts, and hostile tribes to build a nation spanning from sea to shining sea. Yet with time and distance from these events, Americans increasingly recognize that the nation's admirable pioneer spirit came at a tremendous cost in human life, and cultural and environmental destruction. Might the out-

come have been different had the choices that led to it not been so un-
thinking and haphazard? Many of the decisions that relentlessly propelled
America's westward thrust were not the result of considered debate.
Rather, they occurred in immediate reaction to events unfolding on the
frontier—deeply ingrained involuntary reflexes triggered by perceived
threats, whether real or imagined.

At other moments, the decisions that unleashed the westward thrust
and its destructive imperative occurred simply by default, or at the behest
of a few men acting secretly to fulfill their own visions and desires. Those
elite, educated, papery-white Founding Fathers were creating a "nation
of liberty," but for whom was never fully addressed. Native Americans got
a brief nod from Congress during the founding era—"utmost good faith
shall always be observed toward the Indians"—but massive land grabs by
self-enriching politicians and aggressive settlers had already distorted this
high-minded sentiment even before the quill pen scratched the parchment to record it.

In the years bridging the late 1700s and early 1800s, Congress did not
entangle itself with lengthy debates about the fate of Native tribes and
details of so-called treaties. Rather, much of substance was left in the
hands of the early presidents, who powerfully felt the nation's western
destiny, men like George Washington and Thomas Jefferson. Those
presidents, in turn, sat at desks hundreds or thousands of miles away and
relied on territorial officials and U.S. Indian agents to serve as their eyes
and ears on the borderlands where Native nations and westering settlers
collided.

Poised at the epicenter of the clash stood Tecumseh and William
Henry Harrison—literally face-to-face.

William Henry Harrison is often remembered as a footnote, the U.S.
president with the catchy campaign slogan "Tippecanoe and Tyler, too."
Or he is remembered as an answer in countless trivia games—the president with the shortest term. To remind people of his frontier experience,
he refused to wear a coat in the cold rain at his 1841 inauguration—or so

the story goes—then gave a two-hour speech, the longest in presidential history, caught pneumonia, and died.* But Harrison did as much as anyone to create the myth of the rugged American individual forged by the frontier. He also figured out how the U.S. government could sell land, inhabited by Indigenous people, at bargain prices and on credit to poor white settlers, jump-starting the machine that got western expansion rolling. There was a moment when the fate of the West hinged on him. This is how he should be remembered.

He portrayed himself as a hero to these poor white settlers who had pegged their hopes for a new life on claiming land out west, but, in doing so, he, and Thomas Jefferson, deliberately committed genocide to serve both their own ambitions and those of the young United States. Rather than permitting them to live on their homelands as they had for millennia, Harrison and Jefferson gave Native Americans a choice: Give up your lands and become like us or pick up and move. Or, should you choose to resist, fight us and die.†

Tecumseh's life, too, is unfamiliar to many Americans. They might remember his namesakes—affixed to an old Tecumseh-brand gasoline engine, or to the USS *Tecumseh* warship, or as the middle name of a famous Civil War general, William Tecumseh Sherman, whose father greatly admired the Shawnee chief. The name connotes power, strategy, and wisdom. Tecumseh stood as a giant among leaders of his era and remained so for many decades after his death. Many nineteenth-century

---

* The actual cause was probably typhoid from sewage-contaminated White House water.
† Article 2 of the United Nation's Convention on Genocide, adopted unanimously by the UN General Assembly in 1948 in the wake of the atrocities of World War II, defines "genocide" as:

Any of the following acts committed with intent to destroy, in whole or in part, a national, ethnic, racial or religious group, as such:
   (a) Killing members of the group;
   (b) Causing serious bodily or mental harm to members of the group;
   (c) Deliberately inflicting on the group conditions of life calculated to bring about its physical destruction in whole or in part;
   (d) Imposing measures intended to prevent births within the group;
   (e) Forcibly transferring children of the group to another group.

white historians ranked him as the greatest Native leader of the century, greater even than Crazy Horse, Sitting Bull, and Geronimo.

Tecumseh's stature grew from his impressive strategic thinking, his skill and bravery as a warrior, his eloquence, and his remarkable and far-ranging tribal diplomacy. He also possessed great warmth, a ready humor, and an empathy that set him apart from so many leaders, especially in the modern era, who are motivated by their own ambitions. Tecumseh was a visionary who blazed a new path in order to hold on to ancestral traditions and ways of life.

The contest between Tecumseh and Harrison that unfolded soon after the nation's founding—face-to-face, one against one—was the culmination of what early American historian Colin Calloway describes as "a war for America's heart and soul."

Had Tecumseh succeeded, America would be a very different—and perhaps far better—place. We still live with the consequences of that defining moment today.

PART I

CHAPTER 1

THE STRIPLING

A young woman sprinted ahead of the fleeing soldiers on the forest path, her long red hair streaming on the wind as if it were a banner urging them onward to escape their own destruction. As they ran, the soldiers flung their muskets into the underbrush, then their ammunition, their packs, uniforms, rations—anything to lighten their loads and speed their flight. They left behind the wounded who could not help themselves, but not before ensuring that each had a musket charged with powder and ball in order to sell his life as dearly as he could to the Native Americans. Or take his own on his own terms—before they took it for him with war clubs, knives, and tomahawks.

This was the scene that greeted eighteen-year-old William Henry Harrison as he stepped ashore from the Ohio River flatboat in November 1791 at the wilderness outpost known as Fort Washington—at present-day Cincinnati, Ohio. Survivors of the massacre—so humiliating that it never received a proper name in U.S. history—staggered out of the woods toward the fort wearing "clothing reduced to rags," as he described it years later. Their shocked faces and broken bearing showed "the Privations and Suffering encountered."

Young Ensign Harrison's stiff new uniform distinguished him from the survivors wearing shreds. The long blue coat with its scarlet lapels and epaulets draped awkwardly over his slight frame and gangly limbs. A long nose protruding from a long face weighted him with a gravity that bordered on melancholy. Yet Harrison was an earnest, energetic, and conscientious young man with an eye toward self-improvement. Both studious in the classroom and engaged in the outdoor world, he enjoyed the natural sciences and steeping himself in the classics. Nothing in his studies, however, had prepared him for the chaos and desperation of the massacre's survivors as they flung themselves into the muddy safety of Fort Washington's log stockade after a three-day, hundred-mile flight. Breaking into the outpost's casks of grog, they drank themselves into a stupor of oblivion and forgetfulness that stretched for days—they hoped forever.

Only months earlier, as a first-year student, he had walked the hushed corridors and reeking laboratories of the young nation's oldest medical school—the University of Pennsylvania School of Medicine. He was to be tutored by the celebrated Dr. Benjamin Rush, his father's old friend from the heady days of the Revolution. But Harrison had dropped out and left all that behind for this new life in the wilds. He had not felt a great deal of enthusiasm for extracting human blood in precise quantities, or measuring and weighing the copious discharges of other bodily fluids and excretions—sputum, vomit, urine, feces—emitted by patients left in his care. But such was the career his father had chosen for the seventeen-year-old "Master Billy." For a student training to be a "physic"—a doctor—following Dr. Rush's system of medicine, there was no end to the bodily fluids that had to be drawn and catalogued to restore the body's balance of "humors." Worse, it was all done indoors.[*]

---

[*] Dr. Rush was the inventor of the infamous "Thunderclapper Pills" used by the Lewis and Clark expedition in 1804–6 as a laxative of awe-inspiring power. With the toxic metal mercury as an active ingredient, the pills and the excretions they inspired made a significant contribu-

Harrison family fortunes had fallen since British troops had raided their Berkeley Plantation during the Revolutionary War, burned the family paintings, shot its cattle, and freed many of its enslaved people in retribution for the central role that William Henry's father, Virginia planter Benjamin Harrison V, had played in launching the Revolution. Profane in speech and Falstaffian in appetite, Benjamin V had proved helpful in lightening the mood at crucial moments during the rebels' deliberations. After presiding over the final debate of the Declaration of Independence during the Second Continental Congress, Benjamin V had come up to the signing table in the "silence and the gloom" that pervaded the hall that fateful morning in 1776. He famously cracked to Elbridge Gerry, the scrawny Massachusetts delegate lined up next to him: "I shall have a great advantage over you Mr. Gerry when we are all hung for what we are now doing. From the size and weight of my body I shall die in a few minutes, but from the lightness of your body you will dance in the air an hour or two before you are dead."

While he had escaped hanging, Benjamin V's finances were squeezed by the British pillaging of Berkeley. Benjamin V, like other eighteenth-century Virginia plantation owners, was part lord of a medieval fief and part corporate CEO of a complex enterprise, its fortunes swinging on the vagaries of weather, European tobacco prices, credit extended (or denied) by London agents, and other factors beyond his control. But during his long absences pursuing revolutionary politics, he could not track Berkeley's daily business affairs. The plantation's soil no longer sprouted the best crop after a century and a half of the voracious, nutrient-depleting needs of *Nicotiana tabacum*. The elder Harrison came to realize that meager profits from the tired lands of one of the oldest and most esteemed Virginia plantations would no longer sustain his family's lifestyle.

This problem had plagued Virginia planters since the early 1600s. While it could turn a good profit when sold through London merchants,

---

tion to the archaeological record, by allowing modern scientists to precisely locate Lewis and Clark's campsites on the basis of trace metals left in the expedition's latrine holes.

Northwest Territory, 1787

tobacco quickly exhausted the New World's soil. They usually solved this simply by acquiring more land deeper into the forest, clearing it with enslaved labor, and planting tobacco to start the process all over again. This cycle imprinted colonial Virginians with a "land hunger," as it was known, that lured them insatiably inland—westward—from the Atlantic Coast.

For his sons, though, he hoped to break the cycle. Rather than banking on tobacco's fickle needs, Benjamin V had specified a different career for each of his three sons. The eldest, Benjamin VI, apprenticed with a mercantile house, and the second, Carter, joined the Virginia bar. Youngest son Billy would attend medical school according to his father's wishes. Billy loved hunting and riding. He lacked the hulking presence of his meat-fed, wine-saturated old man, and was a good student, also unlike his father, who had argued with a College of William and Mary professor and quit. Decades later, William Henry described himself during his youth as just a "stripling"—"tall, thin, and puerile in his person."

Benjamin V died in 1791, from gout, the "rich man's disease" that particularly afflicted those who overindulged in red meat and drink. Nevertheless, Billy followed the plan and enrolled in medical school.

But it was not to be. Some weeks after his arrival in Philadelphia, Billy received a letter from his older brother Benjamin VI suggesting that Berkeley Plantation had fallen on hard times and the family inheritance might amount to less than expected. While Billy had inherited three thousand acres, overall the estate could not support his tuition, plus room and board, servants, horses, and other gentleman's expenses.

Billy Harrison wasted no time. He had just turned eighteen. Dr. Rush tried to persuade him to stay. But now his father was dead and his family lacked funds. In his mind, Billy was free. He considered his options. His father's old roommate from the Continental Congress, President George Washington, checked in to make sure his friend's son had employment possibilities. A Harrison relative, Edmund Randolph, offered him a job in the newly created U.S. Attorney General's office. Yet this new federal office seemed as claustrophobic as a medical lab. He wanted a life of action and adventure.

Patriotism had just then risen to a high pitch. The newborn nation had thrown off British rule a decade earlier, but now struggled to establish its western boundaries. In the peace treaty ending the Revolutionary War, Britain had ceded to the United States all its land claims from the Atlantic Coast one thousand miles westward to the Mississippi River while retaining its colony of Canada. Beyond the Mississippi, Spain claimed the massive stretch of western lands to the Pacific Coast. In an attempt to administer that newly acquired swath between the Appalachian Mountains and the Mississippi, Congress in 1787 designated much of it as the Northwest Territory. At the same time, Congress spelled out a step-by-step process for which pieces of it, as they reached certain population benchmarks, could be converted into states—a recipe for western growth of the nation.

Previously, the Appalachians had loomed as a geographical and political barrier that stymied would-be settlers. Years before the Revolution, the British had unrolled their map of the thirteen American colonies and inked a line along the mountain range's crest, known as the Proclamation Line of 1763, to prohibit colonial settlers from entering the Ohio wilderness and clashing with Native inhabitants. Gaining its independence from Britain, the infant republic drew no such line—at least at first. A breach quickly opened in the mountain barrier during and after the Revolution. Drawn by hunger for the rich lands beyond, swelling numbers of American settlers migrated from the Atlantic states over the Appalachian Mountains. The tribes who lived there, however, were not eager to see farmers clearing fields on their hunting grounds nor cows and pigs rooting in the forests. As one chief phrased it, the whites' livestock was "pissing in our springs."

Warned to stay away by tribal leaders, land surveyors and settlers came anyway. Soon horrific news accounts arrived in Philadelphia, New York, and Boston of the slaughtering, scalping, and capture of settler families beyond the mountains. Americans suspected the perfidious British of sneaking down from Canada and provoking Indigenous massacres of white settlers in order to prevent the rebellious United States from expanding to the west.

The young country had reached a crucial juncture. What would be its ultimate size? With its eastern boundary delineated by the Atlantic Ocean and its northern boundary by Canada and the Great Lakes, its demarcation to the west was blurred by the presence of Indigenous peoples. By creating the Northwest Territory in 1787, Congress attempted to take this matter in hand by clarifying (or attempting to) that the lands stretching to the Mississippi, as a whole, were part of U.S. territory. But Congress also stipulated that Native lands within the Northwest Territory's boundaries—which meant most of the territory's land at the time—must be respected as legally belonging to the tribes.

Congress's high-flown language in creating the Northwest Territory reflected the warm glow of the recent Revolution's human ideals: "Their lands and property shall never be taken from them without their consent; and, in their property, rights, and liberty, they shall never be invaded or disturbed"—but then came Congress's caveat, with profoundly destructive consequences for the next hundred years—"unless in just and lawful wars authorized by Congress."

Even before the Confederation Congress meeting at New York's City Hall expressed these noble thoughts in 1787 about the tribes, U.S. Indian agents working near the Great Lakes and over the Appalachians were busily engineering several land deals—soon to be infamous as the "conquest treaties." Typically in these sleight-of-hand exchanges, U.S. agents approached one tribe's chiefs or subchiefs and offered to pay them handsomely for a different tribe's homelands. The lopsided deals immediately drew the wrath of Native leaders, who adamantly opposed these transfers of Ohio Valley tribal lands to the United States.

But the settlers kept coming, and retaliatory attacks grew with the number of new arrivals. With U.S. authorities maintaining that the victims were legal settlers on legal U.S. property, something had to be done to stop it. The governor of the Northwest Territory, Arthur St. Clair, urged military action. In retribution for the attacks, President Washington in late 1790 sent troops under General Josiah Harmar into the Ohio wilderness to destroy Native villages. While managing to burn a few villages, Harmar's expedition suffered two costly ambushes and backtracked in humiliation. In the eyes of the nation's highest leader and its towering military hero, George Washington, this would not stand.

A few months later, in early 1791, President Washington asked Congress to authorize raising more troops to punish Native "banditti" beyond the mountains. The force would target the large cluster of Miami and Shawnee villages known as Kekionga along the Maumee and Auglaize rivers, which flow into Lake Erie in present-day northern Ohio. Governor St. Clair, a longtime acquaintance of Washington's from the Revolution and now a general, would command the military force.

At this very moment, having abandoned medical school, Billy Harrison just happened to be in Philadelphia at loose ends. With so much action and opportunity about to unfold on the western frontier, another of Benjamin V's old friends, the Revolutionary War hero Henry "Light-Horse Harry" Lee, suggested that Billy apply for an officer's commission in the recently expanded U.S. military.

This sounded more like the action and adventure he had in mind. Before Billy's appointed guardian, Philadelphia financier Robert Morris, could stop him, young Harrison rushed to apply. He fell well short of the twenty-year-old age requirement for an officer's commission, but Benjamin V's old friend George Washington personally signed the papers to make him an ensign—the lowest officer's rank. Family friends who had opposed his joining the military finally gave in, pointing to the opportunities that lay over the mountains. "You are going to a fine country," Morris advised him, "where, if you should leave the army, you may establish yourself to advantage."

And so the heir to one of America's oldest, most privileged, and aristocratic families of European descent left behind the husk of the old life and started fresh in new lands. The young man headed into the wilds carrying in his bags the tools with which he hoped to forge his path in the world—a work of Cicero's ancient philosophy, a book of rhetoric, and a deep familiarity with Julius Caesar's military victories. Still another tool to carve out his future, he hoped, would be the officer's sword hanging at his side.

One can imagine young William Henry Harrison's surprise, then, that just as he arrived at Fort Washington in November 1791, hundreds of battered, bloodstained, starving soldiers staggered out of the woods, along with those female camp followers who had managed to run fast enough. They represented the shattered remnants of General St. Clair's army who had survived an ambush by a combined force that would become known as the Western (or Northwestern) Confederacy—a large coalition of tribes led by Blue Jacket of the Shawnee, Little Turtle of the Miami, Buckongahelas of the Delaware, and others.

Harrison was taken aback. This primal chaos on the muddy Ohio riverbank did not at all resemble the new life in a "fine country" he thought he had signed up for.

Survivors eventually told a story of stunning arrogance on the part of the U.S. military, which overestimated its own abilities and underestimated the strength and strategy of the Native forces. Hacking a crude trail as it went, St. Clair's army of 2,300, consisting of 1,600 troops plus support personnel and camp followers, had departed from the main post at Fort Washington and traveled northward through damp autumn forests. Late in the day of November 3, 1791, the army had approached within a few dozen miles of Kekionga, where General St. Clair ordered a halt on a low bluff overlooking a small river that they didn't properly identify.

Atop this wooded bluff, they would lay out the main camp, fortify it, and use it as a secure outpost for further advances on Kekionga. He ordered the Kentucky militia to move forward, cross the river, and establish an advance camp on open prairie-and-forest terrain several hundred yards away. Some of St. Clair's subordinates and frontier fighters thought it a more defensible position than the main camp. But with his men exhausted and hungry as they waited for a baggage train of flour to catch up, St. Clair kept the main camp on the wooded bluff, where it was hemmed in by woods, logs, ravines, and other possible hiding places. Many of his obstreperous militiamen claimed they were too tired to build fortifications that night. St. Clair let it pass. The Native warriors seemed a long way off. They were not. Also out somewhere in the surroundings—it's not clear exactly where at that moment—was the young Shawnee warrior Tecumseh leading his own small band.

In the night, nervous sentries sensed movement in the dark forest, but their musket shots were met only by silence. A scouting party ventured a few miles out, and in the darkness exchanged fire with what they identified as a large Native presence. Apparently this report did not reach General St. Clair, who was suffering from a bad case of gout and had been carried for the last several days in a sling suspended between two horses. Yet he took the precaution of ordering troops to "lay on their arms" during the night in readiness for sudden action.

The main camp awakened in the predawn darkness to an early reveille—the military bugle-and-drum wake-up call. The troops were about to start work on the fortifications when an eerie, all-encompassing ringing sound rose from the woods and river bottom—like infinite horse bells ringing together, as a survivor described it. At the 250-man advance camp across the stream, dawn's first grays had lightened the prairie openings where the Kentucky militiamen spotted painted torsos flitting tree to tree, bush to bush. Several discharged their muskets at the torsos with no apparent effect. But an instant later a thunderous volley erupted from a semicircle of hidden warriors facing the advance camp's front, accompanied by "appalling yells from a thousand throats." Warriors with muskets and tomahawks, topknots and fiercely painted faces, leapt from hiding places and rushed at the advance camp. The 250 Kentucky militiamen took a quick look at their fast-approaching fate. Then they turned and ran.

The ambush had been sprung. The strategy worked perfectly.

With Shawnee, Delaware, and Miami warriors hard on their heels, the Kentucky militia sprinted through the brushy river bottom, smashed their way across the thinly frozen stream, and scrambled up the bluff and into St. Clair's main camp, all "helter skelter," in the words of a survivor. They didn't stop there. They bolted through the assembling lines of troops and out the rear of the main camp, seeking the crude road that could lead them ninety-seven miles back through wilderness to Fort Washington and safety. As they exited the camp's rear, however, hundreds of muskets erupted from behind trees and logs and bushes—borne

by Wyandots, Cherokees, Chippewas (also known as Ojibwes), Ottawas, Potawatomis, and Ohio Valley Iroquois.

Realizing they had no avenue of escape, the fleeing militia wheeled
about back into the main camp. They were surrounded. The combined
force of Blue Jacket, Little Turtle, and Buckongahelas had precisely coordinated their numbers to creep through the night and entirely circle
both camps. Now the net had closed. St. Clair's entire 2,300-person
outfit—officers, troops, militia, cooks, camp followers—was squeezed into
a few acres atop the wooded bluff, surrounded by 1,400 hidden warriors.
The once-bold army now resembled an enormous flock of flightless
ducks trapped together in a small pond.

The losses suffered by St. Clair's army in that single defeat on the
morning of November 4, 1791, were appalling. Out of approximately
1,600 troops, about 700 were killed and 300 were wounded, with 150 ci-
vilians either killed or wounded. Many of the women "camp followers"—
officers' wives, nurses, laundresses, prostitutes—did not survive. "The
ground was literally covered with the dead," recalled an officer. Lost, too,
were cannons and ammunition, ox teams and wagons, four hundred
horses and tents, twelve hundred muskets, drums, spades, axes, mattocks,
forges, medicine chests, beef, bread, and on and on. The few survivors
managed to escape only when, deep into the rout, General St. Clair ordered a contingent of troops to unexpectedly wheel and break through a
segment of the hidden Native line. This opened an exit out of the slaughter ground to the crude wilderness road for whomever still possessed the
power to flee. As his own fine horses were targeted by musket balls, General St. Clair barely escaped atop an old pack horse. He soon fell far behind his fleeing troops, like some pathetic Don Quixote in rusting armor
on his broken-down nag. His personal survival probably owed mainly to
the fact that—whether by chance or design—he wore undistinguished civilian dress that morning instead of a bright commander's uniform, thus
depriving Native marksmen of an easy-to-identify Target No. 1.

To this day it remains, by far, the worst massacre the U.S. Army ever suffered at the hands of Native warriors. Three times the number of U.S. troops died on this unsung morning than would die almost a century later at the Battle of the Little Bighorn, aka Custer's Last Stand. It was a loss so humiliating it has been largely swept under the rug of U.S. history with little recognition and without a proper name. Insofar as it is known, the massacre goes by the name "The Battle with No Name," "St. Clair's Defeat," "Battle of the Wabash," or—to the Indigenous victors—"The Battle of a Thousand Slain."

When he received the dispatches of the fatal encounter in the Ohio wilderness at the President's House in Philadelphia, George Washington raged behind closed parlor doors to his astounded private secretary, Tobias Lear, who had never before witnessed this version of his boss.

"Here on this very spot, I took leave of him," Lear recounted Washington saying about St. Clair, the president's voice rising to a shout and his body shaking with fury, "'You have your instructions,' I said . . . 'and will add but one word—*beware of a surprise*. I repeat it, *BEWARE OF A SURPRISE*.' . . . He went off with that as my last solemn warning thrown into his ears. And yet!! to suffer that army to be cut to pieces . . . the very thing I guarded him against!! O God, O God, he's worse than a murderer! . . . the blood of the slain is upon him—the curse of widows and orphans—the curse of Heaven."

After some terrible minutes, this great storm of emotion passed. Pulling himself together, he replaced the unperturbable mask of the wise and judicious leader. Lear recounted: "[He] at length said in an altered voice: 'This must not go beyond this room. . . . General St. Clair shall have justice. . . . I will receive him without displeasure; I will hear him without prejudice; he shall have full justice."

St. Clair received at least a partial measure of justice when Congress launched the nation's first-ever congressional investigation into the disaster, which largely exonerated the general himself and placed blame on lack of supplies and training. President Washington quietly asked for St. Clair's resignation from the army, then reappointed him to the civilian post he had previously held—governor of the Northwest Territory. But the crushing defeat shocked the young nation.

The American experiment had barely launched. When George Washington exploded at the news of St. Clair, so much remained uncertain—most pressingly, whether the experiment would work at all. The Revolutionary War had officially ended only eight years earlier. The signatures had barely dried on the U.S. Constitution, passed just four years earlier, and only in the last months had all the states ratified the first ten amendments—known as the Bill of Rights—guaranteeing freedom of speech, religion, assembly, and so on.

A great deal of tension existed (and still does) over how to balance the relationship between the states and the federal government. Many feared that a too-strong centralized government would simply revert into a monarchy, ruled by a hated king. Others realized that a central government must bind the states together, provide a coordinated foreign policy, and deal with interstate commerce and a national currency. Whether to keep a standing national military fostered a great deal of anxiety—it might be needed for defense from foreign enemies, but also carried the risk that a leader would wield an army for his own purposes against his own people, like the tyrants of Europe. Could individual state militias—working alone or together—defend the nation's interests?*

And now, the nation struggled to defend its western territory. If it couldn't even do that, how was it to defend itself against threats from Atlantic powers to the East? What were its chances of survival?

Washington made a critical choice in this fragile moment. He decided that he needed a real army under a hard-charging fighter to subdue the

---

* Within a few months of the crushing of St. Clair's army, and with Americans fearing that the Northwestern Indian Confederacy might bring war to the East, Congress passed the 1792 Militia Act giving the president emergency powers to call up state militias—"whenever the United States shall be invaded, or be in imminent danger of invasion from any foreign nation or Indian tribe." In certain circumstances, it also allowed the president to call up militias to put down insurrections against state or federal government, which later evolved into the 1807 Insurrection Act.

western tribes. He chose "Mad Anthony" Wayne, a hero of the Revolution, to lead it. Wayne had personally led a nighttime bayonet charge against British troops and earned his nickname for his aggressive temperament. In peacetime, he had fallen on hard luck as a Georgia rice planter—enduring malaria, heavy debt, and abandonment by his wife for his suspected infidelity. He won a U.S. House seat from Georgia in the 1790 election but was later ousted from Congress for voter fraud. Fighting Indians in the northwest wilderness may have appeared a wiser alternative than exposing himself to further risk from the dangerous charms of Savannah's social life.

Vain, egotistical, and driven, Mad Anthony emerged from retirement at his failing Georgia rice plantation and embarked on training a serious professional fighting force headquartered near Pittsburgh—the grandly named Legion of the United States. (Within a few years it would be rechristened with the name it carries to this day, the United States Army.) Soon after taking command, Wayne saw young Ensign Harrison's potential and promoted him to lieutenant.

Drilling the men endlessly in long-range marksmanship and up-close combat with broad swords and bayonets, Wayne assured recruits that fighting Native warriors would ultimately devolve to bloody, man-to-man, hand-to-hand combat—so they had better be ready for it. He would not allow a turn-and-run "helter skelter" debacle. He knew that another loss like St. Clair's could prove catastrophic to the barely formed United States.

Aware of his own reputation for boldness venturing into recklessness, he assured President Washington and Secretary of War Henry Knox that he would not commit the Legion of the United States to combat unnecessarily, "knowing the critical situation of our infant nation."

CHAPTER 2

MAD ANTHONY
AND LITTLE TURTLE

Mad Anthony's efforts to subdue the western tribes—to punish those "banditti," as Washington's secretary of war called them—would receive a great deal of help from an unexpected source. Events half a world away suddenly disrupted the stability of Europe. The shock waves then rolled across the Atlantic and reached deep into the Ohio wilderness.

The French Revolution, erupting in 1789, had crippled the power of Louis XVI. Triumphant French revolutionaries now wanted to export their political upheaval to other European countries. Hoping to retain some of his former power, the French king threw his support to the revolutionary factions targeting other kingdoms, and the monarch officially declared war against Austria and Leopold II. By the summer of 1792, the same time Mad Anthony took command of the Legion of the United States, cosmopolitan Paris had spiraled into a violent frenzy of war fever, political infighting, and purges—all heightened by the invention of the guillotine. Soon much of Europe, including Great Britain, had, in turn, declared war on France.

British war planners eyed the European continent and hoarded their military resources, preparing for what could become an epic struggle. It had been less than a decade since Britain's stinging defeat during the American Revolution. Great Britain had lost its thirteen colonies but still held Canada. It had not, however, come to terms with the upstart colonies-turned-states now beginning to elbow their way westward over the Appalachian Mountains into the vast midsection of North America on lands that Britain had recently possessed. To London authorities, it grew glaringly apparent that the United States could eventually control the heart of the continent—and pinch off the pipeline of wealth flowing to London.

Based out of Montreal, the Crown's beaver-fur trade extended from eastern Canada two thousand miles west to the Rocky Mountains, where British claims ended. Although it had ceded Great Lakes fur outposts to the United States, Britain was reluctant to abandon any of them. Even farther west, beyond Lake Superior, sturdy Highlander Scots managed remote fur posts supported by wilderness-savvy French-Canadian voyageurs and Indigenous hunters.[*] They dispatched the bundles of pelts via a swift network of freight canoes to Montreal and then by sailing ship to Europe, where furriers trimmed them into fashionable hats and robes for the Continent's elite. The British Empire would hate to see its spigot of "black gold" clogged by possible U.S. expansion northward.

---

[*] Canada had been a French colony until 1763 when Britain won it in the Seven Years' War, the most recent major shake-up of European powers. Much of the population of eastern Canada had (and still has) French ancestry.

Eastern North America and Proposed Indian Barrier State, c. 1782

Proposed Barrier State (based on French and British proposals at the close of the American Revolution)

HUDSON'S BAY

C A N A D A
(British)

Lake Superior

Lake Michigan

Lake Huron

L. Ontario

Lake Erie

Mississippi River

S P A N I S H   P O S S E S S I O N S

Mississippi River

(FORMERLY BRITISH)

Ohio River

NEW YORK

N.H.

MASS.

CONN.   R.I.

PENN.

N.J.

MD.

DEL.

VIRGINIA

NORTH CAROLINA

SOUTH CAROLINA

GEORGIA

F O R M E R   A M E R I C A N   C O L O N I E S

(UNITED STATES)

N O R T H   A T L A N T I C   O C E A N

G U L F   O F   M E X I C O

0   MILES   400

0   KILOMETERS   400

But how could Great Britain—facing the outbreak of war in Europe triggered by the French Revolution—stymie the U.S. westward push without risking full-on war in North America, too? Adept at playing the globe's continents like squares on a giant chess board, British strategists landed on what they called an "Indian barrier state." The crushing defeat of St. Clair's U.S. army in 1791 had shown the strength of Little Turtle and Blue Jacket's confederacy of tribes that had gathered at Kekionga to repel the Americans. The St. Clair debacle also laid bare the limits of U.S. power to control its western wilderness lands.

As proposed by British strategists, the Indian barrier state would extend north-south across the continent's middle like a great dam confining the U.S. population to the Eastern Seaboard. Neither under the control of Britain nor the United States, the Indian barrier state would remain open to trade (such as the lucrative fur trade) but closed to white settlement. Britain envisioned it as a giant no-man's-land beyond control of the United States and the empires of Europe as well as permanent homelands for Indian tribes.

The United States, however, had other plans for this great swath of the continent's heart. The western lands represented the young country's bank account, its nest egg for the future, a great pool of capital for the cash-strapped nation and the means for westward expansion. During the Revolution, states like Virginia and the federal government itself, lacking funds, had promised western lands to soldiers as compensation for their military service. Many prominent Americans held land investments in the West, some on disputed land. Not the least of the western land investors was President George Washington himself, who fiercely protected his own claims near Point Pleasant on the Ohio.

Under orders from President Washington and Secretary Knox, General Wayne trained 2,200 regular troops in Native warfare at his camp near Pittsburgh. If necessary, another 1,500 mounted Kentucky militia could supplement the regulars. Wayne then retraced General St. Clair's route of two years earlier—marching his troops from Fort Washington and the village of Cincinnati on the Ohio northwest toward the villages on the Maumee near Lake Erie. At a place they named Greenville, General Anthony had his troops erect one of a secure string of forts running deep into the wilderness. Another twenty miles farther, they gathered up the bleached bones and hundreds of skulls of St. Clair's former army and buried them, erecting another outpost on the haunted spot, optimistically named Fort Recovery.

Employing mounted scouts in every direction, Mad Anthony kept his army at the highest alert while marching deeper in the wilds. With axmen chopping the way for supply wagons, and troops marching in skinny columns that could weave through dense forest and bogs, General Wayne followed a compass bearing northwest like an explorer heading into unmapped regions of the Congo or Amazon.* Recently promoted to lieutenant and named an aide-de-camp to General Wayne was William Henry Harrison of Fort Washington, dashing about doing errands on his expensive new horse, "Fearnought"—a steed, as he proudly put it, of "great strength, activity & fleetness." The general's preparedness and watchfulness on this wilderness march deeply impressed the young aide-de-camp. The example would stay with him in the years ahead.

Mad Anthony moved so maddingly slowly that he tested the patience of certain factions of the Indian confederacy. As Wayne's army left Fort Washington, runners had gone out to distant tribes summoning them to gather at the Maumee villages. Meanwhile, British military parties ventured south from Canada and, in a show of British support for the Indian confederacy, built and manned a fort at the Maumee Rapids, even though its location violated Britain's peace treaty with the United States. The fort,

---

* The going got rough at times, as noted by twenty-four-year-old William Clark, who cut his teeth on this foray for the great western expedition he would undertake two decades later with Meriwether Lewis. According to Clark, the troops shoved through "intolerable thick woods & the earth covered with Snagley underwoods & almost impassible defiles."

in effect, could cover the confederacy's back. If Mad Anthony's army should drive the Native warriors back from the Maumee villages toward Lake Erie and Canada, Fort Maumee (also called Fort Miami) would serve as a backstop to reinforce the Western Confederacy to hold its ground.

But as the days passed, fractures appeared in the Indian confederacy over how to bring the fight to Mad Anthony. The two battle veterans Blue Jacket and Little Turtle strategized to loop around the rear of Wayne's army to cut his supply lines and escape route. Disagreeing were the Ottawa, Chippewa, and Potawatomi chiefs—from the "Three Fires" faction of the confederacy—who urged a quicker, more direct attack on Mad Anthony's forward base at Fort Recovery. (Tecumseh, then a twenty-six-year-old minor chief of a Shawnee war party, attended these deliberations, although his opinion remains unclear.) Blue Jacket and Little Turtle finally relented, concerned that the army's snail's-pace progress would send frustrated warriors back to their distant homes unless battle and its spoils came soon. Without artillery to breach the thick timber walls of Fort Recovery, however, the direct attack failed. As feared, the Three Fires chiefs and warriors returned home.

Blue Jacket and Little Turtle's confederacy quickly frayed. Little Turtle advocated negotiating with Wayne. "We have beaten the enemy twice, under separate commanders," he proclaimed in a war council. "We cannot expect the same good fortune always to attend us." But his fellow chiefs refused.

When Wayne caught up to the remains of the confederacy on August 20, 1794, Blue Jacket and Little Turtle brought only about five hundred warriors to battle against Wayne's 2,200 regulars and 1,500 mounted Kentucky militia. By then, in the face of Wayne's advancing army, the Native Americans had already abandoned their cluster of villages on the Maumee and Auglaize—this "grand emporium of hostile Indians of the West," as Wayne described it. They sent women and children from the villages north to presumed safety in an area beyond Fort Maumee, where the Maumee River empties into Lake Erie (today's

Toledo). The remaining war chiefs chose a spot to make a stand a few miles in front of the British fort amid a windstorm-flattened forest—a place they called Fallen Timbers—hoping the logs would entangle the hooves of mounted militia.

The deadfall did not hinder the horses enough to divert Wayne's army. It was less a battle than an intermittent flurry of shooting as troops advanced and warriors fell back. As musket smoke wafted from forest and meadows and the two sides recovered their dead—about forty each—the skirmish initially did not represent a clear victory for Mad Anthony's forces, nor a clear loss for Blue Jacket and Little Turtle. They could recover the confederacy to fight another day. And so the battle's decisive moment occurred not on the field but beneath the stockade walls of Fort Maumee. Several hundred Shawnee, Miami, Delaware, and Wyandot warriors, as well as some remaining Chippewas, Ottawas, and Potawatomis from the Three Fires, retreated to the British fort for refuge.

The fort's commander, Major William Campbell, may have anticipated better success by the Indian confederacy in turning back the Americans. He understood that if he now let the retreating warriors through the gates, he, too, might be caught trying to stave off Mad Anthony and his Legion of the United States from relentlessly breaking down his walls to get at the warriors inside. A battle between the United States and the British in a time of rising tensions could trigger another all-out war between the two nations in North America. Britain had just allied itself with Prussia, Spain, and others against France and its revolutionary fervor. Even for a great empire, it was too much to go to war in Europe and at the same time fight the United States in North America.

Major Campbell shouted down from the top of the stockade walls to the hundreds of warriors collecting at his gates.

"I cannot let you in! You are painted too much, my children!"

The gates of the fort remained shut fast against the warriors who had painted themselves for battle against U.S. troops. British support to create an Indian barrier state evaporated—at least for now.

General Wayne did not pursue the warriors as they retreated down the Maumee River toward its mouth at Lake Erie, where a thousand Shawnees and other tribes spent a difficult winter sustained by British handouts of pork, salt beef, and flour. Blue Jacket, especially, felt bitter about the British betrayal.

That winter, he approached Wayne to talk about a peace. A council was arranged to take place the following summer, 1795, at Fort Greenville. Many tribal leaders calculated that, lacking British help, they could win more in peace negotiations with the Americans than in further war against Mad Anthony—the "chief who never sleeps." Eleven hundred Natives and dozens of chiefs gathered at Fort Greenville that summer of 1795—from the Wyandot, Delaware, Shawnee, Ottawa, Chippewa, Potawatomi, Miami, Wea, Kickapoo, Piankeshaw, Kaskaskia, and Eel River tribes. The aging war leader Blue Jacket represented the Shawnee, as did Black Hoof and Red Pole. Gathering on grassy council meadows along Greenville Creek, General Wayne offered them peace and cash.

Specifically, Wayne proposed a onetime lump sum of $20,000 plus annual payments of $1,000 or $500 to each of the tribes. He sketched a zigzagging line on the map—soon to be known as the Greenville Treaty Line—that ran from Lake Erie down to the Ohio River, about three hundred miles. The twelve tribes would give more than twenty-five thousand square miles of Native lands to the "Thirteen Fires," as they called the United States in reference to the nation's original thirteen states (now up to fifteen). These were lands that lay to the *east* of the Greenville Treaty Line. (Today, this is the southern and eastern two-thirds of Ohio.) Much of it was Shawnee homelands, where they had established many of their main villages for decades. The Native tribes would retain rights to the lands *west* of the treaty line all the way to the Mississippi River—the boundary between American territory and Spain's claims.

"It will give infinite pleasure to General Washington, the Great Chief of the Fifteen Fires," announced General Wayne to the gathered chiefs, "when I inform him you have thrown the hatchet with so strong an arm, that it has reached the middle, and sunk to the bottom of the great lake, and that it is now so covered with sand, that it can never again be found."

Likewise, the Americans would throw their war hatchet into the center of the ocean. General Wayne promised that if the tribes caused no more trouble or violence, the United States would ensure their happiness. "I now deliver to you the wide and straight path to the Fifteen Fires, to be used by you and your posterity forever. So long as you continue to follow this road, so long will you continue to be a happy people."

With that, General Wayne presented the chiefs with a large beaded wampum belt embroidered with the abstract representation of a road, a symbol that encouraged tribes to abandon their traditional hunting-and-gathering culture and take up "civilization." This meant leaving off their seasonal migrations, settling in place, learning white American agriculture—farming—and selling the vast hunting grounds they would no longer need. In the eyes of Washington and other founders, tribes would quickly see the great superiority of white civilization. Plus, the government would offer the tribes a helping hand toward that goal. They could take treaty settlement money and convert it to farming equipment and farm animals to get them started. Attempting to convince Native hunters of the wisdom of this approach, Mad Anthony observed that farmers could produce a lot of meat quickly if they chose to raise hogs.

This, however, would become a crucial issue in the years ahead. What, then, if they did not want to give up their traditional ways and take up white American agriculture? And, what if they refused to sell their lands?

General Wayne cleverly worked the chiefs, playing them off one another. He promised to recognize chiefs who signed as the designated leaders of their people, and he promised to recognize certain tribes as holding certain lands. And he judiciously placed bribes. One went to Shawnee war chief Blue Jacket, for whom General Wayne promised to build a house and whom, under the table, General Wayne hired.

Blue Jacket agreed to take that "government road" and accept the U.S. offer contained in the treaty. This would draw the Greenville Line as the Indian-settler boundary, and tribes would relinquish lands on the settler side in exchange for annual payments. Little Turtle of the Miami, however, resisted the treaty.

"The print of my ancestors' houses are everywhere to be seen," proclaimed Little Turtle, referring to the earthen mounds, some sculpted into animals, that ancient peoples had built on these lands. To General Wayne's assertion that this Greenville Treaty was based on lands given over to the United States in an earlier treaty, at Fort Harmar in 1789, Little Turtle proclaimed that the faraway Iroquois (in today's upstate New York) had made that deal—not his people. "I beg leave to tell you, that I am entirely ignorant of what was done at that treaty."

William Henry was kept scrambling as an aide to Mad Anthony, supplying the specific tribes with food and drink as Indian hospitality demanded. With his good education and clear handwriting, Lieutenant Harrison was also given the task of copying the treaty several times over with his quill pen. By early August, almost all the chiefs—ninety of them, both minor and important—had agreed to sign.

General Wayne looped his signature on the long document inscribed on parchment with its ten articles and provisions—prisoner exchanges, amounts of compensation. It laid out the Greenville Treaty Line from Lake Erie down to the Ohio River (that zigzagging line, roughly bisecting today's Ohio). Article 4 made it clear that most of today's Upper Midwest—then called the Northwest Territory—still belonged to the tribes: "As the great means of rendering this peace strong and perpetual, the United States relinquish their claims to all other Indian lands, northward of the river Ohio, eastward of the Mississippi, and westward and southward of the Great Lakes." Another official who signed for the United States was Lieutenant William Henry Harrison.

Harrison biographer Robert M. Owens points out that those chiefs signing the treaty sharply disagreed among themselves over which tribe or band possessed which land. General Wayne had negotiated not with a unified Indian confederacy, Owens observes, but with fragmented and infighting groups of villages.

"As chiefs fought for scraps their father [the U.S. government] threw them, they made it easier for him to divide and conquer," Owens writes. "By not selling out one's allies, one risked missing out on valuable trade goods. A chief's authority with his own people rested to a great extent on his ability to be generous to them in distributing gifts."

General Wayne did not see an ethical problem when it came to exploiting the Native Americans' entirely different concepts of land ownership and leadership. In the Native American outlook, no individual or entity "owned" land. An individual could own personal items such as a robe or a bracelet, or trade goods like a musket or furs—"commodities," as modern economists call tradable items. For tribes like the Shawnee, however, the concept of land embraced the earth itself—not a commodity to trade or sell. To Shawnee leaders, the question "Who owns the land?" was like asking "Who owns the air?" The Great Spirit had given the land and things upon it for the use of all.

Tribal homelands existed—a region provided a "common resource" for the use of a particular tribe, as an economist might put it. "Yes, there were conflicts between neighboring tribes over which tribe could enjoy the fruits of the land," write Hans R. Isakson and Shauntreis Sproles in "A Brief History of Native American Land Ownership." But the level of conflict, they write, was not enough to warrant private land ownership in the European sense—those measured slices of the Earth's surface that humans monetarily valued, bought, and sold.

Once Europeans arrived in North America, tribal leaders, often under a great deal of pressure or threat of force, made their marks on legal documents that "sold" pieces of tribal homelands to white authorities in exchange for guns, gifts, or other payments. Even strong-armed treaties often acknowledged traditional uses, specifying that tribes retained their rights to hunting, fishing, and gathering, until white settlers officially claimed it.*

As with the differing concepts of land, tribal leadership was usually dispersed compared to the white and European pattern of centralized government. Among the Shawnee and similar groups, tribes embraced smaller units, or bands, while clans existed within family lineages. All had their own leaders, or councils of leaders. They worked largely on a consensus style of leadership, discussing a matter before coming together on a decision. While some leadership positions passed down through families, most leaders arose by earning the respect of tribal members.

It was difficult to describe to outsiders the supremacy of leaders among the Shawnee, noted a Shawnee who had grown up among his tribe in the mid-1800s and then received a formal white education. "Although we were absolutely democratic . . . we accorded to our leaders and chiefs a deference that was spontaneous," recalled Gay-nwaw-piah-si-ka (or Thomas Wildcat Alford) in a memoir of his Shawnee boyhood. "Once a man established his reputation for bravery, for wisdom and discretion, he became an object of admiration and confidence."

Within the intricate web of interwoven tribes, these concepts, together, maintained a certain equilibrium. Tribes embraced a communal sharing of the earth—despite conflicts that arose—and understood that a tribe could have multiple leaders whose influence grew out of respect they earned. The European arrival in North America, however, left tribes vulnerable to white outsiders who, for their own purposes and often by force, foisted on Native nations their own centralized systems of govern-

---

* Today, as a result of treaties like these, tribal hunting and fishing rights remain political flashpoints in regions of the United States, such as the controversy over whether to remove irrigation and hydroelectric dams built in the 1930s, '40s, and '50s on the Columbia River and its tributaries. Removing the dams would allow salmon to swim freely once again from the Pacific Ocean to their upriver spawning beds and help them rebound from just a few thousand for some species to their former runs in the millions, which had provided a way of life for many Northwestern tribes.

ment and commodified notion of land ownership. By deftly wielding these imported tools, whites discovered they could leverage one tribe against another and claim that they did so legally and even fairly.

"It became increasingly acceptable," writes Owens, "to pay one tribe for another's lands."

General Wayne, like white negotiators before him and after, embraced this tried-and-true formula to acquire Native lands. Several days after Blue Jacket had agreed to Wayne's offer, Little Turtle of the Miami, despite his earlier resistance, made his mark on the treaty. Rival chiefs had gained prestige by signing and winning recognition of their status by the U.S government. If he didn't sign, it could lessen his influence among his own people.

Mad Anthony's magic formula for Native land acquisition had worked. The lesson was not lost on young Lieutenant Harrison. The violent twenty-year-long land dispute now was considered a resolved matter by U.S. officials and nearly one hundred leaders of bands from the Wyandot, Delaware, Shawnee, Miami, Ottawa, Chippewa, Potawatomi, and other tribes. The treaty permanently drew the zigzagging line from Lake Erie to Cincinnati that marked where white settlement ended. Here, at the Greenville Line, the government formally recognized that Native lands began and extended many hundreds of miles to the Mississippi River and Lake Superior—the international western boundaries of the United States.

One young Shawnee war chief, however, sat out the Greenville Treaty negotiations. The final document did not bear Tecumseh's mark. Although he remained neutral in this settlement, in the years ahead he would acknowledge and respect the line. It was only after repeated and flagrant white violations of the Greenville Line's sanctity that Tecumseh's neutrality ended.

CHAPTER 3

FAMILY HONOR

B esides peace, the great gathering at Fort Greenville in 1795 also brought unexpected reunions. Among the hundreds of Native Americans and uniformed officials, an old frontiersman showed up and gave his name as Isaac Ruddell. Fifteen years had passed since a 1780 Shawnee attack on the Kentucky settlement he had founded, Ruddell's Station. The war party had captured his two young sons—Abraham, age six, and Stephen, age twelve. The latter became an intimate companion of Tecumseh's and later wrote a detailed portrait of Tecumseh's youth.

That attack on Ruddell's Station fifteen years earlier was the last time father and sons had seen each other. The two Ruddell brothers attended the 1795 Greenville gathering as full-grown members of the Shawnee tribe while, unbeknownst to them, Ruddell senior had traveled to Greenville after hearing of possible prisoner exchanges.

According to Colonel Daniel Trabue, who witnessed the moment and recorded it in his journal, Isaac Ruddell was utterly stricken to see his now-grown sons painted, ornamented, and dressed as Shawnees. "Old Captain Ruddle cried out aloud, and fell down on the floor crying, and bewailing his condition. Said he, 'My children are Indians.' Stephen took hold of his Father, and said, 'Hold your heart, Father, hold your heart.'"

After the long-ago attack on Ruddell's Station, the Shawnee war party had brought the two captive Ruddell boys to the Shawnee villages on the Little Miami River where Tecumseh, then twelve, and his family lived. The captive brothers had passed the first Shawnee trial for toughness en route to the villages, which were located near today's Xenia, Ohio, about sixty miles from the Ohio River and Kentucky. Along the way, warriors in the party suddenly shoved the brothers over a steep embankment. They tumbled to the bottom, Stephen Ruddell later recounted, showing the alacrity to save themselves without a whimper. They passed. Captives who failed did not fare well.

Stephen Ruddell did not specifically describe his arrival at the Shaw-nee villages. An account by O. M. Spencer, another settler boy captured a few years later by Shawnee warriors, however, portrays a scene of cha-otic joy. The returning warriors waved poles like triumphant flag bearers in a parade to display dangling fresh scalps, scraped clean and stretched on hoops. The villagers who had remained behind—the Shawnee women, children, and elders—sat in a circle on the earth and on logs. A victorious warrior commanded the center and told the heroic story of the raid in the stentorian incantations of formal Shawnee oratory.

Reaching the climax, as the warrior acted out raising his tomahawk to split the enemy's skull, a shriveled old man suddenly pounced on the startled young captive O. M. Spencer and, with a shout, threw him to the ground. The elder proclaimed in a dramatic burst of speech illustrated by violent gestures that he had vanquished the enemy. All the women and children in the circle jumped up, screaming a long, piercing war cry, and gathered around the young white boy.

Weak and suffering from dysentery, Spencer was mercifully spared the traditional "running of the gauntlet," in which villagers would typically form two long rows, standing six or seven feet apart. On a signal, the captive would sprint between the rows for their entire length, sometimes three hundred yards, with arms raised to protect head and face as blows rained down on his back from Shawnees wielding sticks and other cudgels.

If the captive was a young boy, the warriors would withdraw and only Shawnee women and children would deliver the blows. If older, the boy would receive the full force of the welcoming ceremony. An eighteen-year-old Pennsylvanian, James Smith, described in a memoir how he was "flogged the whole way" down the gauntlet and, taking a heavy blow toward the end, staggered and fell, blinded by sand kicked in his eyes, and lost consciousness with a last thought that if they were going to kill him, he wished they would hurry up about it.

Later, a Shawnee who spoke some English helpfully explained to the battered and recovering Smith that this custom was a tribal greeting, the equivalent of saying to the captive, "How do you do?" He would now receive good treatment and full adoption into the tribe. As Smith was of age to be a warrior, he was ritually stripped of his old identity, his hairs plucked by an elder with ashes on his fingers for better grip until his bald head sported only a warrior's topknot, his body pierced, ornamented, and painted, then immersed by women in the river to baptize him as a full-fledged member of the tribe. (He thought the women planned to drown him until they started laughing at his struggles.) Like other captives in this tribal tradition, Smith replaced a fallen warrior or a child who had died.

"My son," the chief explained, "we are now under the same obligations to love, support and defend you."

Stephen Ruddell would stay in this strange new world of the Shawnee for fifteen years. His younger brother Abraham never crossed back to the white world he had left behind. When he eventually reemerged, Stephen recorded his memories of his and Tecumseh's shared youth. Few other written sources exist for Tecumseh's early years.

Tecumseh himself didn't leave a written memoir or "as told to" biography. The Shawnee people preserved their past in stories told around campfires and in lodges over generations. Inscribed on the page, we have memoirs by white men who knew him, early newspaper accounts, letters, diaries, and reports by travelers, settlers, government agents, and military officers. We also have some of his magnificent oration, recorded almost word for word. The early histories of the era portray Tecumseh in his adulthood—as enemy or hero, or not quite either. The captive Ruddell, however, grew as close as a brother to Tecumseh. His reminiscences give us the most intimate look at Tecumseh's passage from boyhood to young warrior to emerging leader.

"I consider him a very great, as well as a very good man," remembered Ruddell, many years later.

Tecumseh and Stephen Ruddell became "inseparable," as Ruddell put it. With his adoption, Stephen received the Shawnee name Sinnamatha—"Big Fish." He and Tecumseh played together, trained as warriors together, and taught each other their native tongues, although Ruddell eventually lost much of his English. They learned how to hunt, to shoot arrows with deadly accuracy, to throw a tomahawk, to wield a knife and war club, and to hide from pursuing enemies by entirely submersing themselves in a river with only a bit of their nostrils protruding above the water's surface like a twig or weed.

Even the games played by Shawnee boys trained them to become great warriors and skilled hunters, recalled Shawnee memoirist and Tecumseh descendant Thomas Wildcat Alford. While his full Shawnee name was Gay-nwaw-piah-si-ka (or, as he translated it, "One of a long following or file, such as the leader of a drove of wild horses"), his family called him Gay-nwah for short. Coming of age in the mid-nineteenth century in what's now Oklahoma, Gay-nwah eventually received a formal education in the East, taking the English name Thomas Wildcat Alford. His memoir *Civilization* survives as a rare firsthand account of traditional Shawnee ways dating back to an era not far removed from the time of Tecumseh, whom Alford claimed as great-grandfather.

The boys would bend a grapevine into a round hoop, Alford recounted, and weave the center with soft, tough strips of bark to create a solid disk. Separating into two teams, they rolled the disk between them, the young contestants unleashing their arrows at this difficult moving target—not unlike a fleeing deer or sprinting enemy warrior. Whichever boy drilled his arrow into the center of the spinning disk claimed victory. He then reaped the spoils of the vanquished team by throwing the disk, Frisbee-like, at an arrangement of their arrows that the losers had stuck upright in the ground. The victor could claim whatever arrows he knocked down, like so many defeated enemy fighters. Much of Shawnee boyhood focused on attaining exalted warrior status as an adult.

A well-rounded education for a young male, Alford recalled, meant gaining knowledge of warfare, tribal history, wild creatures, trees, wild plants, and fruits, and judging weather and foretelling seasons—knowledge that demanded keen observation, a good memory, and close application. "Endurance and self-control were taught so rigidly," observed Alford, "that these qualities had become a part of Indian character."

He recalled with perfect clarity the moment when his father determined he was mature enough for his formal training to begin. With autumn's first frost, his father addressed him early that morning.

"Gay-nwah, take off your shirt and run down to the creek and jump into the water."

"It made me shiver to think of the cold plunge," Alford recalled, "but I never thought of disobeying him, for very well I knew that father had begun to train me to be a man, a brave—possibly a chief. Pride filled my heart!"

He jumped into the frigid creek every morning that winter, sometimes breaking the ice on the surface, until one morning his father told him to jump in four times. After the fourth plunge, he was to grasp the first object to come into contact with his cold-stiffened hand and hold it up to his father for interpretation. Whether feather, leaf, shell, or horsehair, this would reveal his o-pah-wa-ka—the source of his guidance and blessing from the Great Spirit.

In the same manner as Gay-nwah, Shawnee boys like Tecumseh and Big Fish Ruddell learned self-reliance and performance under pressure—or suffered the consequences. In a ritual that occurred about the age of ten, Alford described how the elders rubbed a Shawnee boy's face with black charcoal and sent him out with neither food nor assistance—only a bow and arrow to hunt a small animal such as a squirrel, rabbit, or bird.

"It took me two days to kill the quail my father had sent me out to bring home," he remembered of his test. "After wandering for hours without food, my aim was not steady, and there is something in feeling that so much depends on one's efforts—that a test is being made." When his arrow finally brought down a quail, he swelled with joy and pride returning home with the prize to a family that waited and watched for him. "An Indian boy automatically went on with his own training after such tests," observed Alford, "encouraged and urged on by his father, his friends, and members of his clan."

Training this rigorous and at so young an age rendered them tough to the extreme—a quality that the Shawnee prized. They became great warriors, hunters, and travelers who roamed up and down the entire midsection of the continent. "They are Stout, Bold, Cunning, and the greatest Travellers in America," wrote U.S. Indian agent Edmond Atkin in 1754.

At those seasons when deer fattened and corn ripened and nuts fell to the forest floor, however, the life of the Shawnee people offered an abundance and ease, feasting, storytelling, and dance. They loved games of all sorts—throwing black-and-white dice made of antler, foot races and hunting challenges, and a raucous Shawnee ball game that pitted village men against village women, a kind of blend of rugby and soccer where women could use hands and feet to carry the ball and score a goal, but men feet only.

The elders imbued the youth with a strict ethic of generosity and honesty toward one another and respect for their elders. "Each person was his own judge," Alford said. Rarely was force needed to ensure good behavior. A Shawnee adage embodied the code of conduct: "Do not kill or injure your neighbor," translates Alford, "for it is not him that you injure, you injure yourself. But do good for him, therefore add to his days of happiness as you add to your own."[*]

The accumulation of land or other property, unlike in Old Europe or colonial Virginia, did not represent personal freedom to the Shawnee and other tribes because an individual could not own it. Rather, they placed great importance on sharing goods that came into one's possession as a matter of honor, integrity, and courtesy.

When Shawnee hunters went out together or met each other in the forest, recounted Gay-nwah, the first hunter to kill or trap an animal always offered it to the other, saying "Gi tap-il-wa-ha-la," meaning "I enliven your spirit." The other graciously accepted the offered game, replying "Ni-ya-wa," "I thank you."

It took white captives by surprise to realize how profoundly generosity and sharing—reciprocity—figured in tribal life compared to the distant white world.

"You have behaved just like a Dutchman," an elder rebuked another white adoptee who had neglected to serve prized bear fat and maple sugar to a visiting hunter. "Do you not know that when strangers come to our camp, we ought always to give them the best that we have?" The elder said he could excuse the adoptee, because he was still young. "But," recounted the adoptee, "I must learn to behave like a warrior, and do great things, and never be found in any such little actions."

By implication, in the elder's view, the "Dutchman" (a Pennsylvania German or a white settler generally) cared mainly about accumulating

---

[*] Alford rendered the Shawnee language version of this adage as "Tagi nsi walr mvci-lutvwi mr-pvyaci-grlahkv, xvga mytv inv gi mvci-lutvwv, gi mvci-ludr-geiv gelv. Walv uwas-panvsi inv, wa-ciganv-hi gi gol-utvwv u kvgesakv-namv manwi-lanvwawewa yasi golutv-mvni geyrgi."

and keeping things for himself, rather than sharing. Ultimately, the deeply different ethic of these two cultures would collide over contrary views of the earth itself and humanity's relation to it.

Tecumseh's father, Puckeshinwa, died in 1774 when the boy was six. In early October of that year, Puckeshinwa had left the Shawnee villages near Chillicothe (today's southern Ohio) with six hundred warriors. They planned to slip across the Ohio River (the Eagle River, as they knew it) on rafts, and, at dawn, ambush a large force of British Virginian soldiers encamped on the Kentucky riverbank.

The Shawnee attack was, in fact, a defensive measure against the trickle of whites from the British colonies on the Atlantic Coast that flowed westward over the Appalachian Mountains—initially for animal pelts, then for the rich soils. Led by Virginia "longhunters" like Daniel Boone, they discovered the fertile bluegrass prairies and hardwood forests of the traditional Cherokee and Shawnee hunting grounds that they called Kentucky.

Almost immediately, conflicts erupted. Few and secretive at first, the intruding white hunters detected by the tribes had their furs confiscated and were sent packing back over the Appalachians to the British coastal colonies. Once cracked open, however, the door to the Kentucky country was extremely hard to shut.

London foreign secretaries had tried to lock that door a decade earlier, in 1763, when they drew their "Proclamation Line" down the Appalachian crest—soon to be violated by land-hungry settlers. Likewise pressing against the Proclamation Line, wealthy British and Virginians who speculated in western lands (including the outraged young plantation owner George Washington) felt Britain's policy deprived them of their property rights. British authorities caved to speculator outrage and shoved the Proclamation Line westward—up to several hundred miles in places—by engineering several dubious "treaties" with tribes (or their purported representatives) that "purchased" tribal lands beyond the mountains. In the eyes of the white men, this alleged deal opened much of the Kentucky country to settlement.

Some Cherokees who hunted there accepted the new arrangement. Others fiercely opposed it. Virtually all of the Shawnee people adamantly rejected the notion that white settlers had a right to farm Kentucky.*

The Shawnee leaders made it very clear: *Send no surveyors.*

But teams of surveyors rushed into the Kentucky country in early 1774. Predictably, violence erupted. Virginia's colonial governor, Lord Dunmore, ordered troops raised to teach the Shawnees a lesson. About one thousand colonial soldiers camped in Kentucky on a bucolic plain along the Ohio River called Point Pleasant by the white men who coveted it. They planned to cross the Ohio and attack the Shawnee villages on the far side. Instead, Shawnee warriors, with Tecumseh's father among them, silently crossed the darkened river on log rafts, and launched a preemptive ambush.

The Battle of Point Pleasant—aka the Battle of Kanawha River—ended in a stalemate. (The Shawnees retreated, and the Virginians suffered greater losses.) But as the Virginians, supplemented by reinforcements, continued their march toward the Shawnee villages, Shawnee chief Cornstalk, who had led the warriors into battle, made peace with Lord Dunmore. Cornstalk conceded that Virginians could settle the lands south of the Ohio—the Kentucky country. Many of his fellow Shawnee chiefs, however, passionately opposed Cornstalk's land concession to Virginia's

---

* The so-called Treaty of Fort Stanwix (1768) was signed at a British fort seven hundred miles away from Kentucky in today's Upstate New York by British agents and Iroquois chiefs. The Iroquois (who lived in that upper New York region) claimed to have conquered the Cherokee in the Kentucky region in battle a century earlier. Therefore, the Iroquois chiefs contended, they had the right to dispose of the Kentucky country however they wished, which they did for £10,000.

British governor. Besides the traditional Shawnee hunting grounds in Kentucky, another casualty of the battle was Tecumseh's father, Puckeshinwa, a respected warrior and chief.

As the family story was handed down and recorded by Stephen Ruddell and others, Puckeshinwa, his life ebbing away on the Ohio riverbank, summoned his eldest son, Chiksika, a fourteen-year-old trainee observing the battle. He elicited a promise from the boy that Chiksika carried back to the Shawnee villages on the Scioto River at Chillicothe, where his mother, now pregnant with triplets, and her other children, among them six-year-old Tecumseh, expected a triumphant return of the Shawnee war party.

Chiksika promised his father that he would train his younger brothers well to be Shawnee warriors. He would train them to fight with bravery. He would teach them to uphold the family honor. And he would tell them never to accept peace from the Big Knives.

Cornstalk's diplomacy after the 1774 Battle of Point Pleasant did not end war in Kentucky. Four years later, in September 1778, Shawnee warriors laid siege to the fortified Kentucky settlement of Boonesborough.* The Shawnees finally gave up after nine days and crossed back over the Ohio. It was in retaliation for the Siege of Boonesborough, however, that several hundred mounted Kentuckians launched a midnight surprise attack on a Chillicothe village. As the horsemen dashed about in the darkness shooting into wigwams and torching cornfields, Methoataske and her young children, including Tecumseh, huddled terrified in the village longhouse.

---

* In a much-storied incident in American frontier history, Shawnee warriors had captured Daniel Boone a few months earlier while he gathered salt beyond Boonesborough's stockade walls and took him across the Ohio. At the Chillicothe villages, it is said, Chief Blackfish adopted Boone into the Shawnee tribe. Discovering that the Shawnees planned a raid on Boonesborough, Boone escaped Chillicothe and fled through the wilderness for five days to warn his fellow settlers of the impending attack.

Chief Blackfish and warriors returned fire until the Kentuckians galloped away into the night fearing that mounted warriors rushing from nearby villages might soon surround them.

Methoataske had had enough. She was not alone. With more than a thousand Shawnees she left Chillicothe on a western trek led by Yellow Hawk and Black Stump until, weeks later, they forded the Mississippi River and stepped onto lands claimed by the Spanish Crown. Here, among other tribes on the broad western landscapes, they hoped to live in peace beyond the vengeful Big Knives. Methoataske brought only her nine-year-old daughter on the journey west. She left Tecumseh and his younger twin brothers Lalawethika and Kumskaukau (the third triplet had died) at Chillicothe in the care of her elder daughter, Tecumpease, or "Flying Over the Water."

The Big Knives—Virginians and Kentuckians—had destroyed Tecumseh's family life. By age eleven, he'd lost both his father and his mother. The boy would stay in the Ohio Valley just as two great cultural storm systems were about to collide there—a clash that would shape the boy's life, the future values of a nation, and the destiny of much of the continent.

With his father killed in battle and his mother leaving for safer lands beyond the Mississippi, Tecumseh's education fell to his older brother, Chiksika, along with his older sister, Tecumpease, and her husband, Wahsikegaboe, or "Stands Firm." Tecumseh, sources say, had great respect for Tecumpease, who would become a female chief. Tecumseh's younger brother Lalawethika, "The Loud One," was proving notably inept and uninterested in hunting and warrior life. Tecumseh, however, embraced the Shawnee way, learning honorable and brave behavior in life and warfare from Chiksika, as their father had requested. Chiksika, noted Ruddell, "taught him to look with contempt upon everything that was mean." Tecumseh, he wrote, "was always remarkable from his boyhood up for the dignity & rectitude of his deportment. There was a certain something in his countenance and manners that always commanded respect & at the same time made those about him love him. During his boyhood he used to place himself at the head of the youngsters and divide them, when he would make them fight sham battles, in which he always distinguished himself by his activity, strength & skill."

But at age fourteen Tecumseh failed his first test in combat. He joined older brother Chiksika in a raid on armed Kentuckians threatening the Shawnee villages on the Scioto River. A flurry of musket balls whizzed past. One grazed Chiksika, and blood gushed from the wound. A panicked Tecumseh fled through the forest.

He would have plenty more opportunities, however, to fight the white invaders.

A new pulse of settlers arrived soon after the Revolutionary War. As Britain handed over nearly half a continent, the peace treaty of 1783 mentioned not a word about Native rights or land claims, this despite London's earlier assurances to its allies "of every Support England could render Them."

Native leaders who had helped the British fight the Americans felt bitterly betrayed. "England," the Mohawk leader and British ally Joseph Brant proclaimed furiously, "sold the Indians to Congress."

Brant, looking to the future, understood that neither Britain nor the nascent United States would protect Native land rights if doing so clashed with their own interests. In turn, he passionately advocated for unity among tribes, and for them to agree to hold their lands in common—thus blocking U.S. strategies, writes John Sugden, "to play one tribe off against another in order to buy land." Brant and fellow chiefs metaphorically called this tribal sharing of lands "a dish with one spoon"—meaning many persons (that is, different tribes) sitting together to share a common meal from one great pot.

In response to tribal efforts to unify, the United States quickly made three flimsy treaties—those mentioned earlier, disparagingly called the conquest treaties of the 1780s—in a land grab that played one tribe off

another, just as Brant had feared. The U.S. government pressured individual Wyandot, Delaware, Ottawa, and Chippewa leaders by allowing
them to keep their own villages but insisting they sign away other lands.
While earlier treaties had given up the Kentucky hunting grounds against
fierce Shawnee opposition, now the combined conquest treaties relinquished the Ohio homelands of the Shawnee to the United States.

"We do not understand the measuring out of lands," protested one
Shawnee chief to U.S. agents. "It is all ours."

Offering a thin veneer of legality, the conquest treaties soon attracted
settlers to lands *north* of the Ohio River in addition to earlier dubious
deals that had opened Kentucky to settlement on the river's *south*. Within
just a few years, a huge hole had opened among Native lands—especially
Shawnee lands—in the continent's interior, and settlers rushed in to fill it.

Tecumseh's second chance at combat came soon enough as settler
flatboats drifted down the Ohio River in the late 1780s—sparsely at first,
then by clumps and handfuls, and finally like leaves blown onto the swirling current during an autumn storm. In his mid to late teens, Tecumseh
joined a war party to ambush settler flatboats swinging around a blind riv-
erbend by launching out of hiding with their own stolen flatboat. "In the
action Tecumthe behaved with great bravery," recounted Stephen Ruddell, who was present as a Shawnee adoptee.

Tecumseh distinguished himself far more remarkably after the raid,
however, when fellow warriors burned a flatboat captive alive—a common fate for captives among Eastern Woodland tribes. "[He] expressed
great abhorrence of the deed," remarked Ruddell, "and finally it was concluded among them not to burn any more prisoners that should after-
wards be taken, which was ever after strictly adhered to by him."

He would become famous for this trait—demonstrating fierceness in
combat but treating captives with kindness and warmth once the battle
had ended.

.   .   .

Following older brother Chiksika and his band, Tecumseh spent his late teens and early twenties in nearly perpetual wandering. Making an extended foray into the South, they joined up with the Chickamauga Cherokee—among the South's fiercest and most resilient warriors. Under their leader, Dragging Canoe, they had vehemently rejected earlier "treaties." They split off from Cherokee groups that had accepted the treaties to establish their own remote villages in rugged mountain-and-gorge terrain around Lookout Mountain (near today's Chattanooga, Tennessee).

From this base, they attacked parties of soldiers and settlers floating down southern rivers to stake farms in rich Tennessee and Kentucky hunting grounds. An apprentice in war tactics, Tecumseh studied the terrain in minute detail before placing his camps, slept half-awake propped near the fire, and kept at hand his favorite weapon—the war club, weapon of his ancestors. Now a Shawnee warrior himself, Stephen Ruddell recounted that it was extremely difficult to surprise Tecumseh or best his fierceness and tenacity in battle. In one incident, thirty Kentuckians led by legendary frontiersman Simon Kenton crept up at night on a small hunting party led by Tecumseh. Muzzles flashed in the darkness, aimed at wigwams and tents where the Shawnee hunters slept.

"Sinnamatha—Big Fish!" Tecumseh shouted to Ruddell as he leapt from his place near the fire wielding his war club. "Where are you?"

> "Here I am," says I.
> "You charge on that side and I will charge on this."
> With that he rushed on those on his side, knocked one in the head with his club and drove the rest back. . . . He was a man of great courage and conduct, perfectly fearless of danger.

Having won a fearsome reputation among whites in the Tennessee Valley as the "Shawnee Warrior," brother Chiksika died in a moonlight raid on a fortified settlement when the lowing of a cow betrayed him as he crept beneath its wall. In the darkness, Tecumseh recovered his beloved mentor's body. Chiksika had dreamed of his own death in the previous days but, despite the bad premonitions, insisted on carrying out the attack anyway, preferring his body to be left on the battlefield instead of retiring to a village life and a quiet death.

"[He said] that his father had fell gloriously in battle," recounted Ruddell, "that he considered it an honour to die in battle and that it was what he wished and did not wish to lie buried at home like an old squaw, to which he preferred that the fowls of the air should pick his bones."

Tecumseh honored the loss of his brother by stepping into a leadership role. In the South, Tecumseh gained his own small following of Shawnee warriors attracted to his skill in warfare and genial nature in peace. He proved "a very jovial companion, fond of cracking his jokes," Ruddell recalled. "The women were very fond of him, much more so than he was of them."

He married a Cherokee woman, a tribe with whom the Shawnee had long kept a close relationship. Tecumseh's mother, Methoataske, was Cherokee, according to some early accounts. Tecumseh and his wife settled along the swirling Tennessee River under Lookout Mountain and had a daughter. But a settled village life did not appeal to him, and, as Shawnee marriages were easily dissolved, his soon ended.

In April 1791, when Tecumseh was twenty-two, messengers brought word to the South that a unified force was gathering on the Maumee River, near Lake Erie, at the villages of chiefs Little Turtle of the Miami and Blue Jacket of the Shawnee, and others. Their Indian confederacy would target the next U.S. military incursion into Miami and Shawnee territory.

Tecumseh led an eight-warrior band north to join but apparently was off hunting or scouting on November 4, 1791, and missed the battle that shattered St. Clair's army. With their crushing victory in the Battle of a Thousand Slain, the tribes felt power in unity. Hopes swelled that the Indian confederacy under Little Turtle and Blue Jacket could protect the lands north of the Ohio—the Northwest Territory—from white settlement.

The moment, however, was quickly slipping past. Waving the flimsy "conquest treaties" like banners to lead the westward charge, land speculators purchased huge wedges from the U.S. government in today's eastern and southern Ohio. Settlers scurried along behind them eager to nibble tidbits from this great cake of dark soil. To support them, President Washington recruited Mad Anthony Wayne to build a new national military force, "the Legion of the United States."

For a year or two after St. Clair's 1791 debacle, and while Wayne trained his army, the United States made efforts to compromise with the tribes, at least in appearance. President Washington and Secretary Knox offered to negotiate boundary lines separating Natives and whites in return for frontier peace with Little Turtle and Blue Jacket's powerful tribal confederacy. Reaching out to Joseph Brant—the academy-educated Mohawk chief who straddled Native and white worlds—they invited him and other leaders to meet at the U.S. capital at Philadelphia. Brant returned from his meeting with the president proposing they negotiate a line of settlement. The crux, of course, was where? Both sides clung fiercely to lands they each believed they held in today's eastern and southern Ohio— claiming the same several million acres.

Behind the scenes, the U.S. government had determined to keep all lands already gained through the three conquest treaties of the 1780s. In the Native view, those treaties had cheated them out of their lands. In a clever rhetorical trick, Washington cautioned his negotiators not to speak of "buying" Indian lands. Rather, they should assure chiefs "that we want not a foot of their land," and wish only to respect existing treaties and keep illegal white settlers off Indian lands. In other words, the United States was not offering to give back conquest treaty lands, only to keep settlers off tribal lands that lay *beyond*. In effect, President Washington's "offer" changed nothing.

Joseph Brant suggested drawing the Muskingum River as the boundary between Indian lands and white settlement. This would give settlers the eastern one-third of today's Ohio, and lands to the west would remain in Indigenous hands. But Little Turtle's and Blue Jacket's Shawnee and Miami homelands sat in today's southern Ohio and parts of Indiana. They called out Joseph Brant.

"You chief Mohawk, what are you doing?" Little Turtle exhorted Brant. "Time was when you roused us to war. In a very short time you changed your voice & went to sleep."

Little Turtle, Blue Jacket, and their fellow chiefs would cede *no* land north of the Ohio River and rejected Brant's proposed settler lands in eastern Ohio. Nor did U.S. offers of money for contested lands sway tribal leaders. "You say [President Washington] will make us a compensation if our land was not purchased of the right owner," complained Chief Painted Pole. "We do not want compensation, we want restitution of our country they hold under false pretenses."

The Native consortium, including Wyandot, Chippewa, and other chiefs, came back with a counterproposal to U.S. agents in an April 1793 conference on the Sandusky River: The United States pay settlers to move off the contested lands north of the Ohio and restore it to the tribes, rather than vice versa. That proposal went nowhere. U.S. authorities expected negotiations to fail. They prepared for war.

"We regard this [north] side of the Ohio as our property," said a Wyandot chief through an interpreter to U.S. negotiators. "You say you cannot remove your people; & we cannot give our lands. We are sorry we cannot come to an agreement."

However, neither could the diffuse tribal leadership come to an agreement among themselves. This weakened their ability to negotiate with a centralized entity that could speak with a single voice—the U.S. government. On the U.S. side, negotiations served as a performance, as Thomas

Jefferson put it, "to prove to all our citizens that peace was unattainable on terms which any one of them would admit." In that self-justifying spirit, President Washington assured Congress that he and his people had done everything possible to find a peaceful compromise that would preserve "the essential interests and dignity of the United States."

As Colin Calloway puts it, Washington faulted the tribes for any impasse: "tribes intransigence, not American aggression, was to blame for the impending bloodshed."

Much intransigence, however, rested on the Americans—returning land to the tribes simply wasn't done.

"It would have been extraordinarily difficult for Americans to imagine giving up on the Ohio lands under any circumstances in the 1790s," notes Harrison biographer Robert M. Owens. Poor whites seeking a new life equated "land with liberty and sovereignty."

They would not lightly abandon their own precious piece of soil.

As negotiations predictably failed, Washington ordered Mad Anthony Wayne and his troops into action. They had been trained in expectation of this face-off with Little Turtle and Blue Jacket's confederacy. In late summer 1794, the general set three thousand men of the Legion of the United States marching from Fort Washington north toward the recalcitrant Maumee River villages to bend them to American will.

Tecumseh and his band of warriors joined the Native confederacy to confront the legion as it crawled forward like a giant caterpillar, spinning defensive outposts along the way, its scouts probing outward for danger in all directions. The allied tribes rallied about fifteen hundred warriors, but differences over strategy among the war chiefs (whether to meet Mad Anthony head-on or loop around and attack from behind) caused the confederacy to fracture, then nearly dissolve when many of its members returned to distant homes. This left only about five hundred warriors to fight Wayne's three thousand.

Tecumseh and his warriors held one end of the Native line at Fallen Timbers, but Wayne's organized onslaught finally drove them back to British Fort Maumee like the other warriors. Standing alongside hundreds of warriors still willing to fight for the confederacy, Tecumseh heard Major Campbell as he shouted down from the stockade walls to tell the painted warriors he would not open the gates to them.

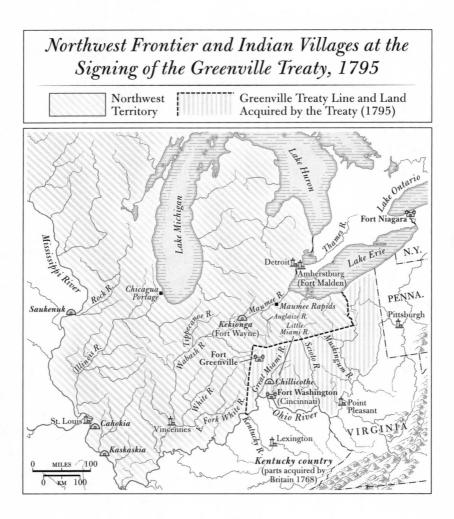

Northwest Frontier and Indian Villages at the Signing of the Greenville Treaty, 1795

| | Northwest Territory | | Greenville Treaty Line and Land Acquired by the Treaty (1795) |

CHAPTER 4

GROUSELAND

White settlers abused the Greenville Treaty boundary from the start. It took several years before the federal government surveyed the line dividing settlement lands from Indian country. In the meantime, Kentuckians forded the Ohio onto treaty-designated Native lands to slaughter herds of bison and other game. Other white settlers carrying axes over their shoulders strode past the unmarked line and chopped out homesteads on Native lands.

One Shawnee faction, however, welcomed white help. Black Hoof and fellow chiefs accepted that the white onrush had ended their hunting way of life, and founded a large village, Wapakoneta, near the headwaters of the Auglaize River, conveniently close to Fort Defiance. The Shawnees at Wapakoneta "took the government road"—meaning they received annual federal payments awarded to tribes who had signed the Greenville Treaty, had relinquished their land claims, and learned white farming methods. The Shawnees under Black Hoof also established a tribal council that could speak with a single voice to the U.S. government.

Tecumseh, however, did not wish to be part of that voice. He moved in the opposite direction—westward, toward traditional tribal life. He relocated his band fifty miles west of the settlers' Greenville Line along the upper White River (in today's central Indiana) at the invitation of the Miami, longtime inhabitants of the region. The Miami had invited other displaced tribes such as the Delaware (Lenape), who had been shoved inland for decades by white settlement that occupied their Atlantic Coast homelands.

Tecumseh's growing Shawnee band now counted about fifty warriors and 250 Shawnees total, among them older sister Tecumpease and her husband, and his younger twin brothers, the affable and skilled Kumskaukau and the poor hunter and boastful "Loud One," Lalawethika. Constructing a village of bark wigwams and planting cornfields in the rich river bottomlands, they attuned their village lives to the seasonal abundance of the White River. The Miami Indians called the river itself Wapahani—"White Sands." The new arrivals fished its waters that swam with everything from pike to paddlefish to eels to otters, gathered turtle eggs on its sandbars, harvested chestnuts and walnuts scattered on the forest floor, tapped maple trees laden with sugary sap, plucked vines bending with wild grapes, and savored bright, nutritious fruits such as persimmon.

A warrior without a war, Tecumseh now won honor and prestige as a superb and generous hunter and rising leader.

"He was particularly attentive to the aged and infirm," recalled Anthony Shane, an interpreter and messenger of French Canadian and Ottawa heritage, and his wife, Lameteshe, in a joint interview years later. "[He attended] personally to the comfort of their houses when winter approached, presenting them with skins for moccasins and clothing, and upon his return from a hunting party the old people in his neighborhood uniformly were presented the choicest game."

Like so many Shawnees—warriors and non-warriors, men and women, young and old—Tecumseh loved competition of all sorts, including stick games, football, and gambling, and happily indulged in a playful side that belied the fierce Indian reputation so heavily promoted by white settlers. On the upper White River, Tecumseh competed in a friendly, three-day hunting contest in which he bagged nearly three times as many deer as any other competitor—killing more than thirty. And he excelled in other Shawnee athletic contests. Frontiersmen later recalled Tecumseh wrestling in good fun in the snow with fellow warriors outside a cabin on a cold winter's night.

When times were good and food abundant, it could be an idyllic life.

"[Tecumseh] was pleased with the peace of Greenville," Stephen Ruddell recounted. "[He] said that now he was happy—that he could pursue his hunting without danger."

A welcome pause in expansion prevailed for the last few years of the 1790s. Large U.S. acquisitions of Native lands in the Ohio Valley mostly ceased. To Shawnees and whites alike it may have appeared that, with the Greenville Treaty of 1795, the Americans had finally sated their lust for land. That document and the line it drew had given twenty-five thousand square miles of tribal land to the United States.

But it still wasn't enough.

Lieutenant Harrison's reputation had grown. He had impressed fellow officers at the Battle of Fallen Timbers in the summer of 1794 by coolly delivering General Wayne's messages in the heat of battle astride his prized horse Fearnought. "If he continues a military man," remarked a senior officer of Wayne's, "he will be a second Washington."

General Wayne granted leave to his young bachelor officers after wintering in the wilds at Fort Greenville to ensure they would be fresh and rested for what promised to be weeks of busy, difficult treaty negotiations in the upcoming summer of 1795. Lieutenant Harrison and a friend, medic John Scott, aimed their horses south two hundred miles toward the brighter lights of Lexington—"the Philadelphia of Kentucky."

Trotting out of the woods astride Fearnought, William Henry was enraptured from the moment they were met by Anna "Nancy" Symmes—the dark-eyed and cultured daughter of a frontier justice and land speculator who had served in the Continental Congress from New Jersey.*

Members of the East Coast aristocracy managed to find one another in the Ohio Valley wilds like mating birds calling through the woods. The fateful encounter took place at the fine Lexington plantation of Peyton Short, who, like Judge Symmes, was an East Coast lawyer turned western land speculator, and, like Harrison, a member of the Virginia gentility. Nancy's older sister, Maria "Polly" Symmes—also a polished East Coast young woman—had come west to the Ohio country a few years earlier to accompany their widowed father and soon met and married Short. Younger sister Nancy had come to visit Polly at the Shorts' Lexington estate when young Lieutenant Harrison rode up on his sleek horse in his dress uniform.

The twenty-two-year-old Harrison soon asked the crusty Judge Symmes—in residence at his would-be city of Symmes on the Ohio—for the hand of his twenty-year-old daughter.

Judge Symmes vehemently objected. He believed that Harrison, despite his aristocratic Virginia pedigree, had few prospects as an army officer—or as anything else for that matter. As the blunt (and often funny)

---

* The example of Judge Symmes illustrates the aristocratic and insider status of those able to acquire—and speculate in—large parcels of western lands in the founding era. A man of bold ideas and big vision, John Cleves Symmes served with distinction during the Revolution in the New Jersey militia. His wife died young, and he disguised himself as a British officer to cross lines and take his young daughter Nancy to her maternal grandparents on Long Island. Well-read and a strong writer, he served on the New Jersey Supreme Court and as a delegate to the Continental Congress in 1785 when it began to consider what to do with the western lands beyond the mountains the United States had won from the British Crown. After seeing for himself the richness of these Ohio lands, Judge Symmes had an audacious vision—that Congress should sell him one million acres in the soon-to-be designated Northwest Territory to start a major settlement. Also approaching Congress to buy a large tract for its own settlement was a New England consortium called the Ohio Company of Associates, led by war-hero Rufus Putnam, Yale-educated lawyer Manasseh Cutler, and others. These settlements became the seeds of modern Ohio.

old man put it in a letter to a business partner back in Philadelphia, "He can neither bleed, plead, or preach."

The couple eloped. It was a "run-away match," in the words of Nancy's close acquaintance.

William Henry's powerful, overbearing father-in-law now came to supplant his powerful, overbearing father. With little to show for future employment, Harrison attempted to prove himself worthy, or so the old stories tell. It is said that an officers' farewell party for General Wayne at Fort Washington in December 1795 marked the first time Judge Symmes and William Henry Harrison actually encountered each other since the lieutenant's "run-away" marriage to the judge's daughter the previous month. Amid the dancing and toasts, the story goes, the red-faced and blunt-spoken Judge Symmes strode up to young Lieutenant Harrison, re-splendent in uniform with dress sword dangling at his side.

"How do you intend to support my daughter, sir?" he demanded.

Lieutenant Harrison reached for the hilt of his sword.

"With my right arm and my sword, sir!" he replied.

Judge Symmes was not impressed.

Over the next four years, Harrison remade himself from Indian fighter into a frontier politician with a little-disguised eagerness—brazenness, by some reckonings—to hop onto the national stage as if aiming for the power centers where his family had climbed to prominence.

It turned out that Harrison's military career in the Ohio country had been a shrewd political move. He rose swiftly in politics once he hitched his fortunes to the quickly evolving fate of the vast Northwest Territory. He had floundered at loose ends with the peace brought by the Greenville Treaty. Without a frontier war to fight, the Legion of the United States had downsized. No officer's promotion would be forthcoming, triggering Harrison's complaints of "very illiberal treatment." Staying on briefly as commander of the now-moldering Fort Washington, he and Nancy lived on the fort's grounds in a wood-framed house painted an uplifting yellow—one of few structures not built of logs.

She gave birth to a child. Soon, another child was on the way. After making a few unsuccessful stabs as entrepreneur—horse breeder, whiskey distiller—William Henry cast about for a steady job. Turning to his late father's personal ties in the U.S. Congress, Harrison managed to nail down the post of secretary to the Northwest Territory. For a few months he worked at the territory's capital in the small town of Cincinnati under the territorial governor—disgraced former general Arthur St. Clair—appointed by former President Washington.

By 1799, the territory had reached a critical threshold in the step-by-step march toward statehood—a population of more than five thousand "free male inhabitants of full age," as the Northwest Ordinance put it.* That triggered "second-stage government" for the territory—political representation for inhabitants. (To achieve the third stage and apply for actual statehood, the territory, or a portion of it, would need to reach a population of sixty thousand.)

At the five thousand benchmark, the territory's citizens could elect representatives to the newly created Northwest Territorial Legislature. Further, their voice could now be heard within the arched windows and green drapes of Congress Hall in Philadelphia, where free white men argued the nation's fate. However, because it was a territory, its single U.S. representative could not actually vote on congressional legislation.

William Henry craved the position. When the territory reached that first population threshold in 1799, he instantly threw his hat into the ring

---

* Congress's phrase "free male inhabitants" made clear that neither women, nor enslaved people, nor Indigenous people were acknowledged as potential citizens or voters in establishing the Northwest Territory. After much debate, Congress also banned slavery in the territory when creating it with its Northwest Ordinance of 1787. Ironically, existing Southern slave states voted *for* the ban on slavery in the Northwest Territory fearing a pool of slave labor in the new states north of the Ohio would allow those states to compete on an even footing in the tobacco-growing business.

as candidate for its single representative to Congress. If elected by the tiny territorial legislature to the office, he could boost his ne'er-do-well status in the eyes of Judge Symmes and simultaneously land in his father's grand arena—the nation's center of power—rather than idling in the Ohio wilderness.

He pushed ahead with smiling tenacity and readiness to game the system. "Mr. H . . . has handsome manners," wrote a future political critic, "[and] in conversation he is sprightly and gay—can repeat a theatrical performance and mimmick a blackguard [that is, a villain] as well as I ever saw a man." Yet the same critic, Isaac Darneille, a young man overlooked for a territorial appointment, also charged that Harrison surrounded himself with "sycophants and parasites" while practicing "art," "intrigue," and "influence."

The latter was certainly true. From the start of his political career, Harrison, a Jeffersonian Republican, cultivated fellow Virginians who had migrated west and now served in the territorial legislature. Bolstered by their support, he edged out his Federalist opponent, Governor St. Clair's son, by an 11 to 10 vote. William Henry had again played the Harrison family's old-boy network to his favor.

The young Harrisons moved east to Philadelphia. He and Nancy conceived their third child amid the city's lamplit urban luxury. He savored success in the House. Named to head a new committee on lands, Harrison engineered a pivotal bill on selling land in U.S. territories. In one sense, it simply adjusted existing land sale laws in earlier legislation that created the Northwest Territory. In another, however, it represented a revolutionary departure—a change in mindset—about the landowning class in the United States.

Previously, only wealthy or well-connected individuals could afford the huge territorial lot sizes sold by the U.S government. The smallest lot measured a mile square, and the next smallest enclosed nearly six thousand acres—nearly half the size of Manhattan Island. But Harrison and the committee proposed that the U.S. government sell off much smaller lots—downsizing the minimum lot by three-quarters, from 640 to 180 acres. No longer would western lands acquired from the Indigenous people go only to big investors and deep-pocketed speculators.

The bill extended a helping hand to whites hoping to become small farmers instead of enduring life as paid fieldhands, indentured servants, or other forms of quasi-slavery under proprietors of the gentry. Truly radical, however, was the notion that the government sell the land to nearly penniless settlers on *credit* with zero interest and four years to pay. This was the equivalent of a modern-day bonanza warehouse sale where cash-poor consumers can cart away major appliances with no money down and forty-eight months to pay off the loan. Now, as the nation pushed west, these dirt-poor, would-be farmers whose only asset was their endless capacity for work could become landed, too.

The dynamic young territorial delegate proved spectacularly successful in making his case. The new law—sometimes called the Harrison Land Act of 1800—passed within five months. The Senate version tweaked it by increasing minimum lot sizes to 320 acres on the argument that Harrison's 180-acre lots would attract shiftless settlers who would do little to improve them. Still, the new law offered remarkably generous terms—selling federal lands to settlers at $2 an acre, with a down payment of one-quarter the total owed, 6 percent interest, and four years to repay at conveniently located frontier offices. It tilted the landscape of western expansion decisively toward the little man, the poor white settler with big ambitions but meager cash. Harrison had reassembled parts from existing land laws to create the dynamo that would power the great western movement.

"This law," he boasted to his territorial constituents in a published letter, "promises to be the foundation of a great increase of population and wealth to our country."

It leaned not on the big investor but the small farmer and entrepreneur to power westward expansion. The mechanism fit perfectly with the ideals of the Jeffersonian republic—small, independent farmers would knit the fabric of a democracy, far from urban cesspools of corruption. Instead of an aristocratic landowning class holding power, as traditionally in Virginia, the nation would shift to a more egalitarian conception of itself, closer to what was envisioned by the original self-governing Puritans who arrived in New England. But it was different, too, in that it would take that Virginia sense of entitlement, that powerful craving for land, that relentless push westward, and meld it with the egalitarian model.

Along with soon-to-be President Jefferson, William Henry Harrison did much to help create this new vision of the nation—powered by what we later came to call pioneer spirit. But in this noble vision there was no place for America's Native inhabitants. On the one hand, tribes were officially treated as independent nations. Yet on the other, the founders believed their lands were absolutely necessary for carrying out the grand experiment—both to pay the nation's outstanding debts and provide room for its growth.

The pace of frontier settlement accelerated. So did the Northwest Territory's political sway in Philadelphia. Rising in tandem with it was William Henry Harrison's surging ambition. With the territory's settler population swelling east of the crucial Greenville Treaty Line, and, beyond the line, the territory's huge, "empty" land mass stretching west nearly one thousand miles and some seven hundred miles north to south, Harrison proposed that Congress split the Northwest Territory into two regions. The smaller and more-settled eastern sector would become a state called Ohio. The massive western reaches would bear a new name: the Indiana Territory.

Congress agreed. In July 1800, just two months after passing Harrison's Land Act, it severed the Northwest Territory in two. Governor St. Clair remained in the Ohio sector. This meant the new Indiana Territory would need its own governor. President John Adams, now nearing the end of his term, appointed the dynamic young William Henry Harrison to the post. The new Indiana territorial governor would be the reigning authority over 260,000 square miles sprawling across the center of the continent, around the Great Lakes to the Mississippi. It was larger than France. He had just turned twenty-seven.

During the same fall of 1799 when Harrison was chatting up his Virginian friends to vote him into Congress, Tecumseh, for the first time, stepped into a leadership role that attracted settlers' notice. Unlike Harrison, he did so reluctantly. Although he hadn't signed it, he respected the peace of the Treaty of Greenville and the dividing line it drew across the Ohio Valley. He and his band had established a traditional village on the upper White River far beyond the settler plow's torn sod. Here he pursued a hunting life.

It didn't last. The disputes of others drew him in.

Fear erupted in the summer of 1799 among nervous settlers along a twenty-mile section of the Ohio Valley frontier on rumors that Shawnees had gathered to paint themselves for war. White militias armed themselves to retaliate with murderous force. Hoping to head off the inevitable spiral of violence, two veteran frontiersmen, Simon Kenton and William Ward, sent a messenger to Shawnee chiefs asking for an explanation. Seven chiefs agreed to meet. It was here that Tecumseh, now thirty-one years old, first walked onto the stage of history as it would be told by whites.

Traveling seventy miles north from the White River to the backcountry home of a French trader, Duchouquet, the chiefs designated Tecumseh their main spokesman. The Shawnees had in fact prepared for war, Tecumseh told the frontiersmen at the trader's house, but had no intention of harming whites. Rather, he explained, they armed against a war party of Choctaws from the South rumored to have been headed north to attack the Shawnees—this in retribution for Shawnees killing Choctaws who had scouted for Mad Anthony's campaign, five years earlier.

Tecumseh's oratory impressed the veteran frontiersmen. Not even the fluent Shawnee speaker Duchouquet could properly interpret his "lofty flights of eloquence." No exact record of his words exists, but whatever he said melted the frontier tension. He and the other chiefs peacefully returned to the White River.

He didn't want trouble. He had removed himself and his swelling band fifty miles west of the legal limit of white settlement along the Greenville Treaty Line. But, like a tilted tub of water sloshing over its brim, the momentum of settlers pouring into the newly opened portions of the Ohio country instantly spilled beyond the Greenville Line and onto Native lands.

With settlers implacably crowding in, Indigenous people continued to lose their hunting lands section by section. With amazing speed, the whites brought them a host of dire problems. Among the most devastating of all was the arrival of William Henry.

The newly named governor of the newly made Indiana Territory arrived ahead of his family in the first days of 1801 at tiny Vincennes—two hundred miles west of the Greenville Line. The U.S. Congress had designated this remote western outpost on the Wabash River to serve as the Indiana territorial capital when it split the former Northwest Territory. The young governor scouted ahead for a place where wife Nancy, their children, and their servants could live in relative comfort far from their former Cincinnati and Philadelphia homes.

Surrounded by a wilderness of forest and prairie, Vincennes retained a French flavor when Harrison arrived nearly a century after its founding. Since the Ice Age, Indigenous people had gathered here for uncounted generations, pursuing herds of buffalo making their seasonal migrations between the Illinois prairies and the eastern forests. The herds followed a "trace" or broad path—Alanantowamiowee, the Shawnees called it—that forded the Wabash River at a shallow spot. Attracted here by Native hunters from whom they bought pelts, French fur traders acquired from the tribes a small parcel of land along the Wabash, and, by mutual agreement, planted a post at the ford soon after their earliest explorations of the North American interior.

Having won much of North America from the French in 1763, British military strategists garrisoned a small fort at the old French fur post during the Revolutionary War to guard their backcountry lands from rebel American marauders. The British strategy failed, however. The Revolutionary American military leader George Rogers Clark of the Virginia militia captured the fort in a bold winter attack in 1779.[*]

The different cultural streams had come to bear on the river's shallow ford. Like the current itself recontouring the river bottom, the shifting dynamics of colonial occupation reshaped the landscape. By the time young Governor Harrison arrived in January 1801, these forces had created a small island of U.S. federal land amid the vast western expanse of Indian territory.

The outpost on the Wabash had a population of about seven hundred—a mere dot compared to East Coast ports such as New York City, with its sixty thousand residents. Residents of French descent occupied Vincennes's log cabins and rows of small clapboard homes with shady verandas and gardens growing out back, separated by dirt paths too primitive to be called streets.

Harrison took temporary lodgings in one of the old settlement's few substantial buildings—the unfinished home of its leading citizen and veteran trader, the Italian-born Francis Vigo, whose handsome white frame house was encircled by a porch and trimmed with slatted green shutters. As the spring of 1801 blossomed and threw a greening cloak of optimism over the remote and wild landscape, Nancy and the family arrived from the cosmopolitan centers back East.

"On the one side we have the delightful Wabash," wrote Nancy's

---

[*] The Clarks were a Virginia planter family that also produced soldiers and explorers. George Rogers Clark was the older brother of William Clark, of the 1804–6 Lewis and Clark Expedition to the Pacific Ocean.

traveling companion, Susan Symmes, to her eastern friends, "on the other the most enchanting landscape of elegant scenery."

Despite the elegant wood-paneled walls and inlaid ash-and-hickory floor, some of the charm in Vigo's house wore off when the entire family had to cram into the single grand parlor room. Badly needing a home—and in the style that befitted a Virginia gentleman and territorial governor—William Henry and Nancy laid plans to build one. They purchased from Vigo three hundred acres on a gentle rise along the Wabash about a half mile upstream from the village. Construction soon began on a large brick home intended to be the grandest in the quarter-million square miles of Indiana Territory—a wilderness Versailles.

For its design, the couple drew on the Harrison family's ancestral Berkeley Plantation on the James River—in effect, dropping that elegant Virginia estate into a clearing hacked from the wilderness on the Wabash's muddy riverbank.

It was not going to be cheap. Harrison would have to pay for the labor. Unlike in his native Virginia, Congress had outlawed slavery in these territorial lands north of the Ohio River. That wouldn't stop Harrison, however, from trying to import it under various guises upon his arrival, first by bringing an enslaved worker from Berkeley to Vincennes in the guise of a servant.

To pay his workers, William Henry had to sell four hundred acres of land he had acquired elsewhere. Laborers hand-dug an enormous cellar and a strategically located well shaft inside the underground chamber. They mortared stones into a foundation, hewed floor joists from logs, dug clay from nearby pits to mold and fire four hundred thousand red bricks, laid exterior walls four bricks thick and two and a half stories high, and built four brick chimneys. They wove mud-and-prairie grass insulation under the floors and smoothed the lath-and-plaster interior walls. Skilled craftsmen from Philadelphia carved the wood moldings and lintels and a banister of black walnut. Harrison planned his mansion on a scale and opulence worthy of the second-wave Founding Father he hoped to become by helping to forge an American identity on western lands for the benefit of the small man. That designation did not include himself. The couple modeled their main staircase on Mount Vernon's and the elliptical arch in the entrance hall on Monticello's, striving to join this vaunted pantheon of founders and the mansions they lovingly built as monuments to themselves. William Henry and Nancy ordered fine glass panes from England for their home's many mullioned windows. They spared no detail for quality and opulence. Nancy chose lemon-yellow walls for the parlor that would serve as William Henry's reception room, and robin's-egg blue for the dining room, requesting silver flecks mixed in with the paint to make it glitter in the candlelight. They named the home Grouse-land after the native bird, the ruffed grouse, that haunts the forest with its rhythmic drumming.

The structure itself mirrored its master's personality and the precariousness of the young couple's toehold in the wilderness. Aboveground, the Virginia-style mansion offered elegance, hospitality, and warmth. Belowground it was a fortress—two-foot-thick stone walls cut with iron-barred gunports offering clear aim in all directions, the interior water well, a full kitchen and fireplace, and an ample powder magazine. A lookout platform topped the roof, while the bowed bay windows of the parlor, where Harrison would conduct his office business, offered a panoramic view of the Wabash—especially upstream, the direction from which the gravest threat might silently arrive in birchbark canoes.

In the event of a siege by Native warriors, the cellar fortress could protect Grouseland's occupants for weeks. It would be due in large part to William Henry's own actions, however, that he felt the need for such a formidable structure. He clearly understood the precariousness of the situation that his emerging policies toward the tribes could create for his family. When someone questioned the wisdom of keeping a large gunpowder magazine in the cellar beneath his family's living quarters, Harrison replied, "I'd rather see them blown to bits than having them taken captive."

CHAPTER 5

THE CHOICE

Thomas Jefferson felt a tremendous sense of urgency. He needed to pin down western lands before Indigenous leaders suspected his intentions.

"The crisis is pressing," he wrote to William Henry Harrison, son of his old colleague from the Revolution. "Whatever can now be obtained, must be obtained quickly. The occupation of New Orleans . . . by the French, is already felt like a light breeze by the Indians."

Jefferson worried that Native leaders eagerly awaited the return of their old French allies to North America. During the 150 years of the New France colony, the French had generally kept good relations with tribes, had intermarried, and, unlike the British and then Americans, did not attempt to pry away vast swathes of their lands. With the possibility of France returning to North America, the tribes, Jefferson feared, would feel French support like a favorable wind and refuse to relinquish more land to the United States.

It was difficult to predict France's strategy. It had suddenly morphed into a volatile global power. An upstart former artillery officer named Napoleon Bonaparte had seized control of the French Army in 1799. Just thirty years old, he wielded this force across Europe with the confident hand of a grandmaster in chess sweeping up his opponents' pieces on the global gaming board.

Bonaparte's armies crossed the snowy Alps in the spring of 1800. He took Northern Italy. He then swung a deal with Spain, trading Northern Italy to Spain in return for Spain's claims to territory in North America. Specifically, he wanted the lands that extended between the Mississippi River and the Rocky Mountains—known as "Louisiana"—and with it the valuable port of New Orleans. In early 1801, Spain handed over the whole package.

It wasn't an arbitrary exercise of power on Napoleon's part. He had a plan—to use the North American lands and the New Orleans port as a base to capture the Caribbean's "sugar islands." With the tropical sun nourishing fields of sugarcane harvested by enslaved labor, these islands generated enormous amounts of cash. Napoleon needed money to fund armies for his grand schemes in Europe and to reestablish France's colonial empire in North America, which it had lost to Britain in 1763.

From President Jefferson's perspective, however, it was one thing to have Spain in the vast Louisiana Territory just across the Mississippi River from the United States. The Spanish Crown had hardly bothered to plant actual colonies during the several decades it had claimed the territory. It was another thing entirely to have the ravenous Bonaparte swinging his sharpened cleaver so close to American lands and controlling the Mississippi's outlet.

With Europe in flux and geopolitical alliances rapidly reshuffling, Jefferson needed to establish the United States as a significant power reaching deep into the North American continent. The West Coast had recently come into play on the global gaming board. Wild and remote to European powers—although not, of course, to the scores of Native nations who had occupied it for millennia—it had attracted Spain, France, Britain, Russia, and the United States, all sniffing around for potential value. This was due in large part to its abundance of fur-bearing mammals, especially the sea otter, which frolicked in icy coastal waters sheathed in an ultra-luxurious coat of one million hairs per square inch. The pelts fetched enormous prices to trim the robes of Chinese mandarins and European aristocrats.[*]

Scottish explorer and fur trader Alexander Mackenzie reached the Pacific Ocean by heading overland from a remote Rocky Mountain fur post, chiseling his name and the date, 1793, on a boulder still visible today at Bella Coola, British Columbia. His account of the expedition, published in 1801, underscored the tremendous commercial potential of the West Coast and the entire Pacific Rim. Whichever nation first established settlements on the West Coast and the Columbia River, and connected them by waterways to the East Coast, he wrote, would possess "the entire command of the fur trade of North America . . . from latitude 48, North to the pole . . . the fishing of both seas, and the markets of the four quarters of the globe."

Jefferson hated to think of the despised British getting across the continent first. Deepening Jefferson's anxiety about establishing a U.S. presence in the North American interior was the fact that, legally, the lands on the American side of the Mississippi River—the east side—did not actually *belong* to the United States. Rather, they belonged to dozens of individual Native nations. And Congress had clearly stated this in the Northwest Ordinance when it created a governing mechanism for future settlement on this same swath of land, the Northwest Territory: "[tribal lands] shall never be taken from them without their consent."

---

[*] With actual wealth at stake rather than merely territorial bragging rights, Britain and Spain nearly came to blows in the 1790s over which empire possessed Vancouver Island and the Northwest Coast. They finally agreed to disagree. They politely settled the matter by raising and lowering each other's flags at a remote outpost on Nootka Sound. Then they both abandoned the post. In European thinking this arrangement left the colonial ownership of the Northwest Coast still undecided.

It had become essential, in President Jefferson's mind, to acquire legal rights, therefore, to Native lands in American territory all the way to the Mississippi River—then the western border of the United States. Only then could he secure this remote border from meddling by foreign powers—whether France, Spain, Britain, or some other European empire entertaining big plans in the New World.

But working from the President's House in Washington, Jefferson was hardly present on the ground to hash out the details of these very delicate matters with the tribes. He needed a dynamic intermediary located in the western territory to carry out this important mission. He would soon identify the perfect front man for his Indian land-acquisition scheme—William Henry Harrison.

Harrison had shown some empathy for a brief moment as he witnessed the advance of frontier "civilization" corroding traditional Native culture. This, however, would not last. Given the timing of his sudden burst of concern, one can't help but wonder whether the women in his life pried opened his eyes—at least temporarily—to the human suffering he would prefer to ignore.

Nancy Harrison and the couple's three children arrived in Vincennes in the spring of 1801, a few months after William Henry. With them was Nancy's good friend, traveling companion, and stepmother, Susan Livingston Symmes.* Although twenty-five years apart, the two women had been raised in the finest institutions and most exalted social circles of the East Coast. Susan belonged to the famed Livingston political family of

---

* A middle-aged widower feeling lonely on the frontier as he tried to develop the massive Ohio land tract he had purchased from Congress, Judge Symmes made a trip back East and, after a whirlwind courtship, married the aristocratic Susan Livingston of New Jersey. Also middle-aged and unmarried, she apparently wed the judge in part for the frontier adventure of it. She would stay about fifteen years in the Ohio country, helping her daughter-in-law Nancy with the many Harrison children, until she permanently returned East.

New Jersey, and her sister was married to John Jay, chief justice of the United States.

Nancy Symmes Harrison had been raised on Long Island by doting maternal grandparents after her mother died young. They provided her with a progressive education at the Clinton Academy, a coed boarding school in East Hampton where children studied the works of the French Enlightenment. She received further polishing at the Isabella Graham School in Manhattan, founded by the famed Scottish feminist and philanthropist who advocated charity to poor widows and female education.

What William Henry saw on the dirt pathways when he first arrived in Vincennes and would soon graphically describe he had probably seen many times before as a veteran of frontier warfare and military life. But when these two cultured eastern women arrived in the spring of 1801, they had not developed his callousness to the human toll visible in Vincennes's muddy roads. They also lived with a man in a position to do something about it.

It would hardly be surprising if that's what they urged. Their intercession on the part of Indigenous people is conjecture, of course, as no written record of this domestic moment survives—almost all personal correspondence between William Henry and Nancy burned decades later in a house fire. But if they did not urge him, it's a pure coincidence of timing that almost immediately after the women's arrival William Henry wrote to his superiors in Washington, D.C., about the shocking condition of Native people near the frontier settlement—as if observing them for the first time.

Citing graphic details, he relayed the bitter complaints of Native leaders to his immediate boss, Secretary of War Henry Dearborn. And he asked Dearborn to communicate them to the first occupant of the President's House at the new capital in Washington, D.C., a man known for his admiration of the humanitarian ideals of the French Enlightenment: Thomas Jefferson.

"They say that their people have been killed—their lands settled on—their game wantonly destroyed—& their young men made drunk & cheated of the peltries which formerly procured them necessary articles of Cloathing, arms and amunition to hunt with. Of the truth of all these charges I am well convinced," Harrison wrote to Jefferson and Dearborn.

The Harrisons' new home of Vincennes sat at the epicenter of Indigenous cultural deterioration in the region. Surrounded by tribal lands, the isolated settlement served as an emporium where white traders plied their goods, selling six thousand gallons of whiskey annually to six hundred Natives whose game and land was vanishing.

> Thousands of the wild animals from which the Indians derive their subsistence have been distroyed by the white people. They complain in their speeches to me that many parts of their Country, which abounded with game when the general peace was made in 1795, now scarcely contains a sufficiency to give food to the few Indians who pass through there.
>
> The people of Kentucky . . . make a constant practice of crossing over [the Ohio River] on the Indian lands opposite to them every fall to kill deer, bear, and buffaloe—the latter from being a great abundance a few year's ago is now scarcely to be met with. . . . One white hunter will distroy more game than five of the common Indians—the latter generally contenting himself with a sufficiency for present subsistance—while the other eager after game, hunt for the skin of the animal alone.

Through Secretary Dearborn, he urged President Jefferson, as soon as possible, to order the survey of the Greenville Line that separated white lands from Native lands. He could do nothing to stop these treaty violations until the line was clearly marked, he wrote.

Untill their boundaries are established it is almost impossible to punish in this quarter the persons who make a practice of Hunting on the lands of the Indians in violation of law and our Treaty with that people. This practice has grown into a monstrous abuse.

Yet the Native people have borne these injuries with "astonishing patience," Harrison wrote. They also face the hostility of frontier settlers, who, he wrote, "consider the murdering of Indians in the highest degree meritorious."

The collapse of their culture, he observed, especially affected the smaller tribes nearest white settlements such as Vincennes. The Natives living nearby were the

greatest Scoundrels in the world—they are dayly in this town in considerable numbers and are frequently intoxicated to the number of thirty or forty at once—they then commit the greatest disorders—drawing their knives and stabing every one they meet with—breaking open the Houses of the Citizens killing their Hogs and cattle and breaking down their fences. But in all their frolicks they generally suffer most severely themselves they kill each other without mercy, some years ago as many as four were found dead in the morning.

All these Horrors are produced to these Unhappy people by their too frequent intercourse with the White people. This is so cirtain that I can at once tell by looking at an Indian whom I chance to meet whether he belong to a Neighbouring or a more distant Tribe. The latter is generally well Clothed healthy and vigorous, the former half naked, filthy and enfeebled with Intoxication, and many of them without arms except a Knife which they carry for the most vilanous purposes.

If matters continued on the present course, Harrison direly predicted, the result would be "the exterpation of so many human beings." With

greater foresight than he likely realized, he suggested that such an extermination would in the future sully the "American Character" with a permanent stain of "reproach." He deferred to President Jefferson, however,
to decide whether anything should be done to stop it:

> Whether some thing ought not to be done to prevent the reproach
> which will attach to the American Character by the exterpation of so
> many human beings, I beg leave most respectfully to submit to the
> Consideration of the President That this exterpation will happen no
> one can doubt who knows the astonishing annual decrease of these
> unhappy beings.

Both William Henry Harrison and Thomas Jefferson were born and
raised in Virginia's plantation elite. Native Americans did not figure into
the social order of the rigid, two-century-old Virginia society from which
they both descended. It customarily recognized a hierarchy of at least
eight classes—from Black slaves to plantation aristocrats. Indigenous people existed in a kind of cruel, parallel universe where the phrase "human
being" did not readily apply, especially when they represented the enemy
lurking in the wilderness. Without a ready social framework and stymied
by the ugly situation in Vincennes, Harrison had decided to consult his
boss and fellow Virginian, President Jefferson, about this looming question and moral quandary. He posed what today would be an inconceiv-
able question: Was extermination—"extirpation" in Harrison's words—the
proper fate for Indians? And should something be done to stop it and prevent the darkening of America's honor forever?

The question put Jefferson in a moral quandary, too. In addition to
Virginia values about class and servitude, he had inherited from his father, Peter—a planter, surveyor, and wilderness mapmaker—a powerful
inclination to look westward for the continent's future. He believed that
acquiring great quantities of additional land was key to the young nation's
strength. Land would nurture a nation of small farmers and prevent its

collapse into sinkholes of moral decay, such as Europe and its poor, packed into pestilential cities.

Getting no immediate response about the moral issues posed by the shifting American frontier, Governor Harrison changed the tack. He now tested Jefferson's "land hunger," as it was then called. Just a few months after expressing worries about stains on the "American Character" from Native "extirpation," Harrison suggested in a general way that the Treaty of Greenville could be interpreted as "much more extensive than is generally imagined." In other words, *We don't have to let the Greenville Line hold us back from getting more Indian lands.* It was as if Harrison baited a hook and tossed it in the water to see if Jefferson would bite. The president hit the lure hard.

Jefferson did not directly answer Harrison's question about Indian extermination. Instead, he put a noble face on his land hunger. A letter in early 1802 written to Harrison on Jefferson's behalf emphasized that in dealing with the Native tribes, the president wanted to respect the "principle of humanity" and the "benevolent views of congress." He also wished to maintain friendship and harmony with them. This could be done best, Jefferson said, by introducing tribes to "civilization"—notably, animal husbandry and domestic manufacturing—encouraging them to forsake their wandering, hunting traditions. Jefferson strove for an enlightened and rational approach . . . while also serving his own purpose.[*]

---

[*] Jefferson interpreted Congress's 1790 passage of the Indian Trade and Intercourse Act as a means to justify his plan to bring agriculture and "civilization" to the nations. The act says nothing about agriculture and civilization, rather that only the U.S. government can negotiate with tribes and all traders must be licensed. As Dearborn wrote to Harrison in his early 1802 letter, on Jefferson's behalf:

> The provisions made by congress, under the heads of intercourse with the Indian nations, and for establishing trading houses among them etc. have for their object, not only the cultivation and establishment of harmony and friendship between the United States and the different nations of Indians, but the introduction of civilization, by encouraging and gradually introducing the arts of husbandry and domestic manufactures among them. The President is more induced to continue to raise all the means in his power for effecting the foregoing object from the happy effects already produced in several of the Indian nations, by the zeal and industry of the agents among them.

"Jefferson probably sincerely intended to carry out his civilization policy, even though it had been initiated by the Federalists," writes Anthony F. C. Wallace in *Jefferson and the Indians*, "but it also functioned in his hand as a public relations device that provided a moral justification for land purchases, which were his primary interest."

Jefferson's stance, in effect, gave Harrison the green light to try to acquire more tribal lands. The young governor blithely ignored whatever moral hesitation he may have felt about "extirpation." Nor did his actions reflect whatever enlightened East Coast sensibilities his wife and mother-in-law may have brought to this frontier outpost. He had all the rationalization he needed. They must be "civilized." And once civilized, they wouldn't need all those hunting lands. It was either get civilized . . . or get out of the way. Jefferson and Harrison framed it as a choice—the tribes could give up their wandering ways and all the land it required, turning it over to white farmers and taking up agriculture themselves. Or leave. Or, if they refused to do either, be exterminated.

"Divide and rule, aid the friendly in peace, exterminate the incorrigibles—this was Jefferson's Indian policy," writes Jefferson biographer Merrill Peterson.

Harrison launched with a vengeance into Indian land acquisition—*beyond* the Greenville Line. He looked for legal loopholes, pitted tribal factions against one another, and employed other tactics short of outright war. At Secretary Dearborn's request, he was first to focus on lands around Vincennes—that federal island far out in Indian country. The tribes signing the Greenville Treaty in 1795 had ceded to the United States an undefined piece of land around Vincennes. How large might this piece be? Dearborn now asked Harrison—more specifically, how much land might local Kickapoo and Piankeshaw tribes be willing to give up? (A larger federal island also offered Governor Harrison the bonus of boosting his own property values in the settlement.)

He first ventured onto shaky ethical ground in the summer of 1802, a little over a year after arriving in Vincennes. He convened chiefs to make the argument that decades-old treaties made between Native nations and early French fur traders, as well as other old deals made by a private land speculation company, remained valid under U.S. administration. The fact that Congress had already twice annulled the private deals with Native nations did not stop Harrison. He argued that the musty deals—however discredited—officially gave the United States lands along the lower White River near Vincennes totaling one million acres.

The gathered chiefs—from the Miami, Potawatomi, Kickapoo, and other tribes—balked at this outlandish proposal. They adamantly contended that the tribes decades earlier had ceded to the old French traders at most eight thousand acres to make their fur post. Harrison cleverly worked the angles—paying off some chiefs, handpicking others who had something to gain, and cutting out the rest. Some villages erupted in anger when they learned that certain chiefs, without consultation, had signed what would become known as Harrison's Treaty of Vincennes (1802–3). But Governor Harrison and President Jefferson had what they wanted, now encoded on a piece of paper signed by at least some chiefs—one million acres along the White and the Wabash rivers to expand white settlement near Vincennes.

With intense focus, Harrison exploited inter-tribal dynamics and loopholes in these old land deals made by the French. Using long leaps of logic, he construed what might be considered a legal rationale for his land grabs. And all the while, he completed his wilderness mansion equipped with its belowground fortress. He knew he might be needing it.

President Jefferson showed no sympathy when word of Native complaints about the 1802–3 Vincennes treaty reached him. The first block in his vision of a much grander edifice had been laid. In the winter of 1803, a few months after Harrison swung the Treaty of Vincennes, Jefferson wrote a secret plan to William Henry on how to acquire tribal lands all the way to the Mississippi River, nearly four hundred miles beyond the

Greenville Line, where white settlement was supposed to stop. The plan would work like this: Squeeze hunting grounds by acquiring piecemeal parcels of lands until game became too scarce to sustain the hunters, push them toward farming, and then force them so deeply into debt to government traders that they would have to sell still more of their lands. He wrote:

> The decrease of game rendering their subsistence by hunting insufficient, we wish to draw them to agriculture, to spinning and weaving. . . . When they withdraw themselves to the culture of a small piece of land, they will perceive how useless to them are their extensive forests, and will be willing to pare them off from time to time in exchange for necessaries for their farms & families. To promote this disposition . . . we shall push our trading houses, and be glad to see the good and influential individuals among them run in debt, because we observe that when these debts get beyond what the individuals can pay, they become willing to lop them off by a cession of lands.

This diabolical strategy came from the pen of a supposedly enlightened humanitarian and champion of individual liberties whose high outrage at his own deprivation of rights by King George III is encoded for the ages in the Declaration of Independence.* Jefferson well knew his Indian strategy was shameful. He warned Harrison that no eyes should see this scheme but his own—"sacredly it must be kept within your own breast."

As one modern historian, Gary B. Nash, summarized it, "Jefferson's

---

* Rather than extending rights and freedoms to Native Americans as it did to white American colonists, the 1776 Declaration demonizes the continent's original inhabitants by accusing the British, among their many other outrageous acts, of inciting "the merciless Indian savages" to attack frontier settlers. As the Declaration's text reads: "[King George III] has excited domestic insurrections amongst us, and has endeavoured to bring on the inhabitants of our frontiers, the merciless Indian Savages whose known rule of warfare, is an undistinguished destruction of all ages, sexes and conditions."

love of minimal government and maximal individual freedom, combined with his insatiable appetite for land, became the perfect formula for seizing Indian land and rationalizing the frontiersmen's ethnic cleansing."

Jefferson urged Harrison to force the treaties on tribes quickly, and so there was no stopping Harrison now. He saw Jefferson's grander vision—securing the nation to its western edges. He wanted to help. He understood that his task was to fill this great space in the continent's center with American settlers, as far west as its border with France along the Mississippi River. He understood he should do whatever it took to extinguish Native title to these lands—and he should do it quickly.

CHAPTER 6

THE FORKED PATH

The Loud One—Lalawethika, the inept younger brother of Tecumseh—deteriorated quickly as white settlement pushed closer. He lived with Tecumseh's band at the village on the headwaters of the White River. As whiskey traders flooded the tributary branches, he became a drunk. Married, with children, and a poor hunter, he could no longer bring home enough game to feed his own family. His surviving siblings—twin brother Kumskaukau, older brother Tecumseh, and Tecumpease and her husband—helped provide. Along with the whiskey traders came disease, especially smallpox. On the river's branches entire villages fell ill. Charges of witchcraft flew. Someone had made the spirits angry—or so believed many traditional Shawnees.

The illness and accusations placed great stress on bands pursuing their hunting and gathering life on the White's upper branches—the Shawnee and Delaware—who struggled with a sense of impotence in face of the onslaught of disease, whiskey, and illegal white hunters who decimated herds of elk, buffalo, and deer, and raided the black bear dens.

Harrison had emphasized this very point to President Jefferson and Secretary Dearborn and how a simple glance at a Native person's physical condition could tell him if they belonged to a tribe near white settlement or one far away.

Tecumseh also felt the stress weighing on Shawnee life and their ancestral hunting, fishing, gathering, and corn-growing. On the White River he married for a second time, to Mamate, and for a second time split up. Half Shawnee and half white, Mamate apparently could not meet his exacting domestic standards. She couldn't neatly sew a new paint pouch for Tecumseh and had to ask another village woman, which finally broke the marriage. That's the story later remembered by Anthony Shane and his Shawnee wife, Lameteshe. Older sister Tecumpease and her husband adopted the son born to Tecumseh's second marriage, Paukeesaa—translated as "Crouched" or "A Panther Stalking Its Prey."

What could Tecumpease have said to her brothers as traditional Shawnee culture began to buckle around them? She had a special relationship with Tecumseh—was "a great favorite with her brother," one acquaintance reported. "She was intelligent and had command of all the women," recalled the Shanes in a joint interview. A captive of the Shawnee remembered that Tecumpease had "much influence over the other females of the tribe."

Among the Eastern Woodland tribes, women wielded an extraordinary amount of power. This was especially the case among the Algonquian-speaking tribes, many of which were matrilineal—meaning they traced descent through the female line. Though speakers of an Algonquian language, the Shawnee were not matrilineal like neighboring tribes, but their society gave women pivotal roles in making decisions of great consequence such as declaring war or seeking peace.

Coming from an exemplary family line of Shawnee leaders on both her mother's and her father's sides, Tecumpease possessed the status of a principal female chief of the band. Male Shawnee chiefs were known as either "war chiefs" or "peace chiefs"—the former having proved themselves in battle, and the latter akin to the civic leaders of a village. Usually related to male chiefs, female chiefs also had powerful sway over making war or peace. A Shawnee "peace woman" could approach a war chief who sought to launch a strike against an enemy. She would ask him to consider the human consequences and back down from his aggression.

"Setting before him the care and anxiety & pain which the women experience in their birth & education [of their children] she appeals to his better feelings and implores him to spare the innocent & unoffending against whom his hand is raised. She seldom fails to dissuade him," wrote C. C. Trowbridge of Shawnee female chiefs, after interviewing Shawnee informants in the 1820s, including Tecumpease and Tecumseh's younger brother.

What role might older sister Tecumpease have played to compel her brothers to stand up to the crisis confronting Shawnee existence in the Ohio Valley? One can only speculate about this as no direct sources exist. Sources have established, however, that a great deal of family honor was at stake. She had raised her younger brothers. They descended from a long and honorable family of Shawnee warriors and leaders. Their older brother Chiksika had died fighting the whites who tried to take Shawnee lands, as had their brother Sauwauseekau and their father, Puckeshinwa, whose dying words elicited from his eldest son the promise that he and his younger brothers would uphold the family honor and never give in.

They had a deep family tradition as warriors and leaders, but could the last three surviving brothers live up to the family's honor? Lalawethika, the Loud One, had proved an incompetent warrior, a poor hunter, a drinker of whiskey, and a loud talker about himself. Of her two other surviving brothers, Kumskaukau, Lalawethika's twin, lived up to the values of a Shawnee male and was a valuable member of the group although known more for affability than leadership. Tecumseh had stood out as a courageous warrior, a skilled hunter, and a respected leader of his band.

But he had come to the White River to pursue a quiet life and indulge his passion for hunting and contests of all kinds.

As the older sister who had raised them, Tecumpease had witnessed the entire arc of their family history, personal growth, and territorial loss. She possessed the influence to urge her younger brothers—all of them— that now was the time to act, before the Shawnee way of life disappeared.

Thousands of miles away, diplomats in European capitals swung deals in American land trades whose effects would ripple across the Atlantic to the upper branches of the White River.

President Jefferson was feeling boxed in by France's sudden control of the entire western U.S. border, the result of Napoleon's Italy-for-Louisiana swap with Spain. He decided to threaten the rising autocrat who then called himself premier consul of France (and would soon crown himself emperor). If France refused to give up New Orleans—the crucial shipping port for the continent's midsection—the United States would form an alliance with France's mortal enemy, Great Britain.

Napoleon, expert at the global gaming table, prepared to make a stunning about-face. His invasion of the rebellious sugar island of Saint-Domingue—today's Haiti—had gotten bogged down in a morass of mosquitoes, mud, and raging yellow fever that annihilated both his troops and his own brother-in-law, French commander Charles Leclerc, in November 1802. With Napoleon's Caribbean sugar-island scheme collapsing by early 1803—the same time that Governor Harrison, on behalf of President Jefferson, completed his first land grab around Vincennes—Napoleon abandoned his plan for a new French colonial empire in North America. He no longer needed New Orleans or the vast Louisiana Territory for logistical support.

In a shocking surprise, Napoleon offered to sell to the United States the claims France held to New Orleans and the entire Louisiana Territory for the absurdly low price of $15 million—or half a billion acres at roughly three cents each.

President Jefferson jumped on it. Among its many advantages for U.S. westward expansion, this bargain could provide Jefferson with a morally defensible way to deal with the "Indian problem." Before, the Louisiana Territory had belonged to a foreign power—France or Spain. Pushing Native people of the Eastern Woodland tribes to move there was, in effect, exiling them from the United States.

But with the Louisiana Purchase, Native peoples who refused to relinquish their lands and "wandering ways" in the Ohio Valley, Great Lakes region, or Southeast and adopt small-scale farming and "civilization" as Jefferson wanted them to do, could now migrate across the Mississippi into this vast, new part of the United States. Assuming the trans-Mississippi tribes welcomed them, the newcomers could roam and hunt all they wanted on U.S. territory until that time—as usual, there would be a hitch—that the United States needed these lands for settlement. Jefferson's representatives in Paris sealed the deal for 828,000 square miles in April 1803. Nearly doubling the existing size of the nation, it placed the United States "among the powers of the first rank," as one of the president's foreign ministers put it.

Jefferson dispatched explorers Meriwether Lewis and William Clark west to find a water route across North America to the Pacific. This out-of-the-blue Louisiana Purchase opened up vast new possibilities for the young country. It allowed Jefferson, always looking westward, a much grander vision of the nation stretching toward the Pacific. Trade routes and settlement could potentially span the continent from the Atlantic Seaboard to the Pacific Coast. But to realize this vision Jefferson needed legal title to lands now held by dozens if not hundreds of Indian tribes—not simply a bill of sale from France.

This had its roots in the U.S. Constitution, in which the Founding Fathers recognized tribes as separate nations that possessed their own national sovereignty. But, consulting the political theories of Switzerland's

Emer de Vattel and his *Law of Nations* (1758), the founders also decided that the sovereignty of nations within U.S. borders was secondary to the sovereignty of the United States itself.

In short, the United States could claim general sovereignty over Native lands within U.S. boundaries. But to gain legal title to actual parcels of their land, the Constitution requires the government to make treaties with each nation. It gives this treaty-making authority to the president, as stated in Article II, Section 2, "with the Advice and Consent" of at least two-thirds of the Senate.* At the time, however, the Senate faced a disadvantage in understanding Indigenous affairs. In that era of slow overland communications, the Senate had few ways of knowing the on-the-ground situation far out in Indian country. The president received information through his network of territorial governors and their Indian agents who reported to his War Department, and so the Senate had to rely heavily on what the executive branch told it about distant affairs.

And far out in Indian country, on that island of federal lands, stood William Henry Harrison. President Jefferson and Governor Harrison quickly discovered that they thought in tandem: Get Native lands. Initially, Jefferson felt the urgency of the French about to take over Louisiana and possibly strengthening the hands of Native nations in disputes with the United States. After he unexpectedly acquired the Louisiana Territory, he was determined to nail down Native lands quickly. The pres-

---

* The "Advice and Consent" of the Senate became a contentious phrase soon after it was written in the Constitution when, in August 1789, President Washington walked down the street with Secretary Knox to seek, for the first time, the "advice" of the Senate on treaties under negotiation with southeastern tribes. The senators could not hear Knox read out the questions to be considered in the hall due to noisy carriages rattling outside. After closing the windows, senators devolved into procedural wrangling over what the phrase meant. Washington exploded in a "violent fret," as one senator described it, with the president exclaiming, "This defeats every purpose of my coming here!" Coming back two days later, Washington obtained the Senate's consent for the treaty in a calmer atmosphere but was heard to remark to someone that he would "be damned if he ever went there again" for Senate consent on Indian treaties. Nor did he, or any president since. Thereafter, he sent a written request for the Senate's approval on Indian treaties only after the treaty had been negotiated and finalized.

ident extended Harrison carte blanche in his usual elegantly veiled prose, "Of the means however of obtaining what we wish you will be the best judge . . . and finally consolidate our whole country into one nation only. . . . For this purpose we have given you a general commission [for making treaties]."

Harrison had first swung the 1802–3 deal to get the 1.1 million acres around Vincennes by digging out the old French treaties, targeting key chiefs, and, if they refused to meet, threatening to cut off their annual payments due from the Greenville Treaty. In mid-1803, employing a similar gambit from the "divide and conquer" playbook, he approached the Kaskaskia tribe whose homelands lay in the Illinois country bordering the Mississippi River. Warfare with Potawatomi, attacks by white fron- tiersmen, and disease had decimated Kaskaskia numbers to a mere thirty or so tribal members. Harrison offered the tiny tribe the protection of the U.S. government from outside threat. He dangled other benefits before them—350 acres of land each, a small reservation of 1,280 acres, and a doubling of their annual Greenville payment to one thousand dollars. Plus a new house and fenced field for their chief Ducoigne, and a new Catholic church with a paid priest (early French fur traders had brought their religion to the Kaskaskia).

It may have sounded like a lot for a tribe of thirty. In return, however, Harrison had them sign away something far, far larger—their rights to eight million acres along the Mississippi and Ohio rivers in today's south- ern Illinois. These lands lay about 250 miles *west* of the Greenville Line— the supposed limit of white settlement.

Harrison was becoming a powerful man. Congress temporarily merged the new Upper Louisiana Territory with Harrison's Indiana Ter- ritory to work out court systems and other details. With the two territories united, William Henry now administered a significant portion of the North American continent. He did not spend these months idly. He rode west with a military escort in October 1804 to arrange details of the trans- fer at St. Louis. That same month, Nancy gave birth to their fifth child back at Grouseland, their children now ranging in age from infancy to eight years old.

Taking care of territorial business and warming to Jefferson's directive, Harrison masterminded one of his most egregious treaties in St. Louis that fall of 1804. Conveniently for Governor Harrison, at the same time five Sauk (or Sac) and Fox warriors and chiefs had traveled to St. Louis on a peace mission delivering up a warrior accused of killing a white man. Given carte blanche by President Jefferson to bag as much real estate as he could get, Governor Harrison spotted a ripe opportunity.

He used as his agents the shrewd and hard-bargaining Chouteau brothers, Pierre and Auguste, wealthy traders in St. Louis. The brothers, according to some accounts, extended the Sauk and Fox visitors a long line of credit at the Chouteau warehouses to buy whiskey, bright cloth, and other luxuries. At the Chouteaus' inflated prices, they quickly ran up a debt that came to $2,234 in the brothers' reckoning. Governor Harrison then struck a deal with the group, who had come to St. Louis on a peace mission, not to negotiate a treaty. He offered to release their accused brother warrior from jail and have the Chouteaus cancel their debts if the Sauk and Fox signed over tribal lands. When totaled, these amounted to an astounding fifteen million acres—encompassing a great stretch of Illinois prairie, north to the forested hills of Wisconsin country, and west to the Mississippi bluffs. These lands lay nearly five hundred miles west of the once-sacred Greenville Line.

In addition to freedom for their warrior and the cancellation of their Chouteau debt, the Sauk and Fox tribes would receive $1,000 annually and the protection of the U.S. government from hostile tribes or aggressive settlers. Ambiguous wording in the treaty rendered it unclear whether the Sauk and Fox could live and hunt there forever—or only until American settlers arrived.

It was absurd on the face of it—the five chiefs and subchiefs had received no authority from their tribal councils to negotiate, nor would they knowingly give away so much land for so little. But, authorized to act on his own and propelled by President Jefferson's urgency, Governor Harrison signed and sealed this travesty of a treaty with the five. If the leaders had had any inkling of how whites would interpret it or a single lawyer to represent them, they would have contemptuously tossed the so-called treaty into the council fire. This land grab would haunt the United States for many years to come—including in the future Black Hawk War—as would other treaties like it engineered by Harrison and his colleagues.

Protests by chiefs who called out Harrison's treaties as unfair had little impact in Washington, D.C.

"Friend and Brother!" Delaware chiefs protested in a March 1805 message to President Jefferson about lands on the White River. "You may judge how our chiefs felt when they returned home and found that the Governor had been shutting up their eyes and stopping their Ears with his good words and got them to sign a Deed for their lands without their knowledge. . . . The [Delaware chiefs] now declare to you from the bottom of their hearts in the presence of God that they never sold Governor Harrison or the United States any land at Vincennes last summer to their knowledge."

These protests didn't stop Harrison from pursuing more of his "treaties," nor his mentor Thomas Jefferson from rationalizing the need for them.

"The inexorable progress of civilization—self-evidently a good thing [in Jefferson's mind]—absolved Americans of agency or moral responsibility for the displacement of indigenous peoples," writes Peter S. Onuf in *Jefferson's Empire*. "White settlers' land hunger [in Jefferson's view] thus was not a threat but a resource Indians should exploit."

With rationales like these overcoming any moral qualms, William Henry in his first five years as territorial governor made an incredible run in acquiring Native lands—or, as he put it, "extinguishing title." This meant getting a piece of paper signed by Natives (or marked in some way) that took legal title to lands so whites could purchase and settle surveyed plots on it.

1.2 million acres—Treaty with the Delaware, June 1803

8 million acres—Treaty with the Kaskaskia, August 1803

1.5 million acres—Treaty with the Delaware, 1804

1.5 million acres—Treaty with the Piankeshaw, 1804

15 million acres—Treaty with the Sauk and Fox, November 1804

2 million acres—Treaty of Grouseland, August 1805

29.2 million—Total acres of Native lands acquired by Harrison, 1802-5

On the tributaries of the White, the Wabash, and other rivers, tribal cultures sagged under the effects of whiskey, lack of game, sickness, and especially encroachment by white settlers. Each year, Harrison's "title extinguishing" further hemmed in lands on which the Shawnee, Delaware, and Miami resided.

During the winter of 1804-5, as William Henry rode home from St. Louis to Grouseland to meet his new son, John Scott, disease leveled villages along the White River upstream of the Wabash. In the spring it killed Buckongahelas, the great Delaware chief living on the White whose age was counted at more than eighty winters and who had helped orchestrate the destruction of St. Clair. Flooding ruined the cornfields that spring. Paranoia rippled through the villages on the White. Some villagers suspected witches—persons harnessing evil spirits—traveled in their midst. Others asked how their own behavior may have offended the Great Spirit and other spirits now wreaking havoc on them.

In this season of distress and profound spiritual imbalance, a prophetess arose in a Delaware village on the White just upriver from Tecumseh's village. An elderly Delaware woman named Beata had heard Christian teachings at a Moravian mission in Pennsylvania as a young girl, when the tribe lived farther east. She may have also learned from Neolin, a famous Delaware prophet of the 1760s.

The tradition of prophets, notes Tecumseh biographer John Sugden,

Harrison Land Acquisitions
Beyond the Greenville Line, 1802–1805

---------- The Greenville Line (1795)

Harrison Land Acquisitions Beyond the Greenville Line

Previous U.S. Land Acquisitions in the Northwest Territory

① From Sauk and Fox (1804)
② From Kaskaskia (1803)
③ From Piankeshaw (1805)

④ Vincennes Tract (1802)
⑤ From Delaware and Piankeshaw (1804)
⑥ Treaty of Fort Wayne (1809)
*(Breaking point for Tecumseh and allies)

went far back with tribes like the Delaware and Shawnee. "At times of extreme public alarm," he writes, "these prophets inspired intense fanaticism in Indians brought face-to-face with the fury of the spirits. In securer days, when the terrors had abated, the tradition survived as an undercurrent."

Younger warriors in the Delaware villages passionately embraced Beata's visions—the Delaware had neglected their old traditions and ceremonies, and succumbed to whiskey, fighting, stealing, abuse, and promiscuity. A time of reckoning neared—a great storm that would punish the wicked and root out witches. Beata claimed she could identify witches among them who dispensed their poison. As her fame spread, distraught individuals in villages up and down the White requested her healing powers.

An elderly Shawnee healer, Penagasha, or "Changing Feathers," had taught Tecumseh's brother Lalawethika some of his powers and incantations and how to use roots and other herbal medicines. Changing Feathers had died recently, so perhaps it was not entirely a surprise that soon after Beata's appearance and Changing Feathers's death, Lalawethika transformed into a prophet, too.

As the story is told, one day in spring 1805 Lalawethika was sitting in his wigwam about to light his pipe. As he brought a coal from the fire to the pipe bowl he suddenly tipped over, unconscious. He remained that way, unmoving, eyes closed, for hours while his wife and other villagers worried that he had died. He finally awoke, sat up, and announced he had undertaken a great journey. The Master of Life had sent two young men to summon his soul into the spirit world. There he saw a beautiful green land rich with clear streams, plentiful game, and fertile cornfields. This awaited the spirits of Shawnees who lived virtuously. The spirits of wicked Shawnees started on the path toward this paradise, but it soon forked and shunted them aside into a great longhouse where fiery tortures awaited them. Only when they renounced their wicked ways could they regain the path leading to paradise.

Lalawethika also announced that he had acquired a new name—no longer "The Loud One" but Tenskwatawa, or "The Open Door." Whites would soon refer to him simply as "The Prophet."

The new religion he espoused immediately struck a deep chord among the Shawnee, Delaware, and other Ohio Valley tribes that had struggled in the face of white settlement. They came from other villages and tribes to see him and hear him, watching as he would convulse with emotion, then sink into a trance, solemnly describe his visions, and deliver instructions from the Great Spirit that would set the world right again.

The Great Spirit told him to relocate his village far from witches—individuals believed to have control over evil spirits—to land near abandoned Fort Greenville, where peace was made a decade earlier. Their spiritual power no longer resided in the pouches around their necks known as "medicine bags," now used by witches, the Prophet told his followers. This revolutionary directive overthrew generations of faith in the potency of medicine pouches. They had to rekindle their fires, give up whiskey, renounce their sins, and return to the traditional ways. His message was repeated up and down the branches of the White.

The Prophet, notes Sugden, "was the voice of an oppressed people. Around him the tribes were losing almost everything—their lands, security, livelihoods, cultures, dignity, and self-respect, even their very identities.... The reform movement had begun long before Lalawethika's intervention, and he was an expression, not a cause of it, its disciple rather than its mentor. He added impetus, but made no changes to the direction of the process; nor was he able to control the energies it released."

Immediately those energies took a dark turn. It was widely believed among some villages that sorcery by witches—and not necessarily contact with whites—caused sudden, inexplicable outbreaks of disease. As word of Tenskwatawa's spiritual powers spread, a Delaware village suspecting witches in its midst summoned him. Whether by coincidence or by choice, he identified as witches two chiefs—Tetepachsit and Hackinkpomska—who had been most responsible for signing away to Harrison a large block of land near Vincennes. In March 1806, warriors with blackened faces tortured Tetepachsit with fire, eliciting a confession of sorcery with his medicine bag, then burned him to death, along with an elderly Delaware headwoman who had been baptized by Moravians.

More executions followed in the days thereafter until the village began to split into factions, and relatives demanded a release of imprisoned witch suspects. Reports of the witch executions soon reached Governor Harrison at Grouseland from his outlying contacts—informants among Moravian missionaries on the White, his Indian agent at Fort Wayne, and allies among the tribes.

Governor Harrison learned of this strange new figure who had suddenly appeared in his Indiana Territory, drawing disciples and executing witches. With alarm, he addressed the Delaware and urged them to stop. He called out this supposed prophet who wantonly advocated murder and whose rise threatened his own vision of western lands.

> *My children*—My heart is filled with grief, and my eyes are dissolved in tears, at the news which has reached me.... My children, tread back the steps you have taken, and endeavor to regain the straight road.... The dark, crooked and thorny one which you are now pursuing will certainly lead to endless woe and misery. But who is this pretended prophet who dares to speak in the name of the Great Creator? Examine him.... Demand of him some proofs.... If God has really employed him he has doubtless authorized him to perform some miracles.... If he is really a prophet, ask of him to cause the sun to stand still—the moon to alter its course.

Lalawethika then did exactly that. That summer he announced to his followers that he would cause the sun to go dark. On June 16, 1806, he entered his wigwam and remained there all morning. Around noon, the full sun of day began to dim, the birds began to chirp, the air began to chill, and the sun's disk went dark. He had predicted the solar eclipse that occurred in the Ohio Valley that June day in 1806. Whether he knew

about it through Shawnee tracking of astronomical events or from European scientists who had trekked to the Ohio Valley to track it remains
unclear. But it provided a direct rebuttal to Harrison's attempt to discredit
his teaching and deepened the passion of his followers as well as sharpened the resistance of some chiefs who saw him as their rival.

"Did I not prophecy truly?" he exclaimed, emerging from his wigwam.
"Behold! Darkness has shrouded the sun!"

Amazing stories of his supernatural powers spread among tribes of the
Ohio Valley. He could make pumpkins as large as a wigwam sprout in village gardens and raise an ear of corn large enough to feed a dozen warriors. It was clear to his followers that neither Governor Harrison at
Vincennes nor the Great Father in Washington could pull off a feat like
that.

CHAPTER 7

A VOICE IN THE MOONLIGHT

A t Grouseland, anxiety wafted like candle smoke through the big house. When Nancy noticed it, perhaps tending to the place settings for guests, the bullet hole in the dining room shutter caused her to pause. Her husband had been walking before the fire cradling their baby son John Scott one chill evening when a muffled shot sounded outside. A musket ball splintered the black walnut shutter and buried itself in the robin's-egg blue plaster wall, barely missing Harrison, who had recently "taken title" to the fifteen million acres "relinquished" by the Sauk and Fox. He had also recently attempted to import a disguised form of slavery to the Indiana Territory, where Congress had explicitly banned it.

Someone wanted William Henry Harrison dead. Nancy didn't know who.

She believed in her husband and in his political career. He was attempting to shape a new world from these forested wilds and tawny prairies, bringing Christ and charity and civilization, farms and towns, schools and churches. His work offered poor white folks a chance to escape fever-ridden cities and servitude to migrate here beyond the mountains and buy rich lands at little cost, creating a new life impossible to imagine while toiling for a master on the East Coast or in Old Europe.

But not everyone shared his vision. That bullet hole in the dining room shutter remained a token—an everyday reminder of her family's precarious foothold. The unknown began just beyond those walnut shutters, where the oaks and hickories edged up to the grassy meadows that fringed Grouseland. The Wabash River slid serenely past only a stone's throw from her elegant entrance hall, brightly papered a lemon yellow in her favorite pattern, "King George III Pillars and Arches." What could ascend or descend that river any day? What fleets of canoes paddled by warriors, bare torsos painted in blacks and reds, heads plucked bald with eagle feathers braided into topknots, silver bands around biceps, and tomahawks in their belts?

Was it worth it—this tenuous destiny they had chosen for themselves and their children?

As the new year of 1807 arrived, dark rumors raced among frontier cabins about a meeting of tribes near abandoned Fort Greenville. Shawnees were gathering on the *wrong* side of the Greenville Line—a few miles into settlers' territory. (Not that *settlers* on the wrong side of the line caused much concern among whites.) Whispers grew that they were plotting a massive attack on white settlements, including those on the proper side of the line.

This frightening talk eventually reached the new Shaker colony at Turtle Creek near Cincinnati. Amid these rumors of war, the Shakers heard that a religious "prophet" led these this group. Despite settlers' warnings they may have heard to stay away, instead of raw terror, this aroused the Shakers' curiosity. In the Shaker way of thinking, the spirit of God might be upon them.

Splitting from the Quakers half a century earlier, Shakers advocated communal living, sexual equality, and pacifism, and celebrated visions, dancing, and ecstatic movement known to outsiders as "the jerks"—thus distinguishing them as the "Shaking Quakers."* The Turtle Creek Shakers' visions told them that the Natives at Greenville suffered persecution like themselves. They selected three young men to locate the rumored prophet's gathering in the belief that he and his followers sought Shaker religious teaching. This trio would leave to history a rare and detailed description of the Prophet's first settlement.

Infused with an epic sense of Old Testament purpose, the three struck blindly into the woods on horseback and spent a week of wrong turns and frigid nights before emerging into a prairie opening. The crumbling stockades of Fort Greenville—made obsolete by Fort Wayne on the Maumee River—rose on a hill at the prairie's north end as the trio rode south toward a large complex of corn plots and pole fences. After a mile of these, they arrived at a settlement of dozens of smoking wigwams and tents that surrounded an "immense building" measuring, they later determined, 150 feet in length—a kind of wood-beamed cathedral in the wilderness.

"What is that great house for?" the Shakers asked when met by a Shawnee villager who spoke English. His name was Peter Cornstalk, son of the great chief Cornstalk.

"To worship the great spirit," Peter Cornstalk replied, as documented by the trio's journal keeper, "Little Benjamin" Youngs.

"Who is your chief speaker?" they asked.

---

* "Another sect, the Shakers, say they worship God best by singing merry tunes and dancing and hornpipes," wrote Judge John Symmes to his daughter Nancy Harrison, of the eclectic religious groups in his neighborhood along the Ohio. "They almost dance themselves to death. . . . There are here too, old Presbyterians . . . Seceders . . . Independents . . . Roman Catholics who have their sins pardoned by their priests, and high-church people, who call all other sects irregular. But the best religion after all is to fear God and do all the good we can."

"Our prophet Lallawasheka, he can converse with the good spirit, & tells us the way to be good. . . . We believe in him, he can dream to God!"

The gravity of the Prophet's followers struck the young Shakers. "All the village seemed to be moved & look'd serious," they noted, "& some appeared very solemn in tears & could scarce take their eyes off us."

A Shawnee chief whose name, as Youngs spelled it phonetically, was "Tekumsaw," guided them a few miles through the forest to the Prophet, who was staying at a maple sugar camp. Tecumseh entered a chief's tent, leaving them outside around a fire. Eventually another English-speaking Shawnee emerged—George Bluejacket, son of the great Shawnee leader whose Western Confederacy destroyed St. Clair's army. White ministers dismiss the things of which the Prophet speaks as foolishness, George Bluejacket told the trio. Therefore, he said, the Shawnees did not wish to speak of it to white people.

"We are not of those kind of ministers," one of the Shakers protested. "We are a people that are separated from them by the work of the great spirit, they count us foolish too & speak against us."

Did the Shakers believe, George Bluejacket asked further, "that a person could have the Knowledge of the good spirit & know what was good by an inward feeling without going to school & learning letters?"

> We told him we believed they might & that was the best kind of knowledge that we felt in the heart. . . .
>
> He told us that their prophet had that knowledge & had been increasing in it for two years & had great understanding & was still seeing more and more wonderful things which he taught the people.

The Shakers assured Bluejacket of their mutual outcast status: "[The ministers] hated us & spoke evil of us because they did not understand the work of [the] good spirit which was among us."

Having established this bond as fellow pariahs from white society, the trio asked to learn the Prophet's teachings. In return, they would answer any questions the Prophet had about Shaker beliefs. George Bluejacket again disappeared into the chief's tent. As the three sat around the smoking fire in the chill March air, Little Benjamin noted the modesty, politeness, and hardworking nature of the women in camp who gathered firewood and did other domestic chores. But they were unsettled by the "heathenish" shaved heads and feather-entwined topknots of the male hunters and warriors, with their painted faces, nose jewels, and tinkling silver earrings.

Waiting anxiously, the Shakers didn't know if friend or enemy would emerge, Little Benjamin reported, but their faith in a universality of spirit had brought them this far. They decided to ride it to the end.

Bluejacket finally reemerged from between the tent flaps, followed by the Shawnee Prophet himself, unadorned but for a large tobacco pipe and a wrap fastened with a clasp. One eye wandered sideways, half-closed, from a long-ago injury. Slim and of average size, he joined the circle around the fire. For a time he sat silently, all eyes upon him, appearing "under great sufferings & in deep labour & distress of mind . . . his countenance grave & solemn."

"He began to speak," recorded Little Benjamin, "& with his eyes closed continued his speech about half an hour in a very eloquent & emphatical manner; he sensibly spake by the power of God—his solemn voice, grave countenance, with every motion of his hand & gesture of his body, were expressive of a deep sence & solemn feeling of eternal things."

"Sequoy!" Other warriors and chiefs who had gathered around the fire and in the tent cried out at his every pause, punctuating his words with passionate agreement. "Sequoy!"

He was a wicked person until two years ago, the Prophet said, sitting trancelike. He then told the story, recorded in detail by Little Benjamin, of how formerly he had been a wicked person, and had one day fallen into a trance, journeyed to the Great Spirit, and returned transformed bearing instructions to live properly.

The Great Spirit had directed him to make a village, he said. Here was the spot chosen by the Great Spirit—far from practitioners of witchcraft, yet near Fort Greenville where peace was made. While it sat ten miles on the American side of the Greenville Line, the land did not belong to the Americans, whatever they claimed otherwise—it belonged to the Great Spirit. The Prophet and his followers came in peace, with the spirit of love and with open hearts. Anyone who thought they came for war was foolish, he told the Shakers. Many Natives of different tribes had traveled here the previous year to listen to his teachings about how they could set their world right by renouncing the white man's path and return to their old ways. While it was early spring now and travel still difficult, he told them, this coming summer thousands more would come from distant red nations to hear him speak.

The three young men listened raptly. After their long wilderness jour-ney to find these people, a spirit of togetherness with the Shawnees and mutual love for the Great Spirit filled the Shakers' hearts, Little Benjamin reported.

That night at the main camp, a full March moon lifted over dark forest groves and the silvery pools of prairie openings. A gossamer veil of woodsmoke rose from campfires smoldering among the wigwams, grouped like a gathering of giant beetles at rest in the moonlight.

A single voice called out in Shawnee, deep and powerful, reverberat-ing across prairie and forest. Given a wigwam in which to sleep, a fire tended by Shawnee women, and wild turkey stew, the young Shaker men quietly observed the evening prayer ritual. Though they did not under-stand the words, the force of the voice astonished them, its stentorian tones rising to shrillness, then deepening. It carried at least two miles, the Shakers estimated.

The voice paused for a moment.

"Sequoy!" replied dozens of answering voices in a single cry—a shout signaling approval—that leapt from wigwams and campfires.

To the three Shakers witnessing it, the moonlit vista on the prairie opening brought to mind scenes from the Old Testament, where the mystery and spirit is present and the divine lives in the most unexpected places.

"Our feelings were like Jacob's when he cried out, 'how terrible is this place, surely God is in this place & the world know it not,'" they recorded.

The Shawnee orator again beseeched under the moonlight.

Again echoed the unified response, "Sequoy!"

From his Grouseland parlor with its curved bay window facing upstream, Governor Harrison kept a watchful eye for any suspicious craft coming down the Wabash. He didn't like what he was hearing from his contacts about the new village at Greenville and the Prophet's swelling followers.

One explanation for trouble stirring came to William Henry's mind—the British. Since their support of the Western Confederacy and construction of Fort Miami in the early 1790s, the British, in his view, had never ceased trying to stir up trouble.* They had convenient bases in nearby Canada from which to dispatch their agents to agitate anti-U.S. sentiment in Indiana Territory tribes, thus stymieing U.S. westward expansion and regaining continental dominance for the British Empire.

The rumors reaching William Henry grew louder. As the Prophet had predicted to the Shakers, with the spring thaw of 1807, his followers began their pilgrimages from distant tribes toward Greenville, in the footsteps of his earlier acolytes who had arrived the previous year. Tenskwatawa's message echoed for a thousand miles across the heart of America that summer of 1807—from the Tennessee Valley to the farthest bays of

* Only reluctantly, after U.S.-British negotiations in the mid-1790s formalized in the Jay Treaty (1794), had the British relinquished Fort Miami and other forts on the American side of the Great Lakes. Fiercely opposed by France and its supporters in the United States, the Jay Treaty also opened trade between the United States and Britain. It triggered the first wave of intense party polarization in U.S. history when politicians fractured into pro-treaty Federalists (Hamiltonians) and anti-treaty Democratic-Republicans (Jeffersonians).

Lake Superior. Potawatomis rode from the prairies of the Illinois country to the Shawnee Prophet's new village. Ottawas from the northern Michigan country canoed down the Great Lakes to hear him speak.

He urged rejection of the white man's whiskey and materialism. He urged respect for elders and kindness toward others. He rejected the white man's spun clothing, livestock, white bread, and fire making with flint and steel instead of kindling a spark with friction and sticks. He even rejected the white man's lethal firearms except for self-defense, and advocated traditional bow and arrow for hunting. The Prophet did not advocate violence. Rather, he wanted his followers "to live in peace with all mankind."

He spoke passionately of generosity rather than succumbing to the white man's lust for accumulation. Those who sought "wealth and ornaments," he said, would "crumble into dust." Those who provided for others would live the afterlife in a well-stocked wigwam.

"Traditionally the Shawnees had been a communal society, but now some tribesmen hoarded food or gunpowder while others went hungry," writes biographer R. David Edmunds. "The Master of Life considered such selfishness to be particularly wicked, since it spread dissension throughout the Indian camps and contributed to the violence that had so decimated his people. Accumulated wealth was only valuable when it was given away. The Shawnees must return to the ways of their fathers."

Yet Tenskwatawa's teachings did not advocate a complete return to traditional Shawnee spirituality. Rather, he espoused a blend—syncretism, in formal terms—of Shawnee and Christian religions. For the Shawnee of the Ohio Valley, traditional spirituality focused on the natural world and its countless spirits—animal spirits, the sun, the moon, the Four Winds, Corn Woman, Earth Mother, and many more. The Shawnee lived in intimate proximity with these spirits, which they perceived all around them. From a young age, a boy or girl on a vision quest would hope that an animal spirit would appear to help guide him or her throughout life. The spirits were everywhere.

"It was the interplay of these spirits which controlled every event, bringing success or failure," writes Tecumseh biographer John Sugden, "and it was essential to invest a great amount of time and effort in securing their goodwill."

Tenskwatawa's teachings also borrowed from earlier prophets such as Neolin and Beata who had woven in certain Catholic beliefs—the notion of Hell, of confession, of monogamy. In one way, according to Tenskwatawa, they were to abandon the custom of their fathers—get rid of their medicine bags that embodied witchcraft. Yet some Shawnee groups adamantly rejected Tenskwatawa's teachings and his spiritual epicenter near Greenville. Black Hoof and other chiefs at Wapakoneta had embraced white agriculture and the government support promised in the Greenville Treaty. They directly challenged the Prophet and Tecumseh as leaders of the Shawnee. At the same time, however, Blue Jacket, the great Shawnee chief who had directed the defeat of St. Clair and signed the Greenville Treaty, committed himself to Tenskwatawa's movement while opposing Black Hoof's Wapakoneta Shawnee faction.

"The battle between the Wapakoneta chiefs and the Shawnee brothers," writes Sugden, "was a sincerely fought contest for the hearts and minds of the Shawnee people."

Northern and western tribes were especially receptive to the Prophet's message, while southeastern tribes would prove more resistant. Ottawa converts paddled back to their northern homes led by a warrior anointed "The Herald" bringing word of the new religion. Traders reported that on the shores of Lake Superior, entire Chippewa villages imbued with the Prophet's teachings erupted with ecstatic dancing that summer of 1807. They heaved their traditional medicine pouches into the lake's crystalline waters, where they bobbed on the waves breaking onto pebbled beaches. The abandoned bags represented a discarding of the old spirits and witchcraft and the acceptance of Tenskwatawa's teachings.

The message traveled by birchbark canoe along rivers and through northern forests nearly to the ice floes of Hudson's Bay. It raced on the small, agile horses westward onto the Plains to the earthen lodges of the Mandan and possibly still farther toward the snowy spine of the Rocky Mountains, where warrior Blackfeet dwelled in tipis along its base. Across the heart of the continent, the message resonated with tribes pressed by white encroachment at their lodges' doors. Thousands began the pilgrimage to the Shawnee village near Fort Greenville's falling stockades to hear the Prophet speak. When four hundred Potawatomi, Ottawa, and Chippewa (Ojibwe) pilgrims arrived at the brothers' village in April, with the ripening of the corn still months away, food grew scarce. Tenskwatawa sent the seekers home bearing the message to send only a few representatives from each village to learn his teachings, and to come at harvest time.

He instructed his followers to pray morning and evening to Waashaa Monetoo—the Great Spirit—asking that the earth provide them with plenty, and with "the Deer, the Bear, and all the wild animals, and the Fish that swim in the river."

If they followed traditional ways and separated from the American "Long Knives," Tenskwatawa proclaimed, they would ultimately prevail.

"I will overturn the land," he announced, "so all the white people will be covered and you alone shall inhabit the land."

All that summer of 1807, U.S. government representatives and white settlers tried to fathom what was happening in the Ohio. Indian agents reported that great numbers of Native people from hundreds—perhaps thousands—of miles away were gathering at the Shawnee brothers' village, passing through Fort Wayne and other isolated outposts en route. Something odd and potentially very dangerous was occurring here, and no one among the white settlers or U.S. agents knew what it was.

It was probably not a surprise to the Shawnee brothers, then, that soon after the Shakers' visit in spring of 1807 a messenger rode into their village. He had been sent by William Wells, U.S. Indian agent at Fort

Wayne, about eighty miles north. Tensions already existed between Tecumseh and Wells, a former white captive who had been raised as a full Miami warrior and had proved his bravery. His red hair had earned him the name Apekonit—"Carrot Top." Wells's allegiances wavered between opposing sides in the wars of the 1790s, and he now spied and scouted for the Americans. Aligning himself with powerful individuals, he married the daughter of Little Turtle, the great Miami war chief of the Western Confederacy who had finally succumbed to U.S. entreaties at the Fort Greenville negotiations.

In the peace following the Treaty of Greenville, Wells's ambitions for power won him an appointment as U.S. Indian agent at Fort Wayne and a trip to Philadelphia with Little Turtle to meet then-President Washington. An untrustworthy, self-dealing opportunist in Tecumseh's eyes, he began to grow rich by taking illicit payments at his government post. He glorified his own importance by sending falsified documents and reports to Secretary Dearborn in Washington, D.C.

The message from Wells demanded that the two Shawnee brothers travel to Fort Wayne to hear a message from the current Great Father, President Jefferson. If they refused to appear, Wells insisted, they must explain in writing why they had located their village on the settlers' side of the Greenville Line. The envoy sent by Wells to the Prophet's village, Anthony Shane, began to translate aloud Wells's message before a full council of chiefs. Part Shawnee, Shane spoke the language fluently. Before he had finished reading the message, however, Tecumseh rose abruptly near the council fire and addressed Shane, who later gave a detailed report of the moment. "Go back to Fort Wayne," said Tecumseh, "and tell Captain Wells, that my fire is kindled on the spot appointed by the Great Spirit above. . . . If he has anything to communicate to me, he must come here."

Tecumseh remained dignified and measured in his bearing. Shane's account of this meeting is one of the first documented descriptions of Tecumseh assuming a prominent role in the Prophet's new spiritual movement. In a manner suggesting that Wells hardly measured up as an equal, Tecumseh added, "I shall expect him in six days from this time."

From roughly this point forward, Tenskwatawa deferred to his older brother in the movement's diplomatic relationship with the white world, and Tecumseh began to see how Tenskwatawa's new religion could reach far beyond the spiritual into the political realm.

As biographer John Sugden puts it, "Why not employ the powerful pulling power of the Prophet's religion to combine moral and cultural re-generation with the long-cherished dream of tribal reunification?" Bring-ing the scattered Shawnee together at Greenville "would place them beneath the direction of Tecumseh, hitherto a minor chief, and his previ-ously disregarded brother. The two were bidding for the blessings of the Great Spirit and tribal leadership at the same time."

Shane departed for Fort Wayne with Tecumseh's message. Six days later he returned with Agent Wells's reply. President Jefferson had re-quested that the Shawnee move their village to the other side of the Greenville Treaty Line, only a few miles away, and off lands now owned by the United States.

Actually, President Jefferson had said no such thing. This was Wells's twisted interpretation of the response from Secretary Dearborn to whom he had addressed complaints about the brothers' Greenville village loca-tion. Secretary Dearborn had simply replied that Wells should take up the matter with Governor Harrison.

Upon hearing Wells's reply, Tecumseh leapt up before the council fire. Speaking this time with indignant passion, recorded Shane, Tecum-seh enumerated the long history of unfair treaties and endless encroach-ments that the United States had committed against the Shawnee and other tribes.

"These lands," he concluded with vehemence and power, "are ours. No one has the right to remove us, because we were the first owners. The Great Spirit above has appointed this place for us to light our fires, and here we will remain. As to boundaries, the Great Spirit above knows no boundaries, nor will his red people acknowledge any."

He paused, turning his attention from the council circle. He gazed straight at the messenger, Shane, perhaps himself sympathetic to Tecumseh. In this key moment in his rise to leadership, Tecumseh now spoke coldly, with disdain—"that stately indifference of manner," as one early biographer puts it, "which he could so gracefully assume when in council."

"If my great father, the President of the Seventeen Fires, has anything more to say to me, he must send a man of note as his messenger. I will hold no further intercourse with Captain Wells."

CHAPTER 8

PRETENDED TREATIES

Tecumseh's cool disdain struck a note of alarm among U.S. authorities in the Indiana Territory. Agent Wells wrote to Governor Harrison that, in his opinion, "the British are at the bottom of this business."

This all made sense to Harrison—the British stirring up trouble with the tribes, never ceasing in their diabolical efforts to restore their American empire. He had seen this on a dramatically personal level at the age of six when Benedict Arnold raided his family's Berkeley Plantation. Reinforcing William Henry's anti-British prejudice was Harrison's boss as territorial governor, Thomas Jefferson, who nurtured a seething hatred of the British, whom he equated with treachery and oppression.

In Harrison's mind, unmistakable confirmation of his suspicions about the British arrived a few months after Tecumseh's rebuff of Agent Wells in spring 1807: the alarming news of an unprovoked attack by a British warship of a U.S. Navy vessel in waters just off the Atlantic Coast.

Early in the summer of 1807, Royal Navy warships plied Chesapeake Bay attempting to blockade two French warships that were undergoing repairs there after a hurricane at sea. The British-French hostilities in Europe had washed across the Atlantic to cause this face-off in Chesapeake Bay. That European showdown in an East Coast estuary sucked in a third power—the young United States—with historic consequences.

One fine June day, a commander in the British Royal Navy, Lord James Townshend, was taking an onshore break at Norfolk, Virginia, from his blockade duties. By chance, he recognized a deserter from his own HMS *Halifax* crew sauntering along the U.S. port's cobbled streets and tarry wharves.

He had jumped ship by stealing a jolly boat in the darkness and rowing to shore. Upon their arrival, he and two fellow culprits had cockily paraded around Norfolk waving an American flag to celebrate their freedom from their British overlord and had signed on as sailors with the U.S. Navy's frigate *Chesapeake*. Confronted in the street by the surprised Lord Townshend, one deserter replied that he would be happy to return to Lord Townshend's *Halifax*. However, one of his coconspirators, Jenkins Ratford, suddenly appeared, grabbed the sailor by the arm, and pulled him away. In parting, Ratford made an obscene gesture at Captain Townshend—the eighteenth-century equivalent of flipping off His Lordship—and brazenly declared that he was "in the land of liberty."

This had become a huge problem for Britain. Deserters from the Royal Navy and other draft-age British males would sign on to American ships wherever they could find them. They believed that once aboard, U.S. sovereignty protected them from being dragooned back into the king's forces to serve as cannon fodder in the Old World.

Europe had grown volatile, largely due to Napoleon's ambition. Giving up on the Caribbean sugar islands, he had massed his French armies near the English Channel and threatened to invade Britain instead. But yet again, he changed his mind. He suddenly swiveled his armies away from England and stormed eastward through Europe. His Grande Armée of 180,000 soldiers invaded the Prussian homelands in order to address threats he saw from eastern Europe and Russia.

Prussia's king Frederick William III balked at facing down Napoleon. The reluctant Prussian king then came under pressure to stand tall from his wife, the young and forthright Queen Louisa, and his advisers. The king marshaled his forces and challenged Napoleon's invading army. But he lost on an epic scale—140,000 Prussian soldiers and 2,000 cannons captured. When the Russian czar sent a force to stop the oncoming French army in Prussia, Napoleon defeated it, too.

Treaty negotiations between Napoleon and Prussia took place that crucial and turbulent summer of 1807. At the same moment that British deserters ducked from *Halifax* officers in Norfolk and William Henry and Nancy worried about a Native attack at Grouseland, Queen Louisa urged her husband not to give up "a hairsbreadth" of Prussian independence to Napoleon during treaty negotiations. "The loss of territory," she warned him in a letter, "is as nothing in comparison with the loss of liberty."

The reluctant Prussian sovereign finally dispatched his persuasive wife to convince, or charm, Napoleon face-to-face into taking leniency on their Prussia.

She asked that he leave western Prussia and the ancient Magdeburg fortress in possession of the Prussian royal couple.

Napoleon was noncommittal—"We will see about it"—and in the end, extracted harsh terms from Prussia, taking nearly half of its territory and a stiff annual levy to keep his French armies on the march.

European kingdoms flipped about at Napoleon's demands. With Emperor Napoleon rolling over duchies and kingdoms, London war planners had to muster every possible British fighting man. Napoleon might turn his armies around to face Britain at any moment. Given this dire need for boots on the ground, when Royal Navy sailor Jenkins Ratford flipped off Lord Townshend in the streets of Norfolk that June claiming he was in the land of liberty, not only was British pride at stake, but the British Empire's future in Europe—and across the globe. Something decisive had to be done. And so dispatches went out to end this sort of nonsense.

Soon thereafter, USS *Chesapeake*, the thirty-eight-gun frigate that Ratford had joined in his defiance of the Royal Navy, sailed out of Chesapeake Bay bound for the Mediterranean. Leaving the bay's protection, she rounded Cape Henry into the open Atlantic. A British warship, the fifty-gun HMS *Leopard*, was cruising offshore. She spotted the *Chesapeake*. The British ship approached and fired a shot across the *Chesapeake*'s bow, hailing her. An officer from each ship talked. Commodore James Barron of the *Chesapeake* refused to turn over any sailors from his sovereign American ship (he had determined three of the four deserters were U.S. citizens).

Captain Salusbury Pryce Humphreys of the Royal Navy's *Leopard* gave the command. His ship unleashed a thundering broadside at close range directly into the American ship. He followed it with six more. Wounded himself, Commodore Barron surrendered what remained of the devastated *Chesapeake* and decimated crew, among them the unharmed Jenkins Ratford, who was indeed a British citizen. The recalcitrant sailor was taken to British Nova Scotia, summarily court-martialed, and, to make a point, hanged from the yardarm of the British warship he had deserted.[*]

The unprovoked (in American eyes) attack on USS *Chesapeake* utterly outraged America. A rebuke wholly without justification! A murderous punishment for minding one's own business! An epic fight brewed between parent and offspring, between this young upstart of a country and the ancient oppressor who had spawned it. President Jefferson wrote that he had not seen Americans this riled up since the Battle of Lexington

---

[*] Many years later, the *Chesapeake*'s Commodore Barron killed the famed U.S. Naval commander Stephen Decatur in a close-range pistol duel, over disparaging remarks Decatur had made to Captain Barron about his lack of preparedness in the *Chesapeake-Leopard* affair.

and Concord. Rather than striking directly back against the British and risking another all-out war, however, Jefferson chose to impose a trade embargo against the import of British goods.

That covered the East Coast ports. But what about the young nation's vast borderlands to the west? The Ohio Valley? The Great Lakes region? The Great Plains beyond the Mississippi, now part of the United States as the Louisiana Territory? The British manned major forts along the Canada-U.S. borderlands in the Great Lakes region. President Jefferson and his agents began to worry that the British would launch operations from these bases to agitate the tribes in the shadowy forest realms, prodding them to pounce on the United States' vaguely defined and weakly guarded West. Using stealthy Native warriors to spring open the back door, the perfidious British would snatch back what they felt was theirs. That was the fear.

William Henry's suspicions of British intrigue in the backcountry deepened as reverberations of the European wars struck the North American interior. Natives and whites fighting on the northwest frontier, however, did not abide by the same gentlemanly European rules of warfare, surrender, and conquest. Rather, they played for keeps. Acutely aware of this, Governor Harrison fixed his watchful eye on his parlor window and kept his cellar-fortress amply stocked with provisions and ammunition for the safety of himself and his growing family.

Reports arrived of great numbers of Native people from near and far congregating at the Shawnee brothers' village near Greenville. *Were the British behind it?* Greenville lay some two hundred miles east of Grouseland and just within Ohio, recently admitted as the seventeenth state. But the little settlement of Vincennes, former French post and now seat of the Indiana Territory, lay farther to the west and was more exposed than any United States capital—like a distant island in a sweeping vision of territorial reach.

A half mile downriver from Grouseland in the heart of Vincennes stood the French-Creole house of trader Antoine Marchal, embellished with airy front and back porches. He rented it out to the territorial legislature when they needed a place to meet. On August 18, 1807, William Henry stood in the Marchal house and formally addressed the fifteen or so territorial legislators of the Second Session. His agenda spanned a broad range of items—from the question of capital punishment for bigamy, to organizing a militia, to the dangers he saw lurking all around, and to the outrageous *Chesapeake-Leopard* incident.

"The situation of our affairs on the Atlantic coast, as well as on this frontier, makes it necessary that there should be no delay in preparing ourselves for the worst that may happen," he told the assembly. "A restless and dissatisfied disposition has manifested itself among some of the neighboring tribes, and a few individuals are believed to be decidedly hostile."

There was no doubt that the Prophet, in William Henry's mind, ranked high among those "few individuals." The territory needed to give the Native people greater justice, he announced to the makeshift hall—not in land deals, but in criminal cases. It would go far to defuse tensions, he suggested, if the Indiana Territory delivered up even a *single* white murderer of an Indigenous person, as it so harshly demanded the tribes give up Native murderers of whites. He asked the territorial government for help in carrying out a humanitarian vision, implying that he led a noble mission to bring civilization's light to these dark, wild realms. "A powerful nation rendering justice to a petty tribe of savages is a sublime spectacle, worthy of a great republic."

He paused for a moment, commending the recent brisk land sales to settlers arriving in the Vincennes district and the opening of more land offices. The expanding population would speed the move toward statehood. He then turned to the British, displaying his outrage that a Royal Navy warship attacked—unprovoked!—an American ship, even after the United States had kept a strict neutrality in the wars storming across Europe. "How deep the humiliation!" he exclaimed. "How lasting the disgrace! How injurious to the cause of republicanism, should the blood of our murdered fellow citizens remain unsatisfied, or unrevenged!"

As a teenage military officer on the frontier, he had witnessed deadly officers' duels over wounded honor far more petty than the *Leopard*'s broadside cannon barrage on the *Chesapeake*. The thirty-four-year-old Governor Harrison expected war to erupt at any moment between the United States and Great Britain over this grave insult at sea. He urged that the citizenry should be prepared to fight, and implored the legislature to pay for a head military officer in every county and provide a "firelock" for every man without his own.

The *Chesapeake-Leopard* incident convinced him absolutely that British agents now roamed among tribes in the Ohio wilds, urging the Native warriors to attack American frontier settlers: "For who does not know that the tomahawk and scalping knife of the savage are always employed as the instruments of British vengeance," he proclaimed to the gathering. "At this moment, fellow citizens, as I sincerely believe, their agents are organizing a combination [that is, conspiracy] amongst the Indians within our limits, for the purposes of assassination and murder" and bringing a grave danger of "slaughter [to] our women and children."

A far less impassioned response to these threats and indignities came from Governor Thomas Kirker, at the new Ohio state capital at Chillicothe, some 250 miles east. Before jumping to alarm, Kirker attempted to actually learn more about the great gathering at the Prophet's village. Instead of commanding the Prophet and his brother to come to him, he dispatched a small delegation to go to them. When the Ohio governor's delegation arrived, Tecumseh and the Prophet discovered with pleasure that its interpreter was their former captive brother Stephen Ruddell, now a Baptist missionary to the Shawnee, Delaware, and others. They knew they could trust their white brother to deliver their words faithfully to the governor.

Nearly two hundred warriors from ten tribes jammed around the council fire beneath the beams of the 150-foot-long council house. Other warriors crowded outside at the four entrances—Shawnees, Wyandots, Potawatomis, Tawas, Chippewas, Winnepaus, Malominese, Malockese,

Secawgoes, "and one more from the north of the Chippewas." Some had traveled from beyond the Mississippi and some nearly from Hudson's Bay.

The assembled warriors and chiefs had authorized Blue Jacket to speak. The Shawnee elder, war chief, and orator had led the Indian confederacy with Little Turtle of the Miami into battle thirteen years before, destroying St. Clair's army. Now, as then, the Americans feared that the tribes would ally themselves with the British if the simmering tensions from the *Chesapeake-Leopard* affair erupted into outright war. In a letter brought by the delegation, Governor Kirker wanted to know: For what purpose were so many tribal members from so far away assembling at Greenville?

The Shawnee elder possessed "an eminently dignified appearance," noted one white observer who had seen him speak, and a "calm persuasive eloquence." Reported word for word by Stephen Ruddell, Blue Jacket's speech in Shawnee to Governor Kirker's delegation contained an eloquent distilled history of decades of shifting dynamics between Ohio Valley tribes and the long arms of white nations reaching for rich lands and Native alliances. The Wyandot (or Huron) near the Great Lakes were known in tribal diplomacy as elder brother to these other tribes. For this reason, it was fitting diplomatic protocol that Blue Jacket's speech quoted a Wyandot elder who had spoken a few days earlier at a council called to discuss how to respond to Kirker. Said the Wyandot elder in the council, according to Blue Jacket:

The French formerly marked a line along the Alleghany mountains. No man was to pass it from either side. When the Americans came to settle over the line, the English told the Indians to unite and drive off the French [that is, the French and Indian War, 1755], until the war came on between the British and the Americans [the Revolutionary War, 1775], when it was told them that king George, by his officers, directed [the Indians] to unite and drive the Americans back.

After the treaty of peace between the English and Americans [Treaty of Paris ending the Revolutionary War in 1783] ... the English held a council with the Indians, and told them if they would turn out and unite as one man, they might surround the Americans like deer in a ring of fire and destroy them all. ... When we could not withstand the army that came against us [Mad Anthony Wayne, 1794], and went to the English fort for refuge, the English told us, "I cannot let you in; you are painted too much, my children." It was then we saw the British dealt treacherously with us. We now see them going to war again. We do not know what they are going to fight for. Let us, my brethern, not interfere, was the speech of the Wyandot.

Blue Jacket concluded his speech to the delegation by again quoting the Wyandot elder: Tribes had gathered at the village near Greenville not to fight the whites but "to serve the Supreme Ruler of the universe." The elder had also thrown his encouragement to Tenskwatawa and Tecumseh's movement. Blue Jacket quoted the Wyandot: "Now send forth your speeches to all our brethren far around us, and let us unite to seek for that which shall be for our eternal welfare, and unite ourselves in a band of perpetual brotherhood."

When Governor Kirker's delegation departed the council house, they had grown convinced that the tribes did not seek war, but rather peace with whites. The Prophet sent a return message and his own delegation to accompany Kirker's back to the Ohio state capital at Chillicothe—Blue Jacket, Roundhead, Panther, and Tecumseh. Tecumseh had spent much of his boyhood playing games and learning the ways of the hunter and warrior at the original Shawnee villages named Chillicothe. Since those days, white settlement had shoved his people one hundred miles west, to the Greenville Line, and now beyond. The urgency of Tecumseh's mission grew from this simple geographical fact.

The governor graciously received them at Chillicothe's two-story courthouse on Saturday, September 19, 1807. Local settlers watched the four chiefs intently to see if they would bring violence to the frontier. The governor's representatives directed the chiefs to seats in the jury box, two on each side of Governor Kirker, who took the clerk's spot at center. Nearby sat the Shawnee-speaking interpreters—the former captive brothers Stephen and Abraham Ruddell. While Stephen had received a white education and become a Baptist missionary since leaving his Shawnee family, younger brother Abraham had kept to his Shawnee ways and a life of the forest. Although racially white, he spoke little English. His ear rims were split like rings of a big onion, draping down to his shoulders and laden with ornaments, to the astonishment of white spectators.

Blue Jacket again delivered an eloquent speech distilling the shifting relations between European empires, the United States, and Ohio Valley tribes for the past half century, and the violence that had spilled from these dynamics. He pledged peace going forward. "We have laid down the tomahawk, never to take it up again."

He sat down in the jury box. It was then that Tecumseh stood, as if the torch had just passed from Blue Jacket's generation to a new generation of Native leaders. He had been rising to this moment of leadership since childhood—first as leader of boys' games, then of a small band of young warriors and a band of families, as an intermediary between tribes and whites to calm frontier tensions, and founder with his brother of a village serving as the epicenter of a movement. That movement had started with Tenskwatawa's spiritual vision and call for a revival of traditional ways, and it remained powerful. But, under Tecumseh's influence, and perhaps that of male and female chiefs such as Blue Jacket and sister Tecumpease, the movement was fast evolving into a pragmatic political force of huge range and potency. Tecumseh now stood up as its leader. The question for whites in the Chillicothe courthouse that day came to this: Was it a political force they had reason to fear?

For three hours Tecumseh spoke passionately. Witnesses described it as an oratorical masterpiece. He gave a detailed account of the entire history of treaties between white governments and tribes dealing with the lands north and west of the Ohio River—what had become the North-west Territory, then split into Ohio State and the Indiana Territory. He systematically examined the treaties, and explained why, one after the other, they were "null and void."

"When Tecumseh rose to speak, as he cast his gaze over [the gathering] he appeared one of the most dignified men I ever beheld," reported witness Colonel John McDonald. "[The] crowd preserved the most profound silence. From the confident manner in which he spoke of the intention of the Indians to adhere to the treaty of Greenville, and live in peace and friendship with their white brethren, he dispelled, as if by magic, the apprehensions of the whites."

Other witnesses, however, sensed a deeper turbulence surging beneath his oratory—one that sprung from the contradictory position into which he and others had been pushed by whites. Tecumseh denied the validity of these "pretended treaties." He openly vowed to resist further white settlement on their lands. Yet at the same time, he renounced "all intention of making war upon the United States."

A civil engineer and frontier surveyor in the audience at the Chillicothe courthouse, John A. Fulton, described Tecumseh's speech: "The utterance of the speaker was rapid and vehement; his manner bold and commanding; his gestures impassioned, quick and violent, and his countenance indicating that there was something more in his mind, struggling for utterance, than he deemed it prudent to express."

This speech represented, in retrospect, a watershed moment. Without saying so directly, Tecumseh adopted a powerful stance. After William Henry Harrison's blitzkrieg of land acquisitions, Tecumseh proclaimed, in effect, *This is enough.*

CHAPTER 9

TWO POWERS
ON THE WABASH

overnor Kirker relaxed, reassured by Blue Jacket and Tecumseh that they had no intention of making war on the United States. He ordered the Ohio militia disbanded in fall of 1807. Unlike Harrison, he had relied on his own research instead of rumors and prejudices. He had personally heard Tecumseh speak at the Chillicothe courthouse. His delegation had returned from the Prophet's village with eyewitness reports of peacefulness—women harvesting the cornfields, men readying gear for the fall hunt. "After the most strict enquiry," the delegation reported, "we could hear of nothing which left a doubt in our minds as to their sincerity. . . . We were treated with great hospitality and kindness in their way from all."

It was clear to Kirker that the Indigenous people gathering at the Shawnee brothers' village did not intend to make war on whites. But Kirker, fourteen years older than Harrison, came with a different perspective. A native-born Irishman with a simple education, he had migrated to the United States at age nineteen and settled with his family in a peaceful region of Pennsylvania. His Irish upbringing had not instilled a deep-rooted fear of Indigenous people, unlike many American-born settlers, and he personally knew what it meant to be oppressed in one's own land by a powerful outsider—the English. When informed of the dark rumors of the threat emanating from the Shawnee brothers' village as the year of 1807 unfolded, Kirker responded with even-tempered reasoning instead of alarm.

But 250 miles west of the Chillicothe courthouse, Indiana territorial governor Harrison at Vincennes believed none of the assurances of peace from the Prophet or his followers. From his parlor desk, he picked up his quill and decided to confront the threat head on.

"My children, I have heard bad news," William Henry wrote, assuming the adoptive voice of a father. Starting with the early Jesuit missionaries in the 1600s, Europe's colonial powers had framed their relationship with Native North Americans in terms of a father taking care of a child, a nomenclature adopted by U.S. authorities. Continued Harrison:

> The sacred spot [at Greenville] where the great council fire was kindled . . . that place has been selected for dark and bloody councils. . . .
>
> My children, this business must be stopped. You have called in [men from] distant tribes, to listen to a fool, who speaks not the words of the Great Spirit, but those of the devil, and of the British agents. My children, your conduct has much alarmed the white settlers near you. They desire that you will send away those people. . . . Let [this imposter] go to the [Great] lakes; he can hear the British more distinctly.

The Prophet kept calm, despite Governor Harrison's accusations. Tecumseh, Blue Jacket, and other chiefs had not yet returned from their mission to Governor Kirker at Chillicothe. Tenskwatawa carefully dictated his own response to Harrison, denying any communication with the

British or that he had summoned people to him. They had come on their own accord to hear him. His purpose was a peaceful one.

"I am very sorry that you listen to the advice of bad birds," he responded to Harrison. "You may rest assured that it is the least of our idea to make disturbance."

The Shawnee brothers had witnessed many times how quickly white fear could mutate into lashing violence. Rather than risking settlers' vengeance over their village placement, Tenskwatawa and Tecumseh consulted on the latter's return and decided to move far west of the Greenville Treaty Line—roughly one hundred miles. The Potawatomi chief Main Poc invited them to settle on lands claimed by his tribe at the juncture of the Tippecanoe and Wabash (near today's Lafayette, Indiana). Far from white settlement, the new site offered richer hunting and greater access to the western and northern tribes. The Tippecanoe location would serve as a "mecca" for tribes of the Great Lakes, Plains, and South, writes Tenskwatawa biographer R. David Edmunds.

They would move with the greening up of spring. That winter of 1808, however, fell heavily on the Shawnees in the village near the old Greenville Fort. The fall hunt had long ended. Snow blanketed the earth, whipped by the north wind in long streamers across the prairie openings, rattling the brittle leaves that still clung to the oaks. The spring hunt lay several months away. The meaty black bears slept peacefully beneath the snow in hollow logs and underground dens. The men spent long days around the fire in their lodges, smoking, talking, sleeping, and repairing weapons and tools. It fell to the women to keep the village alive. Their corn would accomplish that—the corn they had raised in fields around the village and dried and stored for winter.

With so many visitors traveling to hear the Prophet, the village's food supplies ran short that winter, and many returned to their distant homes. As spring neared, the remaining villagers led by the Prophet and Tecumseh packed their belongings, burned their wigwams, and embarked on the westward move to the Wabash and Tippecanoe. As ever, the landscape's drainage patterns determined route and destination. Carrying their dwindling corn reserves and cooking pots by horse and backpack, they trekked overland about fifteen miles northwest of the Greenville village to a thin stream meandering through rich bottomlands—the headwaters of the Mississinewa River. They and their ancestors knew these hydrological highways, and that this small stream, twisting westward, would broaden in size and eventually join the headwaters of the Wabash.

They camped along the skinny Mississinewa, the women erecting temporary bark lodges. The men took on a task that required heavy muscular strength—building canoes.

As April 1808 arrived, melted snow brimmed over the riverbanks and spilled into the bottomlands, depositing more rich silt. Red-winged blackbirds arrived from the South, perching on cattails in the flooded marshes and trilling for mates with their distinctive *oak-a-LEEEE*. The earth softened and grew moist. The streamside willow wands turned green, and buds appeared on forest oaks. As the world came alive and shimmered a minty-green in the warming sun, Tecumseh began the journey down the Mississinewa to start the village at the Wabash and Tippecanoe juncture.

Amid the preparations for the journey, with wood chips flying from the hewing of dugout canoes, and corn stews simmering over fires, the elder Miami war chief Little Turtle arrived in the camp. While the Miami had permitted other tribes to settle there, Miami homelands embraced the region of the Wabash River. Little Turtle flatly forbade the Prophet to settle on the Wabash and Tippecanoe.

Since the signing of the Treaty of Greenville, Little Turtle had become what was known as a "government chief"—aligned with the United States and accepting money and favors. He had visited Washington, D.C., and met with the late President Washington, who gave him a ceremonial sword, a gun, and a specially designed medal of friendship. When President Jefferson came to office he suggested to Governor Harrison that he give personal "liberalities" to Little Turtle to sign land treaties—essentially, government bribes. Little Turtle had gladly accepted annual cash payments and the gift of a Black slave.

The chief and Fort Wayne U.S. Indian agent William Wells had formed an alliance. Little Turtle's daughter was married to Wells, who was suspected of siphoning off treaty money for his personal use. Both Wells and Little Turtle fiercely opposed the Prophet's spiritual movement, as did other "government chiefs" near Fort Wayne, including Shawnee chief Black Hoof, who had established his own villages at Wapakoneta on the Auglaize. Threatened by the Prophet's power, these "government chiefs" claimed that Tenskwatawa would rally western tribes and "commence war against all those Indians that would not Listen to him," as Little Turtle had warned son-in-law Wells. "Then he would attack the white people."

Little Turtle announced to the Shawnees building canoes on the Mississinewa that the Miami—his tribe—held possession of the Wabash all the way down to its middle and lower reaches. The Potawatomi had been only temporary guests on Miami lands. The Prophet was not welcome to paddle there and settle.

Again, the Prophet kept his composure. He told Little Turtle that he did not accept the message.

"[Tenskwatawa's] plans had been layed by all the Indians in america and had been sanctioned by the Great Spirit and it was not in the power of man to interrupt them," Little Turtle recounted of the conversation, which was then relayed by his son-in-law, Agent Wells, to the secretary of war in Washington. Further, the Great Spirit had told the Prophet that the Indians in America were poor because they were not united. "It only requeered the Indians to be united—they would then be able to watch the Boundry Line between the Indians and the white people—and that if a white man put his foot over it that the warriors could Easly put him back."

Face-to-face amid the half-finished canoes, the Prophet told Little Turtle that it was not actually President Jefferson who wanted their land.

Rather, he said, three others sought the lands: "That man at Vincennes [Harrison] the one at Fort Wayne [Wells] and the one at Detroit was always persuading the Indians to Sell their Land and by these means they made thems[elves] great men by cheeting the Indians. . . . [These men] found it necessary to persuade the Indians not to listen to [the Prophet] as they well knew when the Indians was united they would not be able to buy the Indians Lands."

According to Tenskwatawa, the "Great Father"—President Jefferson—planned simply to emasculate them. It was evident that by forcing the warriors to take up agriculture and white ways, the president "intended making women of the Indians . . . but when the Indians was all united they would be respected by the President as men."

In his reply to Little Turtle, the Prophet's emphasis on defining the boundaries between Native people and whites and uniting the tribes, notes Edmunds, marked a major evolution of his movement from strictly spiritual to temporal. "For the first time," he writes, "the Prophet spoke of large numbers of warriors 'united' in a common political or military cause."

Having rejected Little Turtle's message to stay off the Wabash, the Prophet and his followers climbed into canoes and paddled westward down the narrow, winding Mississinewa. Tecumseh had headed downriver in advance. About one hundred miles down the twisting river, the Mississinewa's mouth opened into the broader Wabash. They swung their canoes leftward—southwest—to ride its burgeoning waters to its confluence with the Tippecanoe.

Tecumseh awaited them at the river junction. The Shawnee leaders had chosen this site as deliberately as Congress had chosen an empty stretch of the Potomac River for the new U.S. capital, weighing political interests, accessibility, defensibility, and other factors. The Tippecanoe lay far from the leading edge of white settlement. Fish and game still thrived in this beautiful savanna country where eastern hardwood forests yielded to western prairies dotted with groves of oak and hickory. Western and northern tribes who heeded the Prophet's teachings could reach it easily on horseback across the prairies or by canoeing the Great Lakes to connecting rivers and portages. Humans had identified its attributes from an early date, occupying the Tippecanoe site from the Ice Age's end, twelve thousand years ago, and at some point had erected earthen ceremonial mounds. The Miami called it Kiteepihkwanonk—which early traders adopted as "Tippecanoe."

The Prophet and his followers landed canoes heavy with elders and children and belongings just below the Tippecanoe's mouth on the Wabash's right, or western, riverbank. The Shawnee women examined the soils and slopes. The landscape sang a kind of song to them, a poetry, a rhythm, that wove the best elements—wood, water, sun, earth, sky— together into an exact spot.

They designed the complex to extend a welcome to all, with a large council house, a medicine lodge, and a longhouse known as "House of the Stranger" to lodge travelers from afar who came to hear the Prophet. They placed the village itself on a bench of higher land overlooking the river. Here the women wove pole-and-bark wickiups, dozens of them arranged in neat rows separated by passageways unlike the non-linear layout of many villages.

In his later years, Gay-nwah—the Shawnee memoirist Thomas Wildcat Alford—described in minute detail how, with a deftness and grace that the men couldn't match, Shawnee women and girls plaited together lodges, or we-gi-wa—sturdy, ingenious structures erected in just a few days from the forest's raw materials. They cut saplings, stripped the bark, and planted the thick ends into the ground in two opposing rows of poles. Bending one over toward another in the opposite row, they brought the two saplings together and lashed them to a ridgepole, repeating with saplings all down the row. They then lashed long sticks horizontally across them, creating a barrel-vaulted roof-and-wall framework, like the latticework of an arbor.

To fabricate roofing and siding for this skeleton, they chose youngish trees with few lower branches such as elm, made two slices around the trunk, one low and the other as high as they could reach, and, prying with a special stick that had a flat, bladelike end, peeled off the bark in a large sheet. These sheets they laid on the earth with the inner or "flesh" side down and weighted them with logs to flatten them and let them "cure"— partially dry—until they possessed both toughness and flexibility. The Shawnee women and girls then laid the bark sheeting over the barrel-vaulted latticework and secured them by laying other poles on top of the bark layer. Working with tough strips of bark or roots, they dexterously stitched the whole structure, sandwiching the bark sheeting between the inner and outer framework of poles.

They had now created a sturdy, warm, rain-and-snow-proof lodge, heated by fires placed beneath smoke holes in the roof and furnished with raised beds of lashed-together branches draped with bearskin or buffalo robes. Some lodges stretched one hundred feet or more in length— "longhouses"—if shared by several families or constructed to serve as a village's council house. Early European or American travelers remarked how snug they found these lodges.

For their cornfields and gardens they chose the moist strip of fertile ground along the riverbank. The Shawnee women cleared fields, the men sometimes helping with heavy work. If they could, the women used the natural openings and bits of prairie, the original mosaic of these forests of the Ohio-Kentucky-Indiana region identified today by botanists as "savanna-woodlands." (Native people frequently burned these areas to keep them open prairie.) The women prodded the rich soil with digging tools and planted seeds that sprouted in sun and rains into the "Three Sisters"—corn, beans, and squash. These provided the staple diets of the Shawnee and many Eastern Woodland tribes, supplementing or substituting for the protein of fish and game if the Shawnee males returned empty-handed from the hunt.

Growing together harmoniously, the Three Sisters serve as a focal point for ritual and gratitude in the culture of many Eastern Woodland tribes. The stalk of sister corn grows fast and tall and offers a pole for sister bean to wrap and climb. The broad leaves of sister squash shade the ground to keep the soil moist and weeds from intruding as the Three Sisters ripen to maturity. This "interplanting," as it's called by modern agronomists, provides greater resilience to pest infestations than a uniform crop, and conserves soil fertility. As one sister absorbs certain nutrients, another sister restores them—corn extracts nitrogen from the earth to thrive, while pole beans absorb nitrogen from the air and return it to the soil.

Having originally been domesticated from a grass called teosinte about nine thousand years ago by farmers in central Mexico, maize provided at least half of the annual calories for the Native peoples of the Ohio Valley starting at least a millennium ago, writes Susan Sleeper-Smith, ethnohistorian of Native American women of the Ohio Valley, in her book *Indigenous Prosperity and American Conquest.*

Women picked over each cob for the finest seeds—the best genes—to raise the next generation of crops, selecting for maturity, protein, and sweetness. Scores of generations had gone into refining this body of knowledge that was handed down orally, as if the women corn planters operated a thousand-year-old laboratory that spanned half a continent. Dent corn for grinding, flint corn for hominy, soft corn for flour, plus sweet corn, popcorn, and, among the Iroquois and Miami especially, white seed corn—found to be 50 percent higher in protein than most varieties when tested by modern agronomists. As child bearers, caregivers, and corn growers, women possessed a creative power unavailable to Shawnee men. "Generally, women were not involved in the deaths of animals, since the shedding of blood negated their primary, life-giving function," writes Sleeper-Smith. The year's most sacred celebration, as described by Alford in his memoir of Shawnee life, is the Bread Dance, or Tak-u-wha Nag-a-way, held in the spring to give thanks to the Great Spirit for hunting bounty received over the winter, and for plentiful crops as the growing season begins.

"The Bread dance," notes ethnohistorian Stephen Warren in *The Worlds the Shawnees Made*, "is a prayer for all creation that divides the year between agriculture, and the life-giving powers of women, and hunting, and the life-taking powers of men." In some Shawnee traditions, note other ethnologists, the female power of creation embraces the entire cosmos and supersedes all other deities. The Great Spirit is herself female— "Our Grandmother."

A stick dropped in the river at the newly established Prophetstown would a week or so later drift past the front door of Grouseland and Harrison's bowed parlor window—about two hundred miles down the river's meanders. Harrison held firm to his conviction of Indian trouble. It was rumored that upstream at the Tippecanoe's mouth they mixed religious ceremonies with "warlike sports"—shooting the bow, throwing the tomahawk, wielding the war club. Further, they made these weapons themselves, he heard from a traveler who had visited villages of the Prophet's Potawatomi followers. That alone provided evidence enough of their violent intentions, wrote an alarmed Governor Harrison in May to Secretary Dearborn. He asked for President Jefferson's permission to seize the Prophet and have him "conveyed to the interior of the United States"—in other words, imprisoned—until the danger of war with the British passed.

Tenskwatawa, however, approached Governor Harrison first. In June, soon after establishing the new village at Tippecanoe, the Prophet sent a messenger downriver to explain his good intentions and ask for corn to replenish the village's supplies while their new crop ripened.

"Father—I hope what I now say will be engraven on your heart," his message stated.

It is my determination to obey the voice of great spirit and live in peace with you and your people. I do not mean to do anything to risk the safety of our children, but on the contrary to multiply them as much as possible. This is what the Great Spirit has told us repeatedly. We are all made by him, although we differ a little in colour. We are all his children and should live in peace and friendship with each other.

Harrison softened his stance. In a return message upriver, the governor admitted that he had entertained suspicions that the Prophet and his followers had pursued "bad talks" with "the people on the other side of the great lakes"—the British—to make war on the "17 fires," or United States. He outlined a simple choice. If, as the Prophet claimed, he only wanted to make his people happy and live in peace, he would continue to enjoy the "favor and protection" of the Seventeen Fires. "Very dift'erent however will be your lot if you permit yourselves to be seduced by the British agents." Any tribe joining the British, he wrote emphatically, would be exterminated from this side of the Great Lakes—down to its last member. "The Shawnees . . . are brave warriors but the long knives are not less brave and you know their numbers are as the blades of grass or the grains of sand on the river shore."

Stern warning issued, he welcomed the Prophet. Son of a Founding Father, William Henry proudly noted that "an inviolable rule" of the new nation allowed all people to practice their own religions freely. "Your religious opinions . . . shall never be the cause of dissention and difference between us."

In August 1808, the Prophet came downriver and paid Governor Harrison a two-week visit at Vincennes. He stayed nearby in his own camp. He and the governor spoke frequently and amiably. William Henry watched him regularly exhort his followers to cast away the evils of whiskey and warfare. Harrison quickly reported back to Secretary Dearborn that he believed the Prophet about the whiskey. About renouncing their "passion for war," however, the jury was still out—especially if the British were involved.

.   .   .

And the British were involved—or wanted to be. Messengers had arrived at Prophetstown from Canada with an invitation from senior officers at British Fort Malden to come for a visit. It was a long ride—nearly four hundred miles northeast of Prophetstown. The Prophet and Tecumseh politely declined at first. But by the start of summer, the Shawnee brothers had decided to test the waters on both shores of the lake, so to speak.

In early June, Tecumseh rode northeast toward Fort Malden with a small delegation of chiefs. This sector of the Great Lakes forms a kind of hourglass—Lake Huron representing the upper bulb and Lake Erie the lower. Between the two bulbs flows a short, skinny neck of water—what whites came to call the Detroit River. That hourglass neck separated the United States from Canada. It was also a strategic bottleneck along the major travel route that extended nearly one thousand miles from the Atlantic, up the Great Lakes, into the continent's interior. To defend that narrow passage, the two nations had each built their own installations— the United States occupied Fort Detroit at the upper end of the Detroit River as it comes out of Lake Huron, and Britain erected formidable Fort Malden on the Canadian bank just before it enters Lake Erie.

Fort Malden perched on a low bluff peering across the river toward the American shore, with the river's single deep channel flowing just beneath the fort's walls. In front of the fort, the British had strategically placed a triangular array of cannons that offered a wonderful view out over the river channel, visitors noted. It was also guaranteed to blow to smithereens any unwelcome ship of size trying to pass between the Great Lakes.

Tecumseh and his entourage left their horses grazing on the American side of the river and canoed across. Fort Malden's gates swung open and the fort's officials greeted them warmly, inviting them to council. They listened as the British laid out their case: Relations between Great Britain and the United States balanced on a narrow edge. If they tipped into actual war, the tribes would profit by allying with the British. Tribes had already lost a great deal of land to the Americans. If British forces and allied nations defeated the Americans, they would "probably regain the country taken from you by the Americans" in an "Artful and Clandestine manner," asserted William Claus, British official for Indian affairs in Upper Canada. Only a few months earlier, Claus added, Governor William Hull of the recently designated Michigan Territory had grabbed "upwards of five million acres, for which the Indians will not receive three coppers an acre."

In the existing historical record, this encounter with Claus marks another transformational moment in Tecumseh's rise to leadership. Claus and other British officials in their written reports did not mention Tecumseh's name, calling him "the Prophet's Brother" as if he held lesser status than the Shawnee spiritual leader himself, at least in their eyes. Tecumseh made clear to the Fort Malden officials, however, that he and Tenskwatawa had begun to forge a broad Indian confederacy. And he made it clear that this coalition extended far beyond purely spiritual matters. Recorded one British official at the Fort Malden meeting:

> The Prophet's brother . . . [told us] that they were endeavoring to collect the different Nations to form one settlement on the Wabash . . . in order to preserve their country from all encroachments. That their intention is not to take part in any quarrels: that if the Americans encroach on them they are resolved to strike—but he added that if their father the [British] King should be in earnest and appear in sufficient force they would hold fast to him.

Tecumseh firmly declined to join the British—at least for now. He wanted to stay out of the white man's disputes and would fight the Americans only if necessary for his people's survival. And he vividly remembered the British slamming the gates on the Native retreat at Fallen Timbers.

Stalling for time, the officials asked Tecumseh to wait a week or two for the arrival of their higher-up, Lieutenant Governor Francis Gore. Head of Upper Canada, he oversaw all British lands north of the Great Lakes. Tecumseh agreed. In the meantime, he traveled back across the Detroit River. He consulted with the Wyandot elders. He consulted with Shawnee elder and war chief Blue Jacket, who had assembled the great Western Confederacy that destroyed St. Clair and who now lived on the American side of the Detroit River. Taking in Blue Jacket's advice, he sent Indian delegations on diplomatic visits to tribes in the Michigan country including the formidable trio of tribes known as the Three Fires—the Chippewa, Ottawa, and Potawatomi.

Within a few weeks, showing the forces he could muster for his cause, Tecumseh had assembled a thousand warriors and chiefs. Meanwhile, Governor Gore had traveled via the lakes from Upper Canada's capital at York (now Toronto) to Fort Malden. When Tecumseh and his assemblage of one thousand warriors and chiefs beached their canoes at Fort Malden in early July, they were greeted by flags flying and guns saluting, the white smoke rolling over the river in a spectacular show of both British and Native force. They were reaching out as potential allies.

Gore announced to the assembly that he hoped the Indians and British would renew their "ancient customs and manners." He suggested that British king George III did not recognize the boundaries that the Americans had laid down for the limits of their lands. Britain still regarded the Ohio River as a "sacred" dividing line between Native people to the north and whites to the south and east. This meant, in effect, that King George did not recognize American claims over Native lands in what the United States designated as the Northwest Territory and was energetically trying to populate and dice into states.

At the climax of his speech in front of a thousand warriors, Governor Gore held aloft a massive belt of wampum. Sewn for this moment, it held 11,550 wampum beads, measured perhaps ten feet long, and weighed many pounds. A band of white beading ran its length, edges bordered in black beadwork. The huge belt symbolized the lasting friendship between the British and the Native nations, Governor Gore told the assembly. A beadwork heart lay at the belt's center, flanked by figures representing the governor and the Native leaders. Its sheer size and weight connoted the power of the British Empire and the strength of the commitment it wished to display to forge an alliance with the tribes. It also demonstrated just how badly the British wanted them as their allies—and not their enemies—if war ever broke out with the Americans. The governor hoped the Natives present would carry the symbol of British alliance far and wide across the continent, and to its many tribes.

Gore then hosted twenty-seven of the chiefs for a dinner. In this celebratory atmosphere, young warriors competed in ball games and foot races outside. Gore had heard from British officers at Fort Malden of the Shawnee brothers' plan to gather many Indian nations at the new village and form an alliance to protect their lands. "A very shrewd intelligent man," reported Gore of Tecumseh.

When the meeting broke up, as Gore reported it, Tecumseh carried the belt of alliance out of Fort Malden, bearing it first to Prophetstown. From there, the belt and word of unity among nations would travel to distant tribes. The belt itself carried the message of a possible Indian-British alliance in the event of war. And through his diplomacy both with tribes and the British, Tecumseh had emerged as the leader of a new Indian confederacy. It remained to be seen how far he would actually commit to the British.

CHAPTER 10

THE GOVERNOR'S
NEW BOSS

In early 1809, Thomas Jefferson permanently left the President's House in the federal city to return to his beloved Monticello. He had declined to run for a third term. "Never did a prisoner, released from his chains," he wrote to a friend, "feel such relief as I shall on shaking off the shackles of power." By then, he had overseen a massive expansion of land area of the United States. Directing Harrison and other government officials, he had engineered a policy toward Ohio Valley Indians that, in essence, offered them the choice to give up their lands and adopt white ways . . . or be gone. As president, he had wrought profound changes in the westward thrust of the United States.

In March 1809, James Madison moved into the vacated President's House with his wife, celebrated Washington hostess Dolley Todd Madison. While James Madison was a featherweight in frame at five four and one hundred pounds, he carried a powerful intellect and deep learning in the classics and the architecture of government. Like many other Founding Fathers, he was a Virginia plantation owner, but he lacked the frontier credentials of George Washington, or the geographic passion for the West of Thomas Jefferson, or the hands-on experience of William Henry Harrison with the explosive mix of tribal homelands and white land claims.

Outgoing president Jefferson had relentlessly pursued western lands and had no hesitation for using morally dubious rationales for acquiring them from tribes. Governor Harrison couldn't be sure that incoming president Madison would be so receptive to aggressive western expansion and its perils—such as an Indian war. He decided to take no chances on Madison's possible lack of enthusiasm for acquiring tribal land. James and Dolley Madison had hardly dusted off the furniture in the President's House before Harrison, operating with little oversight 560 miles west, pushed ahead with an extremely aggressive land purchase.

In 1809, he summoned Native leaders to Fort Wayne to discuss another federal acquisition along the Wabash.

"This is the first request your new Father has ever made you [and] it will be the last," Governor Harrison would tell assembled "government chiefs." "[President Madison] wants no more of your land. . . . He will set your Heart at ease. . . . He will never make another proposition to you to sell your lands."

Harrison's statement was a flat-out lie. The "new father"—President Madison—had made no such "first request" to acquire these Indian lands in the Indiana Territory. Rather, it was territorial governor Harrison who urgently wanted them. Nor, as Harrison well knew, would it be the last request he would make for Indian lands in President Madison's name. William Henry had suffered a setback in his drive to make Indiana Territory the eighteenth state. In March 1809, just as President Madison took office, Congress had decided to divide the massive territory into two to make it more manageable, by splitting off the western piece of it as the Illinois Territory (today's Illinois, Wisconsin, and part of Minnesota) and leaving the rest as Indiana Territory, essentially the boundaries of today's state of that name.[*]

This had thwarted Harrison's grand plans. Settlers in the Illinois Territory now were counted separately, meaning the Indiana Territory would have to push that much harder to attract the sixty thousand settlers needed to achieve statehood, as laid out by Congress's Northwest Ordinance of 1787. The Michigan Territory had already been split off a few years earlier. Harrison calculated that the much-reduced Indiana Territory could best lure new settlers by offering up still more rich lands in the Wabash River Valley—lands currently owned by tribes. Once it achieved statehood, Indiana could elect full voting members to Congress and— who knew?—perhaps a U.S. senator Harrison legislating within the beating heart of his father's nation, instead of moldering in a lone mansion-fortress along the Wabash.

Already Harrison had far overstepped the 1795 Greenville Line with his many westward land acquisitions—"extinguishing title" to Native claims, as he so obliquely phrased what amounted to legal chicanery just short of outright theft. The phrase itself simply meant having them sign over their land rights to the United States. Actually getting those signatures—and determining whose signatures did or did not count— required a large bag of tricks, which Harrison cheerfully employed.

Still, a great swath of Native lands remained. In the eyes of William Henry and enablers, this amounted to a gaping hole in the middle of the map of eastern North America, a huge patch of lands beyond the legal claim of settlers where Native tribes still clung to their rights under U.S. policy. And nearly dead center in that yawning gap on the map sat Prophetstown. The three million acres along the Wabash where Harrison now proposed to extinguish Native title resembled a giant fang in shape. With

[*] The original Northwest Territory, established in 1787, was split in 1800 into the Indiana Territory and what became the state of Ohio in 1803. Two years later, in 1805, the Michigan Territory (today's Upper and Lower Peninsulas of Michigan) was split off from the Indiana Territory, and in 1809, the Illinois Territory was carved out from what remained of the Indiana Territory.

its base near Vincennes, the sharpened tooth pointed due north—straight into the heart of Indian country. The tip of that fang was no more than fifty miles from Prophetstown.

He had first written in May 1809 to the new secretary of war, William Eustis, asking for permission to acquire these lands. He falsely claimed that Native threats no longer existed here. The Prophet and his followers, he baldly asserted in his letter, had recently "dispersed" in a state of "terror and alarm."

These three million acres, he argued, were critical to give whites a place to settle and to promote the growth of the Indiana Territory. Without them, white settlement at Vincennes would suffer, remaining "cramped" and "weak." Difficult-to-settle terrain surrounded Vincennes in three directions: marshes to the south and poor soils on the prairies across the Wabash to the west. To the north, Native lands started only twenty-one miles from town, blocking white settlement. He looked to expand in that direction. He told Secretary Eustis that, for some time, he had thought about acquiring these lands along the Wabash. The moment was now. "It appears to me that the time has arrived when the purchase may be attempted with a considerable prospect of success."

President Madison had little firsthand understanding of the on-the-ground reality so far west. He had his hands full juggling rising tensions with the British and other fallout from Napoleon's lightning-fast campaigns in Europe. Madison deferred to Governor Harrison's judgment. The president did, however, make it clear that he wanted any transaction to extinguish Native land title along the Wabash done properly—that all parties come to agreement, and that all tribes who claimed these lands take part in the treaty negotiations.

"Your Excellency [Governor Harrison] will be satisfied that a proposal of this kind, will excite no disagreeable apprehension and produce no undesirable effects before It shall be made," replied Eustis to Harrison in June 1809, writing on President Madison's behalf.

Have no worries, Harrison replied, in effect, one month later: "Permit me to assure you Sir, that no exertions on my part shall be wanting to merit a continuance of the confidence of the Administration."

Despite delays of months in delivering news from across the Atlantic, front-page stories in small newspapers in Kentucky, Ohio, and even the Indiana Territory kept Harrison informed of Napoleon's chess-like strategy to take entire sectors of Europe. Whether directly influenced by Napoleon or not, Harrison's obsession for more settler lands along the Wabash took on a Napoleonic cunning and brazenness—regardless of President Madison's caution about keeping all parties happy.

Napoleon's armies had upended Europe's fashion industry, the turmoil of his wars depressing demand for furs to trim ladies' robes and gentlemen's beaver-felt hats. Across the Atlantic, prices had plummeted for furs that Native people traded for goods at posts in the North American wilderness. William Henry jumped on this market softness knowing that they would have to seek alternatives to income from furs in order to buy guns, ammunition, and other white-made goods. At the same time, he sensed an opportune moment with the new Madison administration while it still lacked experience in frontier matters. He carefully selected Indian chiefs—many of them "government chiefs"—and invited them to a grand council at Fort Wayne to be held in mid-September 1809. Despite President Madison's warning to be all inclusive of tribes and to avoid creating "disagreeable apprehension" or "undesirable effects," he declined to include Tecumseh, the Prophet, the Western Potawatomi, and other less-friendly tribes.

"With astonishing abandon," writes Tecumseh biographer Sugden, "and a disregard for both the mood of the tribes and the need of his country for good Indian relations at a time when war with Britain seemed imminent, the Governor of Indiana Territory pressed ahead with another land treaty."

Leaving Nancy and the children at Grouseland, Harrison arrived at

the Fort Wayne council fire projecting a polite and amiable bearing—
although with his mind made up. He had counterarguments at the ready
like a stack of ammunition, and seemingly had drafted an elaborate strategic plan for the negotiations. Breaking it down for simplicity into three
phases, his plan went like this:

In the strategy's phase one, he met individually with tribal leaders in
their various wigwams and tents. Officials counted 892 Native people
who had traveled to Fort Wayne from several tribes. Some came to receive annuities they had already been promised from earlier treaties,
some to keep their prestige as chiefs, some simply for gifts that the U.S.
authorities would surely hand out, and some because they adamantly opposed sale of their lands. Many belonged to the Eastern Potawatomi (as
distinct from the hostile Western Potawatomi, whom he left off the guest
list). While the Eastern Potawatomi possessed no claim to the Wabash
lands, Harrison had invited them for strategic reasons that would soon
become clear.

He then launched phase two—get them drunk. Despite his proclamation a month earlier banning liquor sales to Native people around Vincennes, he uncorked the whiskey casks at the Fort Wayne gathering. He
would dispense 7,000 gills or 218 gallons of whiskey over the next few
weeks to help loosen and befuddle his tribal counterparts.

In phase three, Harrison split the opposition—picking out the weak-
est, poorest, hungriest, most desperate subtribe, the Eastern Potawatomi,
who lived near the south and eastern side of Lake Michigan and had been
displaced from their original homelands decades earlier. He approached
them with an offer they couldn't refuse: He threatened to withhold the
annual payment already owed to them by the U.S. government for previously ceded lands unless they signed his new treaty.

"The poverty and wretchedness of the Potawatomis made them ex-
tremely desirous of a treaty," he later reported to Secretary Eustis. An
Eastern Potawatomi "government chief" named Winamac agreed to
Harrison's proposal to sell Indian lands along the Wabash—despite Wi-

namac and the Eastern Potawatomi not having an actual claim to those lands. The Delaware (the Lenape, originally from the East Coast) agreed to sell lands along the Wabash as well—also without a real claim.

The Miami, however, did have a strong claim. They had traditionally occupied Wabash lands that were widely acknowledged as Miami home-lands, even by the United States. The Miami had generously allowed dis-placed tribes to live there, too, such as the Delaware.

Many Miami chiefs fiercely objected to Harrison's proposal. Little Turtle himself, who had earlier allied himself with the United States, ob-jected to Harrison's offer. In the run-up to the conference, Harrison had admitted to Secretary Eustis that some Native resistance existed to his treaty proposals—a wild understatement, like saying Britain and France had undergone some rough patches over the centuries in their relation-ship.

He described his recent encounter with a chief. Whether Harrison fully understood its implications or not, the chief's conversation revealed two utterly contrary attitudes toward the land itself. Wrote Harrison to Eustis:

> "You call us" said an old Indian chief to me "your Children why do you not make us happy as our Fathers the French did? They never took from us our lands, indeed they were in common with us—they planted where they pleased and they cut wood where they pleased and so did we—but now if a poor Indian attempts to take a little bark from a tree, to cover him from the rain, up comes a white man and threatens to shoot him, claiming the tree as his own."

Harrison went to work. Even-keeled, smooth in delivery, William Henry appealed to the resisting Miami chiefs to have empathy for the poor East-ern Potawatomi. He employed vivid word pictures to leverage the tribe's desperation to his advantage. "Look at their Woman & Children," he told the Miamis around the council fire, "and see them exposed to the winds & the rain as they will be in a short time to the snows of the Winter."

It left the Miamis in the position of destroying their tribal neighbors if they didn't sell—or so Harrison would make it appear by wielding threats to withhold annual tribal payments. The Miamis met in council among themselves. They responded to Harrison that they would sell land only by the acre, and in smaller parcels instead of in a massive tract. They also wanted to be paid the same price to sell the lands that the government charged to settlers to buy it—two dollars per acre.

Still unflappable, Harrison responded with a tough counterargument: If the United States bought the Miami lands by the acre, instead of a giant block, it would choose only the good acres it wanted and reject the poor ones. He further took the opportunity to slam previous Miami associations with the British, whose duplicitous influence he detected hiding under every rock. The tribe had already lost so much of its land, he told the Miamis, because it had earlier sided with the British in fighting against the United States.

"The loss of the country from Pittsburgh to the Miami was entirely to be attributed to [the British] who urged the Indians to commence all those Wars, which had terminated so fatally to them," reported the interpreter.

Having split the opposition and countered various objections, William Henry then played the urgency card. He hammered home that they had better decide soon about selling the Wabash tract.

"The Governor then told them that he was tired of waiting," reported the interpreter, Joseph Barron, "and that on the next day he would submit to them the form of a Treaty . . . and if they would not agree to it he would extinguish the council fire."

This meant that they would not receive their annual payment for lands they had already sold. To sweeten the deal, Harrison promised he would acknowledge the Miami representatives as the ruling chiefs over all other Miami chiefs, including over their rival, the Miami elder Little Turtle. And he swore to the sacred and inviolable nature of any treaty made by the United States:

> A Treaty was considered by white people as a most solemn thing and those which were made by the United States with the Indian Tribes were considered as binding as those which were made with the most powerful Kings on the other side of the Big Water. They were all concluded with the same forms and printed in the same Book so that all the world might see them and brand with infamy the party which violated them.

Both boxed in and enticed, the holdout Miami chiefs finally gave in.

Harrison had harnessed tribal dynamics to propel his grander scheme for settling the frontier and achieving statehood for the Indiana Territory. In the North American wilderness, his strategy mirrored Napoleon's mastery of Europe's royal rivalries to drive forward his sweep of the Continent.

"[Harrison] invited the Potawatomis and Delawares to use them against the Miamis," observes Harrison biographer Robert M. Owens. "Once Harrison had isolated the Miamis, he dissected them skillfully by exploiting the jealousy and resentment the civil chiefs harbored against Little Turtle."

The grand council continued. Cleverly using other tribes as his proxy agents and messengers, Harrison now went to work on tribes from the upper and western Wabash drainage. These he had not invited to the council. The Eel River tribe, the Wea, and in particular the warrior Kickapoo people had already resisted his land acquisition scheme. He suspected the treacherous Kickapoos of following the Prophet.

Once again, William Henry pitted tribes against one another. He offered bonuses to various tribes to convince the Kickapoos to sign. He forced their hand by making it clear that the treaty—and payments to *any* tribe—were not valid until the Kickapoos signed, too. Governor Harrison also knew when to cut his losses. He did not even bother to try pressuring holdouts so passionately committed to Indian independence and spiritual renewal as the Prophet and his Shawnee followers. He simply tried to keep them in the dark about the entire treaty that would seize a tract of tribal lands shaped like a giant fang aimed toward Prophetstown.

Among the signatories were Chief Beaver for the Delaware, Winamac and Five Medals for the Potawatomi, and Pecan and Little Turtle for the Miami. "These and almost all the other treaty signatories were government chiefs," notes Edmunds. "They shared in the government annuities, but they were despised by the more militant members of their tribes."

William Henry, however, was delighted.

"I have the honor to inform you that a Treaty was yesterday concluded with the Delaware, Potawatomie, Miami and Eel River Tribes by which they have ceded to the United States a Tract of land," he reported to Secretary Eustis and President Madison on October 1, 1809. "These three Tracts will contain upwards of two millions and a half of acres and will cost less than two cents per acre."

This, of course, was one one-hundredth of the price the Miami chiefs had asked for their lands. Harrison proudly trumpeted his achievement of what, in modern parlance, would be called giving the tribes the shaft. But he relied on obfuscation and confusion when reporting his actions to Washington. Without intimate firsthand knowledge, there was no possible way that Eustis and Madison could unravel the knotted details Harrison reported of the tribal rights, sub-rights, arrangements, annuities, sub-arrangements, and so on—all of it mixed up with a tangle of river branches and boundary lines.

"As it is the arrangement which has been made is just to all and is therefore I believe, satisfactory to all," he noted, his prose blithely ignoring reality.

He told Eustis and Madison in a follow-up letter that a "mischievous" story had circulated among the tribes—that the president didn't want these lands, but that Harrison wanted these lands for himself and people of the Vincennes. This so-called rumor was far closer to the truth of the matter than anything Harrison reported. He had countered it, he told his superiors, by inviting the doubtful chiefs to go to Washington to ask the Great Father directly, although he was taking various measures to discourage that possibility, "so I believe there is little danger of your being plagued with them this winter."

If any "ill blood" toward the United States remained among some tribes after the signing, Harrison added, it could be easily remedied with "a little attention" to the influential chiefs. In other words, the federal government could simply bribe the tribe's leaders until they came around. With the consent of the Senate—which was surely unaware of the background details, preoccupied at the time with building roads, canals, and navy frigates in case of war—President Madison ratified the treaty on January 2, 1810. While it may have looked innocuous from Washington, for Tecumseh at Prophetstown, this treaty would prove the breaking point.

Harrison displayed "ruthless pragmatism" and the "zenith" of his negotiating style in this 1809 Treaty of Fort Wayne, notes biographer Owens. "It was, of course," he writes, "wholly consistent with the Jeffersonian reasoning that both Americans and Indians ultimately would be happier if Indians ceded their lands to the United States."

Harrison, observes Owens, was "holding all the cards and dealing from the bottom of the deck."

CHAPTER 11

IN THE WALNUT GROVE

As William Henry quietly plotted his treaty strategy to take the lands along the Wabash, Tecumseh made his own preparations. He rode at least a thousand miles on a recruiting tour that spring and summer of 1809. He first traveled west across the Illinois prairies toward the Mississippi River. Here the Winnebago, Western Potawatomi, and Kickapoo tribes had grown infuriated by white incursions like the building of Fort Madison, the new U.S. outpost on the Mississippi. Likewise, Sauk and Fox along the Mississippi and Rock rivers seethed about Harrison's absurd claim of fifteen million acres unwittingly signed away by a few subchiefs in return for the freeing of a warrior and the cancellation of their trading-post debts to the Chouteau brothers.

"The white devil with his mouth wide open," was how one Potawatomi described the land-hungry United States.

Leaving the large Sauk and Fox settlements like Saukenuk (today's Rock Island, Illinois), Tecumseh turned his warrior entourage east. He possibly rode as far as Upstate New York to recruit members of the Iroquois nation a thousand miles away. On the way, he stopped in Ohio at the Shawnee settlement of Wapakoneta, where Black Hoof encouraged his followers to learn white agriculture and took annual payments from the government. He refused to hear Tecumseh's message. But young warriors rallied to his fiery resistance. At the big Wapakoneta council house Tecumseh explained his cause—unity, resisting white incursions, holding the land as one, and establishing the pan-tribal confederacy based on the Wabash.

Also listening to Tecumseh's impassioned speech before the council fire was his former captive brother Stephen Ruddell, serving as a Baptist missionary among the tribes. Tecumseh's childhood companion in warrior games now disagreed with the outspoken forcefulness of his old friend. Their relationship, once inseparable, now embodied the growing polarization between the white world and the red, the wedge that split them constantly hammered deeper by the relentless land takings of William Henry Harrison.

In the midst of the big gathering, Ruddell produced a letter from Governor Harrison sent to the Shawnee chiefs at Wapakoneta. He began to translate it for the assembled warriors, presumably to illustrate Harrison's peaceful intentions. Tecumseh seized the letter from Ruddell's hands, crumpled it, and threw it into the council fire where it vanished in a burst of flame.

If Governor Harrison were there, Tecumseh declared, according to a report by Indian agent John Johnston, *he would do the same to him.*

"He told the Indians," Johnston's report continued, "that the white people and the Government were deceiving them, and that, for his part, he never would believe them, or put any confidence in them—that he never would be quiet until he effected his purpose, and that, if he was dead, the cause would not die with him."

·   ·   ·

As Tecumseh returned to Prophetstown that autumn from his recruiting tour, news of Harrison's Fort Wayne treaty reached his ears. He may have known a conference was under way but did not anticipate its disastrous outcome. A profound sense of betrayal engulfed him. He grew enraged—not only at Harrison. The "government chiefs," he believed, had sold out the unified tribes. In their anger, he and Tenskwatawa now threatened to kill "government chiefs" or civil chiefs who sold lands to the white government. They regarded Winamac of the Eastern Potawatomi as the worst of the lot. He had helped Harrison recruit other chiefs likely to sign. He had served the governor at the Fort Wayne conference, as some accounts put it, "like a pet dog." The once-great and now unreliable Little Turtle was also among the signers.

A warning emanated from Prophetstown: Any surveyors on the Wabash tract should fear for their safety. Harrison's settlers likewise should stay away. Tenskwatawa "smelt them too strongly already."

The Shawnee brothers had worked out a dynamic relationship—Tenskwatawa spiritual and Tecumseh temporal, diplomatic, political. The Fort Wayne treaty brought a deep urgency to Tecumseh's mission that threw him into the daylight, beyond the shadow of his brother. He suddenly soared in visibility and leadership and drew many toward him. Even to tribes and chiefs who had been friendly to the white government, it became clear that, as Sugden puts it, "no ground upon which they trod seemed safe."

The result of Harrison's sleazy treaty making at Fort Wayne in autumn 1809 was to motivate hundreds of warriors to pour into Prophetstown as the grass turned green in the early spring of 1810.

"Now fully convinced that only assertive political and military leadership could protect the Indian landbase, Tecumseh cast off his mantle as 'The Prophet's brother' to assume the dominant position in the movement," writes Edmunds. "Before the Treaty of Fort Wayne most of the tribesmen who flocked to Greenville and Prophetstown came for religious reasons. After 1809 they came at Tecumseh's beckoning."

·   ·   ·

As spring turned to summer 1810, Governor Harrison responded forcefully. From his informants, he had heard reports of warriors massing at the Tippecanoe. He had heard of the threats to kill government chiefs who sold land to him, of warnings to surveyors to watch out for their lives, and settlers to stay away, even though he had reported to Eustis and President Madison that he expected "several hundred" families to settle this tract as soon as a land office opened.

From his parlor at Grouseland, he dispatched a letter in July with a French trader up the Wabash. It contained his own warning. It declared that the governor believed the Prophet and his followers to be enemies of the United States. But with little damage done so far, the "chain of friendship" could still survive. He asked what harm the Seventeen Fires had ever done to them or when had they taken land unrightfully. He said his ears were open. He would listen to whatever complaints the Prophet and his followers had about the recent Treaty of Fort Wayne purchase. But he warned them not to dare lift up the tomahawk.

"I know your Warriors are brave, ours are not less so, but what can a few brave Warriors do against the innumerable Warriors of the 17 fires," Harrison wrote. "Our blue coats are more numerous than you can count, and our hunting shirts are like the leaves of the forests or the grains of sands on the Wabash."

If tribal leaders still had complaints that he could not answer, he added, he would pay for the Prophet and three chiefs to travel to "the city where your father lives" (Washington, D.C.) and they could deliver their protests directly.

The Frenchman Joseph Barron delivered the message upriver to the Prophet, who, sitting on the ground surrounded by his followers, initially accused Barron of being a spy. "There is your grave," said Tenskwatawa, pointing to the earth at Barron's feet. "Look upon it." But Tecumseh emerged from a lodge and promised safety for the messenger. He and Barron talked late into the night in Tecumseh's lodge.

Barron reported their conversation in detail to Harrison. "[He denied] having intended to make war; but declared most solemnly that it was not possible to remain friends with the United States, unless they would abandon the idea of extending their settlements further to the north and westward; and explicitly acknowledge the principle that all the lands in the western country was the common property of all the tribes."

Barron quoted Tecumseh directly:

> The great spirit said he gave this great island to his red children. He placed the whites on the other side of the big water, they were not contented with their own, but came to take ours from us. They have driven us from the sea to the lakes, we can go no farther. They have taken upon themselves to say this tract belongs to the Miamis, this to the Delawares & so on. but the Great Spirit intended it as the common property of all the Tribes, nor can it be sold without the consent of all. Our father tells us that we have no business on the Wabash, the land belongs to other Tribes, but the great spirit order'd us to come here and we shall stay.

Boldly laid forth, Tecumseh's stance represented an innovative departure from both traditional Native views of the earth as a gift to all from the Great Spirit and European notions of slices of land as an individual's private property. It was a "middle ground" between the two views, notes Edmunds. While he recognized American private property rights up to the Greenville Line, beyond that the land belonged to all tribes in common, he claimed, and no one tribe could sell it without all agreeing— something very difficult to achieve. In effect, the lands would remain as common property of Native Americans.

It was this message that he had traveled so far and so quickly to spread among tribes both east and west. The land does not belong to whites. It belongs to all tribes together. And together we will join our forces to defend that land.

After receiving Barron's report of his Prophetstown visit, Harrison acknowledged for the first time the supremacy of Tecumseh's leadership among the tribal members gathering at the Tippecanoe. He is "the Moses of the family," wrote Harrison to Secretary Eustis and President Madison. "He is however described by all as a bold, active, sensible man daring in the extreme and capable of any undertaking."

Warning bells sounded for Harrison. He regarded the Prophet as a charlatan leading a band of spiritual followers. The brother, however, seemed far more dangerous—a bold and effective military and political leader. His alarm grew further when Barron relayed another message from Tecumseh: He soon would paddle the two hundred miles down the Wabash, accompanied by an entourage of young warriors, to discuss matters with Harrison face-to-face. Harrison immediately dispatched a messenger back upstream telling Tecumseh to bring only the chiefs and a few young men.

The two had not seen each other for fifteen years. After fighting on opposite sides of the battlefield at Fallen Timbers, Harrison and Tecumseh had attended the proceedings at Greenville in 1795 that established the Greenville Line. Harrison had no recollection of Tecumseh. But Tecumseh had told Barron during their long conversation into the night at Prophetstown that he remembered Harrison at the Greenville proceedings as "a very young man setting by the side of Genl. Wayne."

Now as adult men and powerful leaders, the two would take the measure of each other.

For soldiers watching at Fort Knox, three miles upriver of Vincennes on a bluff one hundred feet above the Wabash, the entourage that emerged around the river bend a mile upstream resembled a great raft of leaves swept along on the current. They nearly covered the Wabash bank to bank and extended upriver out of sight—eighty big birchbark canoes, carrying an estimated four hundred warriors stroking together, glints of light flashing off their paddle blades, torsos and faces painted "in the most terrific manner," as one observer put it, and weapons at the ready in the hulls of the canoes. Tecumseh rode at its head.

"One of the finest looking men I ever saw," wrote a Fort Knox army captain to his wife, as the flotilla passed on the way to Vincennes. "About six feet high, straight, with large, fine features, and altogether a daring bold-looking fellow."

The warriors beached their canoes a mile or two above Vincennes village on the same side of the riverbank. As they pitched tents, built wigwams, and kindled fires, Tecumseh went alone to call on Governor Harrison at Grouseland. Every white person who described Tecumseh in detail noted the erectness of his bearing, and the grace of his walk, usually wearing moccasins and fringed deerskin leggings. As he crossed the mansion's broad front lawn for the first time, according to one account, he found William Henry sitting on his pillared front portico like a Virginia gentleman—smoking a pipe and reading a book. Greeting him, the governor offered Tecumseh a room to stay inside the house. Tecumseh replied that it wasn't necessary; he preferred to pitch his tent under an elm tree.

Three days after the casual introduction, the conference at Grouseland between Governor Harrison and Tecumseh officially opened on August 15, 1810. Concerned about a possible outbreak of violence, Harrison again asked Tecumseh to bring only a small entourage. About forty warriors accompanied him while the governor's security detail—at least the visible part—numbered twelve musket-bearing soldiers from Fort Knox under Lieutenant Jesse Jennings of Kentucky. After Tecumseh objected to the meeting's location behind a catalpa fence, William Henry shifted the council to a grassy circle under the walnut grove. The council fire was kindled, and introductions and opening statements made.

Standing and addressing the gathering, Harrison said he had treated the tribes justly. He claimed to have heard no complaints about treaties until Tecumseh stirred up trouble by claiming certain tribes had no right to sign. Yet he and Tecumseh should be able to speak to each other frankly, "under a clear sky, and in an open path."

Harrison sat down in his armchair flanked by government officials.

Tecumseh now rose. He stood before the flaming logs of the fire, its smoke wreathing up into the sun-dappled leaves of the walnut boughs. He faced the American officials on the dais, with the gathered warriors and chiefs sitting on the grassy earth behind him.

"When we were first discover'd it was by the French," called out Tecumseh, emphasizing his words with gestures. Wearing a fringed shirt and quill-embroidered moccasins, he moved gracefully about the council circle—a hawk's feather bobbing in his topknot, three silver crosses swinging from his nose, and his silver tomahawk pipe prominently tucked in his belt. "[The French] told us that they would adopt us as their children and gave us presents without asking anything in return but our considering them as our fathers. . . . They asked us for a small piece of country to live on, which they were not to leave."

"*Brother!*" called out Tecumseh. "This is the manner that the treaty was made by us with the French. Since we have changed our fathers we find it difi'erent."

Tecumseh recounted a brief history of the Europeans' arrival in North America—first the French "fathers" (some of them Jesuit priests), eventually pushed out by the British fathers, who convinced some tribes to help them fight the American revolutionaries. When the British lost to the Americans, settlers pushed over the Appalachian Mountains into the interior. Here the Americans began to clear farms where French and British fathers had made only a few scattered fur outposts.

They bitterly fought the invading settlers and American soldiers until peace was made at the Treaty of Greenville in 1795. The contending parties drew a line on the map that zigzagged from the Ohio River to the

Great Lakes (across present-day Ohio). It was finally agreed—American settlers would not cross west over the Greenville Line onto Native lands.

"You ought to know that after we agreed to bury the Tomahawk at Greenville," Tecumseh continued, "we then found [our] new fathers in the Americans who told us they would treat us well. . . . I want now to remind you of the promises of the white people."

He laid out specific grievances against the "new fathers"—incidents of mass murder by whites of peaceful men, women, and children, including those doing as instructed and waving an American flag to signal their friendliness. He mentioned the American father giving gifts that were contaminated with smallpox, causing many deaths among the Kickapoo.

He then shifted to the deepest grievance—the one at the heart of the council and the movement he had generated. "You have taken our lands from us," he told Governor Harrison and the gathered officials sitting on the dais, "and I do not see how we can remain at peace with you if you continue to do so."

Moving about the council circle as he spoke, but always addressing Governor Harrison, Tecumseh asserted that the Americans had attempted to fragment the tribes and prevent them from uniting. "You try to force the red people to do some injury. It is you who are pushing them on to do mischief. You endeavour to make destructions. You wish to prevent the Indians to do as we wish and unite and consider the land as the common property of the whole. You take tribes aside and advise them not to come into this measure. Until our design is accomplished we do not wish to accept of your invitation to go and visit the President."

He paused to let interpreters translate, to let his words be absorbed.

"The reason I tell you this is—You want by your distinctions of Indian tribes in allotting to each a particular track of land to make them war with each other. You never see an Indian come and endeavor to make the white people do so. You are continually driving the red people," Tecumseh called out. He compared the forced exodus to a galloping horse—

Ne-kat-a-cush-e Ka-top-o-lin-to—being driven westward toward the setting sun. "At last you will drive them into the great lake where they can't either stand or work."

Silence prevailed as he spoke except for occasional assent from the gathered warriors and chiefs at "some eloquent recital of the red man's wrong, and the white man's injustice," according to the detailed account assembled from eyewitnesses by John Law, an early settler and lawyer in Vincennes.

Tecumseh paused to let the interpreter translate. He began again, voice rising, taking on that rhythmic, musical quality. Harrison's most recent claim to Native lands beyond the Greenville Line nearly surrounded Prophetstown with lands the governor claimed for the United States, leaving Prophetstown like an island except toward the northwest.

Addressing Harrison, Tecumseh now emphasized that this most recent illicit treaty was made with chiefs who had no right to sell these lands at Fort Wayne the previous fall. These were a few village chiefs—"civil chiefs" as opposed to "war chiefs." Tecumseh asserted that an Eastern Potawatomi village chief had threatened to harm these other village chiefs unless they signed.

At this moment, that village chief, Winamac, was reclined on the grass near Harrison, as if for protection from Tecumseh and the chiefs and warriors accompanying him. Behind his back Winamac cradled a brace of pistols, visible to Harrison and the U.S. officials but hidden from Tecumseh's line of sight. Surreptitiously, he began to prime his pistols, readying their firing pans to shoot.

Tecumseh demanded that Harrison restore the Treaty of Fort Wayne lands. In the future, he asserted, no village chiefs would have authority in land matters—only warrior chiefs. Village chiefs who sold without consent from all chiefs would face death. If Harrison refused to return the most recent lands, warned Tecumseh, a great meeting of tribes would occur in two moons at the Huron village. This important village kept the wampum belts and had a council fire already lit. Here, village chiefs who sold out at Fort Wayne would be killed. He didn't need to add that Winamac, as a chief who had signed away Indian lands, would be among them. "If you do not restore the land," Tecumseh proclaimed to the governor, "you will have a hand in killing them."

He concluded with both a plea and a warning. He asked Harrison to "take pity on all the red people." He also warned that if white settlement did cross the boundary onto the lands in question, it would "produce great troubles among us." The Indians didn't want war, Tecumseh insisted. But they were prepared to go to war if necessary.

"[This] is the sentiment of all the red people who listen to me.... [The] great spirit has inspired me and I speak nothing but the truth to you."

William Henry Harrison was taken aback, reported Law. During Tecumseh's hour-long speech, which included pauses for translation, Harrison had listened quietly in his chair. The territorial governor had carefully monitored the Prophet and his doings from afar, and had even met with him at Vincennes, but the Prophet's brother—Tecumseh, the Shawnee chief now addressing him personally—had hardly come to his attention.

Until now. He made a powerful figure—in his bearing, in his soaring rhetoric and elegant, cogently laid-out speech, and in his detailed mastery of the history of Native-white relations. But most of all he impressed with his defiance. In Harrison's ten years of dealing with Native leaders as a territorial official, a span in which he had acquired tens of millions of acres for white settlement beyond the Greenville Line, he had never encountered a chief who so audaciously brought such broad, far-reaching claims. Tecumseh objected not simply to the details of a single treaty. He objected to the entire concept of Harrison's U.S. land negotiations.

Most forcefully, he called out Harrison on his targeting of tribes in the divide-and-conquer strategy. The Native nations were united as one people, he boldly asserted. The Great Spirit willed that they hold the land as

one. Assembled in the walnut grove to support him sat Wyandot, Kickapoo, Potawatomi, Ottawa, and Winnebago leaders, among others, while
Creeks, Sauks and Foxes, and Chippewas had recently called at Prophetstown.

It may have sounded outrageous to whites. And while Tecumseh had
assembled a broad coalition of leaders to embrace this concept, not all of
them had joined him—including Black Hoof and other Shawnees at
Wapakoneta. It wasn't hard for even the casual white observer, however,
to see that Tecumseh's concept paralleled the claim that individual states
had banded together in a single federal U.S. authority. Furthermore, Tecumseh dictated to Harrison, any future negotiations would have to be
with the unified tribes. And he was their authorized representative. The
unified tribes wanted peace. But if Harrison refused to withdraw his claim
to the two and a half million acres from this most recent—and wholly
illegitimate—treaty, Tecumseh promised war.

"There was a coolness, and independence, a defiance in the whole
manner and matter of the Chieftain's speech which astonished even
[Governor Harrison]," wrote Law, a Yale-educated lawyer and justice
who arrived in Vincennes a few years after the council and interviewed
many witnesses to Tecumseh's speech. "There was a stillness throughout
the assembly when Tecumseh had done speaking, which was painful.
Not a whisper was to be heard—all eyes were turned from the speaker to
the Governor. The unwarranted and unwarrantable pretensions of the
Chief, and the bold and defiant tone in which he had announced them,
staggered even him. It was some moments before he arose from his armchair."

Meanwhile, Tecumseh sat on the grass alongside his fellow chiefs and
warriors. Addressing him, Harrison justified his conduct. Law recounted
the governor's rebuttal to Tecumseh:

There was "no foundation in fact" to the charges of "bad faith" made
against the government. Rather, the U.S. had dealt with Indians within

"the strictest rules of right and justice." The governor could personally say in the presence of the Great Spirit watching over these deliberations that his own conduct "had been marked with kindness, and all his acts governed by honor, integrity and fair dealing." He had always been a friend of the red man. Tecumseh's assertions marked the first time in the governor's life that "his motives had been questioned" by any chief who cared about the truth or knew anything about Indian-white relations "from the time this continent was first discovered."

Taking a legalistic approach, the governor then challenged the grounds for any Shawnee tribal claims to the lands in question along the Wabash. He also tried to undermine the notion that all tribes held their lands in common. When white people first arrived on the North American continent, the Miami occupied the Wabash lands, Harrison claimed. The Shawnee then lived in Georgia, he asserted, until the Creek drove them away and they traveled north to this region. Thus the U.S. government had purchased the Wabash lands from their rightful owners—the Miami, not the Shawnee.

Additionally, "It was ridiculous to assert that all the Indians were one nation. If such had been the intention of the Great Spirit, he would not have put different tongues in their heads, but have taught them all to speak a language that all could understand."

Harrison returned to his armchair.

As Barron began to translate this into Shawnee, Tecumseh shouted out.

"Tell him . . . HE LIES!"

In that moment Tecumseh and his warriors sprung to their feet, drawing their war clubs and tomahawks, eyewitnesses reported. The soldiers rushed forward from the shady tree. Governor Harrison jumped up from his armchair, his dress sword clanking. He pulled it from its scabbard, thrusting it out to impale any warrior who rushed him. Beside him, Army captain G. R. Floyd yanked out his dagger. Winamac cocked his primed and loaded pistols. Village spectators at the edge of the walnut grove grabbed whatever stick, log, brick, or handy club they could find. The Reverend Winans of the village's Methodist church sprinted across the lawn to Grouseland, grabbed a shotgun inside, and stood at the portico entrance guarding Nancy Harrison and her children sheltered within.

No one spoke. No one moved. A single sudden gesture could erupt in a crescendo of violence from all sides. Each leader weighed the consequences. Was this the time to unleash the fury? Were they each ready to die in this moment for their cause, as they surely would?

Governor Harrison blinked first. He called to the soldiers not to shoot. He asked the interpreter what Tecumseh had said. Barron now translated Tecumseh's words correctly: that Harrison's statements were false—lies—and the United States had cheated them. Harrison responded by telling Tecumseh he was a bad man. He would no longer talk with him. He would extinguish the council fire.

The governor ordered Tecumseh and his entourage to leave. As they had arrived at the gathering in a peaceful manner and under the protection of the council fire, the governor told them, they would not be harmed as they left.

Tecumseh sent a messenger the next day from his upriver canoe camp to Grouseland apologizing for his behavior. He requested that the talks start again. The council resumed, politely and calmly. By agreement each side brought the same number of guards as the day before. In the night, however, Governor Harrison had called up two militia units from the countryside and one from the village. One hundred soldiers, by some accounts, hid themselves inside the Grouseland mansion as a precaution, presumably cramming Nancy's glittering dining room with sweating, blasphemous frontier soldiers.

Down in the shady walnut grove, no change in position occurred on either side of the council fire.

Despite the eruptions of the previous day, Tecumseh retained a calm dignity. He revealed to the gathering with seeming frankness and sincerity some unseen dynamics at work in the territory. White men had recently visited the Prophet's village, he told Governor Harrison, without identifying exactly who they were. These white visitors reported that half the whites in the region sided with Tecumseh and the Prophet in this Wabash land matter. Half stood with Harrison. The white visitors said President Madison did not agree with Governor Harrison's purchase. They advised that the tribes should not accept the white man's annuities and gifts—these were considered payment for the lands. Instead, they should wait two years until Governor Harrison left office. Then a different man—a good man—would arrive and restore their lands.

The white visitor also accused Harrison of trying to conduct the treaty doings at Fort Wayne in "great secrecy" from the Shawnee. Now Harrison again wanted to assemble the Indians, at Vincennes, to take more land from them, the visitor had charged. This time, he would bribe them with horses, saddles, and bridles plated in silver to cheat them out of their lands. The visitor had encouraged Tecumseh to speak up to Harrison "very loud."

"When you wanted land you [were] very smooth with the Indians," Tecumseh quoted his anonymous white source, "but at length became very boistrous."

Tecumseh again addressed Harrison directly. After hearing so many similar stories, Tecumseh could not help but think that Harrison's aim was "to sow discord" among the tribes. "I wish you my Bro. to let alone those distractions. . . . It is doing them a great injury by exciting jealousies between them. I am alone the acknowledged head of all the Indians."

Harrison stood from the dais to speak. He acknowledged none of this. He didn't debate the justness of his actions or future plans to take lands. Rather, he moved straight to practicalities for what he considered a done deal. What were the possible consequences of his taking the Wabash land? he asked Tecumseh. Will there be trouble if we try to survey the lands? And what about the annuities promised for the Kickapoos? He had the gifts and money right here in Vincennes. Would the Kickapoos accept it?

It was another brazen attempt by William Henry to split the tribes—even during a council supposedly working toward conciliation—by trying to buy off the warlike Kickapoos, who were sympathetic to Tecumseh and had fiercely resisted Harrison's acquisitions. Some Kickapoo chiefs were present.

"I am authorized to say that they will not receive them," replied Tecumseh. He added that he pitied the Kickapoo women and children. "*Brother,* they want to save that piece of land, we do not wish you to take it. It is small enough for our purposes." He issued his clear warning again, referring to lands Harrison coveted near Vincennes that the governor had recently claimed with the Fort Wayne treaty. "I want the present boundary line to continue.... Should you cross it ... I assure you it will be productive of bad consequences."

Tecumseh sat down at the conclusion of his speech. Chiefs from other tribes sitting around the council fire stood up in turn—Wyandot, Kickapoo, Potawatomi, Ottawa, Winnebago. They confirmed to Harrison that they had committed their tribes to the Shawnee confederacy. They supported the principles laid out by Tecumseh. They acknowledged him as their leader. The purpose of the great confederacy, an old Winnebago chief said, was "to confine the great water and prevent it from overflowing [us]."

Governor Harrison again stood and addressed the gathered chiefs. He promised Tecumseh he would "faithfully" express to President Madison their "pretensions" to the disputed lands. He pledged to bring back the president's reply. He added, however, that it was extremely unlikely the president would agree.

"The President would never admit that the lands on the Wabash, were the property of any other tribes than those who had occupied and lived upon them," eyewitnesses reported Harrison as saying. The government had purchased them fairly, he added. "[Tecumseh] might rest assured that the right of the United States," he concluded, "would be supported by the sword."

The next day, with the council ended, William Henry faced a crucial decision—whether to return or keep the Wabash lands. During the public proceedings around the council fire, was Tecumseh saying how he truly felt, or was he posturing in front of fellow chiefs to show a hard stance?

That morning, Governor Harrison and interpreter Barron paid a visit to Tecumseh's camp. Tecumseh received the two hospitably, they reported later. Perhaps they all smoked a pipe around the fire. Perhaps Tecumseh served them food as custom demanded. Perhaps a family member, even Tecumpease, helped prepare the meal and serve it—a favorite dish such as tender green corn just ripening for the fall harvest, the kernels stewed with bits of venison or rabbit or bear fat. But Harrison and Joseph Barron, who wrote down the conversation, left no such record of these very human details of the visit. The few hints we have, however, indicate a growing respect for each other. They had a long conversation, the leaders talking one-on-one, absent the necessity of posing before an audience. On such moments, perhaps, the fate of a continent turned.

Governor Harrison asked Tecumseh if he had expressed his true intentions at the council.

"[Tecumseh] said they certainly were," according to the account about the conversation that Harrison later gave to Moses Dawson, an early biographer. Tecumseh declared "that it was with great reluctance he would make war with the United States, against whom he had no other complaint, but their purchasing the Indians' lands; that he was extremely anxious to be their friend, and if he, the Governor, would prevail upon the President to give up the lands lately purchased, and agree never to make another treaty without the consent of all the tribes, he would be their faithful ally, and assist them in all their wars, with the English."

Tecumseh added that he would much rather be the friend of the Seventeen Fires—the United States—and fight alongside them than with the British, who always summoned the Indians to fight their wars. Here Tecumseh clapped his hands and called out, as if calling a dog.

Harrison listened closely. As he had the previous day, he promised to relay Tecumseh's concerns and position to President Madison. But, again, he told Tecumseh, he thought there was no chance whatsoever that the president would accept them. William Henry Harrison neglected to add in this moment, of course, that President Madison surely would agree to return the Wabash lands if Harrison recommended doing so. Nor did he say to Tecumseh that the Great Father had already made clear that he wanted to make sure all tribes were satisfied with whatever land deals Harrison struck.

He neglected to add that it wasn't the president, but William Henry himself who would not accept Tecumseh's and the united tribes' concerns.

Instead, Governor Harrison requested of Tecumseh that in the case of war, he not commit cruel acts on women, children, the wounded, and prisoners. Tecumseh readily agreed. Nearing the end of their conversation, which had made no progress toward agreement, Tecumseh turned wryly philosophical about what he saw coming in the future. He implied that if Harrison had any influence with President Madison's decision it would be best for all concerned to use it now.

"Well," said Tecumseh, "as the great chief is to determine the matter, I hope the Great Spirit will put sense enough into his head to induce him to give up this land: it is true, he is so far off he will not be injured by the war; he may sit still in his town and drink his wine, whilst you and I will have to fight it out."

PART II

CHAPTER 12

THE GOVERNOR'S
DARK THOUGHTS

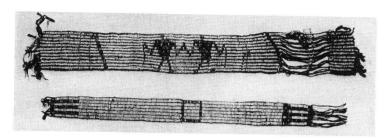

After the meeting in Grouseland's walnut grove, tensions ramped steadily higher. Harrison and the Shawnee brothers viewed each other, as Edmunds puts it, with "mutual suspicion." Following August's Grouseland summit, the fall of 1810 unfolded peacefully through the bright, warm days of September—but ominously.

Traveling on a fast black pony in company with three similarly mounted chiefs, and perhaps also by canoe, Tecumseh, after the meeting, completed a huge arcing recruitment loop that circled the Upper Midwest. From Prophetstown, he traveled north to Menominee villages at Green Bay, on Lake Michigan. He then wended southward down the Wisconsin River to the ancient trading center at Prairie du Chien on the Mississippi. Here tribes from all over traditionally gathered to exchange goods in the precolonial version of a giant shopping mall. He headed down the Mississippi to the Illinois country and the big Sauk village at

Saukenuk, and beyond to Shawnee villages in the Missouri country. All along the way, his message spread.

"If you do not join your friends on the Wabash," Chief Black Hawk remembered hearing as a young Sauk from a representative of the Shawnee Prophet, "the Americans will take this very village from you!" Black Hawk, who would eventually gain his own fame as war chief confronting white intrusion, recalled that he didn't believe it at the time.

By the time he finished this lightning recruiting loop in fall 1810, Tecumseh had brought tribes from across the Upper Midwest into his Indian confederacy: the Shawnee, Miami, Wyandot, Wea, Kickapoo, Western Potawatomi, Winnebago, Menominee, Chippewa (Ojibwe), Sauk, and Fox. This was a good start in the North, although hardly touched on the tribes of the South and the West. Other tribes or bands or chiefs spoke out against Tecumseh and the Prophet, opposed to their ideas or having chosen a different approach to accommodate the U.S. westward push, such as Shawnees under Black Hoof settled at Wapakoneta.

Returning home to Prophetstown, Tecumseh learned that U.S. agents had assembled "government chiefs" from several tribes in a Wyandot village near Detroit, three hundred miles northeast of Prophetstown. The federal agents warned the chiefs that Tecumseh had proclaimed himself leader of all western tribes. Reliant on U.S. annuities for their people, the government chiefs pledged neutrality if war broke out between the United States and Tecumseh's confederacy.

But still another major player in this accelerating contest waited nearby—the British. In response to the government chiefs' pledge of neutrality, Tecumseh rode north from Prophetstown and canoed to the opposite bank of the Detroit River, where he was warmly received at the gates of Fort Malden. He asked British officials for their help in supplying his movement.

"You, Father, have nourished us, and raised us up from childhood," he addressed British officials in early November. "We are now men, and think ourselves capable of defending our country … but expecting you will push forwards towards us what may be necessary to supply our wants."

The British officials tried to remain noncommittal. Strategizing on a global scale as representatives of the king's empire, they did not want to get entangled in an Indian war against the United States while dealing with a volatile Napoleon in Europe. Nevertheless, some partisan officials siphoned supplies Tecumseh's way.

Heavy snows in early 1811 bogged down travelers. Native people and settlers crowded around warming fires in wigwams and cabins, and the Harrisons tucked themselves into their fortified mansion. With the spring thaw, however, a burst of events set the governor in deep opposition to Tecumseh and the Prophet's Indian confederacy. The brothers had repeatedly warned Harrison to send neither surveyors nor settlers to the disputed lands along the Wabash. But now he ordered a crew of surveyors to proceed. Settlers advanced hungrily toward the deep, rich soils. Alarmed, Weas who lived on the Fort Wayne Treaty lands captured the surveyors and threatened their lives, sending them fleeing all the way to Cincinnati. It was clear to anyone paying attention that Harrison had stepped over a clear line drawn by the Shawnee brothers. Even white officials began to question his motives.

Other rumors arrived from Native lands to the west, such as an ominous report from William Clark, U.S. Indian agent for the Louisiana Territory, to Washington about "a talk" supposedly delivered by the Ioway people. "The time is drawing nigh when the murder is to begin," the Ioways reportedly said, "and all the Indians who will not join are to die with the whites."

Clark also dispatched alarming reports to Harrison that Vincennes—perhaps Grouseland itself—was the target. Harrison relayed the alarm to Secretary Eustis in Washington: "On the 2nd of May General William Clarke of Saint Louis wrote to me informing that the Prophet had sent a Belt to the Mississippi tribes inviting them to war against us, and declaring that his intention was to begin the war by an attack on this place."

Tecumseh's Travels to Unify Tribes from Lake Superior to the Gulf of Mexico, 1805–1812

Tecumseh's Routes   *Delaware* Tribes

HUDSON'S BAY

Cree

C A N A D A
(British)

Ojibwe (Chippewa)

Lake Superior

Menominee

Ottawa

Winnebago

Sauk and Fox

Lake Michigan

Lake Huron

Lake Ontario

Mohawk

Seneca

Boston

Mississippi River

Missouri R.

Omaha

Potawatomi

Wyandot

Miami

Lake Erie

Shawnee

New York
Philadelphia

LOUISIANA
PURCHASE
(1803)

Kickapoo

Delaware
Ohio River

Osage

Quapaw

Mississippi R.

Chickasaw

Cherokee

Catawba

Charleston

ATLANTIC OCEAN

Caddo

Creek

Savannah

SPANISH
POSSESSIONS

Seminole

SPANISH FLORIDA

New Orleans

GULF OF MEXICO

0   MILES   400
0   KILOMETERS   400

As spring warmed to summer 1811, Harrison demanded that Tecumseh and the Prophet turn over to U.S. authorities several Potawatomi who were alleged to be allied with the brothers' confederacy, and had murdered settlers out in Illinois country.

The notion now took hold in William Henry's mind that Tecumseh plotted to murder him. The governor claimed to have heard it from tribes out on the Mississippi—perhaps more rumors circling among the Ioway or Potawatomi. It quickly metastasized into an obsession. It's difficult not to wonder whether Harrison's anxiety—or paranoia—that Tecumseh plotted his assassination sprouted in part from his own conscience. He had maneuvered everyone involved so artfully—or, depending on how you looked at it, manipulated them with such duplicity. He would have to be morally blind not to wonder whether his actions against the tribes were justified. He forged ahead, however, convincing himself that he was acting for the greater good. But the greater good did not include Native peoples—at least, not in their "savage" and "uncivilized" state. Only once they had converted to white ways and agriculture—and handed over their vast traditional territories—could he recognize them as part of the fabric of human society.

Until then, William Henry Harrison, like Thomas Jefferson, regarded Indigenous peoples as both opportunity and obstacle—ripe targets to strip of their lands for white settlement, and obstacles because, while they had lived for centuries on those very lands, they now stood in the way. Yet, that same line of thought could have given him pause if he could have mustered even a scintilla of sympathy for the Shawnee view. He would have seen plainly see that, for the Shawnees, among the primary obstacles to their vision of a future were Harrison himself, his Grouseland mansion, and his family.

In his determination to take the disputed land, Governor Harrison continued his use of subterfuge with President Madison, Tecumseh, and other Native leaders throughout the last months of 1810 and first of 1811. Speaking through Secretary Eustis, President Madison had told Governor Harrison plainly that he could acquire tribal lands only under the condition it left no Indian party unhappy. Contrary to Madison's orders, William Henry had pushed through the Fort Wayne Treaty, taking Wabash lands by cutting out some Native leaders and strong-arming others, and leaving a great deal of unhappiness among the tribes. In particular, he enraged Tecumseh, the Prophet, and their many followers. This, although Madison himself had repeatedly warned Harrison that keeping peaceful relations with Native tribes was of the greatest importance—"a primary object," as he put it in October 1810.

William Henry told him not to worry—in so many words, he had it covered. "The President's injunction with regard to the preservation of peace with the Indians shall be faithfully attended to," Harrison replied in December. "I believe indeed that there will be no great difficulty in the affair."

Yet in the same breath—the very same letter—William Henry targeted still more tribal lands beyond the wildly contested Wabash tract. Using every rhetorical trick, he downplayed the unhappiness and anger he had caused. He discounted his purchase of the Fort Wayne Treaty lands as an insignificant parcel, despite the fact that it totaled over two million acres. Further, he cautioned Madison that all those settlers trekking west from Ohio and Pennsylvania would end up at a dead end unless he acquired still more tribal lands.

"The little tract which was purchased to the west of the Greenville boundary will be soon filled up to the very line and our backwoods men are not of a disposition to content themselves with land of an inferior quality when they see in their immediate neighbourhood the finest country as to soil in the world occupied by a few wretched savages," he wrote to President Madison and Secretary Eustis. "For without such further purchase Indiana cannot for many years become a member of the Union and I am heartily tired of living in a Territory."

For exactly a decade he and his family had resided on the Wabash hundreds of miles from the nearest dim specks of city lights and genteel society. He was pushing forty years old. Yes, he could claim achievements such as the Harrison Land Act, winning a territorial governorship in his late twenties, and the millions of acres of Native lands on which he had "extinguished title." But, measured against the background of his family origins, he was a semi-consequential territorial politician operating seven hundred miles through the woods from the U.S. capital—the hot cauldron of power at the center of the nation his father had founded. After ten years in Vincennes, William Henry had to wonder if he would ever get off this muddy Wabash riverbank and back to Washington where his family rightfully belonged.

His most direct path to the echoing halls on the Potomac was to claim more Indigenous land, lure eager settlers to fill it, and vote him their man in Washington, D.C. This struck at the heart of the matter—a population game. Without more Wabash lands for newcomers to settle and boost population to the next level, this was unlikely to happen—at least anytime soon. The population of the Indiana Territory in 1810 was 24,520 people. It needed more than twice that—60,000—to reach statehood.

Harrison vehemently made this point in his annual address to the territorial legislature in November 1810, elevating a lust for land into a moral calling when speaking to his frontier peer: "Is one of the fairest portions of the globe to remain in a state of nature, the haunt of a few wretched savages, when it seems destined by the Creator to give support to a large population, and to be the seat of civilization, of science, and of true religion?"

Making the wildly false claim that "no treaty was ever concluded with the Indians under happier auspices than that of Fort Wayne," he identified two schemers at the bottom of any unhappiness about his land acquisitions: Tecumseh and the Prophet. And these two troublemakers, he argued, were stirred up by *British intriguers*. With indignation, the governor laid out to the frontier politicians that Tecumseh's objections centered on the claim that all land in North America belonged to Native tribes in common, and none could be sold validly "without the consent of all."

"A proposition so extremely absurd," Governor Harrison declaimed, that it "would forever prevent any further purchase of lands by the United States."

Here lay the head-on collision of values, of worldview. In the Shawnee awareness, spirits animated all aspects of the natural world, with the Great Spirit overseeing all. Those spirits—alive in wind, rain, sun, soil, deer, otter, and all creation—needed to be respected and attended to, honored. The Shawnees expressed their gratitude to these spirits in almost every action.

In the white settlers' vision, as Harrison expressed it, these lands were "the province of a few miserable savages." Empowered by their own Creator, an Old Testament God, the newcomers would clear them, settle them, plow them, and make the lands truly fruitful rather than languishing in a primitive "state of nature."*

Among the tribes, rumors continued to circulate. They heard from sympathetic whites that it was not President Madison who wanted the land but Governor Harrison himself. The governor dismissed these reports as intrigue launched by British agents, or put forth by his political enemies. Yet other officials had grown skeptical of Harrison's motives and his unyielding push for land deals. "It is my opinion that Government ought to look closer into this business," wrote land agent John Badollet, at the Vincennes office, to Albert Gallatin, secretary of the treasury. "The Indians want nothing but good treatment to become well disposed to the United States."

But Harrison remained virtually unstoppable, using every possible excuse to justify further extinguishment of title. Every outbreak of frontier violence, even hundreds of miles away, offered up another reason for him

---

* It is ironic that in terms of "fruitfulness"—production—the Native women who grew corn produced far more annually than early white settlers growing corn.

to tell President Madison and Secretary Eustis that the tribes—and especially followers of the Prophet and Tecumseh—must be controlled or removed.

The long lag in communications only exacerbated the situation—a letter and reply took one month. Despite his powerful intellect and deep learning, President Madison lacked the frontier experience to evaluate the pitfalls in the dire scenarios painted by William Henry, as did his secretary of war Eustis, a Boston-based physician who had treated the wounded at Bunker Hill in the Revolutionary War. As a result, Madison and Eustis remained largely silent in response to Harrison—perhaps wary of being manipulated—except for occasional urgings to him to keep the peace.

On the political stage, however, President Madison cast a positive light on whatever news he received from Harrison and others far out in the western territories. During his lengthy annual address to Congress in December 1810, Madison devoted a single sentence to say that all was going swimmingly in relations between the United States and Indigenous tribes, and they would only improve. "With the Indian tribes, also, the peace and friendship of the United States are found to be so eligible that the general disposition to preserve both continues to gain strength."

Madison and Eustis may have failed to grasp from William Henry's obtuse statements—or he may have deliberately left it unclear—that it was his insistence on keeping the disputed lands along the Wabash acquired in the 1809 treaty that was the wellspring of mounting tension. In the absence of instructions from them, he shoved forward. "Having received no orders to the contrary, I have uniformly and positively declared that the Treaty of which they have been made to complain would never be abandoned," he wrote to Secretary Eustis as winter turned to spring 1811, and that the United States would keep the lands "even at the expense of as many lives as there were Trees growing on it."

By June, William Henry was listening to second- and thirdhand rumors from far out in the Illinois and Missouri country that the Prophet had ordered the murders of several whites who had been killed over the past year. He reported that agent William Clark had told Governor Ninian Edwards of the Illinois Territory that he had heard from various sources that the Prophet planned "to make some grand stroke as soon as he has collected a sufficient force." Despite the questionable veracity of these rumors, Harrison now grew certain that Tecumseh and the Prophet had targeted Vincennes itself. He had heard this "from so many different sources that it is impossible to disbelieve."

He bluntly laid out this conviction to Madison and Eustis: "His determination is . . . to come to this place with as many men as he can raise," he wrote to them, "and if the land which was lately purchased is not immediately given up to commence the war."

Then William Henry took a step closer to the precipice. On June 19, 1811, he recommended that Madison and Eustis send federal troops from Pittsburgh to Vincennes. He asked the president and secretary of war for authorization to use the troops in "offensive measures" against the Prophet—"as soon as it is ascertained that he is decidedly hostile." As territorial governor, however, he was the administration's primary source on the subject of the Prophet. And he had no doubt. "For my own part I am so satisfied of his intentions that if I had any discretion on the subject I would attack him on his way hither with any force that I could collect."

His mind was made up. Whatever Tenskwatawa and Tecumseh claimed, they were hostile.

Five days after requesting U.S. troops, Harrison warned Tecumseh to back off from rumored plots that Harrison ascribed to him. He had heard from Mississippi River tribes that Tecumseh planned to assassinate him, then launch warfare against white settlers. "Brothers, your warriors who have lately been here, deny this; but I have received the information from every direction; the tribes on the Mississippi have sent me word that you intended to murder me, and then to commence a war upon our people," wrote Harrison to Tecumseh on June 24, 1811.

"You shall not surprise us as you expect to do," he continued. "You are about to undertake a very rash act; as a friend, I advise you to consider well of it . . . it is not yet too late." He gave Tecumseh a stern warning of his own frontier soldiers' potency: "As soon as they hear my voice, you will see them pouring forth their swarms of hunting-shirt men, as numerous as the mosquitoes on the shores of the Wabash, brothers, take care of their stings."

Harrison grew more anxious by the day. A week after he had dispatched the warning to Tecumseh, he grabbed the quill at his parlor desk for another urgent message to Washington: Another murder reported from the Illinois frontier and the word was—from whom, he didn't say—that the Prophet intended to attack there first as a diversion before attacking his own stronghold at Vincennes. "These events, Sir, require no comment from me. . . . Can the President want any further proof of the Prophet's designs against us?" Trying to show off a proficiency in arcane Indian terminology, he predicted that Tecumseh would probably strike during "the roasting-ear season."

He had plotted his own counterstrategy to the brothers' hostility, William Henry wrote Madison and Eustis a week later, on July 10. If the Prophet and Tecumseh continued to conceal their intentions and delay an imminent attack, Governor Harrison could send—or lead—a large force up the Wabash and "disperse" the "banditti" that the brothers had collected at the Tippecanoe. In other words, if the brothers still refused to admit they had hostile intentions, Harrison would assemble an army and go after them. Unless he had utterly deluded himself, which he may have done, Harrison surely knew that going after them was a surefire way to stir up the brothers' hostile intentions—whether or not they had harbored any before. After he attacked them for not admitting their aggression and they fought to defend themselves, Harrison would then have his "proof" of their aggression.

At Prophetstown, Tecumseh appeared taken aback by Governor Harrison's message and the accusation that Tecumseh intended to murder him. He quickly replied by canoe messenger that he would soon come downriver to Vincennes to clear up these rumors—or, as he put it, to "ease your heart" and "wash away all those bad stories."

Tecumseh's reply did little to quell William Henry's paranoia—if Tecumseh didn't attack Vincennes now, he wrote in a second letter to Madison and Eustis that same day, it was only because Harrison had discovered his scheme. A Native warrior values surprising the enemy above all else, Harrison advised the Washington officials, as this "bestows more eclat upon a warrior than the most brilliant success obtained by other means."

But then he paused, rhetorically, as if he suddenly wondered how Madison and Eustis might interpret this stream of missives detailing his state of high alarm. Some in the federal government, he wrote, might regard his alarm about the Prophet as "premature and unfounded." If he were wrong, he hoped the president would regard it as an honest mistake made in the hopes of avoiding much bloodshed. In a roundabout way, he went on to suggest that the president himself bore the blame for the Indian confederacy's uprising. Despite Harrison's recommendations the previous autumn, William Henry noted, Madison had not sent a speech in direct reply to Tecumseh's main question: Would the United States return the lands it claimed to have purchased along the Wabash?

Because the president did not reply directly and state the U.S. position, "[The Prophet] has been repeatedly told [by others] that the acquirement of more land was no object with the U. States. That they had more than they could possibly settle, that the frequent purchases which have been made for some years past had no other object than to distress the Indians, that the schemes originated with me and that the U. States would give up a considerable part of them rather than go to war with the Indians."

The irony here is almost laughable. William Henry was suggesting that by not responding to the tribal leaders directly, Madison had left him as the fall guy whom the Native peoples blamed for aggressive land grabs, not the U.S. government. But, in fact, that was exactly the case—William Henry *was* the culprit. President Madison had made it crystal clear that he did not want to fight an Indian war, and that Harrison should preserve peace if at all possible. Madison had shown zero interest in acquiring the strip of land along the Wabash that Governor Harrison coveted for white settlement and that so infuriated the tribes. Instead, President Madison took what, for him, may have been the most prudent—or the easiest— course in response to Harrison's flood of entreaties for action: silence.

To bolster Governor Harrison's stance (and surely at the urging of the man they lauded as possessing "the talents which distinguish the states-man"), the leading citizens of Vincennes dispatched a petition to Presi-dent Madison urging strong action against the Prophet, his brother, and their followers, alleging that the British were behind it all: "It is impossible to doubt but that the combination which has been formed on the Wa-bash, is a British scheme; and it is equally certain that this banditti is now about to be let loose upon us, and that nothing but vigorous measures will prevent it. . . . Shall we then quietly wait the stroke, when we see the weapon is suspended over us?"

In early August 1811, William Henry finally got what he wanted— Secretary of War Eustis informed him that a regiment of five hundred U.S. troops would arrive soon at Vincennes and serve under the gover-nor's command. He further instructed the governor that if he did make an attack on the Prophet, to make sure that he had enough forces, both regu-lar and militia, to ensure "the most complete success."

This appeared to give Harrison a complete go-ahead to pursue the Prophet. Only three days later, however, President Madison suddenly equivocated about giving Governor Harrison free rein and five hundred soldiers, like giving a loaded pistol to an angry drunk. Eustis sounded a note of alarm in a follow-up to the original orders. "I have been particu-larly instructed by the President, to communicate to your excellency his earnest desire that peace may, if possible, be preserved with the Indians, and that to this end every proper means may be adopted." Murders of set-tlers should be punished in a way appropriate to the crime. But any attack against "banditti" with the Prophet should be made only if absolutely necessary, as at this time any hostilities should be avoided, unless "indispensable."

True to his word, Tecumseh rushed to reassure Governor Harrison that he meant no harm. One year earlier, they had met in the walnut grove in their first face-to-face encounter. With so many dark rumors circulating about his alleged intentions, Tecumseh now felt all the more urgency to meet again in person and talk it out. This meeting at Grouseland, however, did not go well for either party. Governor Harrison had asked Tecumseh to bring only a small force of warriors. He had started down the Wabash with three hundred, plus families. On Tecumseh's arrival at Vincennes in late July 1811, William Henry displayed every armed man he could summon, marching the troops at Fort Knox up and down so they appeared twice their number. He lined Grouseland's entrance road with hundreds of militia and frontiersmen in fringed hunting shirts, muskets and rifles tipped with bayonets ominously in hand. Tecumseh and 180 warriors filed between them with war clubs and tomahawks.

The governor opened the meeting beneath a shaded arbor. The source of the conflict—the Fort Wayne Treaty lands along the Wabash—Harrison flatly refused to discuss. William Henry said that he hadn't heard from the president on the matter, and wouldn't address it further. If Tecumseh wanted the answer, he said, he should go to Washington "and see the President and hear his determination from his own mouth."

This was a convenient dodge for Harrison. President Madison had left the responsibility for how to proceed in the governor's hands. But now the governor was telling Tecumseh he had no further responsibility in the matter and he should go talk to the president.

Tecumseh replied that he would eventually visit President Madison and settle matters. In the meantime, he said, he would travel south to bring more tribes into his confederacy as he had the northern tribes. To Governor Harrison's rebukes that the gathering of tribes alarmed the settlers, Tecumseh replied that the settlers had no cause for fear—the tribes meant peace, and they followed the example of the United States, the Seventeen Fires, in joining their own tribal fires together. He hoped Governor Harrison did not try to settle the Wabash lands or change anything until he returned from his southern tour in the spring. He expected many Natives to arrive at Prophetstown, and they needed those Wabash lands to hunt. He presented a wampum belt to the governor to atone for any murders attributed to his followers and promised to send out messengers in all directions to tell tribes not to cause trouble. The governor should follow his example, Tecumseh said, and forgive the injuries committed against his people.

Night had now fallen over the arbor. A moon had risen. Tecumseh's declarations did little to satisfy William Henry.

"I made a short reply," he boasted in a report to President Madison, "telling them that the moon which they beheld . . . would sooner fall to the earth than the President would suffer his people to be murdered with impunity—and that he would put his warriors in petticoats sooner than he would give up a country which he had fairly acquired from the rightful owners."

With that, Harrison ended the meeting.

Two days after Tecumseh and a small party of fellow chiefs departed Grouseland and headed south, William Henry wrote to President Madison downplaying what might happen. "I believe Sir that . . . the combination formed by the Prophet will be dissolved. But to ensure success some military force must be brought into view."

The words "brought into view" left it comfortably vague as to specifics. As if preparing President Madison for a grander scheme he had in mind, the governor also wrote eloquently about the formidable leader behind the Prophet—his brother Tecumseh. If not for his own farseeing efforts to counter the Shawnee chief, the governor implied to the president, Te-

cumseh could create a Native empire as powerful as the great Aztec or
Incan states:

> The implicit obedience and respect which the followers of Tecum-
> seh pay to him is really astonishing and more than any other circum-
> stance bespeaks him one of those uncommon geniuses, which spring
> up occasionally to produce revolutions and overturn the established
> order of things. If it were not for the vicinity of the United States, he
> would perhaps be the founder of an Empire that would rival in glory
> that of Mexico or Peru. No difficulties deter him. His activity and in-
> dustry supply the want of letters, for Four years he has been in con-
> stant motion. You see him today on the Wabash and in a short time
> you hear of him on the shores of Lake Erie or Michigan, or on the
> banks of the Mississippi and wherever he goes he makes an impres-
> sion favorable to his purposes. He is now upon the last round to put a
> finishing stroke to his work. I hope, however, before his return that
> that part of the fabrick, which he considered complete will be demol-
> ished and even its foundations rooted up.

During these last weeks of August and into September, New England
troops and Kentucky militiamen gathered at Vincennes as authorized by
a president hard pushed by Harrison's entreaties. On September 26,
1811, with Tecumseh now traveling in the South, William Henry Harrison gave them the order to march—up the Wabash, toward Prophetstown.

CHAPTER 13

TENSKWATAWA
MAKES A GAMBLE

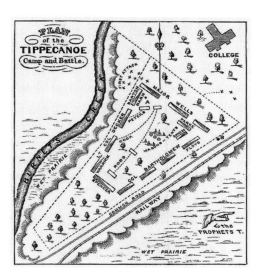

The odd bright spot in the night sky first became visible to the naked eye at summer's end of 1811. As Tecumseh's southbound recruiting party of twenty-one individuals from four different tribes crossed the Ohio in early September, the apparition appeared as a star in the constellation Ursa Major, "the big she-bear."* Everyone who knew the sky, Natives and whites alike, knew a star had not shone there before.

---

* It may be testimony to the ancientness of the world's hunting cultures and their common roots that this constellation is regarded in both Greek and Indigenous mythology as the figure of a bear. Since the distant past, humans dwelling in the Northern Hemisphere have used it to navigate at night. Two of its stars point to Polaris, the North Star, a true and always-visible indicator of the direction north. Embedded in the Great Bear is the constellation we know in the West as "the Big Dipper," representing a water dipper to many cultures. Its orientation—right side up, partially tipped, or upside down—was used to calculate planting and harvest seasons.

Harrison knew that Tecumseh's absence from Prophetstown offered his best chance to threaten the gathered tribes with a show of force into dispersing and destroy the village, although he didn't specify a contingency plan if they refused to leave. As he had put it to Madison and Eustis, before Tecumseh's return, the governor hoped "part of the fabrick . . . will be demolished and even its foundations rooted up." Bolstered by the addition of several hundred troops sent his way by Secretary of War Eustis, Harrison assembled an army of 1,200 composed of both regular army soldiers and temporary militiamen. On the night of October 10, however, two weeks after the governor had given the order to march from Vincennes, Harrison's plan faltered.

His army had advanced on the east bank of the river, about one-third of the way up the Wabash toward Prophetstown, or about sixty-five miles. It was a spectacle on the march. The four hundred regulars of the Fourth Regiment coming from New England via Pittsburgh wore, according to one historian's description, "probably the gaudiest costume ever to appear on the frontier"—brass-buttoned tailcoats, skintight pantaloons, and stovepipe hats tightly strapped under the chin and decorated with cockades in red, white, and blue.

A phalanx of these dandified regulars rode as mounted riflemen at the front of the boxlike column, while a troop of dragoons guarded the box's rear, making up the box's short sides. The eight hundred militiamen, many from the Indiana Territory and Kentucky, and the remaining regulars marched in two single files—"Indian file"—to form each long side of the box. Governor Harrison's idea was that these single files could move easily through the woods and, in case of ambush, pivot like the hand of a clock to face an enemy attacking from any direction.

He called a halt after the eighth day's march beside the Wabash and announced that the troops would stop to build a fort. Flatboats laden with flour struggled along upstream, men hauling them with ropes against the current between sandbars during this season of low water. Food ran low. Men who had enthusiastically joined the militia to fight Indians now grumbled, stopped here one hundred miles from Prophetstown chopping trees and hauling logs to build a fort while on reduced rations. Some deserted. Others fell ill. Harrison sent to Kentucky for more men. His plans slid toward uncertainty. He had calculated that when the Prophet and his followers saw his army marching this far up the Wabash, and with so strong a force, they would disperse on their own. He wouldn't have to attack. He would stay within President Madison's orders to make keeping the peace "a primary object" of any action he took.

That night, a sentry stood guard at the partially finished fort when a yellow flash and musket boom broke the darkness from undergrowth a mere twelve feet away. The sentry fell, wounded, with a ball through both thighs. The camp came to alert. Governor Harrison and the tempestuous Colonel John Boyd of Massachusetts, who had served as a soldier of fortune in India, patrolled the troops' lines in the dark on horseback. At dawn, dragoons led by Major Joseph Daviess, who had served as attorney general of Kentucky before joining Harrison's army, swept the woods for Native warriors. They found none, although a few obviously stalked nearby. Contrary to plans, Harrison's big force had not intimidated the gathered tribes and they gave no indication that they planned to disperse, if that musket shot was any sign. It now appeared Harrison would have to remove them, forcefully. He would have to defy President Madison's injunction, repeated over and over, to keep the peace. What had once been a theoretical proposition now was becoming real.

Did he pause and reconsider? Only ten years earlier, he had expressed to President Jefferson his concerns about the "extirpation" of Native people. It could leave a dark stain on America's history, he had worried. Yet now he was heading perilously close to a place where he might attack a peaceful village, a large gathering, a growing movement. His primary rationale for advancing on Prophetstown was this: The Native people, while peacefully and rightfully living on their own lands, would not disperse when he demanded it.

He had pushed, and pushed, and pushed the tribes, until finally they said *no more*. Did he not understand how far he had pushed them? His personal ambition for higher office had intensified since his appointment to governor of the massive Indiana Territory. He had grown blind to the full consequences of that ambition. He differed little in this respect from the poor white settlers who were awestruck by the rich soils of wilderness lands—Indigenous lands—and determined to settle there, no matter what claim the tribes might have to them.

Harrison had always shown a kind of moral flexibility, a magician's sleight of hand—a poof of smoke and flash of mirrors—for cloaking himself, his personal welfare, and ambition in the guise of a mission of goodwill and a pursuit of the highest calling. A perfect example was his highly ambiguous relationship with slavery. His political enemies knew of his changing stance, and eventually exposed it. His father, Benjamin V, had been an ardent advocate for slavery and a major Virginia slaveholder. In his late teens, however, William Henry had apprenticed in Richmond with a Scottish doctor whose humanitarian leanings extended to treating enslaved people. Whether out of heartfelt empathy for the enslaved, or in reaction to his overbearing father, or simply out of social convenience, William Henry soon attempted to join the Virginia Abolition Society. He had to give up an enslaved person of his own before being allowed to join. Even then, at least one member objected to William Henry's admittance because Benjamin V was such a large slaveholder and powerful advocate for slavery.

Although just what happened remains unclear, he later claimed (when politically convenient) that the Abolition Society had admitted him. A little over a decade later, however, in his early thirties as governor of the Indiana Territory, Harrison tried to introduce slavery to the territory despite Congress's very clear ban in these lands northwest of the Ohio. He had brought his own enslaved people from Virginia to Vincennes under the guise of servants. New settlers would not come to the territory, he argued, unless they could bring their slaves with them.

When Congress refused to pass his proposed suspension for ten years of this prohibition on slavery in the territory, he turned to his own territorial legislature by introducing and then signing "An Act Concerning the Introduction of Negroes and Mulattoes into this Territory." This allowed slavery in fact if not in name. A slaveholder from the South could bring slaves into Indiana Territory, register them as "indentured servants," and keep them working for terms of thirty or forty or more years. (Those under fifteen years old had to work until about age thirty.) If they refused, a slaveholder could send them—or sell them—back to the South. Opponents dubbed it "A Law for the Establishment of disguised slavery."

If it helped boost the territory's population, and, as a result, his own political ambitions, this former would-be member of the Virginia Abolition Society was now willing to impose slavery on lands where Congress had emphatically forbade it. He repeatedly employed this same moral sleight of hand in dispossessing Native people of their lands. Initially warning incoming president Jefferson of this possible dark stain on the American character, William Henry instantly reversed himself when Jefferson conveyed that the United States should acquire as much land as quickly as possible. Harrison had bought wholesale into Jefferson's moral justification for this Indian land grab: The best possible outcome for the Native peoples' future well-being would be for them to take up the ways of "civilization" and give up their lands.

Speaking through Tecumseh, the tribes gathered at Prophetstown said they wanted peace. But Harrison had convinced himself they were hostile. He remained blind to the realization that what he saw as their potential hostility was a direct reflection of his own aggression. He believed something had to be done about the gathering threat he perceived. From the wide spectrum of options available to him—diplomacy, negotiations, deeper investigation, or simple forbearance—his only answer was to meet their supposed hostility with a show of force.

.   .   .

Word—whether true or not—now came to his camp through friendly Delawares that Tenskwatawa had promised to burn alive the first American prisoner taken in a conflict. This only added to the dawning reality that the Native tribes gathered at Prophetstown would not simply disperse at the approach of Harrison's army.

By November 2, Harrison's army had advanced within about eighty miles of Prophetstown and was about to cross into the lands still officially held by tribes. It had left the main trail and forded the Wabash, looping out onto the open Illinois prairies for easier marching. After working to persuade the two for months, Harrison had received more explicit permission from President Madison and Secretary Eustis to attack the Prophet and his Native "combination" if he refused to disperse. As the troops built a small blockhouse at the mouth of the Vermillion River for added protection, a messenger brought news that a Native scout had shot a man lying asleep on the deck of a flatboat. He had been returning downstream after bringing badly needed flour to the hungry army. Harrison sent out expert trackers to pick up the trail of the Native ambushers. They lost it.

That night, Harrison woke up suddenly, alarmed. He had left his family at Grouseland, Nancy due any day with their eighth child. In a burst of paranoia, he pictured the Native scouts whose trail the trackers lost moving stealthily southward to Vincennes, joining with more warriors along the way. He summoned an Indiana militia officer to his tent in the middle of the night, telling him to pick forty of his best men, and proceed immediately to Vincennes with the order to make a fortress of the courthouse and protect the town's women and children within it, if they should attack Vincennes. He also entrusted the officer with a letter for his old friend from Wayne's army, Dr. John Scott, who, as usual, had come to Grouseland from Kentucky to attend to Nancy's delivery.

According to a biography of Harrison published during his lifetime, he wrote in this late-night letter to Dr. Scott "that his only uneasiness was for the wives and children of himself and his brave companions. That he had no fears for the success of the campaign. That he was aware that he was much exposed, because nearly all the Native people knew his person and were hostile to him. That his life was in the hands of his Creator, and Dr. Scott might rest assured that he would bring no disgrace upon the character of a pupil of WAYNE. Should he fall he recommended his family to the care of his friend."

If he hadn't before, in those midnight hours William Henry fully grasped the highly volatile situation he had fostered and now marched toward. He was, in effect, saying a last goodbye to his family and providing for their care. No written record exists of Nancy's awareness of or reaction to this moment—almost all her correspondence with her husband burned many years later in a house fire. But this was the first time since their marriage and first child that William Henry had ridden forth with an army into potential combat. Deeply religious, with seven young children at home and an eighth due any time, she placed her fate—and his—in the hands of a merciful God.

At Prophetstown, Tenskwatawa hesitated. Tecumseh, now many days distant in the South, had always strategized as the war chief of the two brothers. With Harrison's army marching toward him, and the village excited with news of the attack on the flatboats, his young warriors clamored to fight, but Tecumseh had warned him to avoid it. Tenskwatawa deliberated his next move. Harrison gave him an opening, sending a delegation of Delaware and Miami chiefs to Prophetstown with his demands—disperse all Potawatomis, Kickapoos, and Winnebagos from his village, return stolen horses, and turn over the warriors who had attacked frontier settlers.

Tenskwatawa sent a return message with the delegation, telling Harrison to stop his march where he was, and that Tenskwatawa would come and meet him for a peace council. But, partly to deceive Native American scouts, Harrison and his army had unexpectedly crossed to the Illinois

Territory side of the Wabash, while the delegation returned on the Indiana Territory side. The two parties missed each other. Harrison did not receive Tenskwatawa's response. Maybe this was by chance. Or maybe Harrison did not want to hear it, at least not until he had approached Prophetstown closer.

On the afternoon of November 6, Harrison's army emerged from a patch of dense forest and rocky terrain onto open ground near Prophetstown and the Wabash riverbank. Native scouts had tracked them from a distance but would not engage. Harrison's interpreters hailed them, as he hoped to arrange a meeting with the Prophet, but the Native scouts kept their distance. The army marched on, assuming battle order at Harrison's command, reaching the sprawling cornfields surrounding the village. Harrison later reported to President Madison and Secretary Eustis that he kept marching forward toward the village because he was looking for a place to camp, at the recommendation of his officers. As he neared, the warriors at Prophetstown, expecting an imminent attack, ran to the log barricades that the Prophet had ordered for defense. By way of three envoys bearing a flag who'd been sent out to meet him, Harrison relayed the message that he was only looking for a camping site and planned no hostilities until hearing the Prophet's response to his demands. The Prophet's initial reply had not reached him—or so Harrison later would report.

With troops and officers eager to begin to fight immediately, however, Harrison's advance guard kept on marching. It got to within 150 yards of the village when fifty or sixty warriors rushed out and called on them to stop. Harrison rushed to the front. Avoiding what surely would have been a bloody battle on the spot, he ordered his men to halt their march. Asking for a chief to serve as envoy, Harrison again said he was looking for a good camping spot where he could find wood and water. The chief directed him to a low plateau about three-quarters of a mile away covered with an open oak grove and a stream running along one side. His officers went to check it out, found it good, and Harrison and the chief parted, both promising not to begin hostile actions until the sides had talked the next day. Then a drizzle began to fall.

By all accounts it was a chill, soaking, and particularly "dark" night.* The utter blackness pooled so thickly beneath the oak trees, remembered one sentinel, William Brigham, "that no object could be discerned within three feet of me, and I could hear nothing except the rustling noise occasioned by the falling rain among the bushes." At four forty-five A.M., with dawn's light still two hours away, Brigham heard footfalls nearby and was about to shoot when a fellow sentinel identified himself, much alarmed, no doubt using the night's watchword, "wide awake, wide awake." He proposed they run for safety in the camp's interior rather than linger on this precarious edge where, at any moment, he expected Native warriors to attack.

" 'Brigham, let us fire and run in,' " Brigham later recounted his fellow sentinel as saying. " 'You may depend on it there are Indians in the bushes.' I told him not to fire yet for fear we should give a false alarm. While we were standing together, something struck in the brush near us (I suppose an arrow). We were both frightened and run in without firing."

In the absence of Tecumseh's strategic leadership, Tenskwatawa had first stalled for time. It had been agreed with Harrison. Talks would start in the morning. In the meantime, however, he had hatched his own bold—even brazen—plan.

It called for a predawn raid on Harrison's camp by five hundred warriors at Prophetstown—Shawnees, Potawatomis, Kickapoos, Winnebagos. Two Winnebago warriors were designated to slip through the camp's

---

* The infamous opening phrase of a novel penned in 1830 by Edward Bulwer-Lytton that has served as easy target for generations of parody, "It was a dark and stormy night . . ." was not in fact a redundant, overblown, and simple-headedly obvious description of night. It was an accurate description of a particular kind of night and absence of ambient celestial light that characterized navigating outdoors in heavy weather before the advent of artificial lighting.

standing guards as the attack erupted and locate Harrison. As he rushed from his tent to mount his horse to command the battle, they were to kill him.

The battle might not have occurred in the first place if Tecumseh—canny diplomat and seasoned war chief—had been present. He almost surely would have approached Harrison personally long before the army had marched this far and, unless all other options failed, would not have called for violence. But he was a thousand miles away, recruiting southern tribes for his confederacy, and totally unaware of Harrison's march.

The Prophet had been unsure how to respond to the challenge when Harrison's army had threateningly approached Prophetstown the previous afternoon and pitched camp on the nearby plateau. That evening he had embarked on a vision quest, to seek advice from the spirit world. When he emerged late in the evening, he had announced to the eager warriors that Harrison had to die. Initially, he had planned a different ruse. He would meet in the morning with Harrison as agreed and concede to his demands. Above all, Harrison insisted that the warriors from other tribes who had joined the Prophet's movement must disperse. Tenskwatawa and the warriors would then depart the council according to their initial agreement. Two warriors, however, would remain behind. In a moment of surprise, they would assassinate Harrison. Then, he assured his warriors, Harrison's army would fall apart.

Ironically, Harrison's own paranoia about assassination and attack over the past months and his own aggressiveness in marching to Prophetstown had set in motion this actual plot to assassinate him. However, it was hatched spontaneously, on the spot, in response to Harrison's actions—not planned months in advance by the Shawnee brothers as he had feared.

It was a shaky, risky scheme from the start. Nor had it satisfied the warriors—especially the Winnebagos from the distant Wisconsin country, who clamored for battle, honor, and the spoils of war. They wanted to attack Harrison's army immediately. That same drizzly evening, Tenskwatawa went off to have another vision. Guided by this, he had returned to his warriors and proposed they surround Harrison's camp and attack that very night. In the confusion of battle and darkness, warriors would slip into the camp and kill Harrison. Without their leader, Tenskwatawa predicted, Harrison's army would be powerless—their gunpowder would turn to sand, and through the darkness the warriors would see the enemy as clearly as day.

By four-thirty A.M. in cold, drizzly darkness, hundreds of warriors with darkened faces silently looped around the plateau and moved into place to surround the camp, divided in coordinated groups of 125 selected by tribe and language. Harrison had awakened at his usual early hour, and was in his tent, pulling on his boots. The night's campfires still blazed. At nearly the same moment that Brigham and his fellow sentinel heard an arrow whoosh into the brush nearby, another sentry on the camp's periphery, Stephen Mars, detected a slight movement in the shadowy, dripping undergrowth barely illuminated by flickering flames. He fired blindly at it. Then Corporal Mars ran for his life toward the center of camp where General Harrison dressed.

Out of the silent night, ear-ringing blasts and powder flashes erupted from hundreds of muskets. A shrill chorus of war cries overwhelmed the drizzly oak groves atop the plateau. Mars dropped in his tracks, felled by arrow or musket ball. William Brigham and other sentinels at the perimeter's western edge came sprinting for their lives—also toward the presumed safety of the camp's center.

Governor Harrison's big marquee tent sat in the middle of the camp. The camp itself formed a large rectangle outlined by the men's tents, rows of campfires blazing between tents and dark forest. With those first shots from the perimeter, warriors who had already penetrated the camp suddenly appeared at tent flaps and struggled face-to-face with the occupants. Many more remained hidden in the darkness beyond the perimeter, shooting in at the troops as they lined up in battle order. Musket balls whizzed into the coals, tossing showers of sparks upward into the night. Men dropped where they stood.

The attack had begun prematurely with that single movement in the bushes and the sentinel's nervous shot, before all six hundred or seven hundred warriors had fully taken position around the triangular plateau. The closest warriors to the camp, the Kickapoos on the northwest edge, charged inward, having routed the sentinels and guards while two companies of soldiers at that edge tried to take battle order.

Harrison had called to his servant George for his light gray mare to mount and command the erupting battle. But the horse had managed to pull its picket from the wet earth during the night, and George couldn't immediately locate her. Another officer's servant produced a different horse. Harrison took it, joined by his aide-de-camp Major Owen, riding a light colored horse. Almost immediately after they mounted to rush to the collapsing western line, a musket ball knocked Owen from his mount. He fell to the earth, dead. It almost surely had been aimed to kill Harrison, by a native warrior secreted in the camp's interior. The warrior had believed the governor would be astride his usual light gray mare, and mistook Major Owen's horse for Harrison's. How different the outcome might have been if William Henry's horse hadn't pulled its picket and wandered off.

Rushing to the western line, about one hundred yards from his tent, Harrison sought out the highest-ranking officer still standing, and asked what he needed. After returning to the center of camp, he dispatched reinforcements. By now the hundreds of Potawatomis, Winnebagos, Shawnees, and other warriors had taken their positions, and poured fire into the camp from all sides.

Companies all up and down the flanks of the camp organized into battle formation, facing outward, following Harrison's steady commands. They could see little as they shot into the darkness, and yet men dropped where they stood in formation. Some officers and then Harrison himself saw the problem—their orders given the night before had directed the men to assume formation in front of their tents if attacked. But this placed them just behind their blazing campfires. For the Native people looking in from the darkness, firelight illuminated the soldiers, as one account puts it, like actors illuminated on a stage by footlights while peering out into a darkened theater. From that darkened theater musket balls and arrows came whizzing straight at the uniformed actors.

Atop his horse, Governor Harrison shouted out the command to extinguish all fires immediately.

Surrounded by "the yells of the Indians, and the ringing of their fire arms," remembered Captain Peter Funk, "nothing could be seen but the flashes of the enemies guns."

At the northeast corner, a hail of musket balls ripped into camp. A patch of fallen timber and rotted logs protected some Potawatomi warriors from the soldiers' fire. They ducked to reload and shoot again and again. Major Daviess, the attorney general of Kentucky and glory-bound commander of the dragoons, approached Governor Harrison with twenty of the best armed and mounted cavalry. Their exchange was later reported by eyewitness Captain Funk.

"Will you permit me to dislodge those [goddamned] savages behind those logs?" Major Daviess, in his white capote coat with pistols at the ready and sword in hand, asked Harrison.

Permission denied, the governor replied. He didn't know if the gung ho Daviess might send some of Harrison's best soldiers straight into disaster.

Major Daviess asked again. Still the governor denied his request. Still the fire poured into camp.

A short while later, Major Daviess asked a third time—now proposing to lead a foot charge of twenty men.

The fire had intensified. A foot charge led by Daviess might stop the firing without risking any mounts.

Permission granted.

.   .   .

The Native warriors charged repeatedly. The troops fell back in places along the sagging lines, and almost broke. The Native forces retreated into the dripping darkness. For long moments, nothing but silence emerged from the night. Then a high whistling pitch began, and black-painted warriors, screaming, rushed from the darkness and charged at the lines again.

The worst of it came from the warriors hidden among the fallen logs. After finally receiving permission from Governor Harrison, Major Daviess assembled his twenty men, dismounting from horses to present lower targets. With Daviess in the lead wielding his saber and a pistol, they charged on foot toward the logs. The warriors instantly identified the major's long, white cloak even through the rainy dark. As he closed to within thirty or forty yards of the logs three musket balls ripped into him, one perhaps from his own man's gun.

"I am a dead man," he shouted, as the charge failed and his men dragged him, still alive, back to their lines.

As dawn's dim light suffused the gray clouds and cold drizzle, the Native warriors lost their night advantage. Trying another direct charge, they were repelled by Harrison's soldiers holding their lines. The Fourth Regiment and mounted dragoons launched a countercharge in the growing light. The Native warriors fell back, a little at first, and then farther and farther, taking to the marshy open ground below the plateau, and scattering in all directions.

"Huzza! Huzza! Huzza!" shouted the men, the three cheers going up from around the camp in unison.

Later, it became known that Governor Harrison had his own scheme for a night surprise attack. He had planned to hold the morning council with Tenskwatawa, and, however it turned out, attack Prophetstown that following night. But Tenskwatawa and his many warriors had attacked first, in those hours before dawn on November 7, 1811.

That day Harrison's army buried its dead. They reinforced the camp that night with breastworks, bracing for another attack by hundreds of Indian reinforcements said to be en route, possibly under Tecumseh. The attack didn't come. The day after that, they entered Prophetstown and found it deserted. The soldiers carried off all the stored corn they could find, then set its two hundred or so wigwams to flame, in a great conflagration that lit up the night skies.

The U.S. casualties came to 62 dead and 126 wounded. The Indigenous casualties were lower—an estimated from 25 to 50 dead and maybe 100 wounded. Harrison, who had consciously put his army into this confrontational situation, did not want to stay around to see what happened next. Concern mounted that Tecumseh could show up at any moment with many more warriors. Along with eighteen wagons whose contents had been emptied out and burned in order to carry the army's wounded, Harrison quickly marched his men back down the Wabash.

Thus no clear "winner" of the battle emerged, at least initially. The Native tribes had been driven off and, lacking ammunition, had deserted their town, which Harrison's army destroyed. But Harrison had then rushed his army off toward safety over one hundred miles away. The threat remained.

William Henry, however, called it a "glorious victory" at the earliest opportunity. In many accounts and settlers' eyes, and in the praises of Congress and President Madison, William Henry Harrison was a hero. In others, he came under criticism; some newspaper accounts reported it as a "most distressing disaster" and a "horrible butchery." He defended himself at great length in letters after the action.

Under verbal attack, Harrison displayed an early brilliance at what modern political parlance calls "spin"—framing an item of news, an event, or a development in a way that presents oneself or one's cause in the best possible light, often at the expense of accuracy, context, or even truthfulness. In the last decades of the eighteenth century and the first of the nineteenth, newspapers had become widespread in the United States, including several prominent publications on the western frontier. The era of mass communications was dawning, and William Henry Harrison emerged as one of the earliest politicians to learn to work it to his advantage.

In the aftermath of the battle at the Tippecanoe, as it soon came to be called, Harrison did what Richard Nixon and Henry Kissinger, taking a cue from Vermont senator George Aiken, would one day make infamous in their strategy to end American commitment in the long and controversial Vietnam War. As it was phrased in their day, *Declare victory and get out.*

CHAPTER 14

A LAMP IN THE WEST

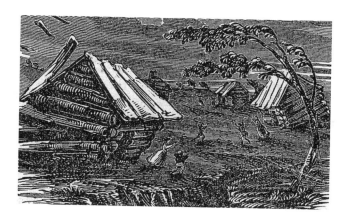

After concentrating his earlier recruiting efforts among the northern tribes, Tecumseh now shifted focus to the South. By early September, he and his entourage had crossed the Ohio River and traversed Chickasaw territory in today's Kentucky and Tennessee. His party numbered six Shawnees, six Kickapoos, and six Winnebagos—all from the Great Lakes region—while two Creeks from the Southeast served as guides. One of them, Seekaboo, a relative of Tecumseh's, knew Indigenous cultures of both North and South.

They made only a cursory effort to recruit among the Chickasaw—longtime enemies of the Shawnee and other northern tribes. With the entourage dressed identically in fringed buckskin shirts and leggings, silver bands around biceps and hawks' feathers braided into the scalp locks that protruded from their shaved heads, they headed still deeper into the South—toward today's Mississippi and Alabama.

Like a diplomatic envoy seeking alliances amid European kingdoms or ancient Chinese states, Tecumseh had specifically targeted the Choctaws. The Choctaws had a confederacy of sorts—interrelated villages spanning a large area, divided into three main districts. Guided by Seeka-boo, who also served as interpreter, the entourage headed down the Six Towns Trail, into what is now central Mississippi and toward the Gulf Coast. The Six Towns was one of the three major districts, led by the celebrated leader, orator, and warrior Pushmataha. From the very start, Pushmataha fiercely tried to block Tecumseh's efforts to create a great confederacy of tribes. The Choctaw and other southern tribes like the Chickasaw had started to take up farming and other white ways.

"In each of the tribes," writes Sugden, "American agents were encouraging the Indians to improve their farming, and to manufacture cloth, rather than to hunt; to produce for the market instead of for mere subsistence; to replace the old values of cooperation and sharing with thrift and acquisitiveness; and to emphasize individual rather than communal ownership of the land."

Here among southern tribes the transformation of values was visibly under way—Native American to Euro-American—with private ownership and acquisition of land at the very center of the equation that could produce such profound change. Several geographical and cultural factors propelled this transformation. The distant southern tribes lacked support from nearby British authorities in Canada who could potentially supply northern tribes with arms and ammunition against U.S. aggression. Instead, to the south of the southern tribes lay the faltering Spanish empire, which struggled to keep its own claims in Florida and the Gulf Coast against expanding U.S. forts and Southeast settlements. Additionally, white traders married Native women on the Southeastern frontier, and their grown children quickly rose to leadership. They "preferred the acquisitive entrepreneurial lifestyles of their merchant forbears to the simple egalitarianism of the Indians," writes Sugden.

Pressure from settlers had eaten at the edge of Choctaw territory and the tribe had ceded land to the United States. Pushmataha and other Choctaw chiefs had aligned themselves with the U.S. government. He had personally pocketed $500 for arranging a land cession to the United

States, receiving a regular pension in addition. As Tecumseh and his fellow chiefs traveled from town to town, Pushmataha kept pace with them, speaking against Tecumseh at every stop. Finally, one of the other three district chiefs called a great council at the main Choctaw town of Mokalusha (near today's Choctaw Indian Reservation, northeast of Jackson, Mississippi).

"Halt! Tecumseh, listen to me," said Pushmataha, according to oral accounts and longstanding legend. "You have come here, as you have often gone elsewhere, with a purpose to involve peaceful people in unnecessary trouble with their neighbors. Our people have no undue friction with the whites. Why? Because we have had no leaders stirring up strife to serve their selfish personal ambitions."

The council deliberated, and went with Pushmataha's argument. If war broke out between the British and United States amid the rising tensions, the Choctaw would not fight on the side of the British against the United States. No description exists of Tecumseh's reaction at this setback—dejection or determination or simple acceptance. He may have expected it, given close ties between Choctaw chiefs and the United States and the growing adoption of white agriculture and commercial production in some Choctaw districts. Nevertheless, the Choctaw, like other southern tribes, had battled disease, alcohol, illegal white settlement, and crashing game populations, and had rapidly lost lands to the United States by selling them to pay off trade debts that the United States had encouraged them to run up. Despite Pushmataha's opposition to Tecumseh, according to some accounts, a number of Choctaw warriors did join his cause.[*]

He pushed onward, still deeper, now into the Southeast and the Creek Nation, in today's Georgia and Alabama. Tecumseh had relatives

---

[*] In 1805, when President Jefferson had begun his second term, his underhanded strategy—get them in debt and take their lands to settle it—bore fruit in a land grab from the Choctaw tribe. The Choctaws gave up four million acres to settle their debt to trading companies and received a $48,000 annuity handed out at the discretion of the chiefs.

here. Both his father and mother probably were born and met in Shawnee enclaves among the Creeks (also known as Muscogees). In the late
1600s, Iroquois invasions had shoved bands of Shawnees out of their
Ohio Valley homelands. Some had migrated southeast to start villages
among the Creeks but kept bonds to the Ohio Valley, like Tecumseh's
parents. It made sense for Tecumseh to aim directly for Tuckabatchee,
one of the main towns of the Upper Creeks, perhaps founded by the
Shawnees and possibly his father's birthplace.

The timing of his entourage's arrival on the evening of September 19
was perfect, and perhaps coordinated by Tecumseh to coincide with a big
council that had already gathered at Tuckabatchee. The main civil chief,
Big Warrior—Tastanagi Tako—served as speaker for the Upper Creeks
and a leader on the Creek Nation's council. The gathering was called to
consider the U.S. request—actually, demand—to build a horse road running north-south through Creek lands all the way from Tennessee to the
Gulf Coast to connect white settlements. U.S. agent Benjamin Hawkins
was making his pitch that day and the next to the Creek Nation, plus dozens of other Choctaw, Seminole, and Cherokee representatives attending the council. Despite the group's initial resistance to the white
settlement that would inevitably follow the road, Hawkins promised they
could keep profits from ferries and toll bridges, apparently funneling some
of these as disguised bribes directly to chiefs, as in the case of Big Warrior,
who personally became wealthy from tolls, according to Edmunds. Nor
did Hawkins offer the tribes much choice, one witness later reported.

"Col. Hawkins, at length, told them he did not come there to ask their
permission to open a road, but merely to inform them that it was now cutting."

Not wanting Hawkins to hear his rallying speech, Tecumseh waited
for the agent to leave the village (permission to build the road in hand).
He then addressed the assembly. He knew how to make an impressive
entrance. He and his entourage had stripped naked except for breech-
cloths and moccasins, their faces painted black, with eagle feathers bob-

bing on their heads and tails from the rare and sacred white buffalo bouncing from the rears of their belts. With Tecumseh in the lead, they circled Tuckabatchee's central plaza several times, as Tecumseh reached out his arm to shake the hands of other tribal leaders and give gifts of tobacco. They then fascinated the assembled leaders and hundreds of onlookers with the Shawnee war dance and war songs in which each warrior in turn recounted and reenacted his heroic deeds to the beat of drums. It climaxed with all the chiefs of Tecumseh's entourage leaping and dancing together, pipe-tomahawks and war clubs and knives in hand, emitting war whoops and cries while acting out the killing of the enemy. Enthusiastically adopted by other Creek villages, it became known as the "Dance of the Lakes."

When Tecumseh finally addressed the large assembly, his powerful speech struck home especially with the Upper Creeks, who had tried to retain their traditional ways, separate from the Lower Creeks. Insofar as this speech to the Creeks can be reconstructed from partial accounts, Tecumseh told them that his own mother and father had lived among them. The Shawnees and Creeks were powerful people, but the white man had taken their lands, over and over, taking their strength. To stand up to the whites, they must return to the ways of their fathers and they must join together, tribes of the North and tribes of the South against the Americans. It was certain that war would erupt between the United States and Britain, he told them, and when it did the British would help defeat the Natives' enemies. "Then their lost lands would be restored," paraphrases Edmunds, "and the Creeks could regain the happiness and prosperity of their forefathers."

Tecumseh's message resonated with a swelling movement among the Creeks to return to traditional roots and receive special powers from the Maker of Breath—the Creek Nation's Great Creator—a spiritual movement perhaps inspired by earlier visits by the Creeks to Prophetstown to hear Tenskwatawa. They soon came to call themselves "Red Sticks" after the red war clubs they carried. Or it might have been, as another version of the name's origin tells it, that Tecumseh gave them a bundle of red sticks when he left. He instructed them to remove one stick each day and throw it away, a traditional Indigenous method of counting days. He told them that a British warship would appear off the coast of Florida (held by the Spanish), loaded with guns and ammunition, to support them. It's not clear if Tecumseh had heard this from the British or had invented the story to inspire his followers. On the day they threw away the last red stick, he told them, the uprising against the Americans would begin.

As Tecumseh and his entourage traveled among the Indigenous villages of the Southeast, bringing word of unification and the new religion, the small, dim star in the Great Bear constellation that had first appeared a few weeks earlier grew brighter. Taking the shape of a comet, a circle of light appeared at its head, and its long, luminous tail reached across the night sky. In midnight ceremonies, Tecumseh—whose name itself meant "Panther Crossing the Sky" or "Shooting Star"—pointed to it as a harbinger of the upheaval to come. This would overturn the whites and their world.

A letter by a white traveler, Francis McHenry, published in *The Georgia Journal* a few months later, gave eyewitness accounts from those who had heard Tecumseh's speeches, although McHenry mistakenly identified Tecumseh as "the Prophet."

"It is certain that an Indian, well known under the appellation of the Prophet, on his embassy to the Creek Nation, in the month of August last, pronounced in the public square, that shortly a lamp would appear in the west to aid him in his hostile attack, upon the whites, and if they would not be influenced by his persuasion, the earth would, ere long, tremble to its centre."

Within just a few weeks of his September visit to the Creek, Seminole, and southeastern tribes, Tecumseh rode west all the way from the Eastern Seaboard to the Great Plains, one thousand miles. Crossing the Mississippi River to the Missouri country, he spoke among the Shawnees there who had fled the Ohio Valley violence decades earlier. The refugees traveling into Spanish territory had included his own mother, who left when he was eleven. She would now be in her seventies, if still alive, and perhaps Tecumseh spoke to her, too. Of this, however, there is no record.

But there is a record of Tecumseh's visit among the Osage, far west of the Mississippi. Originally an Ohio Valley tribe, the Osages, known for their towering stature and independent nature, had migrated west several hundred years earlier to become buffalo hunters on the Great Plains in the region of today's Kansas, Missouri, and Oklahoma, and became closely tied to the Plains tribes. Living among the latter as a member of the Kansa tribe was a young white man, captured somewhere in the Midwest as a boy so small he remembered almost nothing of his parents. In a memoir he wrote years later under the name John Dunn Hunter, he distinctly recalled seeing Tecumseh speak at the Osage villages on the Osage River (near today's Kansas City). Hunter expresses his frustration at his inability to retell Tecumseh's speech with the full language, gestures, and drama that it deserved:

> I wish it was in my power to do justice to the eloquence of this distinguished man; but it is utterly impossible. The richest colours, shaded with a master's pencil, would fall infinitely short of the glowing finish of the original. The occasion and subject were peculiarly adapted to call into action all the powers of genuine patriotism; and such language, such gestures, and such feelings and fulness of soul contending for utterance, were exhibited by this untutored native of the forest in the central wilds of America, as no audience, I am persuaded, either in ancient or modern times ever before witnessed.

Hunter identified both the simplicity of the speech, and its power—"a simple, but vehement narration of the wrongs imposed by the white people on the tribes, and an exhortation for the latter to resist them." But much of the speech's power grew from the receptivity of its audience and how deeply they felt the threat of white encroachment on their remaining lands. Just two years earlier, Osage leaders had agreed to a treaty ceding their claim to the Mississippi's west bank but, already regretting it, had recently sent a delegation to St. Louis asking for its return.

Tecumseh, according to Hunter, aimed his appeal directly at his listeners' emotional core. "The whole addressed to an audience composed of individuals who had been educated to prefer almost any sacrifice to that of personal liberty, and even death to the degradation of their nation."

To open, Tecumseh gazed out calmly for long moments over the great assemblage of warriors, Hunter recounted.

"Brothers," he suddenly cried out, gesturing to embrace the moment. "We all belong to one family; we are all children of the Great Spirit; we walk in the same path; slake our thirst at the same spring." He said the tribes must come together to smoke the pipe around the same council fire. Now "weighty matters" must be decided.

He paused again, then recounted in metaphorical terms the history of white settlement on the continent.

"Brothers," Tecumseh cried out.

When the white men first set foot on our grounds, they were hungry; they had no place on which to spread their blankets, or to kindle their fires. . . . They could do nothing for themselves. Our fathers commiserated their distress, and shared freely with them whatever the Great Spirit had given his red children.

Brothers, the white people came among us feeble; and now we have made them strong, they wish to kill us, or drive us back, as they would wolves and panthers. . . . At first, they only asked for land sufficient for a wigwam; now, nothing will satisfy them but the whole of our hunting grounds, from the rising to the setting sun.

To stop this, Tecumseh said, his people had "taken up the tomahawk."

Brothers—My people are brave and numerous; but the white people are too strong for them alone. I wish you to take up the tomahawk with them. If we all unite, we will cause the rivers to stain the great waters with their blood.

    Brothers—If you do not unite with us, they will first destroy us, and then you will fall an easy prey to them. They have destroyed many nations of red men because they were not united, because they were not friends to each other.

He made an allusion to British support, referring to the British Empire as "our Great Father over the great water." He is angry with the whites and will help the Native Americans in their fight. They should not fear white men—they can't run fast, they're easy marks, and Indian warriors are not women.

Brothers—The Great Spirit is angry with our enemies; he speaks in thunder, and the earth swallows up villages, and drinks up the Mississippi. The great waters will cover their lowlands; their corn cannot grow; and the Great Spirit will sweep those who escape to the hills from the earth with his terrible breath.

    Brothers—We must be united; we must smoke the same pipe; we must fight each other's battles; and more than all, we must love the Great Spirit: he is for us; he will destroy our enemies, and make all his red children happy.

The audience, a very large one consisting of visitors and visiting chiefs, was utterly engrossed, Hunter reported—so much so that when Tecumseh ended his speech, they called a council, and deliberated for the next several days whether to take the major step of joining his confederacy and fighting their battles together.

·   ·   ·

It's not clear exactly where Tecumseh was on the night of December 15–16, 1811, during his recruiting journey. He may have been heading toward Osage villages out on the Plains. He may have been crossing back over the Mississippi before looping through Illinois prairies and Wisconsin lake country on his return to Prophetstown.

The few white witnesses to that night's event along the Mississippi River heard a tremendous roaring at two A.M. It was punctuated by the crack and crashing of trees in the forests along the riverbanks, blasts of sulfur-smelling vapor from deep underground, and wild geese out on the water screaming in alarm. As the earth heaved and soils liquefied, huge slabs of riverbank collapsed into the water, sending out great swells. The Mississippi River itself churned in violent, stormy waves, ran backward, and tumbled over waterfalls where none had existed before, as if the shocks had broken the deep bed of North America's mightiest river.

To John Bradbury, a British botanist collecting plants in the wilderness of what is now Missouri, roused from sleep by the roaring and violent tipping of his small riverboat tied to the shore, it was an earthquake—the largest ever known in eastern North America and one that altered the course of the Mississippi River by many miles. It centered near the tiny settlement of New Madrid, along the river about 150 miles south of St. Louis, but the earth shook violently across thousands of miles—from the Great Plains to the Atlantic. It rang church bells in Richmond, Virginia, and quivered the sandstone walls and brick fireplaces of the just-finished President's House in the new federal capital, Washington City.

At Grouseland, hundreds of miles from the earthquake's epicenter, an officer named Miller lay upstairs in a rope-mattress bed in a spare bedroom, recovering from wounds he had received the month before at Tippecanoe. He later recounted how the earthquake rocked the big brick governor's mansion, and cracks suddenly zipped across the plaster ceiling of his bedroom—cracks that remain to this day.

To the Native tribes across the vast region jolted by the violent shaking, however, it was a sign from the Great Spirit.

Still out in the Mississippi River country, Tecumseh apparently received word of the battle near Prophetstown. No record exists of what he said upon hearing the news, but he now redoubled his recruiting efforts for the confederacy, riding swiftly among tribes already under his influence—Sauk and Fox, Potawatomi, Winnebago. Some of their warriors had just returned from the battle at Tippecanoe and clamored for war against the Americans, wanting to contact British agents for arms. Tecumseh urged them to wait until the proper moment. He rode onward to the northwest, up the Minnesota River toward the Great Plains, to visit the Santee Dakota Sioux.

What Tecumseh made of the earthquake and powerful aftershocks at that moment, it's impossible to know. But, as he completed his three-thousand-mile recruiting loop and headed toward home, lots of signs were emerging—the comet in the sky, the shaking of the earth, the eagerness of the northwestern tribes to fight. It all appeared to foretell a moment of upheaval and change.

When he rode up the Wabash to Prophetstown in early winter 1812, it was not the change he would have liked to see. He had heard about the battle from warriors returning to their distant homes. But the reality came as a shock. No dogs barked. No children ran out to greet him. No women sang songs, nor fires burned under spits of roasting venison and pots of stewing squash and corn. Heaps of sodden ashes marked where hundreds of wigwams had stood along the banks of the Wabash and Tippecanoe. The bulging granary that held dried corn to feed thousands of mouths through the winter was now a charred mound. Human skulls and bones lay scattered about. The living people had scattered.

It was a scene of "great destruction and havoc," Tecumseh later told the British, "the fruits of our labor destroyed, the bodies of my friends laying in the dust, and our village burnt to the ground, and all our kettles carried off."

It was said Tecumseh was so infuriated that his brother had fought against his wishes that he grabbed Tenskwatawa by the hair and threatened his life if he ever did it again. Most of the coalition's warriors had gone home in the wake of the battle and the destruction of Prophetstown, their faith in Tenskwatawa's prophesies shattered. But when his anger had subsided, when the damage was surveyed and the loss grieved, and when others were consulted, acknowledged, and heard—chiefs and advisers, perhaps Tecumpease—Tecumseh resumed his plans to assemble a confederacy.

Tecumseh realized he didn't need his brother the Prophet to carry forward his vision. He had laid the groundwork over the preceding five years across the continent's center, from Florida to the Great Lakes, out on the Great Plains nearly to the Rocky Mountains. He made the leap of faith that he could rally tribal leaders and summon warriors from distant regions if he needed them to fight.

While he didn't know it then, down in the Southeast, among the Creeks, a new movement had already started. This one centered around Tecumseh rather than his brother the Prophet. Tecumseh's vision of tribal unity stopping white encroachment was still alive, if smoldering among ashes and ruins.

The Red Stick medicine men interpreted the shaking of their land. They said that Tecumseh had predicted it. The quaking earth showed his supernatural powers, they recounted; Tecumseh would stamp his foot and the earth would shake. The Great Spirit was angry with their enemies and spoke in thunder, as Tecumseh had phrased it to the Osages. The earth had swallowed up villages. As for those who attempt to escape to the hills and hide, the Great Spirit would sweep them from the earth with his terrible breath.

For the next some months, it seemed that the Red Sticks were right.

CHAPTER 15

A CASE OF NERVES

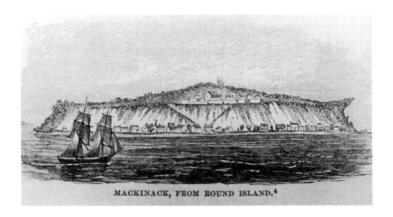

MACKINACK, FROM ROUND ISLAND.[4]

Six months after the burning of Prophetstown and the New Madrid earthquake, another turn of global events suddenly rocked both shores of the Atlantic. It gave a huge boost to Tecumseh's efforts to resurrect the confederacy he had so painstakingly assembled. On June 18, 1812, an angry, exasperated, and impatient United States declared war on Great Britain.

The outrageous British insults to the young nation had finally grown too flagrant to bear—especially for President Madison's Democratic-Republican party. The audacious French emperor had just launched one of history's largest invasions—marching his Grande Armée of nearly three-quarters of a million soldiers into Russia to crush Czar Alexander's army. With this kind of continent-upending madness, the dire need for British bodies to fight in Europe showed no signs of abating. The British relentlessly pursued able-bodied male citizens they suspected of hiding amid the crews of American ships, running them down at sea. It was as if a parental British Empire still felt it could control an adolescent United States and freely barge open the door to its private quarters.

Some U.S. citizens called for a "second war of American independence" against the British tyrant. Among many American politicians, it wasn't just about the rights of U.S. ships on the open sea. They pushed to invade Canada and seize it for the United States. These included the British-hating Thomas Jefferson, who proposed invasion of Canada as a step toward the "final expulsion of England from the American continent."

The outspoken "War Hawks" in Congress added a further grievance—that the British instigated Native tribes to violence against U.S. frontier settlers. Not surprisingly, the most prominent War Hawks blaming Britain for Native violence hailed from frontier states eager to expand west, including Kentucky's Henry Clay, Speaker of the House, and John C. Calhoun from South Carolina. By invading Canada, the United States could wipe the continent clean of British influence and open its entire expanse to America's westward push.

Ironically, a U.S. declaration of war would reenergize Britain's commitment to block American growth. British strategic thinkers revived the idea of an Indian barrier state across the North American midsection. This would contain the American states to the east and give British total control of the Upper Great Lakes. The continent remained far from finished as a political entity. North America's political boundaries were still malleable, open, and unformed, especially toward the sprawling west.

Henry Marie Brackenridge, a journalist and historian who lived through the events, wrote:

> It was foreseen that our Atlantick cities would be much exposed, that the coasts of the southern states would be laid open to the incursions of marauding parties, and that the western frontier would feel all the horrours of a savage and murderous warfare. Many persons, on the other hand, entertained the belief, that the Canadas would fall, and that the Floridas, in case that Spain should be brought into the contest on the side of England, would be ours. Thus should we be freed

from troublesome neighbours, and end forever, that dreadful species of hostility in which we had been so often engaged with the savages. These hopes were not ill founded; but we were not aware, at the time, of our deficiency in experience.

On June 1, 1812, President Madison presented to Congress an account of the brazen wrongs the United States had suffered at the hands of Great Britain. "Thousands of American citizens," railed Madison, "have been torn from their country and from everything dear to them . . . dragged on board ships of war of a foreign nation . . . to be exiled to the most distant and deadly climes, to risk their lives in the battles of their oppressors."

Britain's hostile acts toward the United States, which Madison called a "neutral nation" in Europe's wars, included the blockade of American ports by British ships. Britain claimed the blockades prevented American merchants from trading with Britain's enemies. Madison charged that, in reality, Britain blockaded U.S. ports to keep Britain's own monopoly on Atlantic trade. Evidence for further hostile acts pointed to Britain stirring up "combinations"—conspiracies—among Native tribes on the western frontier and encouraging them to employ against American settlers their "peculiarly shocking" warfare. Or so Madison told Congress. There is little doubt he based this statement partly on William Henry Harrison's suspicions about hostile combinations brewing at Prophetstown.

The House debated the matter in a closed session. It passed a declaration of war, 79 votes to 49, with a strong split between Federalists from New England opposed versus Democratic-Republicans from the South—President Madison's party—supporting it. The Senate took it up and passed a declaration of war 19 to 13, and President Madison signed it on June 18. Some would call it "Mr. Madison's war."

If they remember it at all, most Americans today associate the War of 1812 with two showy events—the sacking and burning of the White House by the British, and the writing of "The Star-Spangled Banner" by Francis Scott Key during the Royal Navy bombardment of Fort

McHenry near Baltimore. Nor do Americans generally remember it as having a clear conclusion or consequence. But at the time, the war—which then had no name, of course—had erupted from American outrage against the British. Passions ran high, and it would indeed have profound consequences for the shape, size, and tenor of the young nation, especially in the far western reaches.

"It was a war," wrote historian Richard Hildreth, who lived through it as a boy, "for the rights of personal freedom—the freedom, suppose, of Britons and other foreigners, as well as Americans, from the domineering insolence of British press-gangs—an idea congenial to every manly soul, and giving to the contest a strong hold on the hearts of the masses; in fact, a just title to the character of a democratic war, in the best sense of that very ambiguous epithet, and even to be called a second war for independence, as its advocates delighted to describe it."

Although the United States declared the war, the British had a faster means of notifying their distant outposts about it through fur-trade networks. The news raced westward out of the Great Lakes via fast voyageur canoe—forty-foot lightweight birchbark craft each powered by fourteen stout French-Canadian paddlers—owned by Canada's Northwest Fur Company. By July 15, news had reached British captain Charles Roberts at Fort St. Joseph, a British outpost on another island at Lake Superior's entrance to that crucial vestibule of the Upper Lakes. Forty miles away at Mackinac Island, U.S. lieutenant Porter Hanks, lacking the speedy canoe network, had no idea that Congress had declared war.

The first reverberations struck far into the North American interior, directly on that juncture of the three Upper Great Lakes. About a month after President Madison signed the declaration of war, a large flotilla of birchbark canoes and wooden bateaux slid quietly onto the beach of the U.S.-held Mackinac Island in the moonlit predawn hours of July 17, 1812. From the craft climbed three hundred British regulars and Canadian militiamen, and nearly seven hundred warriors from a wide spectrum of tribes of the Upper Great Lakes and Great Plains—Winnebago,

Chippewa (Ojibwe), Ottawa, Sioux, and others—their faces painted for war. Two miles around the island's point stretched a crescent of beach cradling the island's village—a centuries-old trading center—with a fortress guarding over it from atop a limestone cliff.

This was Fort Mackinac, currently in possession of the United States, who had won it from Great Britain in peace settlements after the Revolution. The fort's heavy cannons were aimed over the strategic strait linking lakes Huron and Michigan. With Lake Superior's entrance also nearby, Fort Mackinac controlled this watery vestibule to the uppermost lakes and western wilds.

"The situation completely commands the northwest trade," reported a traveler at the time, "which is compelled to pass immediately under the guns of the fort."

Within this impregnable fortress, fifty-seven American troops under the command of Lieutenant Porter Hanks rested easily that morning. They remained utterly unaware that, as the reflection of the full moon gently shimmered on the lake's calm surface, the warriors beyond the point were deftly lifting their canoes onto shore and sliding into the forest that cloaked the island known to Upper Great Lakes tribes as "the Great Turtle."

The hundreds of assembled Native warriors and British soldiers stealthily began their ascent to the island's highest point, a bluff that overlooked Fort Mackinac sitting on its limestone perch over village and straits. En route to the island they had captured an American, a civilian named Daurman who had been sent by boat toward Britain's Fort St. Joseph to learn why it had been so quiet over there lately. The Native and British flotilla had spotted his craft out on the calm, moonlit lake and seized him. Boating him back to Mackinac Island, they released him on the condition that he return to the Mackinac village, gather up the civilian villagers—shopkeepers, fur merchants, grog shop owners—and tell them they were now under British protection. He was to warn them that anyone who went up to the U.S. fort could be massacred.

Accounts vary as to what happened next. According to some, as life at Fort Mackinac awakened that morning, the British and the Native warriors, having climbed to the hilltop above, fired a single shot from a small cannon that whistled over the fort's ramparts, announcing their presence. Others say that at midmorning a messenger was sent down from the hilltop bearing a truce flag and a message to Lieutenant Hanks to surrender the fort.

In either case, Lieutenant Hanks had little choice. Surrender the fort and the fifty-seven troops inside it or face an imminent attack—and certain death—from a force of hundreds of Native warriors.

He surrendered.

"It was a fortunate circumstance," wrote one of the British officers to his superiors back in Canada's East, "that the fort surrendered without firing a single gun, for had they done so I firmly believe not a soul of them would have been saved."

The news raced among the tribes. Over the past five years, Tecumseh, with help from his Potawatomi ally Main Poc, had laid the groundwork for tribes to unify against U.S. encroachment, and combined Native and British forces had finally driven it back. Tribes from across the Upper Great Lakes region now eagerly wanted to go to war against the United States alongside British allies. With Mackinac Island in their possession, they had captured what some strategists called "the Gibraltar of America"—for the anchorlike defensive command it wielded over the portals to the Upper Great Lakes was similar to the famous British rock with its hundreds of cannons guarding the strait between the Mediterranean and Atlantic.

Three hundred miles away by water, down at the foot of Lake Huron, Governor Hull of Michigan Territory teetered on the verge of launching a U.S. invasion of Upper Canada, meaning the British lands north of the Great Lakes (today's Ontario). Following orders from the War Department in Washington to fortify Fort Detroit and prepare to invade Canada,

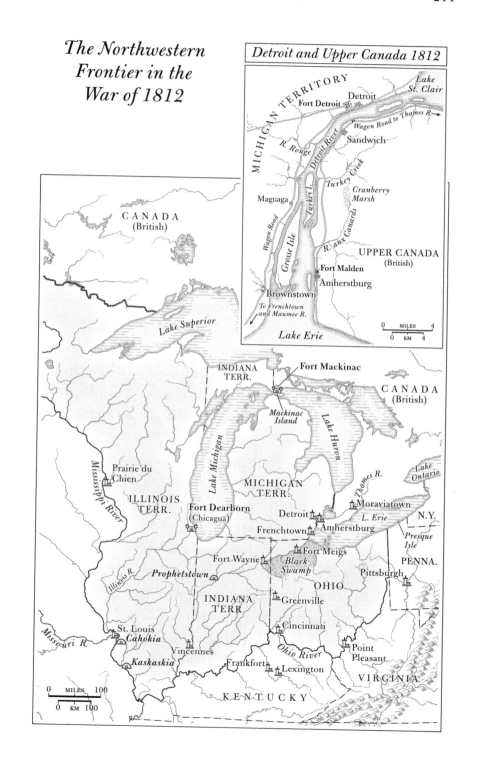

The Northwestern
Frontier in the
War of 1812

Detroit and Upper Canada 1812

Hull summoned 1,200 militiamen in Ohio and the Indiana Territory along with the U.S. Fourth Regiment—known, thanks to Harrison's excellent spin job on the battle's outcome, as "the heroes of Tippecanoe." Hull marched the troops north toward Detroit, slogging through the black-fly-infested Great Black Swamp in northwestern Ohio and ducking the harassment of Native warriors. The men had volunteered eagerly, clamoring for destruction of the tyrant British and thirsting for Native blood in retribution for killings of fellow frontier settlers.

Despite an ambivalence about commanding an army, Hull fired up his troops with patriotic calls of indignation in language recalling the original American Revolution, in which he had fought as a young man thirty-five years earlier: "In marching through a wilderness memorable for savage barbarity," General Hull called out to the men, "you will remember the causes by which that barbarity has been heretofore excited."

It was the fault of the British. Hull, and many other Americans, including President Madison, had become convinced that the British incited the tribes to violence against American settlers—yet another example, the general exclaimed, of the "oppression and injustice which that nation has continually practiced, and which the spirit of an indignant people can no longer endure."

Hull paused for a day as his troops arrived at Fort Detroit slathered with mud and riddled with bug bites from their swamp trudge. Here the grumbling started. Why wasn't General Hull charging immediately into Canada? This is what they had signed up for—to go after the British. General Hull replied to his officers that he would not invade until he had specific orders to proceed.

Hull was old enough to be a grandfather, and indeed had become one several times over. Nearly age sixty, he had studied law at Yale as a young man and served with distinction as an officer in the Revolutionary War. But the intervening decades had tempered his fighting spirit and turned his hair snowy and his soldier's frame pear-shaped. He had received an appointment in 1805 from Thomas Jefferson to the governorship of the new Michigan Territory, making his territorial headquarters at Detroit. Here his family lived with him, including his grown daughter and his several grandchildren. A former Massachusetts judge, Governor Hull had reluctantly agreed to President Madison's wish that he lead the new U.S. Army of the Northwest as tensions with Great Britain soared in early 1812.

Why didn't he keep going to Canada? his officers and men wondered. While his men washed their swamp-stained clothes, General Hull received from Washington what he needed—permission to cross the Detroit River into Canada and capture British Fort Malden. Then, if possible, he should keep going to seize all of Upper Canada.

He first made a feint farther downriver to confuse the commander at Fort Malden. He then launched his troops, now grown to 2,200 men with more Ohio volunteers, in canoes and boats across the boundary channel. Upon landing on the Canadian shore, Hull established his headquarters at a spacious brick farmhouse in the village of Sandwich, his troops quartered nearby. From here it was an eighteen-mile march down the Canadian side of the Detroit riverbank to the British stronghold at Fort Malden. General Hull and his American officers operated under the mistaken assumption that the Canadians living in this British dominion would be only too happy to throw off the repressive yokes of the Crown.

He also seemed to harbor a deep anxiety about hidden Native forces gliding through the region's lakes, rivers, and forests. He had heard they would gather at Fort Malden and elsewhere, recruited by Tecumseh. He faced other unknowns, too—the Canadian wilds and Native fighting techniques lay a long way from his New England background and experiences in the well-mapped battlegrounds of the Revolution.

"After thirty years of peace and prosperity," General Hull wrote in an open letter to the Canadian inhabitants of the region, "the United States have been driven to arms. The injuries and aggressions, the insults and indignities of Great Britain, have once more left . . . no alternative but manly resistance or unconditional submission."

Hoping they would change allegiances, he promised that Canada's residents would prosper under a U.S. government that offered civil, political, and religious liberty. All that was required of the Canadians to earn these "invaluable blessings"—so very unavailable to the king's subjects—was to stay in their own homes as the U.S. Army of the Northwest routed the British forces. No resident should dare to help the British, Hull warned, nor, in company with Native allies, strike out at American troops with tomahawk or musket.

"No white man found fighting by the side of an Indian will be taken prisoner," he wrote ominously. "Instant destruction will be his lot."

Meanwhile, allegiances among tribes shifted and solidified. Tribal leaders, too, declared themselves as this war broke out—pro-British, pro-American, or neutral. The Indigenous peoples of North America found themselves, yet again, caught up in the white men's struggles for control of the continent. Yet again, they had to calculate which Euro-American power afforded them the best chance to survive as strong, sovereign, Indigenous nations.

After years of disappointment and loss from the relentless push of white American settlers, and William Henry Harrison's inflexible forward drive to take Indigenous lands, Tecumseh finally threw his lot firmly to the British side. Earlier in July, just after the war broke out and General Hull invaded Canada, a council of several tribes had gathered at the Wyandot village known as Brownstown, twenty miles south of Detroit on the American side of the river, where they discussed remaining neutral in the conflict between the United States and Great Britain. Tecumseh stayed across the Detroit River at Fort Malden. The council on neutrality sent a delegation to invite him to the discussion.

"No," he said indignantly, according to Anthony Shane's account. "I have taken sides with the King, my father, and I will suffer my bones to bleach upon this shore, before I will recross that stream to join in any council of neutrality."

Tecumseh had gone all in.

.   .   .

Hull sent an advance force of 280 men under Colonel Lewis Cass from his headquarters at the hamlet of Sandwich probing down the wagon road toward Fort Malden, nearly twenty miles away. They were within four miles of Fort Malden when they reached the Rivière aux Canards, a small, deep river with marshy borderlands that flowed into the Detroit. Here the wagon road crossed a bridge over the narrow waterway. As they scouted, however, they saw British soldiers holding the bridge's far side, with Native warriors flitting through the background.

As a diversion, Cass left a smaller detachment on his side of the bridge, taking random shots at the British on the other side. He and the rest of his troops looped upstream on the riverbank to a shallow place, forded it breast-deep, waded through marshes, and attacked the British and Native warriors who held the Fort Malden end of the bridge. The defenders scattered, chased by Cass's soldiers, while drummers beat out "Yankee Doodle." They took two British troops prisoner.

The American invasion of Canada had begun. General Hull would attack this vast outcropping of the British Empire from its western edge, beginning with Fort Malden, regarded as a "nest of vultures" that had launched Native attacks against American settlers. At the same time, other U.S. forces would attack Canada in the East. Soon, it was expected, the entirety of Canada would fall to American hands. U.S. forces would finally—once and for all—drive the British out of North America.

But at this moment, in late July 1812, General Hull paused. It wasn't clear just why. When Colonel Cass requested permission to hold the bridge that spanned the narrow river, word arrived from General Hull's stone-house headquarters at Sandwich for Cass and his men to return the twelve miles to camp. Cass and his men were perplexed.

"I can scarcely restrain my indignation sufficiently while writing to describe the event in deliberate terms," one officer later wrote. "The officers, from this occurrence, began to distrust the views of the general, and their opinion of his abilities began to dwindle into contempt."

Some called him a coward. Others, the rumor went, accused him of treachery. The British forces quickly reclaimed the bridge, ripped it up, raised a defensive barricade, and placed guns on their side of the Canard, sailing a gunship to the river's mouth for extra protection against further invasion. The moment of surprise was lost.

Having survived the battles of White Plains, Trenton, Princeton, Saratoga, Monmouth, Stony Point, and others during the Revolution, perhaps Hull could understand better than his young soldiers the broader consequences of gung ho aggression and the bloody slaughter, destroyed lives, and shattered families that would result on both sides. Regardless, he had lost his fighting edge.

"His appearance was venerable and dignified," attested Judge Wither-ell, who knew him personally and witnessed the events at Detroit. "His heart was the seat of kindness; he was unquestionably an honest man. The general had a most excellent family; Mrs. Hull, a portly, fine-looking woman, made it the principal business of her life to visit the sick and provide for the destitute poor."

General Hull's reasoning to pause his invasion of Canada, insofar as he explained it, was that a small detachment like Cass's wasn't strong enough to hold the bridge. No one knew the size of the British force at Fort Malden and the strength of their Native allies. Still more worrisome, his supply lines could be cut from behind—they led back to Fort Detroit, and then all the way overland across the Black Swamp to Ohio. If the enemy cut the supply line, General Hull and his troops would be trapped inside Canada. So went his reasoning.

From his headquarters, Hull continued to send smaller forces probing toward Fort Malden while he awaited the larger artillery necessary to make a proper assault on the fort. Natives, however, materialized wherever he sent scouting parties. When Hull, inexplicably, left his forward headquarters at Sandwich and returned across the Detroit River for several days to

Shawnee Warrior or *Indian of the Nation of the Shawnoes*, **engraving by Tardieu L'Ainé.** In the 1790s, French military officer (and suspected spy) Victor Collot traveled far into the North American interior and down the Ohio and Mississippi rivers visiting Indigenous villages and frontier settlements. Detailed and elegant engravings by Tardieu l'Ainé illustrated his account of his travels, "A Journey in North America, Containing a Survey of the Countries Watered by the Mississippi, Ohio, Missouri, and Other Affluing Rivers" (1826).

Kaskaskia Warrior or *Indian of the Nation of the Kaskasia*, **engraving by Tardieu L'Ainé.** The Kaskaskias occupied lands in present-day Illinois until William Henry Harrison employed various subterfuges to acquire most of those lands for white settlers. From "Voyage dans l'Amérique Septentrionale, ou, Description des pays arrosés par le Mississipi, l'Ohio, le Missouri et autres rivières affluentes" by Victor Collot (Paris: A. Bertrand, 1826).

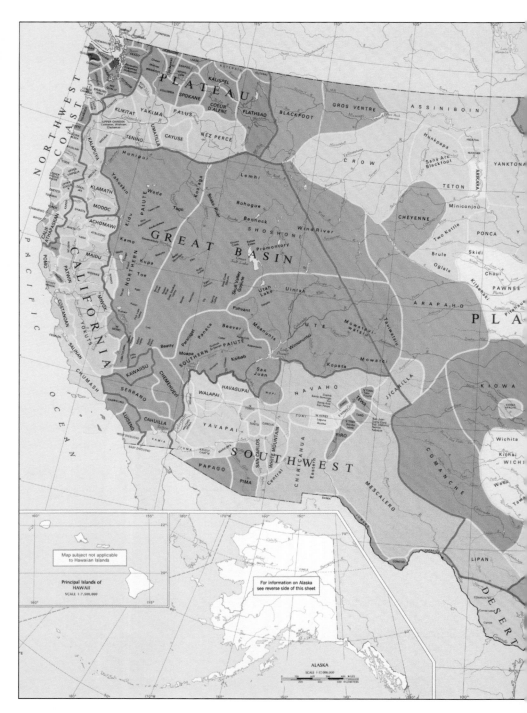

Early Indian Tribes, Cultural Areas, and Linguistic Stocks before the arrival of European colonists. Hundreds of distinct Indigenous groups speaking scores of different languages lived in every part of the North American continent until the arrival of white settlers began to push them westward. These are the geographical areas occupied by various tribes, according to research underlying this map produced in 1967 by the Smithsonian Institution and U.S. Geological Survey.

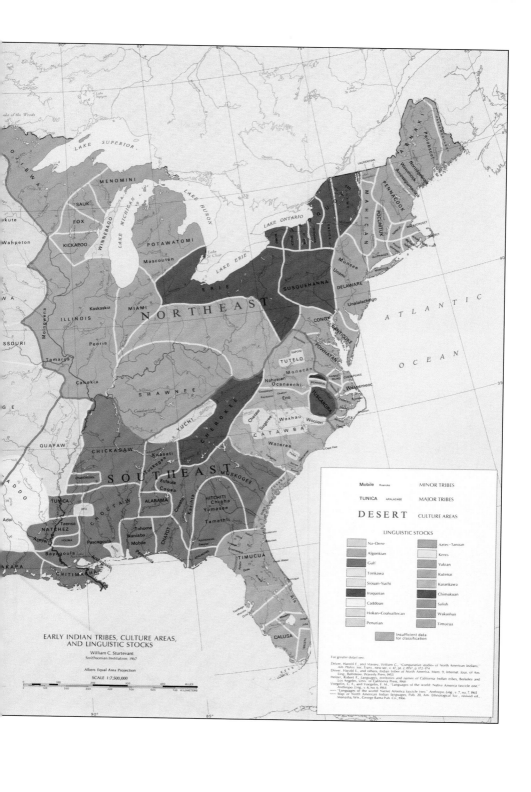

EARLY INDIAN TRIBES, CULTURE AREAS,
AND LINGUISTIC STOCKS

William C. Sturtevant
Smithsonian Institution, 1967

Albers Equal Area Projection

SCALE 1:7,500,000

Mobile Roanoke   MINOR TRIBES

TUNICA APALACHEE   MAJOR TRIBES

DESERT   CULTURE AREAS

LINGUISTIC STOCKS

Na–Dene
Algonkian
Gulf
Tonkawa
Siouan-Yuchi
Iroquoian
Caddoan
Hokan-Coahuiltecan
Penutian

Aztec–Tanoan
Keres
Yukian
Kutenai
Karankawa
Chimakuan
Salish
Wakashan
Timucua

Insufficient data
for classification

Scene on the Wabash, **watercolor by George Winter.** Shawnee homelands centered on today's southern Ohio and Indiana, where the Wabash was an important river for the tribes.

Daniel Boone Leading Settlers Through Cumberland Gap into the Kentucky Country, **painting by George Caleb Bingham, 1851.** The white settlement of the country beyond the Appalachians had taken on an almost mythical quality by the mid-nineteenth century, four decades after Tecumseh and his Native Coalition tried to stop it. Here, Daniel Boone leading white settlers into Kentucky is reminiscent of Moses leading the Israelites through the wilderness toward the Promised Land.

Portrait of the Mohawk Chieftain Thayendanegea, Known as Joseph Brant, by Gilbert Stuart, painting from life in London, 1786. Decades before Tecumseh, Joseph Brant, a Mohawk leader and Loyalist during the Revolution, advocated for unity among tribes to resist American settlement of Indigenous peoples' lands.

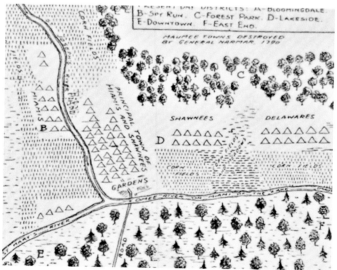

Sketch map of the Shawnee and Miami villages and crops destroyed by General Harmar at Kekionga, drawn by Major Ebenezer Denny in his journal. After attacks by Indigenous groups on settlers coming into the Ohio Valley homelands, President Washington dispatched a force to "punish" villages thought to be dispatching warriors for the attacks. General Harmar burned the villages but his forces were soon routed by Shawnee and Miami warriors.

Painting of the Treaty of Greenville gathering by an officer present, 1795.

General Anthony Wayne, pastel by James Sharples, Sr., c. 1795. A hero in the American Revolution, General "Mad Anthony" Wayne was summoned by President Washington to train a force to subdue the Western Confederacy of Native tribes led by Miami Chief Little Turtle and Shawnee Chief Blue Jacket.

Tenskwatawa, The Open Door, Known as The Prophet, Brother of Tecumseh, painting by George Catlin, c. 1830. By the time George Catlin painted this portrait of Tenskwatawa in his ritual dress, Tecumseh's movement had largely ended with his death and Tenskwatawa himself had moved west of the Mississippi. Catlin's notes on the painting record, "in his right hand he was holding his 'medicine fire,' and his 'sacred string of beads' in the other."

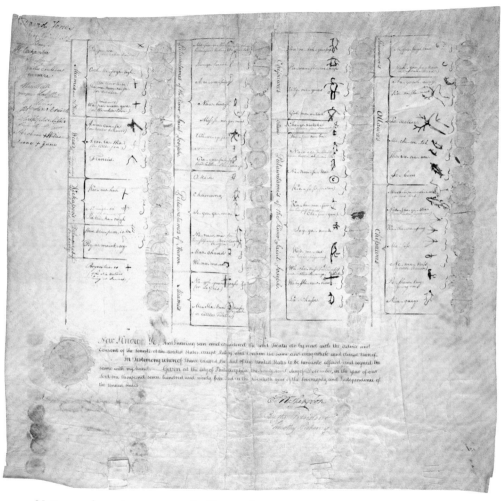

Native marks as signatures on the Treaty of Greenville. This is the treaty that drew the Greenville Line down the center of today's Ohio to settle the conflicts—white settlers were not to cross over it onto Native lands. Little Turtle of the Miamis was one of the last holdouts of chiefs attending the council. His mark is near the bottom of the middle column.

Dining room at Harrison's Grouseland— fortress in the wilderness. Grouseland, Nancy and William Henry Harrison's home, was unique, with elegant living quarters from the ground up, and a virtual fortress underneath. (*Credit: M. Shawn Hennessy*)

Tecumseh in British coat, based on an original sketch (now lost) by Pierre Le Dru. The coat, representing Tecumseh's allegiance to the British, may have been a later addition. Le Dru's now-lost sketch is regarded as the nearest actual likeness to Tecumseh.

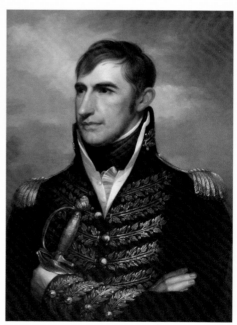

William Henry Harrison in Officer's Uniform, **by Rembrandt Peale, c. 1813.** Rembrandt Peale painted this portrait of William Henry Harrison shortly after his victory over Tecumseh and British forces at the Battle of Thames. (*National Portrait Gallery, Smithsonian Institution; gift of Mrs. Herbert Lee Pratt, Jr.*)

Anna Tuthill Symmes Harrison in later years—the only known existing portrait of her. Pious, reserved, thoughtful, and a committed abolitionist after her husband died, Anna Harrison was both the wife of one president and the grandmother of another, Benjamin Harrison.

Queen Louisa of Prussia Bargains with Napoleon to Keep Part of Her Empire, 1807, early nineteenth-century painting by Nicolas Gosse. British support for Tecumseh's Native Alliance turned in part on Napoleon's military conquests in Europe and negotiations like these.

The Press-Gang, showing forcible seizure of resisting British citizens and sailors on American ships into British military service to fight Napoleon in Europe, oil painting by Luke Clennell.

Mackinac Island and Fort Mackinac, color painting by Seth Eastman, 1872.
A rocky outcrop at a crucial juncture of the Great Lakes, Mackinac Island and its fortress controlled water access to much of the American interior. It was much contested during the War of 1812.

British General Isaac Brock— the Bold Warrior Companion to Tecumseh. Together, they captured U.S. held Detroit and posed a dire threat to the entire Great Lakes region until Brock's death leading the charge against American forces at the Battle of Queenstown Heights.

Map of tiny Chicago, 1812. When the War of 1812 broke out in June of that year, Chicago was an important Native canoe portage between the Great Lakes and Mississippi watersheds and barely the seeds of a settlement. The strategic Indigenous navigation route had been chosen by whites for an isolated fur post and fort but it proved an easy target for tribes opposed to encroachment. Map by Alfred Theodore Andreas.

Battle of Lake Erie, and Oliver Hazard Perry in rowboat, color painting by Edward Percy Moran, 1911. From this moment comes the famous rallying cry, "Don't give up the ship!"—the dying words of Oliver Hazard Perry's U.S. naval officer friend.

Death of Tecumseh, a panel by Filippo Costaggini in the three-hundred-foot-long *Frieze of American History* circling the rotunda of the U.S. Capitol building. A mark of his stature in the nineteenth century, Tecumseh's is one of only nineteen panels in the frieze representing the course of American history up to that point. Most of the panels were originally sketched by Italian artist Constantino Brumidi in 1859, and a few were added later.

Burned-Out U.S. Capitol After British Attack on Washington, August 24th, 1814, **watercolor by British artist George Munger.** Until January 6, 2020, this was the only time the U.S. Capitol had been breached during an assault. It occurred near the end of the War of 1812, which changed little between the U.S. and Great Britain, but had a devastating effect on Native tribes.

View of the Great Treaty Held at Prairie du Chien, Sept. 1825, by James Otto Lewis. Twelve years after Tecumseh's death at the Battle of Thames, representatives of many tribes of the Upper Mississippi gathered at the confluence of the Wisconsin and Mississippi rivers to work out with federal agents boundaries between individual tribes to reduce inter-tribal friction as natives were pushed west, and also with white settlers. In effect, it served to reduce each tribe's hunting territory. These boundaries were later used to make further tribal land cessions. (*Credit: Library of Congress*)

Payta Kootha, or Flying Cloud — Shawnee Warrior who signed the Treaty of Greenville and engaged in other diplomatic activities, painted by Albert Newsam, after Henry Inman, after Charles Bird King. This work is a copy of a copy of an original portrait of Payta-Kootha by Charles Bird King, who was commissioned in the 1820s by Thomas L. McKenny to paint the portraits of Indigenous leaders visiting Washington, D.C. After other artists reworked Bird's many portraits into colored lithographs, they were published in McKenny and Hall's "Indian Tribes of North America" (1836). King's original paintings burned in an 1865 fire at the Smithsonian, but the colored lithographs of the originals survived. (*Credit: Image courtesy of the National Gallery of Art, Washington, D.C.*)

Lehman & Duval Lith.ers Philad.a

Billy Shane, a Shawnee Chief, at a treaty council in Indiana, 1827. Shane fought
on the American side under William Henry Harrison in the War of 1812 and was
wounded at the Battle of the Thames in Upper Canada.

The Son—Miami Chief, by James Otto Lewis. Miami chiefs and warriors had been allies and neighbors of the Shawnees for decades and formed a core part of the Native coalitions built by Little Turtle and Blue Jacket in the 1780s and 1790s and that Tecumseh rallied two decades later. This portrait from life was one of many painted of Native leaders by James Otto Lewis starting in the 1820s (a decade after Tecumseh's death) during government excursions to treaty sites on the frontier in Indiana and today's Wisconsin and Minnesota—Green Bay, Fond du Lac (Lake Superior), and Prairie du Chien. His works were published in *The Aboriginal Portfolio, or A Collection of Portraits of the Most Celebrated Chiefs of the North American Indians* (1835) as well as in McKenny and Hall's *Indian Tribes of North America.*

Wa-Pa-Laa, or the Playing Fox, Prince of the Fox Tribe, **by James Otto Lewis.** The Fox and Sauk Nations had been victims of an egregious land grab by William Henry Harrison in 1804–5, and their tribal members willingly joined the Native Coalition to stop the westward advance of white settlement. Twenty years after Tecumseh's death, as settlement relentlessly advanced into their homelands in Illinois and Wisconsin, Fox and Sauk warriors fought under Chief Black Hawk to take some of those lands back in what became known as the Black Hawk War.

Fort Detroit, another officer, Colonel Duncan McArthur, took over command. He resolved to attack Fort Malden even if Hull would not.

Colonel McArthur sent out a detachment of Rangers to discover a means to transport artillery across the River Canard. When the Ranger patrol encountered Native scouts, Colonel McArthur dispatched a hefty force of 120 Ohio militia under Major James Denny to drive the Native forces back.

Major Denny and his men encountered a small band of warriors who had advanced several miles beyond the Canard toward Hull's headquarters. They chased the scattered Native warriors back toward the River Canard and Fort Malden. In the midst of this hot pursuit, another, far larger force of Native warriors suddenly came rushing at them on horseback, faces painted, shouting war cries.

The charge was led by Tecumseh. He had set the trap.

Jumping off their horses, Tecumseh's warriors and the Ohio militia made a footrace toward a wooded grove that could provide cover. Arriving first, the militia established a position within the copse. Tecumseh and his warriors started to circle around behind Denny to cut off the wagon road that led back to the safety of Hull's camp, several miles away. Grasping their danger as the warriors encircled them, sure to result in their total destruction by musket ball, tomahawk, war club, and knife, Denny's men broke position and sprinted toward the wagon road and the small farmsteads that bordered it.

"As the soldiers fled," writes Sugden, "the Indians ran alongside, jamming guns through fences or from beside farmhouses and fruit trees to fire, while the bemused Canadian inhabitants gazed from their windows with apparent indifference to the drama outside."

It seems the Canadian homesteaders did not regard the invading American army as liberators and were happy enough to leave them to their fate. Occurring on July 25, 1812, and orchestrated by Tecumseh, this was the first American bloodshed on land in what would become known as the War of 1812.

CHAPTER 16

WARRIOR FROM THE EAST

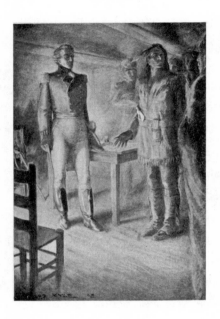

G eneral Hull had invaded Upper Canada in mid-July. He had staked out a staging ground for his U.S. troops at Sandwich. He had made probes at taking Fort Malden and the village of Amherstburg and appeared on the verge of launching the decisive blow. But then, again, he paused. He had not secured his supply line running two hundred miles through the Black Swamp all the way back to Ohio. He knew it presented a vulnerability. So did Tecumseh, his fellow war chiefs, and his British allies at Fort Malden. As July turned to August 1812, they struck relentlessly.

John Richardson, then a young British soldier, took part in one raid. Richardson's details of the British march through wild and forested terrain toward an unsuspecting column of U.S. troops remain vivid and haunting more than two centuries later, capturing the essence of the difference between European and Indigenous warfare:

> No other sound than the measured step of [our] troops interrupted the solitude of the scene, rendered more imposing by the wild appearance of the warriors, whose bodies, stained and painted in the most frightful manner for the occasion, glided by us with almost noiseless velocity, without order and without a chief; some painted white, some black, others half black, half red; half black, half white; all with their hair plastered in such a way as to resemble the bristling quills of the porcupine, with no other covering than a cloth around their loins, yet armed to the teeth, with rifles, tomahawks, war-clubs, spears, bows, arrows, and scalping-knives. Uttering no sound, and intent only on reaching the enemy unperceived, they might have passed for the spectres of those wilds, the ruthless demons which War had unchained for the punishment and oppression of man.

While to Richardson's eyes they glided by without order or a chief, in fact Tecumseh and his fellow war chiefs moved silently along with the warriors in complete control. Tecumseh had emerged as a leader among leaders, both in warfare and in diplomacy. With relentless focus and drive, he had rebuilt the Indian confederacy out of the ashes of Prophetstown and wreckage of Harrison's Battle of Tippecanoe.

Tecumseh had not been idle in the nine months since returning from his southern and western recruiting tour. After discovering the destruction left by Harrison's army, he had reestablished villages near Prophetstown, where followers had gathered during the winter and spring of 1812. He had reached out to Harrison, despite Harrison's insistence that Tecumseh and Tenskwatawa break up villages and disperse followers. He had sent a delegation down the Wabash to Grouseland. He had also blamed the Potawatomis and their attacks on frontier settlers the previous spring for provoking Harrison's march up the Wabash. He had made it clear that the razing of Prophetstown would not have occurred in his presence, and that warriors under his leadership either would have made peace or destroyed Harrison and his army.

"Had I been at home and heard of the advance of the American Troops towards our Village, I should have gone to meet them and shaking them by the hand, have asked them the reason of their appearance in such hostile guise. . . . Those I left at home were (I cannot call them men) a poor set of people, and their scuffle with the Big Knives I compare to a struggle between little children who only scratch each others faces."

As tensions had climbed between the United States and Great Britain that spring of 1812 before the formal declaration of war, authorities in Washington had worried—with good reason—that if hostilities between the two nations erupted, the Native nations of the Northwest would join the British forces based in Canada. Secretary of War Eustis ordered Harrison to "re-establish the relations of peace and friendship with the Indians." This, of course, was after Harrison had marched on and destroyed Prophetstown. But Harrison went further and tried to subvert any direct peace dealings between Tecumseh, his Native allies, and federal authorities in Washington, D.C. On returning from the South, Tecumseh announced he was ready to visit the president in Washington. But Governor Harrison stymied it. As the territory's highest federal official, he refused to permit Tecumseh to serve as leader of an American Indian delegation to the federal city. He insisted only a small party go with Tecumseh, not the body of warriors who usually accompanied the Shawnee chief. He also suggested a possible quick way to resolve the "Indian problem"—kidnap Tecumseh and use him as a hostage.

Tecumseh had tried to keep the peace while rebuilding his confederacy in the aftermath of Prophetstown's destruction. Little violence had occurred during the hard, cold winter of 1812. But with the thaws of March, angry young warriors from other tribes had attacked settlers across a five-hundred-mile arc of the northwestern frontier in retribution for Harrison's destruction the previous fall of Prophetstown. Winnebagos attacked lead mines along the Mississippi and the small outpost at Chicago. Kickapoos killed settlers in Louisiana Territory. Potawatomis raided homesteads near Vincennes in the Indiana Territory. These raids had killed nearly fifty settlers by the end of that spring, when, according to some interpretations of these events, the blood debt for Tippecanoe had been paid.

Accused by Harrison and other officials of provoking this violence against frontier settlers, Tecumseh had angrily denied it. "We defy a living creature to say we ever advised anyone, directly or indirectly, to make war on our white brothers," he proclaimed to a council of chiefs convened in May 1812 to address the attacks. "It has constantly been our misfortune to have our views misrepresented to our white brethren; this has been done by pretended chiefs of the Potawatamis and others, that have been in the habit of selling land to the white people that did not belong to them."

In early June, however, two weeks before Congress authorized war, Tecumseh issued a stern warning of what he would do if provoked. He emphatically stated it in a message delivered to the British authorities at Fort Malden, who, in the previous months, had been urging him to keep the peace:

Father & Brothers! We will now in a few words declare to You our whole hearts—If we hear of the Big Knives coming towards our villages to speak peace, we will receive them; but If We hear of any of our people being hurt by them, or if they unprovokedly advance against us in a hostile manner, be assured we will defend ourselves like men. And if we hear of any of our people having been killed. We will immediately send to all the Nations on or towards the Mississippi, and all this Island will rise as one man—Then Father and Brothers it will be impossible for . . . either of You to restore peace between us.

Tecumseh, nevertheless, had prepared for war against the Americans. Working with fellow chiefs Main Poc, Roundhead, Split Log, and others, he sent envoys to tribes that he had cultivated across the massive span of North America. They carried red wampum—signaling to prepare for war. Several thousand warriors moved toward designated gathering spots: the Minnesota River valley, Lake Koshkonong in today's Wisconsin, Lake Peoria in today's Illinois, and the rebuilt Prophetstown.

In late June, Tecumseh headed north toward the British stronghold at Fort Malden and Amherstburg village. He arrived on July 1, at the same time that messages from the East Coast brought word that the United States had declared war on Great Britain. Many warriors had already gathered near Fort Malden under Main Poc of the Potawatomi and other war chiefs. They crafted wigwams on Bois Blanc Island in the Detroit River, just across the channel from Fort Malden and Amherstburg, the island literally straddling the water border between the United States and the British Empire.

With war openly declared between the two white powers, Tecumseh dispatched messengers to his brother Tenskwatawa, according to U.S. Indian agent William Wells, who may or may not have reported accurately, given his own allegiance with the Americans and enmity toward Tecumseh. He instructed Tenskwatawa to send all women and children from Prophetstown toward the Mississippi River or beyond it. Here, presumably, they would find safety from the storm that was about to descend. Tecumseh also told Tenskwatawa, according to Wells, to gather warriors and "strike a heavy blow at the inhabitants of Vincennes, that he Tecumseh if he lived would join him in the country of the Winabagoes."

Tecumseh's messenger—if indeed there was one—apparently was questioned by Wells, who reported these alarming developments to Governor Harrison. Whatever the accuracy of Wells's report, by mid-July 1812, a month after the United States had declared war and as British and Native forces took to the moonlit lake and surprised U.S. Fort Mackinac, no doubt remained that Tecumseh had thrown himself and the full weight of the Indian confederacy against the Americans and allied himself and his people with the British. By July 25, when he drew the first blood with the ambush on American troops at the River Canard, there was no turning back.

On August 8, now seven weeks after the war declaration, Colonel James Miller left Fort Detroit heading a U.S. detachment to secure Hull's supply lines southward to Ohio through the Black Swamp. The colonel led with gusto—boldly, bravely, decisively—in direct contrast with General Hull's leadership style.

Hull's officers grumbled that the general had not shown enough aggression in aiding his supply trains struggling toward Detroit through the swampy wilds or in executing a direct attack on Fort Malden. His vacillation had surfaced again the previous day, August 7—he had abruptly ordered an attack on Fort Malden, only to call it off a few hours later. He had then ordered all troops to row back across the Detroit River to U.S. territory. Once they returned and assembled in a sheep pasture behind the fort, General Hull had suddenly shown a little spine, in Colonel Miller's eyes. He ordered a large detachment to go to the relief of a supply train from Ohio, now beset by the threat of Native attack and stuck at the River Raisin some thirty-five miles south of Fort Detroit.

Hull had good reason to act at this moment. He had just received an intelligence report that a large force of British soldiers was coming from the East to reinforce Fort Malden. If he expected to keep his army intact and fed at Fort Detroit, he badly needed to secure the Ohio supply line.

After getting his orders from Hull to rescue the stuck supply train, Colonel Miller brought his men on parade down the streets of Detroit, then a village of 160 houses along the riverfront. Assembling them into marching order on Jefferson Street, he paused to give them stern warning and steel their courage. Only a few days earlier, a previous relief column under Major Thomas Van Horne had been ambushed by Native forces and British while trying to help the same supply train. With Tecumseh directing warriors, the combined Native and British forces had routed Van Horne.

Colonel Miller's speech implied a harsh rebuke of the shameful behavior he believed Hull had displayed over the last few weeks.

"Soldiers," Colonel Miller called out to the group, "we are now going to meet the enemy, and to *beat* them. . . . The blood of our brethren, spilt by the savages, must be avenged. I shall lead you. You shall not disgrace yourselves nor me. Every man who shall leave the ranks or fall back without orders will be instantly put to death." He then turned to address the regular troops of the Fourth Regiment, which had marched on Prophetstown the previous fall. Their commander in that battle, William Henry Harrison, was currently dashing about several hundred miles to the south offering to lead Kentucky troops in the just-declared war.

"My brave soldiers, you will add another victory to that of Tippecanoe," Colonel Miller announced confidently to his troops. "If there is now any man in the ranks of the detachment who fears to meet the enemy, let him fall out and stay behind."

"Huzza! Huzza! Huzza!" called out the troops, followed by "I'll not stay! I'll not stay!"

With that, this column of six hundred men, including cavalry and artillery, got under way, crossing the River Rouge that day and camping on the far side. The next morning, they began their march again.

"On the morning of Sunday, the 9th [of August]," remembered John Richardson, marching with British troops of the Forty-first Regiment, "the wild and distant cry of our Indian scouts gave us to understand that the enemy were advancing. [The scouts] appeared issuing from the wood, bounding like wild deer chased by the huntsman, and uttering that peculiar shout which is known among themselves as the news-cry."

Just a few days earlier, the first wave of British reinforcements, under Colonel Henry Procter of the Forty-first Regiment of Foot, had arrived at Fort Malden. Almost immediately upon landing, Colonel Procter ordered a detachment to cross the Detroit River. He had received intelligence that Hull struggled to keep his supply line open to Ohio and that he'd sent troops to escort his provisions train from the River Raisin.

The combined force numbered about 450—about 150 regulars of the Forty-first Regiment and Canadian militia under Captain Adam Muir, and around three hundred Native warriors led by Tecumseh, Walk-in-the-Water of the Wyandot, Lame Hand, Split Log, and more. The chiefs together with Muir had decided to meet the U.S. column, advancing south from Fort Detroit toward the River Raisin, on terrain near the village of Maguaga (near Grosse Ile, in today's Michigan).

Richardson later described that march north to Maguaga—the heavy forest closing overhead, the mud ankle-deep along the wagon road, the unmoving air and putrid smell emanating from the dead horses and naked corpses of American soldiers left behind from Tecumseh's ambush of Van Horne, wooden stakes driven triumphantly through their bodies, the rhythmic sound of the marching troops, and the gliding silence of the Native warriors.

In late afternoon, the skies heavy with dark rain clouds, the U.S. advance troops led by Captain Josiah Snelling had nearly reached the village of Maguaga along the Detroit River. They marched from the forest of big old oaks into a clearing surrounded by the forest on three sides and with a fourth opening onto the brushy riverbank.

Thwack!

A single musket shot rang from the bushes near the riverbank. Even as its hollow echo rolled across the river's dark waters, the war cries of hundreds of hidden Native warriors ripped apart the pastoral serenity of the spot while a thundering volley erupted from the wood's edge.

Snelling's advance troops held their ground while Colonel Miller galloped from the rear toward the sound of the action. He ordered the main body of troops to follow at double time, marching in two columns, two hundred yards apart, with cavalry in the center and trailing behind the two cannons, bogging down in marshy ground. The pounding of musket fire resumed up and down the British and Native line as troops and warriors reloaded, fired into the blue coats and white pantaloons of the U.S. troops, and reloaded again.

"Charge! boys, charge!" Colonel Miller shouted from horseback, waving his sword in the air.

Volunteer soldiers from Ohio and Michigan grouped for a charge at the Native warriors concealed near the brushy riverbank. U.S. gunners dragged the six-pounder cannon into firing position, loading it with powder and grapeshot. The thundering concussion sent metal balls shrieking through the air, splintering the ancient oak bark, clipping off leaves, and ripping human flesh. Ohio and Michigan volunteers rushed with bayonets at the warriors near the river.

The warriors dropped back to regroup—a common Native fighting tactic to avoid loss rather than contest a piece of ground. British redcoats mistook the falling-back warriors for attackers and opened fire on their allies. In the confusion, and with the six-pounder booming grapeshot straight at them, the Native and British line paused, then wavered. The troops at the British center jumped up from their positions and ran back through the forest and glades.

A quarter mile back, Muir mounted a small hilltop and rallied his British redcoats and Canadian militiamen. From the oak forest to his left, away from the riverbank, he heard intense firing. The battle had shifted there as Tecumseh and his warriors drew the attention of Colonel Miller, shooting at his soldiers from behind trees, flattened on the earth, crouched under bushes, and probably perched up in the oak limbs themselves.

It was a moment of fruition for Tecumseh—of both his experience and the deep knowledge of his ancestors. Knowing the woods, knowing weaponry, knowing his enemy, knowing his strengths, deeply understanding his terrain. As warrior and strategist, he had learned how to fight superbly, both from personal experience and from the passed-on knowledge of generations of warriors and war chiefs before him, like the women knowing how to grow corn.

All that came to bear in this moment. He knew that, in the woods at least, he and his warriors could outfight anyone. For this reason he had chosen to take an ambush position in the line's left flank in the ancient oak forest. If the British under Muir ran into difficulty in the line's center, or the Native warriors in the meadows along the river faltered, Tecumseh knew he could hold fast among the ancient oaks. And he did. Miller and his U.S. troops had little choice but to engage Tecumseh and his warriors shooting out from the wood, as Tecumseh had predicted. Tecumseh and his warriors melted deeper into the oak forest. Miller's horse threw him. Collecting himself, he ordered a cavalry charge. A cavalry officer, Captain Sloan, froze. Captain Snelling ordered him to dismount and leapt on Sloan's horse. His hat was shot away, his red hair flew, and he went on the chase at the head of the cavalry. They pursued the Native warriors deeper into the forest until the warriors slowly vanished amid heavy growth. Suddenly fearing a possible ambush, Snelling broke off the chase.

By now all of Captain Muir's British and Canadian troops had made it to the boats they had beached on the river's shore. Soon followed by warriors in their canoes, they recrossed the Detroit to Amherstburg village and Fort Malden.

The U.S. officers declared a victory—a rout. But it wasn't. Far from that. Colonel Miller's forces suffered eighty-two dead and wounded. The combined forces suffered about thirty dead and wounded. Both Tecumseh and Muir received wounds. Although not large, the battle had much greater implications.

"Ultimately, then, Tecumseh and Muir had suffered a tactical defeat," writes Sugden, "only to win a far more important strategic triumph."

The heavy losses in the battle seem to have further rattled U.S. general William Hull while giving a tremendous boost to the enthusiasm of Tecumseh's warriors and British troops. In the next few days, General Hull ordered Colonel Miller and his troops back to Fort Detroit. Suddenly on the defensive, he also withdrew the last American troops left in Canada from his attempted invasion. Now Hull was totally isolated from the rest of the United States. His supply line remained broken. Fort Detroit's reach had shrunk to an island in the wilderness surrounded by hostile forces.

As the battle of Maguaga unfolded, British general Isaac Brock raced as quickly as his small boats could sail, night and day, down the two-hundred-mile length of Lake Erie, from its eastern end, which lay near Upper Canada's capital at York (Toronto), west toward distant Fort Malden and Amherstburg. Bringing six hundred troops, he planned to halt Hull's attempted invasion of Upper Canada.

"A great part of the banks of the lake," he warned the flotilla toward the end, "is much more dangerous and difficult of access than any we have passed; the boats will, therefore, not land except in the most extreme necessity."

Isaac Brock had hungered for this kind of action his entire life, having joined the British Royal Army at age fifteen. He came from a prominent family on the island of Guernsey in the English Channel and a line of ancestors with military honors. His father had died young. Brock, the youngest of eight sons and a good swimmer and boxer, had left formal schooling when his older brother received a Royal Army promotion. As was common then among the British upper classes, the family bought Isaac a vacant spot as a Royal Army ensign. He had won some recognition in 1799 at age thirty when he led a charge on horseback across the sand dunes of the North Sea beaches as Britain and her allies tried to drive the French out of Holland. A musket ball had slammed him in the neck and knocked him off his horse, senseless, but the thick scarves he wore against the cold, wet North Sea weather had absorbed the ball's impact. A half hour later he was back in the action.

Posted to Canada, he rose in the ranks to general and acting head of the government of Upper Canada based at York. At first, he had lamented his exile to this distant outpost across the Atlantic, yearning for opportunities to win eternal glory fighting Napoleon in Europe. From his post at York, however, he foresaw war looming between the United States and Great Britain. Before it erupted, he laid out a far-reaching strategy to his superiors. The very first thing to do, he asserted, was to capture Mackinac Island and Detroit—and thereby control the Upper Lakes while winning the Native people from the entire western region to the British side. As soon as he got word at York of the U.S. declaration of war, General Brock had written to the commander of British troops at St. Joseph Island, far north at the juncture of lakes Superior, Michigan, and Huron. It was Brock's letter that had launched British troops and Native warriors from St. Joseph Island on the moonlit raid to take the U.S. fort at nearby Mackinac Island.

Yet Brock faced two threats of his own—two possible U.S. invasions of Upper Canada, one at Niagara, on the eastern end of Lake Erie, and, on the western end, invasion at Fort Malden and Amherstburg. When the threat at Fort Malden had materialized with Hull menacing from Fort Detroit, General Brock rallied a reluctant Upper Canada legislature at York. Receiving funding, he collected all the men that could be spared—regulars and militiamen—from that eastern end of Lake Erie and rushed westward down the lake to rescue Fort Malden from General Hull's invasion.

After five nights and days afloat, his boats of reinforcements landed at Amherstburg's waterfront late in the night of August 13, a few days after the Native and British ambushes of Van Horne and Miller on the American shore at the Battle of Maguaga. As General Brock entered Fort Malden, musket shots began to echo across the water from an island in the middle of the Detroit River, separating Canada and Fort Malden from the United States and Fort Detroit. He first heard a few reports, then more and more in a mounting crescendo. General Brock asked what it was, and Indian agent Matthew Elliott explained that the hundreds of Native warriors camped on Bois Blanc Island were welcoming General Brock's midnight arrival. The general asked Elliott to go to the island and request that they conserve their ammunition.

"Do, pray, Elliott, fully explain my wishes and motives, and tell the Indians that I will speak to them to-morrow on this subject."

Elliott disappeared, crossing in the dark to the island, and a half hour later reappeared at Brock's quarters, accompanied by Tecumseh himself. At General Brock's side that night was Brock's aide-de-camp, J. B. Glegg.* Tecumseh's powerful presence struck him instantly that night in the candlelight at the general's quarters. He recorded it in minute detail:

> Tecumseh's appearance was very prepossessing; his figure light and finely proportioned; five feet nine or ten inches; his complexion, light copper; countenance, oval, with bright hazle eyes, beaming cheerfulness, energy, and decision. Three small silver crowns, or coronets, were suspended from the lower cartilage of his aquiline nose; and a large silver medallion of George the Third, which I believe his ancestor had received from Lord Dorchester, when governor-general of Canada, was attached to a mixed coloured wampum string, and hung round his neck. His dress consisted of a plain, neat uniform, tanned deer skin jacket, with long trousers of the same material, the seams of both being covered with neatly cut fringe; and he had on his feet leather mocassins, much ornamented with work made from the dyed quills of the porcupine.

General Brock and Tecumseh extended their hands and grasped each other's. One imagines that they may have perceived something spe-

---

* Aide-de-camp Glegg descended from an ancient landed family, some of whom had arrived in England with William the Conqueror. He received a formal education at the Royal Military College. It is to his eyes and ears and literacy that we owe the details of the interactions between Tecumseh and Brock.

cial in the other, immediately. Tecumseh knew that Brock had just swept virtually nonstop down the two-hundred-mile-length of Lake Erie with his reinforcements and surely sensed his eagerness to engage and the easy confidence of his manner. Brock likewise knew that Tecumseh had led Native warriors in the recent attacks on Hull's columns with boldness, intelligence, and devastating effect. As so many British officers would testify, Tecumseh projected an almost instantaneous magnetism and confidence of purpose that persuaded many to follow him.

Tecumseh cheerfully agreed with Brock that the Native warriors blasting salutes should save their ammunition, Captain Glegg recorded, and promised to relay the message to the warriors on the island. The two leaders then agreed to resume their meeting in the morning with Native warriors present.

The next morning, a thousand Native warriors paddled in hundreds of birchbark canoes across the channel from the island and entered the gates of Fort Malden, draped with tomahawks, war clubs, muskets, scalping knives, and bows and arrows—warriors, as aide-de-camp Glegg put it, "whose equipment might generally be considered very imposing."

General Brock—well over six feet tall with a powerful torso and sandy, windblown hair—likewise cut an imposing figure with his scarlet officer's coat and general's shimmering gold epaulets. Born only a year apart, both in their early forties, Isaac Brock of Guernsey and Tecumseh of the Panther clan had reached the prime of their lives—they still had their youthful physical vigor melded with life's and combat's hard-won experience.

General Brock called out to the gathered warriors and soldiers, probably with Elliott and Tecumseh or others helping translate, that their Great Father—the British Crown—had ordered him to come to the assistance of the Native warriors, and, with their help, "to drive the Americans from Fort Detroit."

Great cries of assent went up from the warriors.

The time for vacillation between powers—the Americans or the British—had passed. The Indian forces had gone all in with the king. Warriors had come from far away—not only Shawnees and Wyandots, but Sauks, Winnebagos, Menominees, Ottawas, Kickapoos, Ojibwes, and more—to join the confederacy led by Tecumseh and his allied chiefs. Their numbers had surged as word spread of the British and Native victories at Michilimackinac, Sandwich, and Maguaga.

By their agreement, Tecumseh spoke for the gathered chiefs, among them the Potawatomi Main Poc and Roundhead of the Wyandot.

Tecumseh gave "expressions of joy," recorded Glegg, "that their father beyond the great salt lake (meaning the king of England) had at length awoke from his long sleep, and permitted his warriors to come to the assistance of his red children, who had never ceased to remain steady in their friendship, and were now all ready to shed their last drop of blood in their great father's service."

When Tecumseh had finished, other chiefs spoke to the gathered warriors, who again cried out their assent.

As the meeting broke up, General Brock, having now witnessed "the superior sagacity and intrepidity of Tecumseh," in Glegg's words, sent Agent Elliott to the Shawnee war chief asking him to meet separately and bring some of the other most respected chiefs. They retired to the privacy of Elliott's quarters. General Brock spelled out exactly how he planned, with the help of the Native warriors, to cross the river and capture Fort Detroit. If Tecumseh and the chiefs gave their assent, the operation would start the next day.

Tecumseh heard Brock's words through the interpreter. Then he held up his hand and turned to his fellow chiefs.

"Ho-yo-o-e!" he exclaimed. "This is a man!"

Brock marched his troops from Fort Malden to Sandwich village, only three-quarters of a mile away from Detroit, directly across the river's width. On August 15, the day after the meeting at Fort Malden and just two months after the declaration of war in Washington, a boat flying a white flag of truce and carrying two British officers, including aide-de-camp Glegg, rowed across the river to Detroit village, which itself was surrounded by a log stockade fourteen feet high. Met by American troops, the British officers handed off a letter for delivery to General Hull at Fort Detroit, which sat on a rise about 250 yards behind the village. Not large, the fort itself enclosed about two acres and could not hold all the U.S. troops General Hull had brought from Ohio. That morning, the general had left his regular quarters inside the fort and pitched his headquarters tent—visible for its red and blue stripes—among the white tents of the troops outside the walls in order to be close to command.

General Hull opened the letter. It came from General Brock. This was the first Hull knew that Brock had arrived at Fort Malden after sailing the length of Lake Erie, and now, surprisingly, was just across the river.

It was dated that day, written from "Head Quarters, Sandwich."

Sir—The force at my disposal authorizes me to require of you the immediate surrender of Fort Detroit. It is far from my inclination to join in a war of extermination; but you must be aware, that the numerous body of Indians who have attached themselves to my troops, will be beyond my control the moment the contest commences. You will find me disposed to enter into such conditions as will satisfy the most scrupulous sense of honor. [The bearers of this letter] are fully authorized to conclude any arrangement that may lead to prevent the unnecessary effusion of blood.

—Isaac Brock, Major-General.

General Hull read the letter and consulted with his officers. At the same time, across the river at Sandwich, British troops and Canadian militiamen hastily tore down a house, revealing a battery of five cannons that the British Royal Engineers had moved in, undetected, including two eighteen-pounders and an eight-inch howitzer. On their side, American soldiers at Detroit went to work readying a battery of their own big twenty-four-pounders aimed to respond to the threat from the village across the river.

For two hours, General Hull kept the two British officers waiting. His troops laughed out loud when they learned that General Brock demanded Detroit's surrender. Hull, however, vacillated. He spoke to his officers gloomily of the superior size of the British force compared to his own, the threat posed by Indigenous tribes, and problems with supply lines. Finally, General Hull decided to stand firm. His response was delivered by the waiting British officers via boat to his counterpart just across the river.

> Sir—I have received your letter of this date. I have no other reply to make, than to inform you that I am ready to meet any force which may be at your disposal, and any consequences which may result from its execution in any way you may think proper to use it.
> —William Hull, Brigadier-General

The American troops at the fort and camp watched closely as the boat with the white flag bearing the British officers and Hull's reply made its way back across the river. When it touched the Canadian shore, they cheered—three loud "Huzzas!"—ready to fight the British who assembled across the water.

Soon thereafter, the British battery opened fire on Fort Detroit and Detroit village around it. Shells lobbed over the river whistled through the late-afternoon sky accompanied by a steady procession of heavy thuds from the cannons, and the sharper bursts of shells exploding overhead like massive fireworks displays.

Thud! ... Boom! ... Thud! ... Boom!

At General Hull's orders, most of the American troops hurried from the tent camp into the fort. General Hull abandoned his blue-and-red striped marquee tent and took shelter within solid walls. The village's women, children, and elders—its population was estimated at eight hundred, many of French descent—rushed into the fort from their houses below its walls and crammed into its small center yard nearly elbow to elbow.

The big American force answered back with a thundering roar, its discharges shaking the air within the fort and thudding against every chest as it tried to take out the British battery across the river.

The deafening exchange kept up until midnight. One British shell, the story was later told, arced across the river and over Detroit's main street, crashed through the roof of the two-story house of Augustus Langdon, splintered through the center of the main-floor table where the family was dining, and buried itself in the cellar. The family abandoned their dinners and sprinted outdoors to safety just as their cellar exploded.

In the disconcerting midnight silence following the day's bombardment, unbeknownst to the Americans, nearly one thousand Native warriors under the direction of Tecumseh, Roundhead, Walk-in-the-Water, Main Poc, Split Log, and other leaders, including Agent Elliott, noiselessly climbed into hundreds of canoes and paddled across the river, landing at a creek mouth several miles below the fort. Painted and armed to the teeth, as John Richardson put it, they traced a wide loop around the fort to the forest behind it. Then they waited.

Earlier that day, Brock, in planning the attack, had asked Tecumseh if he knew the lay of the land across the river in a broad area around Detroit. Writes early Tecumseh biographer Benjamin Drake, who interviewed witnesses:

> Tecumseh, taking a roll of elm bark and extending it on the ground by means of four stones, drew forth his scalping knife, and with the point presently etched upon the bark a plan of the country, its hills, rivers, woods, morasses and roads; a plan which, if not as neat, was for the purpose required, fully as intelligible as if Arrowsmith [a master London cartographer] himself had prepared it.

The barest eastern light colored the sky in the predawn hour of the following day when lookouts for General Hull spotted hundreds of bateaux, rowboats, barges, and ferries gliding across the waters of the Detroit River from Sandwich on the Canadian side. The seventeen cannons of the British gunship *Queen Charlotte* out on the river gave defensive cover to the flotilla, along with the ten guns of the brig *General Hunter.* The craft landed on the riverbank at Springwell, about three miles downriver from Detroit and sheltered by the cover of a hill. After eating breakfast in a ravine out of the line of fire, General Brock's 750 troops assembled in a column and marched up the wagon road toward Fort Detroit with a few light cannons in tow.

General Hull's engineers had placed a battery of his heaviest cannons—two of the twenty-four-pounders—on a high point outside the fort aiming down on the wagon road that they had anticipated might be the British line of march. Loading the guns with massive charges of powder and grapeshot, and with artillerists standing by with lit fuses in their hands to touch them off, they waited for Brock's column to approach closer before they unleashed what was sure to be massive slaughter of the British formation.

But the British didn't flinch.

"Nothing but the boldness of the enterprize could have ensured its success," wrote Richardson of the British plan, with its column marching fearlessly toward the twenty-four-pounders.

At the same time, British batteries at Sandwich on the Canadian side opened up their barrage again, although most shells exploded too high above the fort and did little damage. As if swinging down an upraised hammer, however, soon the firing from Sandwich grew more intense and more lethal, launching fewer bursting shells and more solid cannonballs, aimed lower—directly at the fort—packed full of soldiers and townspeople. General Hull's wife, their daughter, and her children had taken refuge inside the fort in an officer's house squeezed alongside many other women and children.

Thud . . . thud . . . thud, the cannons from across the river thumped.

The British column had now marched within a mile of the fort itself. General Brock gave the order for the column to turn off the road to a nearby farmstead and assemble in assault order. The U.S. artillerists with the loaded twenty-four-pounders waited on a hill in front of the fort for their prime moment, confident they could drive back the invading British army, kill many, capture many more.

Hull paced. The gunners wanted permission to put their fuses to the touchholes unleashing sheets of flame and smoke, the muzzle roar, and a winging spray of death.

There were so many uncertainties, and Hull was short of men. Some 350 of his troops were still marching back from yet another failed attempt to rescue the Ohio supply train. His men and the huddled villagers would soon run short of food. He knew that in the event of a long siege it was two hundred miles through wilderness controlled by "savages," as he put it, to resupply. Looking eastward from the fort's heights, he could see British warships plying the river—the *Queen Charlotte* and smaller gunboats—that also controlled Lake Erie. Looking southward, he could see a column of 750 British redcoats and militiamen led by General Isaac Brock advancing to within a mile of his fortress's walls. Looking westward, he could see scores—perhaps hundreds—of Native peoples moving from the forest toward the fort and village and surrounding it. He'd heard that there were many more—perhaps thousands more—from a multitude of western tribes coming his way. He had about 1,500 men under his command and was responsible for the safety of the village's hundreds of women and children, including his own wife, their daughter, and grandchildren, huddled in various quarters within the fort's walls. He also knew that once he opened fire—a single gun—on any of the advancing British or Native troops, all bets were off. The rules of war, as General Brock had amply warned him, would no longer hold. The uncontrollable "bands of savages"—as Hull later explained his plight to the secretary of war—would set upon his people with all their fury, and no carefully choreographed European-style surrender with drumrolls and flags and proffered swords would hold them back.

At least that was what he feared: the unknown—a continent full of hidden, barbarous warriors, who were as much a concept in the European mind as a reality. He feared horrible massacre and slow torture, ending in lingering, excruciating death.

In direct contrast, many Native warriors perhaps feared their own massacre, torture, and death at the hands of an enemy the least. To withstand unimaginable pain and succumb to a tortured death conferred honor on a Native warrior. White witnesses among many tribes recorded excruciating accounts of the capture and torture of warriors by enemy tribes. The captive warrior took pride in standing up to the worst pain and mutilation, and even taunted the torturers, which in some cases were women.

"I killed your husband," one captured Omaha chief taunted his torturer, according to John Dunn Hunter's memoir of his many years as an adopted member of the Osage. "I took his scalp, I drank his blood: I owe my country nothing; I have fought many battles for her, killed many of her enemies, and leave behind me warriors enough to revenge my death, to defend their hunting grounds, squaws, and little ones. I am a man: the fate of war is against me:—I die like a warrior."

Rather, the great fear for Shawnee and Osage warriors was loss of freedom. The Osage warriors, noted Hunter, "had been educated to prefer almost any sacrifice to that of personal liberty, and even death to the degradation of their nation."

If Tecumseh and his allies didn't work with the British to stop the Americans, freedom was exactly what they would lose. The Shawnee leader had taken advantage of the dynamics now in play and wanted the Americans to know that they could be struck brutally, forcefully, and en masse by his united warriors. He had orchestrated his campaign against

Hull and masterfully taken advantage of the general's fears. He and his warriors had constantly appeared out of nowhere—in the forest, in the glades, in the swamps—to ambush and destroy Hull's men. Tecumseh and his warriors, in Hull's mind, lurked everywhere.

Stand fast or surrender? Give permission to the men to touch off the fuses on the big guns square in the face of the advancing British? All was uncertainty.

The room in the house where Hull's daughter and her children and others huddled suddenly exploded into chaos and blood. A cannonball ripped through the wall and across the room, literally cutting Lieutenant Hanks in half, tearing off Surgeon Reynolds's legs from the knees down, and severely wounding the grimly named Surgeon Blood. The spraying carnage splattered over the dresses of the women and girls and onto the walls. Some women fainted. They were carried away to a special vault built to withstand shells and cannonballs, although it could not fit the many villagers who needed protection.

General Hull was standing on the fort's parade when the cannonball smashed through the officer's house below. He had no idea whether his family had survived.

Just then, an officer with the Michigan militia rushed up to Hull to tell him Native warriors and British troops had reached the leather tanning yards and were about to enter the village itself. The officer asked Hull whether the Michigan militia alone had to defend the village—no one else was shooting at the invaders.

General Hull did not answer. He stepped into a room of the barracks, it was later reported. He took a quill and scribbled a note. He summoned his son, Captain Hull, and, handing him the note, told him to go outside and suspend a white flag from the walls of the fort so that Captain Dixon of the British artillery across the river could clearly see it.

The only thing handy was a white tablecloth. It was August 16, 1812.

CHAPTER 17

A SECRET PASSAGE OUT

In mid-August, while Brock's cannons pounded the grandfatherly Hull at Fort Detroit, William Henry Harrison, three hundred miles south, pushed his horse hard in a shuttle between Vincennes, Cincinnati, and Kentucky. His urgent, self-appointed mission entailed checking in with his family, which had temporarily moved to Cincinnati, and glad-handing prominent Kentuckians to win appointment as head of the Kentucky militia.

Several months earlier, William Henry had grown worried about his family's safety at Grouseland. When alarming reports had arrived at Vincennes in the spring of 1812 of Native attacks on frontier settlers, he had ordered his workers to dig a secret escape tunnel from the fortress-cellar of Grouseland to a hidden exit on its grounds. Other craftsmen built a passageway leading from the second-floor bedrooms of the house to the cellar. If Tecumseh or others launched a surprise attack, William Henry could rush Nancy, the children, and his household staff down the hidden staircase to the cellar, and then through the escape tunnel to safety beyond the encircling Native warriors. Mad Anthony Wayne—"the general who never sleeps"—had taught him as a young officer twenty years earlier how to prepare for the worst eventuality: *alertness.*

Yet he was blind to how deeply he bore personal responsibility for the growing Native hostility—or perhaps he had chosen not to acknowledge it. For a decade he had employed every ruse he could conjure to force Native leaders to give up their lands. Behind the genial manner he had inherited from his affable father, William Henry showed a voracious and bottomless appetite for acreage—in the tens of millions. Tract after tract after tract. By now it was abundantly clear to Native leaders like Tecumseh that it would never be enough. They had finally drawn a single, clear line—do not take this latest Wabash tract and settle it. And still Harrison would not back off. Rather, he pushed forward, leading an army up the Wabash to confront the Shawnees, Potawatomis, Kickapoos, Winnebagos, and others gathering at Prophetstown.

What could have stopped him and made him reconsider? It seems nothing could have. He misled his commander in chief, President Madison, about his aggressiveness in taking Indigenous lands, and his aggressiveness in confronting Tenskwatawa and the Native people gathered at Prophetstown with his army—notably, while Tecumseh was away. He feared Tecumseh's leadership. He feared the sweeping way the Shawnee leader could gather up tribes into a single powerful force—tribes who respected his intelligence, diplomacy, oratory. Harrison understood that with unified tribes, and the support of the British, his own army might not prevail. So he had to strike soon, as he had at Tippecanoe. But what he had done at Tippecanoe, and all the land grabs leading up to it, had pushed Tecumseh and his allies straight into British hands. It didn't have to be that way.

Despite his escape tunnels, the violence on the frontier finally approached too close for William Henry's comfort. Early in the summer he sent Nancy and their eight children by stagecoach to Cincinnati, a fast-growing town of several thousand that lay two hundred miles east of the frontier raids. Nancy's ailing father, Judge Symmes, lived only twenty miles away from Cincinnati at North Bend and the neighboring settlement of Cleves, where William Henry and Nancy still owned a four-room cabin from their early marriage.

A pause—an ominous one, in William Henry's mind—came in the attacks from Native warriors on frontier settlers at the end of the spring of 1812, shortly before the U.S. declaration of war on Great Britain. He rode off from Grouseland to visit his family in Cincinnati, by way of Kentucky. American outrage against Great Britain had grown steadily since the *Chesapeake-Leopard* affair. When William Henry arrived in Kentucky in early summer 1812, war fever had reached a high pitch, fueled by the Kentucky "War Hawks," although word of the actual declaration of war had not.

Throughout the violent history of carving a state from the wilderness, Kentuckians generally demonized American Indians and despised British enablers. They greeted Governor Harrison as a hero for his "victory" the previous fall at Tippecanoe (although Kentuckians had initially disputed his performance). Arriving at the capital of Frankfort on June 26, he received a "national salute"—a gun fired to represent each state—and a lively tavern celebration. Friendly, well-mannered, and trim, William Henry magnetically drew the guests toward him. "Each member of the company vied in their attentions to a man so highly esteemed throughout the state," reported Frankfort's local newspaper.

Big news from the East Coast just then arrived in Kentucky, having taken some days in transit: The United States had declared war on Britain on June 18. (It would be another month before the fall of Fort Mackinac and Hull's invasion of Canada, followed by the fall of Fort Detroit in mid-August.) Never shy about promoting himself—discreetly, of course, and within the strictures of good manners—William Henry immediately dashed off a letter to Kentucky governor Charles Scott suggesting that the hundreds of Kentucky troops now being raised for the war could just as soon serve under William Henry "as under any person." In other words, give him the command. Governor Scott responded that it would give him "the highest pleasure" to have such an accomplished military man as Harrison to lead Kentucky's troops. The war had already begun. William Henry Harrison wanted to be sure not to miss it.

Leaving Kentucky, he recrossed the Ohio River and reunited with Nancy and their eight children in Cincinnati. They had rented a spacious house near the corner of Fourth and Broadway, which ended a few blocks downhill at the riverfront's ferry landings and warehouses, with churches and the central market nearby.

One can imagine William Henry riding up, briskly dismounting, servants in attendance to take his horse, and being happily swarmed by the four smaller children—from three-year-old Mary to ten-year-old William Henry II—while the older children looked on, and Nancy, pleased, held their nine-month-old Carter Bassett securely in her arms. Judge Symmes had also moved into the Harrisons' big rented house on Broadway—his health failing, his real estate scheme ruined by clouded titles, and his midlife marriage to Susan Livingston Symmes having essentially ended after fifteen years when she moved back East.

Even as William Henry rejoined his sprawling family, wife, and father-in-law, a bittersweet note underlay the warm boisterousness of a collective family embrace at the Broadway house. War was afoot. Though there was not yet word of major action, William Henry surely would serve. He had survived Tippecanoe but now these moments could mark his last gathering with wife and children in this lifetime.

And yet his blood was rising. He prepared to fight. The citizens of Cincinnati knew he would play a major role in whatever came next. They threw a dinner in Governor Harrison's honor in early July, three weeks after the declaration of war. William Henry stood and gave a toast that exuded confidence and thundered with the proud refrains of frontier independence.

"The American Backwoodsman—Clad in his hunting shirt, the product of his domestic industry, and fighting for the country he loves, he is more than a match for the vile but splendid mercenary of an European despot," he boasted to the enraptured audience, reported the Cincinnati *Gazette.*

From today's perspective, with the benefit of two centuries of hindsight, this appears to be a defining moment—both for William Henry and, it would turn out, for American politics many decades into the future. If the American Revolution represented a breaking free of British monarchical rule, the freshly declared War of 1812 would establish the American identity—independent, homegrown, frontier-toughened, and vastly superior to the decaying and immoral Europe.

This "second war of independence" forged the young nation's transition from youth to adulthood. In a parallel transformation, William Henry Harrison—this son of Virginia aristocracy born into an East Coast, transatlantic culture—refashioned himself into a wilderness fighter and leader of frontiersmen against corrupt foreign influences and the yoke of oppressive governments. The powerful motif would echo through the centuries, until today.

While Harrison had sequestered his family in the safety of Cincinnati due to the threat of Native attack on Vincennes that spring of 1812, out on the frontier the settlers hacking small farms from the wilds lacked the means to flee to a secure town and rent a comfortable house. Under the growing threat of violence from Native attack, they took their families and what belongings they could carry to "fort up" in secure wooden blockhouses. Harrison had issued orders back in Vincennes to fortify the village's stoutest houses as makeshift forts to shelter settlers. Not since the days of Little Turtle and Blue Jacket's coalition, before the Greenville Treaty, had the northwestern frontier come under such dire threat. But now the settlers numbered far more and had struck ever more boldly into lands still claimed by tribes, whatever Harrison's "treaties" may have said.

Toward the end of July, while Harrison shuttled back and forth between Cincinnati and Kentucky on political and family matters, news arrived of the first American defeat—Michilimackinac, or Fort Mackinac, had fallen to a force of British and nearly one thousand war-painted Native warriors in canoes. This was ominous. Sensing victory, more war chiefs would now rally to the British side—"pour down in swarms upon Detroit," as Harrison put it in a letter to Secretary of War Eustis. With the fall of Michilimackinac, the British now substantially controlled the waters of the Upper Great Lakes.

In a letter to the secretary of war on August 12, Harrison suggested a strategy to Eustis to immediately build a string of forts along the Illinois River between St. Louis and the small U.S. outpost of Chicago—a kind of barrier blocking distant tribes living to the west and north from coming east. When he heard of General Hull's underway invasion of Canada, he understood Hull's vulnerability at Detroit with the British controlling Lake Erie and Native warriors able to attack his overland supply lines. Harrison urged sending a large body of troops immediately to Fort Wayne to keep Hull's supply lines to Detroit intact.

But then urgent mounted messengers several days in transit brought dire news—General Hull had suddenly called off his invasion of Canada, recrossed the river, and retreated into Fort Detroit. Tecumseh and Brock in mid-August had joined their forces to target Fort Detroit itself. It appeared in imminent danger.

The news got still worse. Warriors threatened the small, far-west post of Chicago. Tecumseh and others had brought Tenskwatawa's teachings to the Western Potawatomi, winning over many warriors. If the Americans didn't accede and relinquish their ill-gotten Illinois and Indiana land claims, the Western Potawatomi were to prepare for an uprising against the white invaders. The moment had arrived. Once Michilimackinac fell, Main Poc, the revered Potawatomi chief allied with Tecumseh, sent red wampum belts to the Western Potawatomi. Some five hundred warriors—mostly Potawatomis, but also Winnebagos, Ojibwes, and Kickapoos—gathered near Fort Dearborn, on a bend of the Chicago River near Lake Michigan.[*]

The U.S. officers there had received an urgent message from General Hull, still in command of Fort Detroit, to abandon the post at Chicago. The post amounted to a new stockade and a few traders' cabins at a key portage spot along southern Lake Michigan that the Native peoples called Chigauga. According to Hull's orders, the troops were to immediately march 160 miles east to the safety of Fort Wayne in the Indiana Territory. Meanwhile, at Fort Wayne, U.S. Indian agent and officer William Wells, who was raised a Miami warrior and was deeply familiar with tribal dynamics, knew that Chicago would come under dire threat from the Western Potawatomi as soon as they heard about the fall of Michilimackinac Island and its fort at Lake Michigan's northern end. A small rescue party of Miami warriors organized by Wells rushed from Fort Wayne toward Chicago to help in the fort's defense.

The traders living next to the Chicago fort, who had better relations with the Native peoples, warned the U.S. officers to stay put inside the stockade and not venture out among the clamoring warriors. However, the officer in charge, Captain Nathan Heald, insisted on following Hull's orders and striking out. He struck a deal with the Native warriors that he believed would ensure the occupants' safety. Captain Heald would leave the warriors all the fort's goods and a monetary reward in exchange for a safe passage to Fort Wayne. But the night before departure, Captain Heald ordered the fort's extra muskets surreptitiously smashed and

---

[*] One anecdote about these incidents at Fort Dearborn reveals a fun-loving dimension of life on the frontier, as well as raw terror. In the spring of 1812, while peaceful relations still prevailed, two Calumet leaders and an interpreter walked through the Chicago post and saw two officers' wives playing battledore and shuttlecock—a forerunner of badminton played with racquets. "The white chiefs' wives are amusing themselves very much," one said to the interpreter, he later reported. "It will not be long before they are living in our corn-fields."

tossed down the well, and barrels of gunpowder and whiskey dumped in the middle of the night into the Chicago River.

Unseen Native warriors witnessed this betrayal. At dawn they detected the skim of gunpowder on the river's surface and the taste of whiskey in its sluggish waters. Soon after sunrise, the rescue party from Fort Wayne bound for the beleaguered fort emerged from the lakeshore's sand dunes—William Wells leading a small body of Miami warriors friendly to Americans.

But without the arms and ammunition that Captain Heald had destroyed there was little hope of holding the fort, Wells realized. Abandoning it presented the only option. Deeply familiar with Native warfare, Wells, according to some accounts, blackened his face with wet gunpowder—a color that indicated he had prepared for war—before leaving the fort. He knew what lay ahead.

With the post's little military band striking up a tune, the stockade gates swung open and the procession marched out of Fort Dearborn on a hot, sunny Saturday morning, August 15, 1812, the day before Hull's surrender at Fort Detroit. Wells rode a white thoroughbred at the front. About two miles out, the trail passed through a narrow spot—with beach dunes on the right and the Lake Michigan shoreline on the left. As the party passed through it, five hundred Potawatomis and other Native warriors came charging over the dunes' crests.

The battle ended in less than fifteen minutes. Scattered about the dunes lay the dead: William Wells, plus thirty-seven soldiers and militiamen, twelve children, and two women, one of them Mrs. Heald's Black enslaved woman, Cicely. In the heat of battle, one blood-crazed young warrior had tomahawked most of the children riding in a wagon. Some of the women, eyewitnesses later reported, fought on horseback like "Amazons," one swinging her husband's sword at Native warriors trying to knock her down. The remainder were taken prisoner. Some of the wounded were tortured or scalped.

Upon finally arriving in Fort Wayne weeks later, one captured officer,

Walter Jordan, who managed to escape from his captors wrote to his wife:

> First they shot the feather off my cap, next the epaulet from my shoulder, and then the handle from my sword. I then surrendered to four savage rascals. [The chief], taking me by the hand and speaking English said, "Jordan, I know you; you gave me tobacco at Fort Wayne. We won't kill you, but come and see what we will do with your captain." So leading me to where Wells lay, they cut off his head and put it on a long pole, while another took out his heart and divided it among the chiefs and ate it up raw.*

It was as if the back door to the young nation had suddenly sprung open that summer of 1812. First it was the capture of Michilimackinac Island and its Fort Mackinac in mid-July. Now the news of the fall of Detroit and Fort Dearborn at Chicago stunned the East Coast. The Ohio Valley and Upper Midwest were suddenly up for grabs. The young United States had defeated the British Army in the Revolution and an Indian confederacy at Fallen Timbers. But this was potentially a more powerful enemy. Allied warriors together with fully committed British forces could possibly drive the United States back to something approaching the size of the original thirteen colonies.

Hull's sudden retreat out of Canada and his surrender of Detroit, in particular, caused a paroxysm of "mortification and intense indignation throughout the country," as one nineteenth-century historian phrased it. Among the outraged were the citizens of Greensborough, North Caro-

---

* The eating of William Wells's heart (while still "palpitating," according to some accounts) to imbibe his courage occurred in the vicinity of today's Field Museum on the Chicago lakeshore. Wells gave his name to one of the principal streets in Chicago's Loop. The battle site itself is marked by Battle of Fort Dearborn Park.

lina, who voted at a public meeting to hang and burn U.S. General Hull in effigy.*

Along the northwest frontier, the threat loomed over every homestead, village, and fort. If Fort Detroit could fall, they all could fall. Settlers began to flee by the hundreds from the Indiana and Illinois territories south across the Ohio to the relative safety of Kentucky. One homesteader who stayed reported that whenever he stepped from his cabin, he carried his rifle, tomahawk, and butcher knife, plus a loaded pistol stuck in his belt. "When I went to plow, I laid my gun on the plowed ground, and stuck up a stick by it for a mark, so that I could get it quick in case it was wanted."

To Americans' horror, the British now moved into Detroit. They had captured 2,188 men, plus thirty-nine cannons, three thousand rifles and muskets, and a U.S. warship under construction for use on Lake Erie, patriotically named the *John Adams*.

Having instantly bonded, Brock and Tecumseh took over a pleasant white house on the main street, where the two war chiefs conducted postsurrender operations. Several rooms featured the frontier luxury of wallpaper and they were attended by a waitstaff.

Tecumseh had now become a legend to the British as well as the Native peoples. "The Indian General," the British soldiers called him. "A

---

* General Hull's surrender of Fort Detroit outraged his troops and officers—one of whom ripped the epaulets off his own shoulders and broke his sword on the ground—but he bore up for the rest of his life under the weight of the humiliation and stain on his reputation. Made a prisoner and paraded through the streets of Montreal to cheering crowds, then lodged in the formal hospitality of the governor's mansion, he returned to his farm in Newton, Massachusetts, and was summoned to a court-martial (which he had requested) some months later. Convicted of cowardice, sentenced to be shot, with his name obliterated from army rolls, he was eventually recommended for leniency by the court and pardoned by President Madison. He wrote an extensive series of essays defending his actions, and to his dying words said he had no regrets. "When he could perceive no alternative but surrender or destruction," writes historian Lossing, who interviewed witnesses and examined evidence in depth, "he bravely determined to choose the most courageous and humane course; so he faced the taunts of his soldiers, and the expected scorn of his countrymen, rather than fill the beautiful land of the Ohio, and the settlements of Michigan, with mourning."

more sagacious or more gallant warrior does not, I believe, exist," General Brock wrote to the British prime minister, Lord Liverpool, two weeks after they had captured Detroit. "He was the admiration of everyone who conversed with him."

General Brock made a public ceremony of removing his scarlet sash and presenting it to Tecumseh. With characteristic diplomacy, Tecumseh presented the sash in turn to the highly respected Chief Roundhead, a fellow leader of the attack on Detroit and a member of the Wyandots, the tribe considered the "elder brothers" of the Shawnees.

At Detroit, Tecumseh greeted prisoners and U.S. officials with good manners and notable cordiality. A junior aide to the defeated General Hull called on Brock with some matter of business, and the British general introduced him to Tecumseh. Always dressing with a sense of elegance and panache, he wore a Moroccan sword belt over a fringed deerskin hunting shirt. "He was tall and commanding and straight as an arrow," reported Hull's aide, Robert Wallace, who considered Tecumseh the best general in the country.

"Well," Tecumseh told Wallace, "you are a prisoner, but it is the fortune of war, and you are in very good hands."

Fort Wayne became the next target. The Western Potawatomis poised to strike. They had received more red wampum belts from Main Poc, connoting war. Moving east toward Fort Wayne, they made their initial attack on September 5, while the same day Sauks and Winnebagos some three hundred miles to the west assaulted Fort Madison on the Mississippi. The red wampum belts apparently had coordinated the two attacks.

Tecumseh and Roundhead prepared warriors at Detroit to help the assault on Fort Wayne, backed by British troops and artillery. The British, however, paused. General Brock had abruptly rushed back to the East to help with the defense of Niagara. The commander left in charge of Detroit and Fort Malden, Colonel Procter, lacked the dash and boldness of Brock. He hesitated to send British troops because the admiralty in London had suspended its stop-and-search policy of U.S. vessels and Canada's governor-general George Prévost hoped this would at least pause hostilities.

The Americans, however, did not pause.

After a week's delay, the big Native-British military entourage left Fort Malden—nearly one thousand warriors under Tecumseh and Round-head, including several hundred Ottawas and Ojibwes, supported by 250 British troops and two cannons. In a sign of gathering momentum, they had paddled down from Michilimackinac Island to join Tecumseh's confederacy and oust the Americans from the North American heartland. Adding still more momentum, the great Miami war chief Little Turtle had died suddenly of gout, and many of his Miami warriors now switched from the U.S. to the British side.

Tecumseh's moment—seeded by Little Turtle and Blue Jacket's confederacy and before them by great war chiefs like Pontiac—had arrived. If Fort Wayne were to fall, it would open up another enormous swath of North American territory to Native and British control. Before his departure for the East, Brock had promised Tecumseh that in the peaceful settlement of the war—assuming that it occurred—the British would ensure Native land claims were prominently recognized. London authorities had agreed to Brock's recommendation. The political geography of North America was about to be upended.

"Difficulty, argument, and intimidation had not bowed Tecumseh," writes Sugden, "and suddenly his dream seemed to be coming to life. In the heat of conflict Indians and British began catching his wild spirit. The Indians began to wonder whether, after all, the Great Spirit had not reserved the lands north of the Ohio for his red children; the British resurrected the idea of an Indian buffer state that would keep the northwest out of the American hands."

Tecumseh and Harrison vied to outplay each other on a chessboard that spanned the central swath of North America. Events suddenly moved at lightning speed, and William Henry with them. Each dispatch from the north brought ever more alarming reports down to Cincinnati and Kentucky. Citizens, officials, and soldiers looked toward Governor Harrison for military leadership.

He happily obliged them. William Henry had recently asked the Kentucky governor to tell President Madison that Harrison would be just the man to lead the Kentucky militia. On August 24, as Harrison dashed back and forth on horseback between Cincinnati and Kentucky, Kentucky's outgoing governor, Charles Scott, appointed him a general in the Kentucky militia.

The newly minted General Harrison organized his Kentucky troops in Cincinnati. He called on the citizens to make twelve thousand cartridges. His ambition gloved with polite tact as usual, he also tried to nudge aside a rival for the army command, General James Winchester, an easy-living, laid-back, sixty-year-old from Tennessee who had never met the troops.

"The backwoodsmen are a singular people," he wrote of the Kentucky troops to Secretary Eustis. "From their affection and attachment everything may be expected but I will venture to say they never did nor never will perform anything brilliant under a stranger."

He had traipsed these wilds since a young ensign, he added. "No general can act in this country without a personal knowledge. . . . Beyond the survey there is no map that can at all be relied upon."

Reports arrived that Native warriors and British troops were marching from Fort Detroit to Fort Wayne, a journey of 160 miles. Cincinnati lay almost that exact distance to the south of Fort Wayne. The race was on for who would get to Fort Wayne first.

General Harrison's first men marched out of Cincinnati on August 29. By September 3 he and over two thousand troops had reached Piqua, the last of the white settlements, in western Ohio midway between Cincinnati and Fort Wayne. An urgent message arrived from friendly Indian scouts that Potawatomis, perhaps numbering three hundred, had already besieged it. By September 10, forced marches on reduced rations had brought them within striking distance of Fort Wayne. The Kentuckians clamored for a fight. Although skilled with their horses and guns, and eager to kill Native peoples, they lacked order and discipline. General Harrison issued detailed instructions on how to swing the marching columns to face outward to counter a Native ambush.

As Tecumseh had shown with warriors and fellow chiefs, Harrison likewise had a bearing and a manner—a steadiness, bravery, and intelligence—that almost wordlessly inspired the respect of his men. "In an army but one can rule," remarked one of the Kentuckians on the march. "Harrison, with a look, can awe and convince, or persuade, where some would be refractory. He . . . makes all do their duty. . . . All are afraid and unwilling to meet with his censure."

He soon learned that he had edged out Winchester. An official dispatch from Washington announced that on August 22, President Madison had appointed him commander in chief of the Army of the Northwest.

On the night of September 11, twenty miles from Fort Wayne, they built a fortified camp, and troops "lay on their arms" during sleep. Natives moved in the darkness outside the pickets. No attack came. Only a few miles and a swamp now separated them from Fort Wayne. On the morning of the twelfth, General Harrison sent scouts to probe the swamp, a likely place for hidden warriors to launch an ambush. No one there.

They marched on. As they reached Fort Wayne's stockade, the gates suddenly swung open and cheers broke out to greet them. About seventy or eighty Potawatomis had just left in frustration after burning the settlers' cornfields and houses.

The Potawatomis had waited as long as they could for Tecumseh, Roundhead, Main Poc, Split Log, and united warriors, and the 250 British troops hauling cannons to smash down the walls. Without artillery and much greater numbers, the Potawatomis could not breach the tall stockade of Fort Wayne. Procter's hesitation had delayed the reinforcements' departure from Fort Malden for a week. Tecumseh and Roundhead and their warriors were finally en route when Native runners brought the news that Harrison had arrived and the Kentuckians at Fort Wayne were now "as numerous as the trees."

The moment for Tecumseh to take it had passed. If Brock had been in charge, they would have left on September 1, beat Harrison and his Kentucky army to Fort Wayne, and captured it. They would have sprung the back door to America wide open, backward on its hinges.

The rest of that fall of 1812, the fights on the western frontier teetered back and forth, inconclusively—and for Tecumseh frustratingly. Years earlier, just out of his teenaged years, he had broken his leg when thrown from his horse during an autumn buffalo hunt with older brother Chiksika in the Illinois prairie country. Confined to the campfire circle over winter, Tecumseh had grown despondent—some reports say he even tried to kill himself—but with spring he had healed enough to fashion a set of crutches and hobble onward with Chiksika's party.

It seems that now, two decades later, another bout of depression hit. Again, an injury played a role. In August's battle at Maguaga he had taken a buckshot pellet to the leg. As autumn 1812 wore on, the wound would not heal, and his leg, according to some accounts, was withering.

At the same time, the combined Native forces struggled to take American forts. Without British cannoneers to blast down the walls, Fort Wayne had held against the Potawatomis. Likewise, Fort Harrison on the Wabash. Tenskwatawa's followers from Prophetstown attacked Fort Harrison on the dark night of September 4, sneaking up and shoving bundles of flaming kindling through loopholes in a corner blockhouse. The fire touched off the fort's 150 barrels of whiskey—twenty-five thousand rations—whose flames jumped into the blackness to illuminate soldiers as targets for showers of arrows and musket balls.

Despite the twenty-foot-wide hole burned through the stockade wall, the commander of the fort, a young Captain Zachary Taylor, managed to plug the hole and keep the fort together. (Like Harrison, he was the third son of a Virginia plantation family and had chosen a military career, eventually going into politics.) After another ten days, the Prophetstown tribes gave up their siege of Fort Harrison as they had Fort Wayne. The Native warriors could harass the forts and ravage the white settlements but not overcome them. Countering, General Harrison, establishing his headquarters in northern Ohio, sent parties to burn Indigenous villages and dispatched one thousand men to destroy (again) the rebuilt Prophetstown. Another Tecumseh brother, Kumskaukau, and a handful of warriors lured sixty of the American horsemen into an ambush among bluffs and ravines near Prophetstown, killing sixteen, but the main force was too large for their little party.

The Native people suffered little loss of life, as they had abandoned most villages before the army's arrival, but this did not lift Tecumseh's gloom. Unable to fight or lead and perhaps exhausted after his years of unremitting travels, he spent most of the fall on headwater streams above Prophetstown, where Indigenous tribes had taken refuge. The powerful momentum of just a few weeks earlier had seemingly stalled, and Tecumseh's energy, dynamism, and hope seeped away as the fighting season faded into winter's dark and cold. The darkness deepened when he learned that his soul brother Brock had taken a musket ball directly through the heart at the Battle of Queenston Heights while leading a foot charge against the Americans trying to invade Canada across the Niagara River. Though the battle ultimately proved a jubilant victory for the British, at the cost of Brock's life it did not lift Tecumseh's spirits.

In those long-ago times of deeper snows, colder winters, and thinner uniforms, the "fighting season" for European-style armies typically ended in late autumn, after which they stayed put in winter camps, such as Washington did at Valley Forge. Likewise, in the rhythms of traditional Native warfare, men returned to their families in winter to hunt for them.

William Henry had a deep and painful familiarity with the difficulties of winter travel by an army in the wilderness, from his first months as a young ensign at Fort Washington in the winter of 1791–92. He had served in the detail attempting to recover cannons from the battle site of St. Clair's destroyed army. He had vivid memories of plodding through deep snow, all-night guard duty without a warming fire, and stumbling upon a massive tangle of mutilated bodies lying two feet beneath an icy crust.

Yet the American public and President Madison insisted that the United States regain immediately what it had lost to the British and Native people—especially Fort Detroit. Feeling the pressure, General Harrison sketched out a plan for a winter campaign to take back Detroit and recapture Fort Malden. But he recognized that none of these plans could fully succeed without controlling the waters of the Great Lakes by warship—and especially Lake Erie.

From his army headquarters in northern Ohio, just shy of Lake Erie, he wrote to Secretary Eustis in December that if the straits separating the United States and Canada—meaning parts of Lake Erie and the Detroit River—froze in the coming winter, he could easily advance with troops and sleds across the ice and take Fort Malden, and then Fort Detroit. But if the straits didn't freeze—frequently the case—he would have to wait until spring. Time and expenses better spent, he suggested to the War Department, would be to build a small fleet of warships to control Lake Erie.

The winter expedition went forward, nevertheless. By January 10, 1813, after struggling through the Black Swamp of northern Ohio, Harrison's former rival General Winchester and his Kentuckians reached the Maumee Rapids, and built a fortification there, Fort Meigs. Winchester then launched an attack against British forces holding Frenchtown on the River Raisin, where it flowed into Lake Erie. His troops marched across the frozen river under fire, then, to a drumroll, charged up the far bank and slowly pushed a force of British militia and Native fighters from the hamlet and into a forest.

The Americans considered it a victory. Winchester had now successfully brought one large wing of Harrison's Army of the Northwest in position to launch an expedition across the Lake Erie ice and frozen Detroit River for the capture of Fort Malden and glorious retaking of Detroit. Winchester's nearly one thousand troops camped in the hamlet on the Raisin's north bank, while the general himself—known for his taste for good living—lodged a half mile back to the rear in a small but comfortable log house with a large fireplace to warm him.

At Fort Malden, eighteen miles across the Lake Erie ice, Procter acted with a decisiveness he had lacked the previous fall. As one participant, Squire Reynolds, later recounted, the "lads and lasses" of Fort Malden and nearby village of Amherstburg were holding a ball on the night of January 18, 1813, at Mrs. Draper's Tavern to celebrate Queen Charlotte's Birthday, an annual event in the British Empire. In the midst of the dancing and fun, Squire Reynolds recounted, a British colonel walked into the tavern dressed for battle:

> "My boys," said he, in a loud voice, "you must prepare to dance to a different tune; the enemy is upon us, and we are going to surprise them. We shall take the route about four in the morning, so get ready at once." Of course there was some confusion and surprise, but I believe the fellows liked the fighting as much as the dancing. The ball broke up at once, and every man was at his appointed post at the proper time.

A young British soldier, John Richardson, later described the glorious moment.

> No sight could be more beautiful than the departure of this little army from Amherstburg. It was the depth of winter; and the river at the point we crossed being four miles in breadth, the deep rumbling noise of the guns prolonging their reverberations like the roar of distant thunder, as they moved along the ice, mingled with the wild cries of the Indians, seemed to threaten some convulsion of nature; while the

appearance of the troops winding along the road, now lost behind
some cliff of rugged ice, now emerging into view, their polished arms
glittering in the sunbeams, gave an air of romantic grandeur to the
scene.

Three days later at four-thirty A.M., deep cold and predawn darkness
blanketed the American camp on the River Raisin, and reveille was
sounding with the drummer boys thumping out "The Three Camps,"
when canister shot and shells fired from nearby British cannons started to
explode overhead. With a chorus of war cries, Native warriors charged in
from the darkness with tomahawks, and charging British troops opened
fire with muskets, as a combined force of seven hundred Native warriors
under Roundhead and six hundred British troops under Procter attacked
the Americans at Frenchtown, caught completely unaware. The easy-
living General Winchester of Tennessee soon came rushing up to rally
his troops with his uniform thrown over his nightshirt.

The snow, witnesses said, became stained crimson in the pale light of
dawn. Only thirty of the Americans made it back to the Maumee Rapids.
John Richardson painted a vivid picture of the Kentuckian backwoods
fighters who survived the battle:

> The appearance of the American prisoners captured at Frenchtown
> was miserable to the last degree. They had the air of men to whom
> cleanliness was a virtue unknown, and their squalid bodies were cov-
> ered by habiliments that had evidently undergone every change of
> season, and were arrived at the last stage of repair. . . . It was the depth
> of winter; but scarcely an individual was in possession of a great coat
> or cloak, and few of them wore garments of wool of any description.
> They still retained their summer dress, consisting of cotton stuff of
> various colors, shaped into frocks, and descending to the knee: their
> trowsers were of the same material. They were covered with slouched
> hats, worn bare by constant use, beneath which their long hair fell

matted and uncombed over their cheeks; and these, together with the dirty blankets wrapped around their loins to protect them against the inclemency of the season, and fastened by broad leathern belts, into which were thrust axes and knives of an enormous length, gave them an air of wildness and savageness, which in Italy would have caused them to pass for brigands of the Apennines.

In the end, American losses amounted to about 290 killed and nearly 600 captured. Had he been there, Tecumseh, known since his teenaged years for his kindness to those he captured, surely would have done everything in his power to stop the scalpings and killing of prisoners and those trying to surrender that followed. It outraged the American public, and especially Kentuckians.

"Never, dear mother," one Kentucky prisoner wrote home from captivity at Fort Malden, "if I should live a thousand years, can I forget the frightful sight of this morning, when handsomely-painted Indians came into the fort, some of them carrying half a dozen scalps of my countrymen fastened upon sticks, and yet covered with blood, and were congratulated by Colonel Proctor for their bravery."

The calls for revenge came instantly. "Remember the River Raisin!"

CHAPTER 18

GENERAL JANUARY

It had been a bad several months for Napoleon, too, who had thrown the bulk of his army toward the East. British military fortunes in Continental Europe—and by extension the Royal Army's capacity to fight simultaneously in North America—rose and fell inversely to the French emperor's glorious victories and crushing defeats.

While General Hull invaded Canada in July 1812, Napoleon was invading Russia to secure the eastern flank of his ever-expanding empire from the armies of Czar Alexander. This, too, quickly became a supply line issue for the invading army. The difference was that while General Hull had to worry about keeping provisions coming to his army of 2,200, Napoleon had around half a million troops in his Grande Armée to feed on the march. He anticipated a relatively short march and a victory within thirty days. Used to living off the land in the fertile farm country of Europe, Napoleon had his commissariat lay in enough bread and beef to last for fifty days. For so huge an army, this required a provision train of nearly ten thousand wagons and a herd of fifty thousand beef cattle trailing the invaders. But a fifty-day supply, it turned out, was not nearly enough.

Employing tactics not unlike those of a Shawnee war chief, the Russian generals engaged Napoleon with their much smaller armies only a bit at a time, and then withdrew a bit farther, in retreat, luring Napoleon and his half million men and 180,000 horses ever deeper into the vast Eurasian landmass. General Winchester, in bringing one thousand men to the Maumee Rapids, had relied on a two-hundred-mile-long supply line that crossed the Great Black Swamp wilderness inhabited by hostile forces. By comparison, Napoleon's supply lines reached back nearly one thousand miles over bad, muddy roads to Poland. Despite losing battles, the Russian army never conceded defeat. It kept backing up until Napoleon finally reached Moscow. When he invaded it, he found the city abandoned, stripped clean of food, and its wooden structures blazing.

By now it was mid-September 1812, and in the heart of North America, allied Native and British forces were celebrating their recent capture of Michilimackinac Island, Detroit, and Chicago. In the vastness of Russia, Napoleon's army had no victory to claim, no food at hand, no place to sleep except among the ashes, and was more than one thousand miles from home. In mid-October, without a good alternative, Napoleon simply turned his Grande Armée around and left. It had now fallen to 110,000 men, due to battles along the way into Russia, illness, and desertions. Smart Russian generals guided their armies to prevent Napoleon from seeking an alternate route home—forcing him to march through the same devastated countryside that both the retreating Russian army and his own advancing troops had just stripped clean of food and forage.

General January, as they like to say in Russia, then got on the move. By November 14, the temperature had fallen to -15 degrees Fahrenheit and plummeted from there. Far more soldiers died from freezing to death— hypothermia—and starvation, or a combination of the two, than from battle wounds. It is one of the most striking features of human physiology that in winter, during heavy exertion like marching, the human body needs twice—or even higher—the caloric intake that it does in warmer weather. In other words, if Napoleon's troops needed fifty thousand beef cattle to feed them on the way into Moscow, on the way out they would need another one hundred thousand. They had zero.

At his winter camp in northern Ohio, William Henry Harrison confronted the same problem in those last months of 1812 and early 1813. Not only did his supply lines stretch long distances, especially to provide Fort Meigs at the Maumee Rapids beyond the Black Swamp, but he was feeling pressure from his superiors in Washington to retake Fort Detroit immediately. Before General Winchester had advanced to the Maumee Rapids to build Fort Meigs, Harrison had written Secretary Eustis in early December to underscore the hazards of winter warfare. He would need to get one million rations of flour to the Maumee Rapids to feed the men, and feeding and keeping the horses healthy presented a nearly insurmountable logistical problem.

"The prodigious destruction of Horses can only be conceived by those who have been accustomed to Military Operations in a Wilderness in the Winter Season," he warned. "I fear that the Expenses of this Army will greatly exceed the calculations of the Government."

Disaster did result when General Winchester pushed forward in the dead of winter from Fort Meigs and the Maumee Rapids toward Detroit—the slaughter of American forces at the River Raisin by Native warriors under Roundhead and British troops under Procter.

The troops and animals in Napoleon's winter invasion of Russia were suffering on a far grander scale. The French army killed and ate its own horses, which were starving to death, too, like the human body devouring its own fat stores and finally its own muscle in a desperate attempt to survive without food. The once-magnificent cavalry stumbled along on foot through cold and snow, the artillerists abandoned their cannons, the drivers left their horseless wagons, and deserters drifted off, happy to be taken prisoner to escape from this frozen hell, while Russian Cossacks nipped like wolves at the army's flanks and rear.

On December 5, learning of an attempted coup in France, Napoleon leapt in a sleigh and bolted off for Paris to save his empire, despite his shattered army. Estimates vary over how many perished out of a Grande Armée estimated at 500,000 to 600,000 on the way into Russia. The starving wraiths who stumbled out in December 1812 numbered between 10,000 and 70,000. Of those who remained behind in Russia, many had been taken prisoner. But many more were dead.

Wrote the Marquis de Caulaincourt, officer in Napoleon's army:

> The cold was so intense that bivouacking was no longer supportable. . . . One constantly found men who, overcome by the cold, had been forced to drop out and had fallen to the ground, too weak or too numb to stand. Ought one to help them along—which practically meant carrying them? They begged one to let them alone. . . . Sleep comes inevitably, and sleep is to die. I tried in vain to save a number of these unfortunates. The only words they uttered were to beg me, for the love of God, to go away and let them sleep. . . . I saw [this] happen to thousands of individuals. The road was covered with their corpses.

By January 1813, for the British, at least, things were looking good on two continents—a favorable omen for Tecumseh and his confederacy who expected British support to fight the Americans.

Tecumseh's exact whereabouts during this winter of 1812–13 remain uncertain, most likely on the upper tributaries of the Wabash and Tippecanoe with warriors and families.

His family was with him during this emotional slump—his wife, his son, his sister, Tecumpease, and his younger brothers, Tenskwatawa and Kumskaukau. One can't help picturing Kumskaukau, the good-natured younger brother, trying to cheer him with stories of former times, funny stories, stories of hope for the future. Tecumseh's relationship with Tenskwatawa had grown deeply strained since the debacle with Harrison's advancing troops at Tippecanoe and Prophetstown. He had become dismissive toward Tenskwatawa, whatever his prophesies. Tecumseh's confederacy had evolved into something that ranged beyond a spiritual movement to cast a wide net in a cultural and political sphere.

He remained closer than ever to Tecumpease. In her, perhaps, he could truly confide, and to him, perhaps, she could give her truest insights. What could she tell him at this moment? That he'd come so far and brought the people so far? That there was still further to go? That he was the one to take them—that this was his destiny? That the moment was at hand, and not to give up?

Whatever it was, he slowly gained strength and spirit. It emanated outward, through the tribes. By the middle of winter, nearly one thousand warriors had gathered again with him in the upper reaches of the Wabash and Tippecanoe. Celebratory news from the South then started to filter into these northern river valleys so remote from white settlement.

Tecumseh's revolt had spread south all the way to Florida, a thousand miles away, where Red Stick warriors from the Creeks had joined with Seminoles and Blacks living with tribes to help the Spanish fight U.S. territorial aggression. Parties of American troops from neighboring Georgia had entered Spanish-held Florida to annex pieces of it by force. In the spirit of Tecumseh's confederacy, whose disciples had worked the Southeast, the united Red Sticks, Seminoles, and Blacks broke the American siege of St. Augustine and drove Georgian troops out of Florida.

Along with this good news came word of U.S. general James Winchester's defeat at the River Raisin. Tecumseh's close ally Roundhead had excelled, and Procter and his British troops, this time, had risen to the occasion to confront Harrison's American forces.

Tecumseh now began to heal, in both body and spirit, and, once again, the great movement revived.

The site of the showdown soon became clear—the rapids of the Maumee River—a key spot in the continental geography that, for thousands of years, had provided a natural transit passage for humans on the move. The Maumee River and its rapids sat near a kind of roof peak—a long, gentle ridge extending east-west across northern Ohio, Indiana, and Illinois. From this ridge crest, like the two slopes of a roof, some rivers flow north into the Great Lakes and eventually the North Atlantic Ocean, others south into the Ohio and Mississippi rivers and eventually the Gulf of Mexico. In some places, the headwater streams drain from the same swamp in opposite directions toward these distant seas, like the transit hub at the center of a sprawling subway system.

For this reason, Native tribes located many villages and trading grounds along this gentle crest. And for the same reason, William Henry Harrison aimed to dominate these spots, hoping to stymie the attempts of Native and British forces to cross from the Great Lakes over that divide and push south into lands claimed by the United States. Fort Wayne represented one key spot; Harrison strategized that the Maumee Rapids could be another. Before their massacre at the River Raisin, U.S. troops under General Winchester had started a base, soon named Fort Meigs, overlooking the rapids. It could serve as Harrison's army's advance base to retake Detroit and launch an invasion into Canada.

But, just as surely, Henry Procter at Fort Malden—now promoted to British general—understood the strategic importance of this gentle divide between watersheds. Taking a page from the late, great Isaac Brock, he chose boldness over inaction. He determined to hit Fort Meigs at the Maumee Rapids before Harrison could finish its construction and bring in a full complement of U.S. troops to defend it.

Tecumseh provided an essential element of Procter's strategy. As he emerged from his low ebb of darkness and injury over the winter, he brought his band and its women, children, and elders north from the seclusion of the upper Wabash to the Detroit River, near Fort Malden. Once settled, in mid-April 1813, he was ready. Like all the Native allies, he expected the big guns of the British to make all the difference in pounding Fort Meigs into submission—unlike the musket fire that had harmlessly pocked Fort Wayne's stockade logs with small leaden balls. Native warriors would cut off any U.S. troops General Harrison marched toward the fort to try to reinforce it.

In late April, one thousand British troops in bateaux, ships, and gunboats and 1,200 warriors under Tecumseh and Roundhead launched in canoes from Amherstburg across the western end of Lake Erie to where the Maumee River spilled off that roof peak and emptied into the lake at today's Toledo, Ohio. Other warriors rode on horseback around the end of Lake Erie. Boats hauled the heavy twenty-four-pounder cannons up the Maumee and deposited them at the British camp on the north bank and only two and a half miles short of U.S. Fort Meigs on the south bank, which sat on a low bluff overlooking the river. Warriors camped near the British leather tents, crafting bark shelters and kindling campfires against early spring's cold and mud. They then performed war dances and built sweat lodges to purify themselves for battle.

On April 29, 1813, the British artillerists hauled the big guns with oxen teams up a muddy path to emplacements on a bluff overlooking Fort Meigs from the other side of the river. In outline, Fort Meigs formed an oval four hundred yards long and two hundred yards wide, with twelve blockhouses and gun batteries, protected by a tall stockade, a dry ditch, and the rows of sharpened stakes known as an abatis. To the British artillerists and Native warriors, it presented a ripe target from their gunsights on the bluff across the river and above. Like a bull's-eye target, its stockade encircled scores of canvas tents that housed 1,200 U.S. troops. For the moment, they looked like sitting ducks. The Native warriors under

Tecumseh and Roundhead took particular satisfaction as the circle tightened.

"Emotions ran particularly high," writes Sugden, "because they knew that behind those powerful walls their enemies were led by a man widely regarded as a major author of their misfortunes, William Henry Harrison. There was an immense feeling of anticipation and grim satisfaction that their greatest adversary was about to be delivered up to them."

First, the Native forces crossed the Maumee in canoes and slipped through the woods around the fort. To start, they picked off the cattle and pigs that grazed and rooted in the open area Harrison had ordered cleared around the fort's walls.

Gathering his troops, summoning up his most eloquent outrage, and comparing them to Mad Anthony's army when it had routed Little Turtle and Blue Jacket's confederacy at nearby Fallen Timbers two decades before, Harrison called out to his men:

Can the citizens of a free country, who have taken up arms to defend its rights, think of submitting to an army composed of mercenary soldiers, reluctant Canadians goaded to the field by the [British] bayonet, and of wretched, naked savages? Can the breast of an American soldier, when he casts his eyes to the opposite shore, the scene of his country's triumphs over the same foe, be influenced by any other feelings than the hope of glory?

On May 1, the big British guns on the bluff across the river opened up. Warriors screamed their war cries as the forest shook and shells arced over the Maumee while the artillerists found their range to drop their bombs straight into the tent encampment within the stockade.

But as those first shells exploded, the tent encampment suddenly seemed to vanish. Down in the fort, scrambling U.S. soldiers dismantled the tents, revealing in their place a massive earthwork resembling an ancient snake-like mound. They quickly restaked their tents behind the earthwork and out of sight—and harm—from the British bombardment.

This was the brainchild of Captain Eleazer D. Wood, a recent West Point graduate and army engineer who had helped fortify Governors Island in New York Harbor.* With a deep understanding of firing angles and trajectories and shock dispersion, he had dug what is known as a "traverse"—a trench containing curves and angles to prevent shells or the shock of explosions from traveling its length. What's more, he had hidden the work of digging the traverse behind the tent encampment.

British shells began dropping into the fort, exploding, but the blasts, the shrapnel, the massive twenty-four-pound cannonballs, and the nine-pound balls heated red-hot, were largely absorbed by the traverse, whacking and sizzling into the earth, or passing harmlessly over the heads of soldiers tucked behind the mounded earth or huddled in the muddy burrows they had dug for extra protection. Even the horses remained hidden and unharmed.

Meanwhile, the British artillerists were having a grand time shelling the fort's visible features from their gun emplacements across the river and above, anticipating heavy damage to the U.S. defenses. Young John Richardson watched alongside the British artillerists:

> The fire of the 24-pounder battery was principally directed against the powder magazine, which the besieged were busily occupied in covering and protecting from our hot shot. It was impossible to have artillery better served; every ball that was fired sank into the roof of the magazine, scattering the earth to a considerable distance, and burying many of the workmen in its bed, from whence we could distinctly perceive the survivors dragging forth the bodies of their slaughtered comrades.

---

* The pedestal for the Statue of Liberty is built atop an eleven-pointed star-shaped fortification, formerly named Fort Wood, after Eleazer D. Wood.

Or so it looked from above. British officers, Richardson noted, visited the gun emplacement and asked the artillerists for the chance to touch off the big guns themselves and personally drop a shell straight down on the Americans. In return for this delightful favor, they gave the artillerists a glass of whiskey.

Still, after three days of bombardment and a thousand or so shells and cannonballs launched at and within the stockade, the British had not inflicted much damage to Eleazer Wood's fort. They now tried a new approach—ferrying cannons across the river and setting them only three hundred yards from the stockade walls. But engineer Wood and his troops, working like burrowing animals, busily shoveled up new traverses to protect the fort from that direction.

The siege of Fort Meigs would have ended in a total stalemate if not for the sudden arrival on May 5 of eighteen big flatboats that bounced down the foaming shelves of the Maumee Rapids carrying 1,400 Kentucky troops champing at the bit to fight Native warriors and Brits. With them arrived the chaos of battle. Working by secret courier, Harrison had laid his own plans to surprise the British batteries with these reinforcements. Six of the flatboats landed on the side of the river where Fort Meigs stood. The troops jumped off and, covered by the fort's guns, rushed inside the gates.

The other twelve flatboats with eight hundred troops landed on the river's other bank about two miles above the main British batteries. Under the command of Colonel William Dudley, a forty-six-year-old Kentucky magistrate, they marched toward the batteries in three powerful columns. At the same time across the river, Harrison released from the fort another 350-man detachment of his now-reinforced troops to attack the newer British battery near the stockade. They quickly overran it, capturing forty-one British redcoats. Tecumseh, nearby with his warriors, swiftly counterattacked and retook the battery, inflicting heavy losses on the Americans of thirty dead and ninety wounded. Then, it is said, he swam across the river to help on the other side.

On the bluff opposite the fort, Colonel Dudley's Kentuckians and Ohioans rushed up on the main British batteries with a yell, although the few British defenders had already fled. Colonel Dudley's gung ho Kentuckians, however, still had not seen enough action. Eager to shoot Indians, they noticed warriors taking potshots from the forest. They returned fire, causing the Native warriors to retreat. The eager Kentuckians set off in pursuit—hundreds of militiamen pushing into the forest, shooting, reloading, and pushing forward again, as the warriors, still pausing to shoot back at the Kentuckians, retreated each time a bit deeper into the woods.

One moment they were driving those they considered savages boldly back, and the next the Kentuckians realized they were surrounded. Fire poured in from the woods on all sides. Men dropped, rapidly. George Carter Dale, one of the militiamen, described what he saw next, rushing at him wielding tomahawks and knives: "[Indians rushed in] painted almost every color; their heads tipped with bird wings, huge bunches of feathers, and skins of animals . . . their faces being black as black as coal and grease could make them, the upper and lower lips marked with white stripes."

His wounded comrade had a broken leg and couldn't run. Dale threw a pile of brush and leaves over him and ran. As he did, having thrown aside his musket, he fled past a dead, mangled, scalped Kentuckian, then another downed soldier, still alive but knowing he was doomed. The soldier gave Dale his gun and told him to run.

As Dale looked back, he saw warriors drag his comrade with the broken leg from under the brush pile. They then tomahawked him. Dale did not stay to see what happened next.

The first siege of Fort Meigs ended inconclusively with this May 5 counterattack by the Kentuckians in flatboats. Harrison and his Army of the Northwest managed to hold the fort on the one hand, but Native warriors had lured Dudley's reinforcements into a forest ambush and decimated them. Harrison's forces suffered 135 dead, 188 wounded, and nearly 650 taken prisoner by British troops—for total casualties of nearly one thousand. The prisoners were filed inside the ruins of the old British fort at the Rapids as a makeshift holding area. Carnage erupted when warriors who had showed up too late for the battle but who still wanted a share of the spoils began to shoot and scalp the American prisoners. Tecumseh arrived in the midst of this chaos, raised his tomahawk, and threatened to kill the next warrior who killed or scalped a prisoner. The killing and scalping instantly stopped.

"In any other country," Richardson later wrote, "and governing any other men, Tecumseh would have been a hero; at the head of this uncivilized and untractable people he was a savage; but a savage such as civilization herself might not blush to acknowledge for her child."

CHAPTER 19

THE FLEET IN
THE WILDERNESS

A natural hook of sand—like a mini Cape Cod—projects into Lake Erie from its southern shoreline. For centuries this had provided a sheltered harbor for Native canoes and then voyageurs following the Great Lakes water route into the continent's center. It was at this natural harbor that a merchant captain named Daniel Dobbins insisted that the United States build warships in late 1812 to challenge British naval superiority on Lake Erie, despite all the bureaucratic pushback from U.S. military higher-ups who wanted to build the warships somewhere less remote.

Up to that point, autumn of 1812, the United States had fared poorly in the war it had declared three months earlier on Great Britain. War Hawks in Congress had predicted U.S. troops would sweep into Canada and seize large chunks of it. That had ended in disaster and humiliation on the western frontier—the fall of Fort Detroit under Hull, and the rapid losses of Chicago and Fort Mackinac.

These faltering western defenses left the United States vulnerable to a British-Native invasion by land from the Northwest. The U.S. fortunes also looked grim on the populous East Coast. In early fall 1812, Royal Navy ships blockaded American seaports to choke off trade and strangle the nation's economy. At the time, European powers widely dismissed the U.S. Navy as a proverbial ninety-eight-pound-weakling against the heavyweight British Royal Navy with their nearly one thousand warships mounted with countless cannons against the paltry dozen or so vessels of the American fleet. Several of the U.S. ships, while large and heavily armed, sported innovative designs rendering them fast and maneuverable.

Hopelessly outnumbered in ships, U.S. naval strategists focused on carefully choosing sea battles that might use the few American ships to best advantage. As a result, in that fall of 1812, American vessels faced down His Majesty's bristling warships in a series of one-on-one sea duels that riveted the public attention like a bloody, major league championship series with all its gruesome box scores listing statistics such as numbers of dead and wounded, poundage of cannonballs thrown, and vessels captured, burned to the waterline, or sunk to the deep.[*]

With so much attention focused on Atlantic sea duels and blockaded U.S. ports, it was easy to lose sight of the dire situation on the western frontier. The most astute British and American war strategists, however, understood the crucial importance of the inland waterway formed by the Great Lakes. Whoever controlled that—and especially Lake Erie—controlled the key route to the North American interior.

Captain Dobbins understood this on the most fundamental level. Dobbins had sailed his own small trading vessel, the *Salina*, on the Upper Great Lakes for years, hauling salt to places like Michilimackinac. Cap-

---

[*]

Frolic	vs.	*Wasp*
18 guns		18 guns
Broadside, 262 lbs.		Broadside, 268 lbs
Crew, 92. 75 hors de combat		Crew, 135. 5 killed, 5 wounded
Tonnage, 384		Tonnage, 434

tured by the British at the fall of Michilimackinac Island and Fort Mackinac early in the summer of 1812, he was released, captured again at the
fall of Detroit in August 1812, and released again. He quickly made his
way home to that hook of sand named by the early French "Presque
Isle"—or "almost island"—where recent American settlers had established a village named Erie. As a veteran seaman on the lakes, Dobbins
brought news of the fall of Detroit. With it came his alarming observation
that Lake Erie's entire south shore (the American shore) now lay vulnerable to British ships and invasion. The local militia commander told him
to proceed directly to Washington, D.C., and sound the alarm to President Madison.

This is exactly what Captain Dobbins did, arriving in September
1812 to meet with President Madison and his cabinet. Months earlier,
General Hull had strongly advised Washington authorities of the need
for the United States to have a naval fleet on Lake Erie, in order to maintain supply lines. But nothing had happened. Now, after Hull's disastrous
invasion of Canada and the fall of Detroit, the alarm from Dobbins rang
loudly in War Department ears. With remarkable speed, President Madison authorized four ships and had $2,000 appropriated to start their con-
struction. The secretary of the navy put Dobbins in charge of building
them and choosing the location for the shipyard. The U.S. naval officer in
charge of Lake Erie, however, insisted to Dobbins that it would be impossible to build ships at Presque Isle. Instead, he would refit five merchant
ships at Black Rock naval station at the lake's eastern end.

"I believe I have as perfect a knowledge of this lake as any other man
on it," Dobbins wrote to Lieutenant Jesse Duncan Elliot at Black Rock,
"and I believe this [Presque Isle] is the place for a naval station."

Dobbins carried on, understanding the superiorities of Presque Isle
and constructing new ships there. A shallow sandbar guarded the entrance to the natural harbor and would prevent heavy, deep-drafted British warships from entering and blowing the new shipyard to smithereens

before the U.S. ships could launch. Dobbins also knew that the dense hardwood forests that grew nearly to the Lake Erie shoreline at Presque Isle could provide the timber needed to frame the ships. His plan won out.

Dobbins tried repeatedly to get guidance from Navy higher-ups on what kind of hulls to lay down. He received little response. With $2,000, he hired an expert shipwright, Ebenezer Crosby. Where the foot of the sandy streets of Erie village, population four hundred, met the shoreline of Presque Isle Harbor, the pair laid out two makeshift boatyards. Dobbins and Crosby decided on four stout gunboats, fifty feet long and seventeen feet broad. They started from scratch—hiring blacksmiths to forge the axes out of bits of scrap iron, laborers to fell the huge oaks from the hardwood forest (paying owners one dollar per tree, the equivalent of a day's wage at that time), and horse teams to haul the trunks to the sandy shore. Woodworkers brought from New York and Philadelphia swung away with sharp adzes, chips flying from the fresh, green wood, to shape heavy timbers for the hulls. Lacking enough iron for nails so far out in the wilderness, the shipbuilders instead carved wooden dowels, cranking on hand drills to bore holes through the timber frames, pounding in the dowels—trunnels, in shipbuilder's language—to pin the ships' hulls together.

Everything manufactured had to be sent via river and wilderness path from Pittsburgh or beyond—rope, canvas, paint, cannonballs. Partway through construction, on New Year's Eve, 1812, a naval official appeared with a naval architect. Before leaving the following day after their brief visit, they told Dobbins and Crosby to lengthen the hulls by ten feet and lay down two larger ships—two-masted, twenty-gun brigs of 118 feet in length and 30 feet in beam, with graceful lines like a clipper ship, to be christened USS *Lawrence* and USS *Niagara*. The local Erie courthouse served as a sail loft to spread out and cut the canvas that would billow from their yardarms. At the same time, the navy contracted with a foundry in Georgetown for thirty-seven carronades—short, stout cannons, in this case capable of hurling a volley of thirty-two-pound iron balls into the hull of an opposing ship.*

The hulls for this "Fleet in the Wilderness" took shape on the beach at Presque Isle through the winter of 1813 and into the spring—still half finished, vulnerable, like sea creatures caught out of their watery element. This was the moment to attack, before the ships could launch. The British had the armed ships to destroy them, especially the powerful *Queen Charlotte*, at Amherstburg, 150 miles down the lake on the opposite shore. But Dobbins had chosen wisely. The sandbar blocking the entrance to Presque Isle Harbor had a maximum water depth of six feet while the *Queen Charlotte* had a draft—the depth the hull lies under the water's surface—of twelve feet. She would run aground trying to enter to attack Dobbins's vessels. On the landside, however, the shipyards faced greater peril with the heavy forest extending to the village and water's edge. This left the shipyards exposed to Native attack. And far across the lake at Amherstburg, the British were working furiously in their own shipyards.

The British controlled the waters of Lake Erie, but Procter, at Fort Malden, worried that he might lose his advantage. By now, huge numbers of Native people—warriors and their families, ten thousand or more individuals in all—had gathered and built villages in the region around Amherstburg and Detroit, preparing to go up against the Americans. With so many people gathered so closely, they could not feed themselves only by hunting or fishing or gathering. As winter turned to spring 1813, the corn that could sustain them had barely sprouted. Procter, recently promoted

* The foundry's owner, Henry Foxall, sent the newly forged carronades in fourteen wagons from Washington to Pittsburgh and thence by boat to Erie, pledging that if "the Fleet in the Wilderness" defeated British naval forces on Lake Erie, he would build a new church. It stands to this day as Foundry United Methodist Church on Sixteenth Street, ten blocks due north of the White House in Washington, D.C.

to general, had to keep them fed—mainly with Irish mess pork doled out by his commissariat. His main supply line arrived via boat from Lake Erie's eastern end, more than two hundred miles away. If that line were cut, he knew that he—and all those around him relying on his support— would find themselves in deep trouble.

He had received the intelligence reports of American ships under construction at Presque Isle. To bolster his hold on the lake, Procter set his own shipwrights hard at work not simply on a lake-sized gunboat but a full-scale British Royal Navy warship—HMS *Detroit*. It made Dobbins's first efforts to build fifty-foot boats look puny by comparison—*Detroit* was a "Cruiser-class sloop" ninety-two feet long, weighing three hundred tons, deep hulled and stoutly built to carry twenty guns. Like Dobbins at Presque Isle, the master shipwright at Amherstburg struggled to find skilled craftsmen and had to order heavy guns from Canada's East and have them shipped up Lake Erie. With its sister ship, HMS *Queen Charlotte*, HMS *Detroit* made a formidable pair that matched USS *Lawrence* and USS *Niagara*, both fleets supplemented by smaller merchants turned gunboats and other armed vessels.

The moment hung in the balance as winter turned to spring, then spring toward summer, at this wilderness juncture between the British Empire and the young United States. In this stasis, there arose a sense of foreboding—a naval battle looming. Procter pondered attacking the American shipyards at Presque Isle to destroy this U.S. fleet-to-be while they still remained beached, whale-like skeletons of timber framing overrun with scurrying carpenters.

Tecumseh and Roundhead, however, had other priorities—Fort Meigs, Harrison's stronghold and forward base for his Army of the Northwest on the rapids of the Maumee River. With the clever earthwork of Eleazer Wood's traverse, Harrison had repelled the first Native and British attack on the fort in early May. The U.S. outpost lay only forty miles from the Native villages where warrior families had gathered on the Huron River near Detroit. In order to keep their villages and families safe from an American attack in their absence, Tecumseh and other chiefs urged another assault on Fort Meigs.

Fifty big canoes of warriors paddled from the Upper Great Lakes to bolster the thousands of warriors already gathered early in the summer of 1813 near Detroit. The canoe flotilla, headed by British Indian agent Robert Dickson, brought Ojibwes, Sioux, Menominees, and Winnebagos—all wanting battle and spoils. And they wanted battle now. Just across the Detroit River on the Canadian side, General Procter delayed at Fort Malden, saying he needed troop reinforcements. He tried to convince the chiefs to choose an easier target than the heavy earthworks of Fort Meigs—a target such as the smaller Fort Stephenson about forty miles east of Meigs and on the Sandusky River near Lake Erie's south shore. Also arriving at Fort Malden was the new commander of British naval forces on Lake Erie, Robert Heriot Barclay, who had still other targets in mind.

Tecumseh called Commodore Barclay "Our Father with One Arm," due to his uniform's empty left sleeve. He had joined the Royal Navy as an eleven-year-old Scottish lad. He served under Lord Nelson and, unlike Nelson, survived the Battle of Trafalgar against the French and Spanish fleets but lost his arm in a later sea battle against the French. Instead of attacking Fort Meigs, Commodore Barclay urged General Procter and his Native allies to destroy the American ships under construction at Presque Isle.

A big council gathered at Fort Malden in mid-June to hash out the next target of attack. A British witness to this council, Robert Reynolds, later recalled Tecumseh standing to make a speech in favor of a second attack on Fort Meigs, "calm, cool, deliberate, thinking in look, very hard in what he said."

"Our father has brought us here to take the fort, why don't we take it?" Tecumseh said, with Indian agent Matthew Elliott interpreting. "If his children can't do it, give us spades, and we will work like beavers; we'll eat a way in for him."

He then calmly sat, reported Reynolds, and slowly filled his tomahawk pipe.

Agent Elliott, who had little respect for General Procter, argued with him about the next target. Procter suddenly burst out, "Sir, you are a traitor!"

Elliott instantly reached for his sword, half drew it from its scabbard, and shot back an insult, while Procter reached for his own sword hilt. A duel over honor looked to be in the works. Tecumseh, who may have found it amusing to see his British "father" going at it like this, slowly stood up, Reynolds reported, and casually knocked the spent tobacco out of his tomahawk pipe's bowl.

"What does he say?" Tecumseh asked Elliott.

"Sit down," replied Elliott, putting his hand on Tecumseh's arm. "Never mind what he says."

Other officers stepped between the two British officials, and the tension subsided. But General Procter had shown, not for the first time, his awkwardness as a leader of men.

The second attack on Fort Meigs almost worked. Tecumseh and Roundhead had hatched an elaborate plan to pry the Americans out of the fort's earthworks. General Harrison had left the fort in charge of Green Clay, a general from Kentucky, and moved with two hundred dragoons to an outpost on the Sandusky River to bide his time. War Department orders barred Harrison from mounting any offensive operations against the British until the U.S. fleet at Presque Isle had launched on Lake Erie. By attacking Fort Meigs on the Maumee River, however, Tecumseh and his fellow war chiefs hoped to lure Harrison to rush from the Sandusky River to its relief. But Harrison did not show.

Nor was Tecumseh able to lure General Clay out of Fort Meigs. The chiefs and warriors organized a fake battle in the woods a half mile to the fort's rear, with ferocious shooting and war cries, as if ambushing a relief party coming from Sandusky led by Harrison. They hoped that Clay would let loose a rescue party from Fort Meigs, at which point hundreds of hidden British redcoats would charge through the fort's open gates. Hearing the shooting and war cries, American soldiers on the fort's ramparts grew convinced a battle raged in the woods, and Native forces were being driven back. General Clay, however, held fast inside, having just received a message from Harrison saying he was confident Clay could hold the fort on his own. In other words, he wasn't on the way.

The allied Indian-British forces were eager to fight, but it was as if they had nowhere to go. General Procter proposed again that they attack the smaller and less heavily defended Fort Stephenson, about forty miles away from Fort Meigs, in part to capture its cattle to feed all the mouths at Amherstburg. Tecumseh and other chiefs argued against traveling so far from their women and children, leaving their villages vulnerable to American attack. It was agreed that part of the Native force would stay closer to the villages and part would accompany Procter and his redcoats to attack Fort Stephenson.

This foray ended in disaster for Procter and the British when it became clear that the little garrison of 160 soldiers at Fort Stephenson, under twenty-one-year-old Major George Croghan, would not be intimidated by the approaching British troops and artillery, nor by the hundreds of Native warriors sheltered in the woods. Procter sent a message to Croghan to surrender, or risk massacre at the hands of the waiting "savages."

"When the fort shall be taken, there will be none to massacre," came the reply from Croghan and his officers. "It will not be given up while a man is able to resist."

In a burst of boldness, as if to compensate for his earlier caution, General Procter ordered a direct charge by his redcoats across the fort's dry ditch—eight feet wide and eight feet deep—and upon its stockade walls, after his six-pounder cannons had hammered them from only 250 yards away although without doing much damage. The watching Native warriors thought the plan suicidal and didn't take part. Anticipating just such a charge, young Major Croghan under cover of darkness the previous night, had cleverly concealed his single cannon, packed with a massive load of grapeshot, in one of the fort's blockhouses. It aimed right down the length of the ditch. Late on the afternoon of August 2, 1813, as thunder rumbled in the distance and the impatient Native warriors threatened to leave, Procter gave the order and his redcoats boldly stormed across the ditch at the stockade walls. Croghan gave the counterorder for his men to touch fire to the hidden cannon in the blockhouse. The spray of high-velocity metal shot down the ditch like an invisible paw swatting flat the redcoat charge. Kentucky sharpshooters picked off the stragglers. The toll came to twenty-nine British dead, twenty-eight missing, and forty-four wounded.[*]

Some accounts say that the inexperienced Procter was near to tears at the sudden, startling loss of his men. Writing to his superiors, Procter explained his decision to charge as a means to keep Native forces on the British side, as his superiors had requested. As if to implicate his higher-ups for this bad idea of trying to placate the Native allies, he wrote that he considered the losses of his men "a more than adequate sacrifice . . . to Indian opinion."

Whatever the sacrifice to their opinion, many of the Indian warriors now began to lose confidence in Procter, despite the big guns at his command, after his failures to take any of the forts. Some returned to distant homes on the Upper Lakes; others believed that they had a better chance on the American side.

Harrison now saw an opportunity. Shuttling from fort to fort to orga-

---

[*] In what surely was a heady moment embodying the glory and romance of warfare for a young man of the era, the "Ladies of Chillicothe" presented to George Croghan an elegant ceremonial sword along with a message signed by twenty-nine ladies "impressed with a high sense of your merits as a soldier and gentleman." Croghan wrote a modest and graceful reply, pledging that his "exertions shall be such as never to cause you in the least to regret the honors" conferred on him. "A mark of distinction so flattering and unexpected," he wrote, in what was probably an understatement, "has excited feelings which I cannot express."

nize scattered militiamen and volunteers and anticipating a land attack on the Presque Isle shipyards, he met with Native people who had previously been friendly to the American side, such as Tarhe, a Wyandot chief. He asked them to go to the Wyandot villages at Brownstown in the Michigan Territory and warn the Wyandots who had sided with Roundhead, Tecumseh, and the British that General Harrison would soon arrive with a powerful army and a fleet of U.S. warships. The Wyandots, suggested Harrison, should leave the British and "step forward and take [Harrison] by the hand."

But Roundhead and Tecumseh were at Brownstown and heard Harrison's message, and knew they could still bring at least two thousand warriors to fight—from the Shawnee, Wyandot, Potawatomi, Winnebago, Menominee, and other tribes. The British, with Indian help, still held key points and resources throughout the Upper Great Lakes, including Fort Detroit and Fort Malden, along with warships waiting nearby at Amherstburg. They anticipated the launching of another big ship, the HMS *Detroit*, still under construction. In addition, they possessed the forts at Chicago and Michilimackinac, and Fort St. Joseph at Lake Superior's entrance.

Roundhead made it clear to Tarhe that the British-allied Natives led by Tecumseh and himself would not switch to the American side or become neutral and withdraw. "We are happy to learn your Father [Harrison] is coming out of his hole," he said, "as he has been like a ground hog under ground and will save us much trouble in traveling to meet him."

However, another prominent Wyandot chief, Walk-in-the-Water, privately relayed to the messengers that if Harrison and his army came north and invaded Canada, his warriors would switch sides to join the Americans.

As Procter made his disastrous British attack on U.S. Fort Stephenson, 160 miles to the east Captain Dobbins and shipwright Ebenezer Crosby

prepared to launch the U.S. warships at Presque Isle. A major barrier
loomed in the way—the same sandbar that guarded the natural harbor's
entrance from British attack. Dobbins and Crosby had originally designed
the warships at only fifty feet in length, with a draft of five feet. A five-foot
draft would allow a ship to glide over the six-foot-deep sandbar with one
foot to spare. But when U.S. naval officials showed up and enlarged the
original ship designs, adding two large ones (by lake standards) with a
great deal of firepower, the new hulls would sit much lower in the water.
The draft of the *Lawrence* and *Niagara* measured nine feet in depth.
There was no way they could simply sail out of Presque Isle Harbor.

But Captain Dobbins had that figured out. He instructed his work-
men to construct devices called "camels." Like belting on a giant life
jacket, two barges were maneuvered along each side of the *Lawrence* with
plugs opened in the bottom so they filled with water and partially sank.
Poles were shoved through the gunports of the ship and attached to the
barges. Once the sunken barges and ship had formed a single rigid mass,
workers pumped the water from the barges, so they began to rise higher.
Once fully afloat, they literally lifted the three-hundred-ton ship higher in
the water. With her heavy cannons unloaded to lighten her further, she
was raised just enough to clear the bar and float out into the broad, blue
waters of Lake Erie.

Within a few days, Dobbins and his workers had floated the whole
fleet over the sandbar. British ships appeared several miles offshore, and
British officers studied Presque Isle Harbor through their spyglasses. Apparently due to hazy air and glaring sun, however, they did not realize the
vulnerability in that moment of the unarmed U.S. ships—or surely they
would have sailed closer, blasted them with cannon fire, and captured
them.

Taking command of the U.S. fleet on Lake Erie was a twenty-eight-
year-old veteran of the wars against the Barbary pirates, Oliver Hazard
Perry. An action-ready officer, he had stepped forward for the Lake Erie
command in order to escape a "backwater" posting at Newport, Rhode

Island. He immediately embarked on practice cruises to train a largely green crew of foot soldiers in the complex and precise task of maneuvering and firing a warship in a sea battle. He then sailed his newly constructed fleet to the Bass Islands, an archipelago at Lake Erie's western end where he waited for the British fleet to appear from Amherstburg, thirty miles across the open water.

Nothing happened. No billowing square sails appeared over the lake's horizon. No ships bore down on his fleet with "bones in their teeth"—a mighty, white bow wave crashing with foam and speed. Instead, only empty blue water. Perry waited.

Tecumseh and his warriors at Fort Malden could see the American ships far out in the lake near the islands and wondered why Procter didn't send the British ships under Commodore Robert Barclay to challenge the U.S. fleet.

"From Tecumseh's perspective," writes R. David Edmunds, "the Americans had thrown down the gauntlet and Procter had refused to accept it." Still more Native leaders questioned Procter's leadership and some, including Walk-in-the-Water, began to switch their loyalties to the American side.

But Procter had suffered delays. At the Amherstburg shipyards, craftsmen worked furiously to complete the *Detroit*. The master shipbuilder, William Bell, had worked meticulously and constructed a formidable vessel—a true Royal Navy warship. He faced many of the same problems as the Americans, using green timber and lacking skilled craftsmen, but the biggest was armaments. The big cannons destined for HMS *Detroit* had been captured en route by the Americans in fighting at York on Lake Ontario. Making matters more urgent still, Perry's fleet now sailing on Lake Erie out at the Bass Islands had cut Amherstburg's supply line. Provisions ran low at a stunning rate, given the ten to fifteen thousand mouths to feed in the nearby Indigenous villages. Something had to be done immediately, so Barclay finally took the long-range cannons off Fort Malden's walls and mounted them into the *Detroit*'s gunports.

.   .   .

Early on the brilliant blue day of September 10, 1813, lookouts on Perry's ships at Put-in-Bay in the Bass Islands spotted the British fleet bearing down on them from the Canadian shore, six vessels with sails bellying on a light wind. Perry gave the command for his nine ships and gunboats, including the powerful *Lawrence* and *Niagara*, to sail out to meet them. He ordered each of his American ships to match a like-sized British ship and then pull in close—the idea being to simply overpower the enemy ship in fierce, face-to-face combat, a literal duel to the death. The previous night, Perry had quoted the British admiral Horatio Nelson to sum up his strategy: "If you lay your enemy close alongside, you cannot be out of your place. Goodnight."

In naval warfare fashion, each fleet swung into formation, the British ships forming a line, and the *Detroit*, using a "long gun" taken from the ramparts of Fort Malden, opening fire on the American fleet at a distance of one and a half miles. That first big ball splashed into the lake short of its target.

As the breeze shifted to the south, now coming off the American shore, it gave Perry an advantage. He ordered the decks sprinkled with wet sand to give his men's feet traction in the blood about to spill. The two parallel lines converged, opening fire on each other with long guns and heavy short-range carronades that fired massive cannonballs designed to crush ships' hulls.

Unlike so much of the current era of drones and missiles and laser-guided projectiles, this was in-your-face warfare. It strains the modern imagination to picture the sheer noise and chaos of a close-range sea battle like this, fought with ponderous sailing ships, and the incredible violence of 117 cannons on fifteen vessels carrying nearly one thousand men, firing directly into one another with sheets of flame and great billows of smoke. Cannonballs ripping through the air, tearing through canvas sails, shredding ropes and rigging, shattering gaping holes into thick oak planking, ripping limbs from sailors, or sweeping them away in an instant. Captains shouting commands, men hauling on lines, swiveling the big yardarms to move the sails as the ships try to maneuver, cutting off the enemy and positioning their guns to deadliest advantage. The day is bright and sunny and the wind blows gently, propelling the ships slowly, but determining all.

Captain Barclay commanded the British fleet from his flagship *Detroit*. A ball whistled across the ship's deck and tore off his leg, and another projectile wounded his remaining arm. Yet he and his officers had managed to maneuver their two big warships into position to fire direct broadsides into Perry's flagship, the *Lawrence*, one after the other. Inexplicably, Perry's other big warship, the *Niagara*, lingered toward the rear of his battle line, giving him no help.

Broadside after broadside tore into the *Lawrence*, literally smashing the ten cannons on her starboard side from their mountings, blasting holes in her hull, slicing through the lines that held her masts and rigging aloft. She was finished—no longer able to maneuver—a sitting target in the water.

Perry, still perplexed by why the *Niagara* sat mysteriously out of the action, realized she was unharmed. He called for a small boat from his shattered vessel and oarsmen to propel it, jumped in, and ordered them to row with everything they had to the *Niagara*. With him, he took the battle flag from the *Lawrence*. The ladies of the village had sewn it the night before out of a piece of muslin nine feet square. At Perry's request, they embroidered it with letters a foot high memorializing the last words of his dear late friend Captain James Lawrence, for whom Oliver Hazard Perry had christened the now-shattered U.S. flagship.

Perry stood upright in the rowboat, the men madly pulling at the oars, with the blue battle flag defiantly wrapped around him as the rowboat passed through a flurry of British cannon fire trying to take him down.

It read, *"Don't give up the ship."*

CHAPTER 20

IN THE HANDS
OF THE GREAT SPIRIT

The heavy thuds of the ships' cannons rolled across the placid water all the way to Amherstburg and Fort Malden on the Canadian shore, thirty miles off. Hearing the first distant booms, Tecumseh jumped into his canoe at the Fort Malden waterfront, according to some accounts, and paddled the three miles downstream to where the Detroit River opened into the lake in hopes of seeing the battle's shifts and turns. British officers hurried from the fort to nearby hilltops along the lakefront, spyglasses in hand. Mushrooming billows of white smoke flowered over the water like low, distant clouds, obscuring all, while it rumbled with a constant thunder.

After nearly three hours, in midafternoon, the thunder suddenly stopped. The smoke lingered, in silence. Tecumseh could not see who had won, if anyone at all. Looking through his glass atop the bluff, it appeared to one British officer that Commander Barclay had won. But he couldn't be sure.

Over the next two days, a strange atmosphere fell over Fort Malden.

No British ships returned from the distant battle. No British officer announced to the gathered Native forces and troops the outcome, or even whether the outcome remained unknown. There was no news at all.

Tecumseh had nothing to tell the nearly ten thousand assembled Natives—warriors and their families—in wigwams at Grosse Isle and Bois Blanc Island. Food was running low. Sister Tecumpease was there at Grosse Isle, with all the family's belongings and horses, with her husband, Wahsikegaboe, and Tecumseh's son, Paukeesaa, now seventeen, having moved from the Wabash headwaters with other Shawnee families.

Tecumpease had watched her now-forty-five-year-old younger brother's ascent into leadership from the time he was a child of twelve. She had helped steer that ascent and, as a female chief, had brought Shawnee women and families along in support of his movement. But now he could tell her nothing. It was as if his life's work, her life's work, the fate of their people, hovered over a deep chasm. Would they pass to the other side?

They had unified the tribes to stop the land encroachments by the Americans. They had started a movement spanning north to south, across the continent from Canada to the Gulf of Mexico, and east to west from the Appalachian Mountains to the Great Plains. She had lived longer than her younger brother, through more of the changes that came when whites entered their world. With the French, the Shawnee world had remained in balance. When the British arrived so had uncertainty. And yet still the rhythms of village life had gone on. At Chillicothe, she had helped her mother grow the corn and weave the wigwams; had observed the ceremonies of the Bread Dance and the I-la-ni-wag-a-way—the male dance for warriors—and the thanksgiving ceremony in the fall. She had taken part in the intimate choreography of the everyday. The females embodied the power of creation that brought that world to life, over and over, despite the never-ending press of destruction.

Since her girlhood, she had watched the men go off to war—first her father to fight Lord Dunmore's Long Knives coming over the mountains.

He had not returned. Then came the night raids on Chillicothe by the Kentuckians on their horses. Her mother had left. Tecumpease became the one woman in charge of caring for her younger brothers, her own children, her husband. The fighting went on, against the Kentuckians, year after year. Then one brother, Chiksika, had not returned. Her brothers kept fighting, joining Blue Jacket and Little Turtle's warriors to destroy St. Clair's army. And then Wayne, the American general who never sleeps, came after them. At the great council at Greenville, the Americans had promised to leave the tribes in peace, had said no more settlers would clear Indigenous lands. But every year, Harrison took more. Finally, he brought his Long Knives to the village they had built on the Tippecanoe far from whites, where they had planted the Three Sisters up and down the river plain, and he burned it.

The British, again, had promised to take them by the hand, and so they had moved yet again, now to Grosse Isle, to this island between. With the thunder of the big ships' guns across the lake, the British father and the American father were fighting it out, and the Native people on this island in the river between two countries claimed by white men were left with their fate hanging in the balance.

No answer was forthcoming.

It was not until four days after the lake battle that Native messengers rushed from Fort Malden to the sprawling wigwam encampments on the river islands. General Procter was packing up his belongings in trunks. British soldiers cut apart the stockade walls and toppled them into the dry ditch around the fort. It appeared the British were preparing to run.

Perry had made his escape from the shattered *Lawrence* aboard the little rowboat with his battle flag wrapped around his body, serving as a flagpole.

Through whistling balls and shot, the rowboat survived the half-mile journey to the USS *Niagara*, which inexplicably lagged out of action behind the rest of the U.S. fleet, and then moved ahead of it. Perry climbed aboard the ship. He sent its commander off in a rowboat to direct the smaller vessels and ordered the *Niagara* to bear directly toward the big British warships, *Detroit* and *Queen Charlotte*. A favorable wind now rose from the American shore, propelling the *Niagara* toward the enemy battle line with her prow churning up a white wave.

Cannon fire had quieted. Commander Barclay assumed that when Perry deserted the *Lawrence*, he had surrendered the flagship, leaving Barclay the victor. Now he realized his mistake. The *Niagara* was bearing down on him on a good breeze, cannons loaded, and trailing a V-wake. The one-armed British commander, now also missing a leg but still conscious, ordered *Detroit* and *Queen Charlotte* to swing into position to intercept *Niagara* and blast the oncoming American ship with devastating broadsides of simultaneous cannon fire. Both British ships, however, had suffered damage to their rigging and did not respond agilely to Barclay's commands. Lacking enough experienced sailors from the start, they had now lost many of their officers to combat.

The two big British ships drifted toward each other, their hundreds of tons of oak and iron and cannonballs inexorably propelled by momentum and lake breeze. With a shrill ripping of canvas, squealing of ropes, and clunking of heavy wood, they collided, interlocking their rigging into a nest of tangled lines and cockeyed yardarms. They drifted aimlessly, unable to swing about and point their guns.

Oliver Hazard Perry at the command of the *Niagara* came at them, cutting across their bows. As he did, he unleashed thundering broadsides at close range. A broadside from the other side of his ship kept the smaller British gunboats from approaching. Like a hungry animal defending its prey in order to consume it, he polished off the *Detroit* and *Queen Charlotte*. Wrote John Richardson of the moment:

Captain Finnis, commanding the *Queen Charlotte*, was killed by a round shot . . . and the same ball carried off Lieutenant Garden, a promising young officer of the Newfoundland Regiment, mingling the blood of the one and the brains of the other, on the bulwark, in one melancholy and undistinguishable mass.... The decks were literally filled with the wounded; and such was the crippled state of the *Detroit*, that not a mast was left standing: almost all the guns were dismounted, and it was impossible to place a hand on that side which had been exposed to the enemy's fire, without covering part of a wound, either from grape, canister, or round shot.

The battle was over in three hours. An hour later, Perry scribbled out his dispatch from the deck of the *Niagara*, writing in pencil on the back of an old envelope pressed against his stiff hat as an impromptu desk. He sent it by express messenger with all possible haste to General Harrison.

Dear General,

We have met the enemy and they are ours. Two ships, two brigs, one schooner and one sloop.

Yours with great respect and esteem,

O. H. Perry

When the messengers arrived at the wigwam camps four days after the battle with the news that Procter was packing his trunks and ordering troops to destroy Fort Malden, it was clear to Tecumseh that the one-armed Barclay had lost, the Americans had captured the British fleet, and Procter was preparing to retreat deeper into Canada.

Tecumseh angrily confronted one of Procter's officers, demanding to know Procter's plans. He received no answer.

It enraged him that Procter was even considering a retreat without making a stand, as it enraged hundreds—thousands—of other warriors on the islands. Fury erupted through the camps. Tecumseh had urged warriors and families to move here, closer to the British stronghold, with the promise that they would receive their own homelands under British protection. Now the British, seeming to walk away from the promise, wanted to retreat. Feeling betrayed, some of the warriors urged turning on the British to attack them in revenge. Tecumseh calmed them, but, furious himself, demanded that Indian agent Matthew Elliott arrange a council with General Procter.

It took place on September 18, 1813, in the big council house on Fort Malden's grounds. Used at times as a warehouse, its high, vaulted ceilings enclosed a dim, spacious interior. The Battle of Lake Erie had occurred eight days previous, and the participants still did not officially know its outcome. Nor had General Procter revealed any of his plans. Tecumseh brought with him a big wampum belt that symbolized the lasting friendship between the Native peoples and British, its embroidered beads portraying a hand at each of the belt's two ends and a heart in the belt's middle, uniting the two in lasting friendship. Tecumseh had determined that, if necessary, he would slash the belt in two and throw it at Procter's feet.

The many chieftains gathered and sat in the center of the big council house while the British officers stood along the walls, recalled John Richardson, who stood among them. Standing in the center, Procter addressed them.

He told them that the British fleet had been lost. He told them that William Henry Harrison was amassing a large American army to invade Canada. And he told them that he planned to abandon Amherstburg, Detroit, and Fort Malden, and leave this part of Canada to the American general Harrison. He would retreat eastward several hundred miles to Niagara and the head of Lake Ontario and join with the British stationed there. Tecumseh and his warriors were welcome to come along.

Tecumseh had devoted his entire life to this moment. He came from a line of famous warriors, and a father and older brother who told him never to give in. Since his teens, he had fought battle after battle, at a distance with musket, at close quarters with tomahawk and war club, against the relentless American drive to take Indigenous lands and give them to white settlers. He had become a warrior, a leader of warriors. He had traveled thousands of miles to recruit distant tribes, given countless speeches to persuade former Native enemies to join his confederacy. He had fostered a vision created by earlier war chiefs—a united confederacy of tribes—and made it a reality. He had brought the concept of central authority, matching white central authority. He had countered the white concept of land as inviolable property that belonged to individuals with the Indigenous idea of land held in common. He had tried endless diplomatic approaches with the Americans, and Harrison in particular, to reach a compromise over their claims to the continent's center. He had worked with the British, over and over, as they approached him to make alliances, as they urged him to stand firm against America's westward push, as they encouraged him to create an Indian barrier state to stop the United States from spreading across North America.

And he had succeeded. He and his confederacy, had, with British support, stopped the American push west—taking Detroit, Chicago, and the Upper Great Lakes at Michilimackinac Island and Fort Mackinac. They had made their great stand.

And after that, all that, British general Henry Procter was telling Tecumseh and his hundreds of assembled warriors, in effect, *We're done.* We're leaving all this land, these thousands of miles, to the Americans. We're going back East to our friends. Join us if you want. We'll feed you while supplies last.

When General Procter had finished, Tecumseh rose in front of the hundreds of sitting warriors, with their tomahawks and knives and war clubs, their war paint and bear claw necklaces. Lean, wiry, strong, carrying himself with an upright and soft-stepping grace, he wore his fringed deerskin shirt and leggings that revealed his compact physique, and moccasins. A plume of white ostrich feathers arched down over his forehead and over his piercing, coal-black eyes, giving his dark features, John Richardson recorded, "a singularly wild and terrific expression."

His presence provoked awe. "It was evident," wrote Richardson, "that he could be terrible."

Samuel Saunders interpreted. Holding aloft the wampum belt, gesturing to its symbols to mark his points, Tecumseh began to speak in thundering tones:

> Father, Listen to your children! You see them now all before you. The war before this, our British father gave the hatchet to his red children when our old chiefs were alive. They are now all dead. In that war, our father was thrown on his back by the Americans, and our father took them by the hand without our knowledge, and we are afraid our father will do so again at this time. . . .
>
> Listen! When [this current] war was declared, our father stood up and gave us the tomahawk, and told us that he was now ready to strike the Americans—that he wanted our assistance; and that he would certainly get us our lands back. . . .
>
> Listen! You told us . . . to bring forward our families to this place. . . . You promised to take care of them, and that they should want for nothing, while the men would go and fight the enemy. . . .
>
> Father—Listen! Our fleet has gone out; we know they have fought; we have heard the great guns; but know nothing of what has happened to our father with one arm. Our ships have gone one way, and we are much astonished to see our father tying up everything and preparing to run away the other, without letting his red children know what his intentions are. You always told us to remain here and take care of our lands; it made our hearts glad to hear that was your wish. Our great father, the king, is our head, and you represent him. You always told us you would never draw your foot off British ground; but now, father, we see you are drawing back, and we are sorry to see our father doing so without seeing the enemy. We must compare our father's conduct to a fat animal, that carries its tail upon its back, but

when affrighted, it drops it between its legs and runs off. [Laughter erupted from both Indian warriors and British soldiers.]

Listen, father! The Americans have not yet defeated us by land; neither are we sure that they have done so by water; we therefore wish to remain here, and fight our enemy, should they make their appearance. If they defeat us, we will then retreat with our father. At the [Battle of Fallen Timbers], last war, the Americans certainly defeated us; and when we retreated to our father's fort at that place, the gates were shut against us. We were afraid that it would now be the case; but instead of that we now see our British father preparing to march out of his garrison.

Father! You have got the arms and ammunition which our great father sent for his red children. If you have any idea of going away, give them to us, and you may go in welcome, for us. Our lives are in the hands of the Great Spirit. We are determined to defend our lands, and if it is his will, we wish to leave our bones upon them.

Tecumseh concluded his speech. The instant he spoke the last words, Richardson reported, the feathered chiefs and painted warriors leapt to their feet, wielding their tomahawks in the air. Their piercing war cries reverberated against the high, vaulted ceiling to create a deafening din inside the big council house, while British officers and soldiers, neatly dressed in their uniforms, looked on from around the walls. It took some time for Agent Elliott to restore calm.

Tecumseh gazed into the bed of orange coals and yellow flames of the campfire, dancing in the October night, as if in their depthless glow he could see far into the past, and into the future. His warriors were with him around the campfire, along with many more out in the autumnal darkness. The whole continent spread out before him, its forests rolling away

toward the east, over the Appalachians, to the Atlantic. The tribes there—
the Wampanoag, the Nanticoke, the Powhatan, and others—had greeted
those first great sailing ships from across the sea with a wavering blend of
hospitality and hostility, but always finally accommodated, accommodated, accommodated, until the white settlers making their homes on
tribal lands pushed the tribes themselves to the west, to the foot of the
mountains, and then over the mountains. Many finally scattered or simply disappeared. The whites had followed them, taken their and their ancestors' hunting grounds, and pushed them, until there was nowhere
farther to go.

This was it. This was the stopping point.

This moment was not his choice. He would not have retreated and
would have fought sooner. But Procter, like the fat animal with its tail
dropped between its legs, wanted to retreat all the way to the East to Niagara and give up these lands to Harrison's army—these lands and this
world Tecumseh had fought so hard to keep. He and Procter had argued
back at Fort Malden. General Procter had unfurled his maps on the table
in his quarters, and with his finger traced for Tecumseh the dwindling options. When Captain Perry's American fleet had captured Captain Barclay's British fleet, the Americans had cut General Procter's supply line
by water on Lake Erie. The alternative supply route through the woods
north of the lake presented problems even more daunting.

One writer of the period, William Foster Coffin, remembered the difficulties of travel through that kind of forested Canadian wilderness and
the obstacles facing Procter in moving people and provisions through it,
whether supplying his army overland or retreating on foot.

> Whether for advance or for retreat, the by-paths of the forest . . . were
> such as the macadamized and locomotive imagination of the present
> day cannot encompass. A backwoodsman, laden with his axe, wading
> here, ploutering there, stumbling over rotted trees, protruding stumps,

a bit of a half submerged corduroy road for one short space—then an adhesive clay bank—then a mile, or two, or more, of black muck swamp,—may possibly, clay-clogged and footsore, and with much pain in the small of his back, find himself by sundown at the foot of a hemlock or cedar, with a fire at his feet, having done manfully about ten miles for his day's work.

And that was for a single male, largely unencumbered, not a soldier with a sixty-pound pack of supplies and ammunition, not to mention women, children, arms, and all the other accoutrements of a traveling army. The Battle of Lake Erie had left General Procter and his army stranded, out here alone in the forested wilderness of the North American heartlands, without support.

Tracing over Procter's maps, Tecumseh well understood the problems of geography and terrain (although his people were surely more adept at forest travel). But he disagreed with Procter's choice. Regardless of supply line issues, instead of retreating and abandoning Fort Malden and Detroit, quitting these lands and this life, the moment had come to make a stand against the advancing General Harrison and his three thousand American troops and cavalry.

After much discussion, Procter and Tecumseh and other war chiefs had finally reached a compromise. They would retreat from Fort Malden on Lake Erie and travel about fifty miles eastward into Canada's interior, establish fortifications at a defensible spot on the Thames River, and, if the Americans pursued them, make a stand there.

So, they had retreated eastward, everyone, some three thousand Native people, including the women and children and his own sister Tecumpease, loading the family's belongings on horses and moving up the Thames. British troops had gone first, with the Native people trailing behind—880 British regulars and more than 1,500 Native warriors, from at least a dozen Indigenous nations. Procter traveled ahead of the army, riding at times in his carriage rather than on horseback, to the shock of warriors who saw little evidence of a battle leader in a white man at rest in a wheeled conveyance.

Harrison and his American army had already started in hard pursuit. Procter had lost the luxury of time due to his secrecy and indecision. It was more than a week after the Battle of Lake Erie before Procter agreed to a council forced by Tecumseh, and another week passed before Native and British troops left Fort Malden and the wigwam villages en masse to head for the Canadian interior. On September 27, two and a half weeks after the Battle of Lake Erie, the last British lookouts near the abandoned Fort Malden spotted a fleet of sails coming across the lake.

These were the ships that had survived the lake battle. Along with smaller boats sailing and rowing beside them, they now carried Harrison's five thousand American troops to the Canadian shore. With spectacular coordination, one hundred landing boats manned with oarsmen lined up side by side, each craft twenty-five yards apart, stretching nearly two miles in breadth. At the firing of a signal gun at four P.M., they rowed in unison toward the beach, expecting to face Native warriors and British troops charging over the tops of the sand dunes at the American soldiers wading through the shallows and storming the beach.

"The landing of our army . . . surpassed anything of the kind ever witnessed," wrote one American officer. "All of our boats landed at one and the same time. In less than 2 minutes after the first boat struck the shore, no less than 4,000 troops and 6 pieces of artillery all landed, completely formed in a line of battle."

Fifty miles into the Canadian interior, Tecumseh arrived at the spot upstream on the Thames River where he and Procter had agreed to make a stand. He was astounded to find the British had done nothing at all to reinforce the place, known as the Forks of the Thames. British cannons lay scattered about, as if waiting for someone to assemble them, and a hut contained a store of small arms, but no palisades, no earthworks, no gun emplacements—nothing to suggest that Procter intended to make a stand here.

And he didn't. After vacillating with indecision, he had gone ahead to a hamlet several miles deeper into the interior and farther up the Thames, thinking it a better spot.

Tecumseh erupted in rage. He and his Native warriors felt utterly betrayed by British promises to stand firm. In anger and chaos, Tecumseh met with fellow chiefs and decided to retreat to the hamlet, Moraviantown, a few miles farther upriver, where Procter might be forced to stick to his agreement.

Scouts reported the quick advance of the American army. Harrison was riding at the head of three thousand men coming up the bank of the Thames, including one thousand mounted Kentucky volunteers under Colonel Richard Mentor Johnson, an outspoken War Hawk in the U.S. Congress. The Native warriors set an ambush and fought a skirmish against the mounted Kentuckians, attempting to delay the American advance so the 2,400 Native women and children, now running out of food, could reach Moraviantown and British provisions there.

Already some warriors and chiefs had started to drift away from the great retreat.

At seven P.M. on October 4, 1813, Colonel Johnson summoned officers together at their army camp. "Gen. Harrison soon came up and directed us to furnish ourselves with beef for a forced march tomorrow," recorded one American officer. "He was determined if possible to bring them to a stand."

The two rivals, Tecumseh and Harrison, sat that night in the dancing light of campfires only a few miles apart. They both knew that tomorrow would be the day they squared off face-to-face, as Tecumseh had predicted two years earlier in the walnut grove at Grouseland. If the Great Spirit didn't put enough sense in the great chief Madison's head so that he would give up the contested lands, "you and I will have to fight it out."

Now that moment had arrived. There were the practical issues—the logistics, the order of battle, the arraying of warriors, soldiers, cavalry, cannons. They let their minds run over the terrain, envisioning every advantageous spot in river, forest, swamp, meadow, hillock, thinking through every place where their rival might set a trap. One imagines they thought of their families, and their people, the thousands they each led, with the life and values each group embraced.

And they thought of each other, perhaps even with a flash of sentimentality, of the life that ironically bound them to each other. It was their destiny. The Great Creator—or Providence—had set Tecumseh and Harrison, two leaders, two warriors, against each other, each fighting for a people and a vision that would determine what America would become.

But especially they wondered how the other thought in this moment. What kind of feints, or ruses, or full-on attacks might the other employ to prevail? What kind of warriors, or weaponry, or tactics of courage and fear? How would the other try to embolden his men and strike terror in the enemy?

Both Tecumseh and Harrison gazed into the coals. This is where it had all led.

"Father, tell your men to be firm and all will be well," Tecumseh said to General Procter, as they arrayed their men in battle formation along the Thames River.

The British troops and Native warriors had stopped about two miles short of Moraviantown. Procter had hoped to make his stand there, but General Harrison and his troops had marched hard, closing in on the British. On the morning of October 5, General Procter and Tecumseh decided to position their warriors and troops in an advantageous spot and face the American army. Procter stretched his redcoats in two lines perpendicular from the riverbank, across the wagon road, where he placed a single six-pounder cannon facing down the track, and into the woods beyond. Tecumseh arrayed his eight hundred Native warriors—the force now diminished by warriors and chiefs who sensed the futility of the fight and had simply left—in a dense cedar swamp where, they hoped, the hooves of the one thousand mounted Kentuckians would bog in the mud.

Tecumseh unbelted his sword and gave it to a fellow warrior, asking that it be kept for his seventeen-year-old son, Paukeesaa, if ever he grew up to be a warrior. With his white ostrich plume bobbing, he climbed out of the swamp to check once more on the British troops. Perhaps he sensed reticence in Procter. The general recognized that he was badly wanted by Americans, that they blamed Procter for instigating the torturing, scalping, and death of American prisoners by Native warriors in earlier battles, even paying for scalps.

"Remember the River Raisin!" had become the battle cry of the revenge-bent Kentuckians. Now they approached. Procter could imagine how he might be treated if they captured him—in like fashion.

"Father," Tecumseh encouraged Procter, "have a big heart!"

Tecumseh walked along the British line, recalled John Richardson, and pressed the hand of every British officer. He then disappeared into the swamp to join his warriors. General Harrison's 3,500-man army came marching up the wagon road, the Kentuckians thirsty to engage the Native Americans, and spotted the British line and cannon.

Harrison, eyeing the river to his right and the swamp to his left, had a good guess that the swamp concealed Indian warriors. He ordered his foot soldiers to advance slowly toward it, giving it caution and respect. At the same time, he ordered the first battalion of his cavalry to charge directly at the British lines holding the road, as if he sensed a weakness or lack of commitment to face death for the Native cause.

He gave the command. The cavalry thundered up the road, accompanied by bugle blasts and battle cries. As they closed, Procter gave the command for his British soldiers. The front line of redcoats erupted in flashes and smoke as it fired a volley in unison, then dropped to a knee as the rear line fired a volley. But still the charging horses came on, some knocking aside the redcoats and smashing through the lines, others sweeping off to the sides and around the ends.

The British lines suddenly broke into hundreds of running fragments of red. Some redcoats simply surrendered. After a moment's attempt to rally his troops, crying out and waving his sword, General Procter turned his horse's tail to the action and galloped away up the road, gulped down a few swallows of water at Moraviantown two miles away, and kept going. The British had not lingered long enough even to fire their single cannon before the Americans captured it.

Richard Mentor Johnson rallied his horsemen. Leading a charge of twenty mounted Kentucky volunteers, with many more foot soldiers coming behind him, he went crashing into the swamp after the Native leader and his warriors. As his advance guard bogged in muck and thick brush, Tecumseh's forces opened fire from their hiding places.

The two sides exchanged intense gunfire amid the tangle. Tecumseh took a wound. The horsemen pulled back to higher ground. Tecumseh had shot a Kentuckian mounted on a fine horse, with a cocked hat, draped with an elaborate wampum belt. Believing it to be Harrison, he advanced to scalp his great rival and the author of so many Native people's woes. As he did, a Kentuckian fired a gun loaded with a musket ball and buckshot. Tecumseh took the ball squarely in the chest. He fell, dead.

Word quickly spread along the Native lines of Tecumseh's death. Some accounts say the warriors gave a deafening cry, "the loudest yells I ever heard from human beings," and retreated. They had lost their leader and along with him their fighting spirit. Soon the battle ended, with Americans and Native forces each having lost about thirty men killed or wounded. The British casualty rate made clear the magnitude of the disaster for Procter—634 men killed or captured.

The battle had lasted only about forty minutes. The War of 1812, however, would lurch onward—in fits and starts, defeats and victories, in battles scattered across the continent all the way to the Mississippi River and Gulf Coast. Even a year after Tecumseh's death, a kind of roving stalemate shrouded the conflict. Amid the seesawing action, British troops torched the U.S. Capitol in August 1814, but just three weeks later U.S. troops stood firm under the Royal Navy's nighttime bombardment of Baltimore's Fort McHenry, the standoff inspiring Francis Scott Key's poem that became "The Star Spangled Banner."

Nor did Tecumseh's legacy end in the swamp beside the Thames. His spirit still burned brightly in the South and West. The message he had delivered in person—to unify and hold the land together—inspired the Creeks' Red Stick warriors, supported by the British and Spanish, to fight U.S. militias bent on taking swathes of the Southeast. To the west, along the Mississippi, unified Sauk, Fox, and Kickapoo forces who had taken part in Tecumseh's movement reclaimed much of the Illinois Territory and Wisconsin regions William Henry Harrison had tricked them out of a decade earlier. At the same time, a Royal Navy fleet aimed toward the mouth of the Mississippi and New Orleans with plans to wrest the Louisiana Purchase away from the United States.

It appeared that an Indian barrier state could still block U.S. westward expansion—and that's where things stood when the war simply ended.

EPILOGUE

We Indians . . . perhaps the Master of Life would give us more luck if we stick together as we formerly did. . . . [We] might go back and tread again upon our own lands . . . since our great chief Tecumtha has been killed we do not listen to one another. We do not rise together.

—CHIEF NAIWASH of the Ottawa, second chief in the
Battle of the Thames, speaking in the 1840s

The wonder is not that he did not succeed, but that he was enabled to accomplish so much.

—BENJAMIN DRAKE, *The Life of Tecumseh, and
His Brother the Prophet* (1841)

oday in the Smithsonian Institution's National Portrait Gallery gleams a brilliantly white marble statue of Tecumseh sculpted by Ferdinand Pettrich in 1856, forty or so years after Tecumseh's death. Titled *The Dying Tecumseh*, it is less a literal representation of Tecumseh than a moment in the nation's history frozen for the ages in a single striking image. For its white American viewers, the statue both celebrates and mourns a glorious warrior fallen to the earth, prone, clutching the shaft of his tomahawk like a staff to support his torso from settling into its final resting place—struggling, still alive, a heroic warrior about to die, nobly, and with dignity. It connotes the death of something much greater than just this individual warrior—the supposed end of a noble but doomed people.

For the first thirty years after Tecumseh's death, no commissioned sculptor would have proposed this heroic rendering of the famous Shawnee leader. Rather than nobility, a sculpted Tecumseh would have represented bloody violence and inhuman cruelty. It would take several decades for the United States to win its final battles against the Native tribes occupying the North American continent, and for the possibility of viewing the Native resistance as anything but something to be destroyed to emerge. Until then, the specter of Tecumseh, or some new rising leader who could unify the tribes, posed a direct threat to the nation's vision of westward expansion. Native Americans could be seen as "noble" only in defeat.

Even after death Tecumseh remained a foreboding image for whites. For many of the Indigenous peoples of the continent, however, Tecumseh represented something far brighter, as luminescent as the sculptor's marble—a vision of unity, strength, and hope.

Neither Britain nor the United States won the War of 1812, but it soon became clear that Native nations lost. After two and a half years of battles up and down the continent, the two powers had failed to vanquish the other—or even gain decisive advantage. In the autumn of 1814—one year after Tecumseh's death along the Thames River—British and American negotiators sat down together and hashed out a cease to hostilities while outlining possible terms of settlement. Britain and the United States basically called it a draw. Each nation would revert to the North American boundaries that had prevailed at the time the war began. For Britain and the United States, in terms of territory, *nothing had changed.*

Not so for Indigenous tribes. They lost enormously—territorially, politically, culturally. As in the past, when it worked to Great Britain's advantage, she had backed these nations against the United States. When it no longer worked in her favor, she deserted them. It had happened in the peace settlement after the Revolution—*Britain sold the Indians to Congress,* Joseph Brant had protested; again when the British gates remained shut fast to Native warriors at Fallen Timbers, and still again with Procter's retreat into Canada and his abandonment of Tecumseh's forces at the Battle of the Thames. Now, again, in the peace negotiations ending the War of 1812, the commitment that Tecumseh's allied tribes had made to the British came to naught. Because of the Native-British alliance, the United States felt it had all the more reason to punish Indigenous tribes or drive them out.

In peace talks with the United States, Britain asked for an Indian barrier state starting at the Greenville Line that would remain the sole possession of the tribes, as British authorities had promised Tecumseh they would during the war. In effect, this would push the frontier of white American settlement back eastward to its location in 1795, around the middle of Ohio. U.S. negotiators flatly rejected the idea, and, in yet another betrayal, the British relented.

Unlike the American Revolution, which carved out the physical boundaries of a new nation, little territory was gained or lost in the War of 1812. But it became a "second war of independence" in other ways.

The war and its conclusion sent a strong message from the United States to European powers: *Either lay off, or expect us to fight back*—not unlike a maturing adolescent who stands up to their parents. At least that was the American perspective. The British pretended not to really care.

The war did much to forge an American identity—an identity celebrated as one shaped by the frontier. It told Americans that they were independent, rugged, self-made, had started with nothing. Americans came to think of themselves as *Can do!* people energized by a dynamism distinct from an exhausted Old Europe mired in tradition.

The mythology contains some truth. Americans can be bold and innovative, although it is a flagrant self-deception for Americans to believe they are entirely self-made. They did not do it all on their own. The nation got its start with a great deal of capital, in the form of land. Many of its early arrivals benefited hugely from the free labor of enslaved workers. Native peoples sacrificed their lands to these newcomers' prosperity and to the economic and global strength America enjoys these many years later.

William Henry Harrison was pivotal in unleashing the gritty, relentless forces that powered the westward movement. In his Harrison Land Act of 1800, he engineered a process encoded in law by Congress to acquire huge tracts of land from the Indigenous people for little money—or, depending on one's point view, to steal it or cheat them out of it—and then sell it in small lots, cheaply and largely on credit, to poor whites from the crowded East eager to start a new life as independent farmers. This proved to be a magical formula. The frontier of land acquisition and settlement shifted west with amazing speed—sweeping from the Greenville Line in the middle of Ohio, across Indiana, and into Illinois toward the Mississippi—until Tecumseh rose to stop it. Their two visions clashed along a seam that ran down the center of the continent.

Harrison would eventually realize his ambition to rise to the halls of power in the capital of the nation that his father had played a key role in founding. After the war's end, he returned to North Bend, Ohio, where he and Nancy had a farm that could provide some income. His political prospects may have looked rosier in the state of Ohio, as the Indiana Territory still had not achieved statehood, and in Ohio he would be closer to the center of power in Washington than on the Indiana and Illinois frontier.

In 1816, Harrison won national office as a U.S. congressman from Ohio, then as a U.S. senator in 1824. He ran for president in 1836 but lost to Martin Van Buren. He tried again for the presidency in 1840 and changed the way presidential candidates campaign.

His opponent—Van Buren again—attempted to belittle Harrison by painting him as an unsophisticated backwoods hick who did little but sit in his log cabin drinking hard cider—this despite Harrison's background as an educated Virginia aristocrat from one of America's most prominent families and son of a Founding Father. Ever adept at transforming himself or his ideology to suit the moment and his best advantage, Harrison embraced the backwoods image. His campaign produced memorabilia featuring log cabins and cider jugs. He leveraged his frontier and fighter background by highlighting the memorable slogan "Tippecanoe and Tyler, too." (John Tyler was his running mate.) Historians consider it the first modern presidential campaign.

The irony is that this frontier public relations image ultimately led to Harrison's death, or so the old stories say. He won the presidency in the election of 1840 and traveled to Washington (leaving Nancy back in North Bend) to attend his inauguration in early March 1841. A cold winter rain fell steadily on Inauguration Day. Continuing to buff his frontiersman image, Harrison did not bother to wear a coat or hat, and he forwent an enclosed carriage to ride a horse to the ceremony. He then gave a record two-hour-long inauguration speech. Three weeks later he fell seriously ill with fever and chills. He died exactly one month after his inauguration—of pneumonia, which, it was assumed, he had contracted during his hatless frontiersman parade in the cold rain. Recent research indicates that typhoid from contaminated water caused his death. History remembers his actual time in office not for any accomplishments, but as the shortest presidency ever.

Yet it was what he accomplished years before that really matters. William Henry Harrison laid the groundwork for decades of wars with Native peoples and removal as the dynamic young governor of the Indiana Territory. Where Thomas Jefferson had taken an inchoate Federalist policy of "civilizing" tribes and made it into a governing ideology— "civilize," or move on, or be exterminated—Harrison had made that policy real.

The uncompromising westward push that Harrison began in Indiana reached its logical conclusion at a national level during the Jackson administration. By the time of Harrison's election, in 1840, Andrew Jackson had already served two terms (1829–37) as president. Jackson had put down uprisings in the South, including major battles against the Creek "Red Sticks." In the treaty that Jackson forced on them afterward, the Creek bitterly relinquished twenty-three million acres of their land. He then crushed Seminole forces in Florida in the Seminole Wars. By 1830, he had signed the infamous "Indian Removal Act"—removing tribes from the eastern United States to lands far beyond the Mississippi. Tens of thousands of American Indians underwent forced migrations to the West during and soon after Jackson's tenure, including the infamous Cherokee exodus known as the Trail of Tears and the Potawatomi Trail of Death.

Some of the last to leave were Black Hoof's followers at Wapakoneta—those who had chosen the government road and taken up white agriculture. The federal government took the last bits of their fertile homelands in northern Ohio in 1830 and forced them west across the Mississippi where it gave them new lands—until it wanted those, too.

"I heard a very intelligent Indian chief declare . . . that he had been engaged, in the course of his life, in making three treaties with the United States," wrote a Quaker missionary among the Shawnee in 1854, "that in all these treaties they used this term, 'forever.' . . . [This treaty] had only lasted for about twenty-one years."

Harrison branded himself, as Jackson would, too, the champion of the little man in the Jeffersonian vision of a nation of small farmers. Yet Harrison, like Jefferson and his aristocratic Virginia father and so many other whites of the era, could not broaden that vision of free and independent American individuals to reach beyond himself and others who looked like him to embrace Indigenous Americans, enslaved Africans, and people of color generally. Rather than champion of the little man, one can see William Henry as a perpetrator of genocide against the Native peoples of this country.

Who spoke up for the American Indians in Harrison's era? Very few white people. We have those words of John Badollet, land agent at Vincennes, which haunt the nation's history two and a half centuries after its founding more than ever before.

"It is my opinion that Government ought to look closer into this business," he warned high Washington officials in 1810. "The Indians want nothing but good treatment to become well disposed to the United States."

But, as ever, before and since, higher national priorities—in this case the outbreak of the War of 1812—subsumed any serious investigation into the abusive treatment of American Indians by federal officials. As they were in future decades, these concerns probably would have been pushed aside regardless of national priorities.

The United States and its peoples have accomplished monumental and wonderful things over the past two and a half centuries, ushering in, among other things, a new world era in which individual rights and liberties are encoded in law. Americans are coming to understand with more urgency now than ever before that the application of those rights has been flawed, but over those 250 years, progress has been made to extend those rights to all individuals. Nevertheless, the nation's treatment of Indigenous people remains a dark stain on the American character—as William Henry Harrison warned President Thomas Jefferson it would, before he, too, so eagerly jumped on board. The stain needs to be acknowledged if its hurt is ever to have a chance to heal.

The Dying Tecumseh could not have been sculpted any earlier than a certain moment in the nation's history. If Harrison had lived into the 1850s to see Pettrich's portrayal, would he have objected to his "savage" opponent glorified as noble and dignified as his earthly power slips away? By the time Pettrich carved Tecumseh's exquisitely sculpted physique, the threat that Native tribes would block America's westward movement was fading. Jackson's forced removal of eastern tribes was followed in quick succession by the Black Hawk War (securing Illinois and Wisconsin), then the Mexican War (securing much of the Southwest), the Oregon Trail, and the California Gold Rush.

Vast expanses of the West's interior still remained in control of the Lakota Sioux and other tribes, and powerful war chiefs like Sitting Bull, Crazy Horse, and Geronimo would still arise among them. But by the early 1850s, Manifest Destiny had brought the nation to what most Americans considered its rightful farthest extent—the Pacific Ocean, nearly three thousand miles from the first colonial landings at Jamestown and Plymouth. It was now certain the United States would embrace the continent from sea to sea.

Reviled and feared by many white Americans while alive, in death Tecumseh transformed into a symbol—the embodiment of what had once been, as some put it, "a noble but doomed race." White Americans told themselves that the race was doomed by the overpowering forces of a so-called superior civilization as they made their final push westward across the continent. Its inevitability morally absolved them from guilt or blame. Theirs was the superior civilization, they told themselves, and the superior civilization would always win out.

For many Native inhabitants of the continent, Tecumseh embodied precisely the opposite—not a dying hope but a rising one, like the comet in the sky that announced his appearance, that the tribes could defend their lands and ancestral ways against the voracious and insatiable white hunger for more land to clear. While some tribes in the East and Southeast took up white agriculture and domestic manufacturing, and other tribes adamantly refused to take his path and followed their own, many tribes farther west beyond the line of settlement enthusiastically embraced Tecumseh's vision. For them he represented a future in continuity with the past, a hope rather than an utter shattering of what they had known.

From the 1860s to the 1880s, the U.S. Army conducted major campaigns to defeat the Lakota Sioux, Northern Cheyenne, Nez Perce, Apache, and others. After the United States subdued these final, resisting tribes in the interior West, the Indigenous nations themselves largely fell from white American consciousness. Pettrich's *Dying Tecumseh* received its greatest public exposure when it was displayed in the Capitol Rotunda from 1864 to 1878—just as the Plains Indian Wars were winding down. After that, at least in the popular white consciousness, the image of the American Indian went dark—or was frozen in time.

In reality, what came next for the tribes was a series of deep humiliations and further injustices. They were rounded up and placed on reservations and told that these were lands of their own. Then the U.S. government opened up their reservations to white homesteaders with the 1887 Dawes Act, fragmenting the communal ownership of Native lands, while sending Native children to far-off white-run boarding schools where they were forbidden to speak their Native languages or practice their Native culture and religion. As one former U.S. officer in the Indian Wars put it in an 1892 speech, "All the Indian there is in the race should be dead. Kill the Indian in him, and save the man."

A still deeper symbolism underlies Pettrich's *Dying Tecumseh* as it reflects the American society that created it. He modeled it on a renowned sculpture from ancient Greece—*The Dying Gaul*. Every conglomeration of humans that calls itself civilized identifies its dark counterpart—the "barbarians" or "savages" that live beyond its boundaries or outside the wall it erects around itself, such as the Great Wall of China, Hadrian's Wall, and many others. *The Dying Gaul* glorifies these dark forces that oppose civilization and holds this sculpted embodiment of them up as a worthy adversary who gave fierce battle, with barbarian strength and cunning, but whom the forces of light and civilization ultimately vanquished, bringing about the ascendancy of the Hellenistic period or the Roman Empire.

The irony is that ancient Greece and Rome thought of themselves as everlasting bastions of civilization and permanent bulwarks against the barbarian tribes. They, however, crumbled into dust some two thousand years ago while the "barbarian tribes" and so-called savages who inspired the statues and who were supposedly vanquished remain these millennia later—the Celtic peoples (of which the Gauls were one) in places such as Brittany, Ireland, and Scotland, and the hundreds of Native nations in North America.

These Native nations are not "noble but doomed." They are very much alive.

Despite two centuries of U.S. policies aimed at subduing, corralling, and ultimately extinguishing Native tribes—including the "tribal termination" policy of the 1940s and '50s—the tribes themselves have remained remarkably resilient. Some were "terminated" never to officially reappear, but others regained tribal status, are working to regain it, or never lost it. In the past few decades, many tribes have undergone a cultural resurgence and launched widespread efforts to renew their ancestral languages and cultural and spiritual traditions. The difficulties they have suffered in the centuries since the European arrival on the continent have not simply disappeared. But tribes have begun to develop in new ways economically and wield their strength politically and legally while upholding tribal sovereignty.

"If you have a ten-thousand-year history, two hundred years is nothing," says Mark Trahant, a citizen of the Shoshone-Bannock tribe and editor-at-large of *Indian Country Today.* He notes, for example, that his people have already been through climate change, starting a long, long time ago. "The Shoshones once hunted mastodon. To go through that transition to hunting buffalo and other animals shows there is a route."

Tribes are now thinking about their lands, though diminished, as a source of strength. "How can any people be poor," says Trahant, quoting a Navajo leader, "when they own 5 percent of the land? That idea of having a sense of capital is a pretty powerful one. Five percent is a really big number."

Tecumseh, in some ways, anticipated the revival of tribal strength. He saw unity among the Indigenous peoples of North America as their best hope—to work together, to hold the land as one, to care for it the way the Great Spirit intended. These were values he espoused not simply to cling to a glorious or traditional past but to usher in an enduring future. In that way, he succeeded.

Recently, a three-thousand-year-old canoe fashioned of white oak was discovered by a diver in Lake Mendota, Wisconsin, and carefully raised by archaeologists from the muddy sediment in which it was embedded, along with the polished stones that weighted the fishing nets it once contained. Ho-Chunk (or Winnebago) elders—members of the Ho-Chunk Nation of Wisconsin—ceremonially greeted the canoe as it appeared above the lake's surface.

"We're here and we're staying here," said a tribal spokesperson present at the occasion. "We're here for the long run."

Tecumseh knew this, too.

—*Missoula, Montana, and Chenequa, Wisconsin*
September 2022

ACKNOWLEDGMENTS

In the summer of 1977 my brother Ted and I, both in our early twenties, launched a lightweight racing canoe from the front lawn of our family house on Pine Lake, in Chenequa, Wisconsin. From the lawn's shoreline, we paddled a mile and a half to the far end of Pine Lake, portaged our canoe across a swamp to another lake, followed its outlet stream to still another lake, where we battled choppy waves and a ferocious headwind that nearly sank our delicate craft.

Several arduous hours into our journey, wearily stroking our way across more swampland, we glimpsed an odd roofline beyond the reeds.

Ted stood up in the canoe to check it out. He sat back down in disgust. "It's the Kiltie," he said dishearteningly.

Neither of us needed to state aloud that, after most of a day of hard paddling and near disaster, we had canoed only as far as the iconic local drive-in. You could almost *walk* to the Kiltie from our house.

And so went the first day of a six-week, fifteen-hundred-mile epic canoe trip from our front lawn to New Orleans, via lakes, streams, and rivers that brought us to the Mississippi River, and then down it.

We didn't have any particular reason *why* we made this journey. As the saying goes, it sounded like a good idea at the time. Or we did it because it was there. Or because I had just finished my senior year of college and Ted had just finished his freshman year and we had few other prospects that summer besides painting houses. We had added incentive from our father and grandfather, passionate canoeists of Wisconsin's beautiful rivers. Normally sticklers for us taking summer jobs, they thought this voyage was a great idea. They even contributed to it.

My father also had a passion for history—especially early frontier history. He was captivated by the image of the Native tribes—Potawatomi, Sac, Fox, Winnebago, Menominee, and others—paddling these waters. He told countless stories about the early days of the fur trade, about the tribes who took part, and about the big birchbark canoes of the French-Canadian voyageurs.

This is the world I grew up in—steeped in frontier history and in the outdoors, via canoe, skis, foot, sail, and other means. When I eventually started writing about early exploration, initial contacts between Euro-Americans and Native people, and frontier history, I felt as if it came almost naturally to me. While this book is carefully researched from historical records, some of the most important "original research" I bring to it are my own many experiences in the North American outdoors and wilds. I've tried to inform each page with my understanding of the outdoors and bring it to life as vividly as possible, while keeping the account historically accurate.

My first debt, then, is to my grandfather and father, and to my many companions over decades of outdoor adventures and expeditions. I would especially like to acknowledge my brother, Ted Stark, paddler of hundreds of thousands of strokes in tandem with me and many other adventures, and an astute reader of historical biography.

So many individuals and institutions have helped me along the journey that is this book. I would like to acknowledge some of the teachers I met along the way—those who have made a deep commitment to teach history to a younger generation, both at the middle school and high school level. These dedicated teachers are Karen McClain, Keith Robinson, and John Robinson, and Tammy Elser, professor at Salish Kootenai College.

I've had great conversations about historical matters and the subject of this book with great conversationalists who have regular radio shows, especially Jimmy Mac and Clare Marie of Dave Nemo Radio, and Bob Seidenschwarz of the Montana World Affairs Council and KGVO radio show, *Talk Back*.

Jim Mackenzie is a dear friend and fellow writer who read this manuscript in various stages and inevitably brought to it (and to many other things) his keen insights. J. "Bill" T. Youngs, professor of history at Eastern Washington University, introduced me years ago to the Northwest Indian War, or "Little Turtle's War," and imparted how relatively unrecognized it is in U.S. history. Colin Calloway, professor of history and Native American studies at Dartmouth College, an expert in Native-U.S. relations during this era and a prolific author, provided helpful comments on the manuscript and inspiration.

I am very grateful and honored to have had the help of several Native readers who read parts or all of the manuscript and gave valuable comments. These include Julie Cajune, coordinator of the tribal history program at Salish Kootenai College, fellow writer Chris La Tray, member of the Little Shell Tribe of Chippewa Indians, and Kim Vigue, executive director of the Mitchell Museum of the American Indian in Evanston, Illinois, and an enrolled member of the Oneida Nation and descendant of the Menominee Tribe of Wisconsin.

Robert T. (Tim) Coulter, executive director of the Indian Law Resource Center in Helena, Montana, member of the Potawatomi Nation, and longtime advocate throughout the Americas for Indigenous land rights, gave a sense of legal history and Native nations. Mark Trahant, editor at large for *Indian Country Today* and member of the Shoshone-Bannock tribe, offered his invaluable perspective on Native nations and their long view of history.

I would like to thank John Carter, longtime attorney for the Confederated Salish and Kootenai Tribes of the Flathead Reservation, located in Montana. I am also grateful to Matthew C. Waxman, professor of law at Columbia University and specialist on Constitutional issues, war powers, and national security.

Helpful in writing and envisioning this book was listening to the speakers, comments, and presentations at two literary conferences in Missoula in the summer of 2022. I would like to thank the organizers and participants of the James Welch Native Lit Festival and In the Footsteps of Norman Maclean Literary Festival, and especially my fellow panelists in the latter, Debra Magpie Earling, Mandy Smoker Broadus, and Annick Smith.

Many friends, family, and professional acquaintances have read versions of this book while it was still in manuscript. They are: Noel Ragsdale, Ted Stark, Bob Hayssen, Mike Kadas, Sally Thompson, Kate Stark Damsgaard, Jim Ritter, Jon Reichard, John Onzick, Roy O'Connor, Dick Osborne, Forrest Horton, and Rick Fuhry. Generous in giving their time and energy to reading and commenting on this manuscript and others are University of Montana professor of English (and my fellow Old Boys soccer player) Ashby Kinch and his book club: John McKay, John Bardsley, Jesse Johnson, Dave Calkin, Colin Bishop, and Tom Webster. They also serve up a sumptuous dinner and drinks to accompany the discussion.

I've relied on a number of archives and online resources for research on primary sources that inform this book. Of particular help have been the Draper Manuscript Collection at the Wisconsin Historical Society (the major collection of documents regarding Tecumseh), the Indiana Historical Society, the Newberry Library of Chicago, and the Filson Historical Society of Louisville, Kentucky. As with my previous books, I've also relied for early documents on the remarkable Founders Online project of the National Archives, in conjunction with the University of Virginia Press. The Papers of John Jay, digital collection, at Columbia University provided access to letters of the Symmes and Livingston families.

In the course of research for *Gallop Toward the Sun*, I visited many of the sites where the actual events occurred. Among these are: Fort Recovery, Tippecanoe, Point Pleasant and murals, Hopewell mounds, Presque Isle, and Chillicothe.

I would like to single out in particular Grouseland, the luxurious mansion-in-the-wilderness of William Henry Harrison when he was territorial governor, located in Vincennes, Indiana. Well worth a visit, Grouseland is surely one of the most unique and captivating official homes in the nation, with its graceful parlors and dining rooms and bedrooms aboveground, and its stone-walled fortress in the cellar, cut with gunports and containing a powder magazine. I want to thank especially Lisa Ice-Jones, executive director of the Grouseland Foundation, who welcomed my wife, Amy, and me graciously and provided a detailed tour once she got over her surprise at seeing two mud-caked canoeists show up at Grouseland's front door after we had paddled a section of the Wabash River, on the trail of Tecumseh.

Words can't adequately express my gratitude to Random House editor Hilary Redmon, who commissioned and edited this book, and her colleague, editor Molly Turpin, who worked with me closely on the manuscript over several drafts. When acquaintances would ask me "How's the book coming?" I would answer "I'm doing more revisions." And I would always add "I feel enormously grateful to have two editors who are so smart." In particular, their guidance helped me find the shape and voice for this book.

Many others at Random House contributed to this book, including Miriam Khanukaev; managing editor Rebecca Berlant; production editor Dennis Ambrose; interior book designer Jo Anne Metsch; David Stevenson, who designed the beautiful cover; and David Lindroth, designer of the striking maps.

My agent, Stuart Krichevsky, and his staff at Stuart Krichevsky Literary Agency, have been enormously helpful through the entire process. Many thanks in a thousand different ways to my publicist, James Faccinto of Full Complement Publicity and Communications Agency, who has arranged countless media appearances and events for me. My longtime friends and editors Mark Bryant and Laura Hohnhold worked closely with me and my spouse, Amy Ragsdale, on an essay for the digital publication Scribd, "Sins of the Founding Father" (at scribd.com) that centers on the "Battle With No Name" and its political repercussions today.

Finally, my love and gratitude to my spouse and life partner, Amy Ragsdale, who both physically and emotionally accompanied me on this journey, and to our children, Molly Stark-Ragsdale and Skyler Stark-Ragsdale, who inspire me to paddle onward.

NOTES

PROLOGUE

xvii **Approaching Grouseland** Cleaves, *Old Tippecanoe*, 73. Dawson, in *Historical Narrative of the Civil and Military Service of Major-General William H. Harrison* (written in 1824 with Harrison's cooperation and hereinafter referred to as *Historical Narrative of WHH*) has the chairs and benches set out in the portico.

xviii **Twelve U.S. soldiers armed with muskets** Dawson, *Historical Narrative of WHH*, 156.

xviii **"My father?"** Law, *Colonial History of Vincennes*, 83. Similar versions appear in Dawson, *Historical Narrative of WHH*, 159, and Cleaves, *Old Tippecanoe*, 73.

xviii **The effect was "electrical"** Law, *Colonial History of Vincennes*, 84.

xx **"Brother! I wish"** "Tecumseh's Speech to Governor Harrison, August 20th, 1810," in WHH, *Messages and Letters*, 1:463–67.

xx **He moved gracefully about the council** See Brock, *Life and Correspondence*, 227–28, for a detailed description of Tecumseh's dress, including silver crosses dangling from his nose. Lossing gives a similar description in his *Pictorial Field-Book*.

xx **the men were silent** Law, *Colonial History of Vincennes*, 86–87.

xx **There was "no foundation in fact"** Ibid., 87–88.

xxiii **Any of the following acts** United Nations Convention on the Prevention and Punishment of the Crime of Genocide, Article 2. See Legal Information Institute, "genocide," Cornell Law School, www.law.cornell.edu/wex/genocide.

xxiv **The contest between Tecumseh and Harrison** Calloway, *The Shawnees*, xxxvi.

CHAPTER 1: THE STRIPLING

3 **A young woman sprinted ahead** Cleaves, *Old Tippecanoe*, 9, citing the statement of Major Whitlock of Crawfordsville, Indiana, as quoted in Lossing, *Pictorial Field-Book*, 48n3.

3 **This was the scene** Ibid., 9. Cleaves quotes from the WHH letter of July 20, 1839, to editor James Brooks describing what he had witnessed on his arrival at Fort Washington.

4 **Young Ensign Harrison's stiff new uniform** For a description of WHH's uniform as a young ensign, see Booraem, *Child*, loc 973.

4 **Both studious in the classroom** Cleaves, *Old Tippecanoe*, 10.

4 **But such was the career** Skaggs, *Conquest*, 29.

5 **Harrison family fortunes had fallen** See "Life of General Harrison," *The Port Folio*, 308-10, and Skaggs, *Conquest*, 28-30.

5 **"I shall have a great advantage"** Benjamin Rush to John Adams, July 20, 1811, National Park Service, Independence National Historical Park, www .nps.gov/inde/.

7 **Decades later, William Henry described** Skaggs, *Conquest*, 29.

7 **Some weeks after his arrival** Cleaves, *Old Tippecanoe*, 7.

10 **He fell well short** Owens, *Hammer*, 15.

10 **"You are going to a fine country"** "Life of General Harrison," 310.

10 **The young man headed** Skaggs, *Conquest*, 30-31. For Julius Caesar's battles and writings, see 29-30.

12 **The troops were about to start work** Sargent, "Diary," 34.

12 **But an instant later** Robert Branshaw, *Indiana Herald*, April 13, 1864, in Fort Wayne Museum pamphlet, 27.

13 **"The ground was literally covered with the dead"** See Denny, *Military Journal*, 17-18.

13 **Lost, too, were cannons** Sargent, "Diary," 43.

15 **"whenever the United States shall be invaded"** See "Militia Act of 1792," George Washington's Mount Vernon, www.mountvernon.org. See also "Insurrection Act Explained," Brennan Center for Justice, www.brennancenter.org.

16 **In peacetime, he had fallen** Victor, *Life of Wayne*, 68. For Wayne's ousting for voter fraud, see "To George Washington from Anthony Wayne, April 6, 1789," n1, https://founders.archives.gov/documents/Washington/05-02-02 -0035, accessed August 14, 2022.

16 **Soon after taking command** Cleaves, *Old Tippecanoe*, 14.

16 **Aware of his own reputation** Wayne to Secretary of War Knox, October 5, 1793, in Victor, *Life of Wayne*, 75.

CHAPTER 2: MAD ANTHONY AND LITTLE TURTLE

20 **Neither under the control** Calloway, *Indian World*, 396.

21 **Recently promoted** Cleaves, *Old Tippecanoe*, 14.

21 "intolerable thick woods"   Booraem, *Child*, loc 2803, citing William Clark's journal, 422–23, in chap. 15, n8.

22 The two battle veterans   Sugden, *Life*, 88–90.

22 "We cannot expect"   Lossing, *Pictorial Field-Book*, 53n3.

22 "grand emporium of hostile Indians"   Cleaves, *Old Tippecanoe*, 17. Wayne to Secretary of War Knox, August 14, 1794, quoted in Lossing, *Pictorial Field-Book*, 53.

23 Chippewas, Ottawas, and Potawatomis   Sugden, *Life*, 88.

23 "I cannot let you in"   Ibid., 90, attributing the account to Blue Jacket.

24 General Wayne did not pursue   Ibid., 91.

24 Specifically, Wayne proposed   See "Treaty with the Wyandot, etc.," First People of America and Canada, https://www.firstpeople.us/FP-Html-Treaties/TreatyWithTheWyandotetc1795.html, accessed January 10, 2020.

24 The twelve tribes would give   Lossing, *Pictorial Field-Book*, 57n2.

24 Much of it was Shawnee homelands   Tanner, *Atlas of Great Lakes Indian History*, 58–59.

24 "It will give infinite pleasure"   For Treaty of Greenville speeches, see http://historymatters.gmu.edu/d/6525/, accessed January 9, 2020.

25 They could take treaty settlement   Owens, *Hammer*, 30.

25 playing them off one another   Ibid., 31.

26 "The print of my ancestors' houses"   Speech of Little Turtle at Treaty of Greenville; see http://historymatters.gmu.edu/d/6525/, accessed January 9, 2020.

26 To General Wayne's assertion   Owens, *Hammer*, 29.

26 "As the great means of rendering"   "Treaty of Greenville," American State Papers, Indian Affairs, 1:562–63.

27 "As chiefs fought for scraps"   Owens, *Hammer*, 31–32. Owens also quotes Richard White, *The Middle Ground*, on the fragmentation of the tribes. See Owens, *Hammer*, 31.

27 "Yes, there were conflicts"   Hans R. Isakson and Shauntreis Sproles, "A Brief History of Native American Land Ownership," 66, in Robert Simons, Rachel Malmgren, and Garrick Small, eds., *Indigenous Peoples and Real Estate Valuation*, Research Issues in Real Estate, vol. 10 (New York: Springer, 2008).

28 "Although we were absolutely democratic"   Alford, *Civilization*, 45.

29 If he didn't sign   Owens, *Hammer*, 31.

CHAPTER 3: FAMILY HONOR

31 "Old Captain Ruddle cried out aloud"   Pauline Ruddle Harman, "Ruddle-Riddle Genealogy and Biography," L.C. #84-52275, 21–26 in "The

Ruddell Family," *Virginia Genealogist*. Part of this history of the Ruddell family, notes Harman, can be found in Collins's *History of Kentucky*, and part from the journal of Colonel Daniel Trabue, an eyewitness to the reunion of the Ruddell brothers and their father at Greenville in 1795. More details of the Ruddell family's initial capture are in "Local Notices," *Virginia Gazette*, Richmond, 1783, 296–97, also available at the above website.

31 **The captive brothers had passed** Sugden, *Life*, 34–35. Sugden also describes how Shawnee villagers greeted the victorious war parties bringing captives and scalps.

31 **An account by O. M. Spencer** See *The Indian Captivity of O. M. Spencer*, ed. Milo Milton Quaife (Chicago: Lakeside Press, 1918), 72.

32 **On a signal, the captive would sprint** Howard, *Shawnee!*, 122–23.

32 **An eighteen-year-old Pennsylvanian** Smith, *Remarkable Occurrences*, 8–9.

33 **"I consider him a very great"** Stephen Ruddell, "Reminiscences of Tecumseh's Youth," 132. These are Stephen Ruddell's handwritten memoirs, held in the Draper Collection at Wisconsin Historical Society, http://content.wisconsinhistory.org/cdm/ref/collection/aj/id/17916, accessed May 28, 2018.

33 **Sinnamatha** Ibid., 131.

33 **Even the games played by Shawnee boys** Alford, *Civilization*, 22.

34 **The boys would bend a grapevine** Ibid.

34 **Whether feather, leaf, shell** Ibid., 25.

35 **"They are Stout, Bold, Cunning"** Laura Keenan Spero, "Stout, Bold, Cunning and the Greatest Travellers in America": The Colonial Shawnee Diaspora" (PhD diss., University of Pennsylvania, 2010), 2, https://www.proquest.com/docview/759984560, accessed January 3, 2022.

36 **When Shawnee hunters went out together** Alford, *Civilization*, 53.

36 **"You have behaved just like a Dutchman"** Smith, *Remarkable Occurrences*, 8–9.

37 **Tecumseh's father, Puckeshinwa, died in 1774** Calloway, *Indian World*, 210, and Edmunds, *Tecumseh*, 15–16.

37 **London foreign secretaries had tried** See "Proclamation Line of 1763" in Digital Encyclopedia, George Washington's Mount Vernon, https://www.mountvernon.org, accessed February 20, 2022. This article discusses planter and land investor George Washington's opposition to the Proclamation Line and his efforts to have it removed.

38 **The Shawnee leaders made it very clear** See Edmunds, *Tecumseh*, 12.

38 **Many of his fellow Shawnee chiefs** Sugden, *Life*, 29.

38 **The so-called Treaty of Fort Stanwix** "The Treaties of Fort Stanwix: 1768 Boundary Line Treaty of Fort Stanwix," Cumberland Gap National Histori-

cal Park, Fort Stanwix National Monument, National Park Service, https://
www.nps.gov/articles/000/1768-boundary-line-treaty-of-fort-stanwix.htm
(accessed January 6, 2023).

39 **He elicited a promise** Ibid., 28, and Edmunds, *Tecumseh*, 20, give slightly
different accounts of just what promise Chiksika made, but the general sentiment is the same.

39 **Chiksika promised** Stephen Ruddell, "Reminiscences," 120–21. As Stephen Ruddell recalled the story, "At his dying moment, he called to him his
oldest son a youth of twelve or thirteen years named [Chiksika] and strongly
enjoined on him to preserve unsullied the dignity and honour of the family and
directed him in the future to lead forth to battle his younger brothers."

40 **With more than a thousand** See Edmunds, *Tecumseh*, 22, on Shawnee
migration in summer of 1779, and also Calloway, *Shawnees*, 69. Edmunds puts
Methoataske's departure in the summer of 1779, 22. Sugden puts arrival of
Stephen Ruddell in 1780, 34–35.

40 **Methoataske brought only her nine-year-old daughter** Edmunds, *Tecumseh*, 19, states that a third daughter, Nehaaeemo, was born about 1770.

40 **She left Tecumseh and his younger** See Edmunds, *Tecumseh*, 19–20, for
a listing of Tecumseh's siblings. He was the fifth child, after Chiksika, Tecumpease, son Sauwauseekau, and another daughter, and was followed by daughter Nehaaeemo (born ca. 1770) and triplets (born in 1775 after father's death),
two of whom survived infancy, Lalawethika and Kumskaukau.

40 **Tecumpease, or "Flying Over the Water"** Sugden, *Life*, 19.

40 **The Big Knives—Virginians and Kentuckians** Sugden, *Life*, 27, says
some eastern tribes called Virginians "Big Knives" and that the term came to be
applied to Americans generally. They were also called "Long Knives."

40 **Chiksika, noted Ruddell, "taught him"** Stephen Ruddell, "Reminiscences," 121.

41 **A flurry of musket balls whizzed past** See Edmunds, *Tecumseh*, 25, for
details of Tecumseh's role in the skirmish.

41 **A panicked Tecumseh fled** Drake, *Tecumseh*, 68, and Sugden, *Life*, 47,
state that Tecumseh became frightened without his older brother's guidance
and ran. Sugden dates the action as likely in 1786, based on place of fighting
and says that it was led by Benjamin Logan. Edmunds dates it as 1782.

41 **Native leaders who had helped the British** See "Joseph Brant (Thayendanegea)," *The Canadian Encyclopedia*, https://www.thecanadianencyclopedia
.ca/en/article/joseph-brant, accessed July 11, 2020.

41 **"England," the Mohawk leader** Paxton, *Joseph Brant*, 47.

41 **In turn, he passionately advocated** Sugden, *Life*, 44.

42 "We do not understand the measuring"   Ibid., 45.

42 "In the action Tecumthe behaved"   Stephen Ruddell, "Reminiscences," 124.

43 They split off from   Sugden, *Life*, 55–57, discusses the Chickamauga and their history.

43 "Here I am," says I   Stephen Ruddell, "Reminiscences," 129.

44 "[He said] that his father had fell gloriously"   Ibid., 126.

44 "The women were very fond of him"   Ibid., 124.

44 He married a Cherokee woman   See Sugden, *Life*, 61, for details of Tecumseh's marriage and his descendants living in Arkansas.

45 Rather, they should assure chiefs   Calloway, Indian World, 414.

46 "You say [President Washington] will make us"   Ibid., 417–21.

47 "It would have been extraordinarily difficult"   Owens, *Hammer*, 20–22.

CHAPTER 4: GROUSELAND

49 In the meantime, Kentuckians forded   WHH to Secretary of War Dearborn, July 15, 1801, in WHH, *Messages and Letters*, 1:25–31. See also WHH to Dearborn, February 26, 1802, ibid., 41.

49 Black Hoof and fellow chiefs   Sugden, *Life*, 97.

50 Tecumseh's growing Shawnee band   Ibid., 94–95. See also 98–100, for life at the White.

50 "He was particularly attentive"   Ibid., quoting Shane's account in the Draper Collection. See also ibid., 413n1 and n2, discussing the significance of the Shane interview, and that his Shawnee wife was involved.

50 Like so many Shawnees   Burnet, *Notes on the Early Settlement of the North-Western Territory*, 68–69.

51 Frontiersmen later recalled   See Sugden, *Life*, 100, for Simon Kenton's memory of the snow wrestling.

51 "[Tecumseh] was pleased with the peace"   Stephen Ruddell, "Reminiscences," 132.

51 "If he continues a military man"   Cleaves, *Old Tippecanoe*, 21, quoting an officer recording the statement of Major Mills, in "Journal of Lieutenant Thomas J. Underwood" in Draper Collection, Wisconsin Historical Society.

52 The example of Judge Symmes   For details on the timing of Symmes's and the Ohio Company's purchases, see the introduction to Symmes, *Intimate Letters*, 7–12.

53 "He can neither bleed, plead, or preach"   Quoted in Booraem, *Child*, loc 3084.

53 **It was a "run-away match"**   Susan Livingston Symmes to Sarah Livingston Jay, March 13, 1796, Jay Papers, Columbia Digital Library Collections. Sarah Livingston Jay was the wife of John Jay. https://dlc.library.columbia.edu/jay/ldpd:80968, accessed January 5, 2020.

53 **No officer's promotion**   Booraem, *Child*, loc 3116, quoting WHH to Wayne, July 11, 1796.

54 **By 1799, the territory**   Owens, *Hammer*, 44–45.

54 **Congress's phrase "free male inhabitants"**   "Northwest Ordinance 1787," Section 9. https://www.archives.gov/milestone-documents/northwest-ordinance accessed, August 19, 2022.

55 **"Mr. H . . . has handsome manners"**   Cleaves, *Old Tippecanoe*, 36, quoting letter of Isaac Darneille, October 10, 1805.

55 **The smallest lot measured**   Treat, *National Land System*, 85.

56 **"This law," he boasted**   "Harrison to His Constituents," Philadelphia, May 14, 1800, in WHH, *Messages and Letters*, 1:12–18.

56 **It leaned not on the big**   See Owens, *Hammer*, 45–49, for more perspective on the changes wrought by the Land Act of 1800.

57 **With the territory's settler**   These measurements, 1,000 miles east to west and 700 miles north to south, were cited in the debate on the issue, as put forth by Representative Harper when speaking in favor of the bill to split the territory. See "Annals of Congress," Friday, March 28, 1800, col. 649, https://memory.loc.gov/cgi-bin/ampage, accessed May 8, 2020.

57 **The smaller and more-settled eastern sector**   Cleaves, *Old Tippecanoe*, 30–31.

58 **The Shawnees had in fact**   Sugden, *Life*, 102.

59 **The herds followed a "trace"**   Sleeper-Smith, *Indigenous Prosperity*, 47.

60 **Residents of French descent occupied**   Cleaves, *Old Tippecanoe*, 33.

60 **"On the one side we have"**   Susan Symmes to Maria Short, June 21, 1801, quoted in Cleaves, *Old Tippecanoe*, 34.

61 **That wouldn't stop Harrison**   Cleaves, *Old Tippecanoe*, 33.

61 **To pay his workers**   Owens, *Hammer*, 56. Cleaves, *Old Tippecanoe*, 45, gives more Grouseland details. See also "William Henry Harrison's Grouseland" website. http://grouseland.org/explore-history, accessed March 19, 2021.

62 **The couple modeled their main staircase**   Grouseland tour given by Lisa Ice-Jones, August 6, 2019.

62 **A lookout platform topped the roof**   Ibid.

62 **When someone questioned**   Ibid. This quote appears in somewhat different versions in various sources.

CHAPTER 5: THE CHOICE

63   "The crisis is pressing"   Jefferson to WHH, February 27, 1803, in WHH, *Messages and Letters*, 1:69–73.

63   **During the 150 years**   "Indigenous-French Relations," *The Canadian Encyclopedia*, www.thecanadianencyclopedia.ca/en/article/aboriginal-french -relations, accessed August 26, 2022.

65   **Whichever nation first established**   Alexander Mackenzie, *Voyages from Montreal Through the Continent of North America to the Frozen and Pacific Oceans in 1789 and 1793* (New York: Allerton, 1922), 2:358.

66   **He would soon identify the perfect**   Owens, *Hammer*, 78.

66   **Susan belonged to the famed Livingston**   Sarah Livingston Jay letters are in the John Jay Papers of the Columbia Digital Library Collections, https://dlc. library.columbia.edu/jay/, accessed January 5, 2010.

67   **They provided her**   For more details on Clinton Academy in Easthampton, see https://easthampton.com/history/clinton-academy/, accessed September 30, 2019.

67   **Citing graphic details**   WHH to Henry Dearborn, July 15, 1801, in WHH, *Messages and Letters*, 1:25–31.

70   **It customarily recognized**   Freeman, *George Washington*, 1:79.

70   **He believed that acquiring**   Owens, *Hammer*, 47. Jeffersonian Republicans, following contemporary European political theory, assumed that "continual expansion was the only hope for the survival of the republic." Otherwise people settle in cities, and social decay occurs.

71   **Just a few months after**   WHH to Henry Dearborn, February 26, 1802, quoted in Owens, *Hammer*, 62, citing *The Papers of William Henry Harrison, 1800–1815*, ed. Douglas E. Clanin and Ruth Dorrel (Indianapolis: Indiana Historical Society, 1999).

71   **A letter in early 1802 written to Harrison**   Dearborn to WHH, February 23, 1802, in WHH, *Messages and Letters*, 1:39–41.

71   **Jefferson strove**   Owens, *Hammer*, 66, points out that it was an "inherently self-serving" view that Indigenous people's lifestyle was outmoded and they needed to change or head to extinction.

71   **The provisions made by congress**   See "An Act to Regulate Trade and Intercourse with the Indian Tribes," https://avalon.law.yale.edu/18th_century /na024.asp.

72   **"Jefferson probably sincerely intended"**   Wallace, *Jefferson and the Indians*, 20. Also see Calloway, *Indian World*, 229–30. "The formula they [Wash-

ington, Knox, and Jefferson] developed—land for civilization—became a strategy for American expansion and a hallmark of U.S. Indian policy for one hundred years. So did the readiness to wage war on Indians who refused the deal."

72 **"Divide and rule"** Wallace, *Jefferson and the Indians*, 59, quoting Merrill Peterson, *Thomas Jefferson and the New Nation*.

72 **At Secretary Dearborn's request** Owens, *Hammer*, 62–65, citing Dearborn to Harrison in June 1802, some three months after Harrison had first suggested a much more "extensive" interpretation of the Greenville Treaty.

73 **The fact that Congress had already twice** Ibid., 63.

74 **The plan would work like this** See summary of TJ's strategy in Wallace, *Jefferson and the Indians*, 225. Wallace summarizes one aspect of Jefferson's strategy as follows: "Encircle the eastern tribes by first acquiring the land on the east bank of the Mississippi, compressing them into a vast but ever-shrinking enclave between the Mississippi and the Appalachian mountains."

74 **The decrease of game rendering their subsistence** Cleaves, *Old Tippecanoe*, 38, and Jefferson to WHH, February 27, 1803, in WHH, *Messages and Letters*, 1:69–73.

74 **As one modern historian, Gary B. Nash** In this quote, Nash is describing the "master lesson" of the powerfully revealing book *Jefferson and the Indians* by Anthony F. C. Wallace.

CHAPTER 6: THE FORKED PATH

77 **On the White River he married** Sugden, *Life*, 98–99.

77 **That's the story later remembered** Edmunds, *Tecumseh*, 91.

77 **She had a special relationship** Ibid., 22–23. Edmunds also discusses Chiksika's close relationship with Tecumseh.

77 **"She was intelligent"** Sugden, *Life*, 99.

77 **Though speakers of an Algonquian** Howard, *Shawnee!*, 98–101.

77 **Coming from an exemplary** Sugden, *Life*, 94. C. C. Trowbridge in his account of Shawnee society states that there are female chiefs and gives some detail.

78 **"Setting before him the care and anxiety"** Howard, *Shawnee!*, 109, quoting Trowbridge in *Shawnese Traditions*.

80 **the Founding Fathers recognized tribes** Calloway, *Indian World*, 325. See also "Commerce Clause," Cornell Law School, Legal Information Institute, www.law.cornell.edu/wex/commerce_clause, accessed July 21, 2022. See also "Powers & Procedures: About Treaties," United States Senate,

https://www.senate.gov/about/powers-procedures/treaties, accessed July 21, 2022. For the U.S. Constitution specifying that the president has the power to make treaties, with the advice and consent of Congress, see https://www.archives.gov/founding-docs/constitution-transcript, accessed August 28, 2022, and https://www.archives.gov/founding-docs/constitution-transcript, accessed August 28, 2022. For a discussion of the history of Senate treaty approval, see Bureau of Indian Affairs, "Does the United States Still Make Treaties with Indian Tribes?" https://www.bia.gov/faqs/does-united-states-still-make-treaties-indian-tribes, accessed August 28, 2022.

81 **It gives this treaty-making**   Calloway, *Indian World*, 357.

81 **The president received information**   Dearborn to WHH, February 23, 1802, in WHH, *Messages and Letters*, 1:39–41. Dearborn reports that orders from Jefferson state that territorial governors are in charge of Indian affairs, and agents and subagents report to the territorial governors who report to the secretary of war. This same letter discusses bringing civilization to the Indians through agriculture and small manufacturing. See also Owens, *Hammer*, 58.

81 **"This defeats every purpose"**   Ibid., 357–60.

82 **"Of the means however of obtaining"**   Jefferson to WHH, February 27, 1803, in WHH, *Messages and Letters*, 1:69–73.

82 **Harrison had first swung**   Owens, *Hammer*, 78, writes that WHH threatened to withhold Greenville Treaty payments.

82 **In mid-1803, employing a similar gambit**   Ibid., 80–81.

83 **Ambiguous wording in the treaty**   See ibid., 85–90, for details of the Sauk and Fox treaty and Sauk and Fox homelands.

83 **But, authorized to act on his own**   Ibid., 78.

84 **"Friend and Brother!"**   Wallace, *Jefferson and the Indians*, 230.

84 **"The inexorable progress of civilization"**   Onuf, *Jefferson's Empire*, 47, as quoted in Owens, *Hammer*, 77.

85 **29.2 million—Total acres**   These treaties and acreages are based on details in Owens, *Hammer*, Sugden, *Life*, and Cleaves, *Old Tippecanoe*. The acreages of some of the smaller treaties, such as the Treaty with the Piankeshaw, 1804, are approximate. Several of the treaties go by two or more different names and slightly different dates, depending whether they were negotiated or ratified in any particular year.

85 **During the winter of 1804-5**   See Sugden, *Life*, 109–20, for a depiction of this onslaught of disease and other maladies on White River villages and the accusations of witchcraft.

87 **An elderly Shawnee healer, Penagasha**   Edmunds, *Tecumseh*, 75.

87 **As the story is told**   Edmunds, *Shawnee Prophet*, 28–33. Similar versions are

found in other sources, such as Andrews, "Shaker Mission," and Lossing, *Pictorial Field-Book*, which is based on the author's interviews with witnesses to the era and other sources, 188-89 and 189n3.

88 **It was widely believed**   Sugden, *Life*, 126.

89 **"*My children*—My heart is filled"**   WHH to Delawares, early 1806, in WHH, *Messages and Letters*, 1:183.

90 **"Did I not prophecy truly?"**   Drake, *Tecumseh*, 91.

90 **He could make pumpkins as large**   Lossing, *Pictorial Field-Book*, 189n3.

CHAPTER 7: A VOICE IN THE MOONLIGHT

91 **Her husband had been walking**   Interview at Grouseland with Lisa Ice-Jones, August 2019, quoting story told at Grouseland. Cleaves, *Old Tippecanoe*, 55, states that baby John Scott was in WHH's arms.

93 **Infused with an epic sense**   Andrews, "Shaker Mission to the Shawnee Indians," 116.

93 **"They almost dance themselves"**   Judge John Symmes to Anna (Nancy) Harrison, September 11-19, 1809, in Symmes, *Correspondence of John Cleves Symmes*, 297-310.

94 **"[The ministers] hated us & spoke evil of us"**   Symmes, *Correspondence of John Cleves Symmes*, 119-20.

95 **"He began to speak"**   Ibid., 122-23.

97 **"Our feelings were like Jacob's"**   Ibid., 124.

98 **Potawatomis rode from the prairies**   Edmunds, *Shawnee Prophet*, 50-54.

98 **"Traditionally the Shawnees had been"**   See ibid., 34-37, and Edmunds, *Tecumseh*, 77, for description of Tenskwatawa's teachings compared to traditional beliefs.

98 **Rather, he espoused a blend—syncretism**   Sugden, *Life*, 120.

98 **"It was the interplay of these spirits"**   Ibid., 16-17.

99 **"The battle between the Wapakoneta chiefs"**   Ibid., 130.

100 **When four hundred Potawatomi**   Ibid., 143-48.

100 **He instructed his followers**   Edmunds, *Shawnee Prophet*, 36-37; Sugden, *Life*, 118.

100 **"I will overturn the land"**   Edmunds, *Tecumseh*, 79, and Edmunds, *Shawnee Prophet*, 38.

101 **Tensions already existed**   For Wells's description and background, see Sugden, *Life*, 148-49, and Edmunds, *Tecumseh*, 93. For a detailed biography of Wells, see William Heath, *William Wells and the Struggle for the Old Northwest* (Norman: University of Oklahoma, 2015).

101 "Go back to Fort Wayne"   Drake, *Tecumseh*, 92–93. See also original Shane transcript in Draper Collection, 13–14.

102 **Actually, President Jefferson had said**   Sugden, *Life*, 149–50.

102 **"These lands," he concluded**   Shane transcript in Draper Collection, 14. See also Drake, *Tecumseh*, 92–93, citing Shane's report.

CHAPTER 8: PRETENDED TREATIES

104 **In Harrison's mind**   Wells to Harrison, August 20, 1807, quoted in Cleaves, *Old Tippecanoe*, 57.

105 **By chance, he recognized a deserter**   Details of the Jenkins Ratford incident are from the official testimony of the commander, Lord James Townshend, given at Ratford's court-martial in Halifax, Nova Scotia, in Nicholas Tracy, *The Naval Chronicle, 1799-1804: The Contemporary Record of the Royal Navy at War* (London: Stackpole Books, 1998).

106 **She asked that he leave**   Moffat, *Queen Louisa*, 202.

107 **utterly outraged America**   For details on reaction to Chesapeake affair, see Sugden, *Life*, 166–68.

107 **killed the famed U.S. Naval commander Stephen Decatur**   Joel D. Treese and Evan Phifer, "Commodore Stephen Decatur: An Early American Naval War Hero," White House Historical Association, https://www.white househistory.org/commodore-stephen-decatur-an-early-american-naval-war -hero, accessed January 7, 2023.

109 **"A restless and dissatisfied disposition"**   WHH to Territorial Legislature, August 17, 1807, in WHH, *Messages and Letters*, 1:229–36.

110 **When the Ohio governor's**   For accounts of this meeting, see Drake, *Tecumseh*, 94–96; Edmunds, *Shawnee Prophet*, 60–61; Sugden, *Life*, 3–10, 160–61.

110 **Stephen Ruddell, now a Baptist**   See Lankford, "Losing the Past," 214–39; "The Ruddell Family," *Virginia Genealogist*; and www.genealogy.com/forum /surnames/topics/ruddell/797/.

111 **Some had traveled from beyond**   Sugden, *Life*, 161, notes that some of the warriors came from north of the Ojibwe, possibly the Cree.

111 **Said the Wyandot elder**   Drake, *Tecumseh*, 94–96. See also Sugden, *Life*, 160–61.

112 **The governor graciously received them**   Sugden, *Life*, 5–6.

113 **For three hours Tecumseh spoke passionately**   Drake, *Tecumseh*, 85, 96–97.

114 **"When Tecumseh rose to speak"**   See Sugden's quotation of McDonald's

remark in *Life*, 7. Sugden writes that McDonald's quote has appeared in earlier historical accounts out of its proper chronology. Sugden, in chap. 1, 7n6, places the McDonald quote in 1807 when Tecumseh speaks at Chillicothe, not in 1803, as in Drake, *Tecumseh*, 85.

114 **A civil engineer and frontier surveyor** Drake, *Tecumseh*, 97 and 97n, attributing the description of Tecumseh's speech to John A. Fulton, via General James T. Worthington.

CHAPTER 9: TWO POWERS ON THE WABASH

115 **He ordered the Ohio militia disbanded in fall of 1807** Sugden, *Life*, 7.
115 **"After the most strict enquiry"** Ibid., 162.
116 **"My children, I have heard bad news"** This message from WHH to Tenskwatawa was in September 1807, according to Edmunds in *Shawnee Prophet*, 61. Tenskwatawa responded soon after.
117 **The Tippecanoe location** Ibid., 68.
118 **Since the signing of the Treaty** See Owens, *Hammer*, 99–100, for bribes given to Little Turtle in 1805 to get him to agree to treaties, and how Jefferson advocated these bribes or "liberalities."
118 **He had visited Washington, D.C.** Calloway, *Indian World*, 461.
119 **Little Turtle's daughter** Sugden, *Life*, 148–50.
119 **Threatened by the Prophet's power** William Wells to Secretary of War Henry Dearborn, April 22, 1808, *Territorial Papers*, 6:558–59.
119 **"[Tenskwatawa's] plans had been layed"** Ibid.
120 **"For the first time"** Edmunds, *Shawnee Prophet*, 70.
121 **The Miami called it Kiteepihkwanonk** From signage in Tippecanoe Battlefield Museum, August 2019.
121 **They cut saplings** Alford, *Civilization*, 15–16.
123 **This "interplanting"** Eames-Sheavly, *Three Sisters*, 4.
123 **Having originally been domesticated** Brigit Katz, "Rethinking the Corny History of Maize," *Smithsonian Magazine*, December 14, 2018, https://www.smithsonianmag.com/smart-news/rethinking-corny-history-maize-180971038/, accessed June 29, 2020. See also Sleeper-Smith, *Indigenous Prosperity*, 26–32.
123 **Dent corn for grinding** Eames-Sheavly, *Three Sisters*, 8.
123 **"Generally, women were not involved"** Sleeper-Smith, *Indigenous Prosperity*, 26.
123 **Bread Dance, or Tak-u-wha Nag-a-way** Alford, *Civilization*, 56–61.

124 **"The Bread dance"**   Warren, *Worlds the Shawnees Made*, 7.

124 **In some Shawnee traditions**   Voegelin and Voegelin, "Shawnee Female Deity in Historical Perspective," 370.

124 **Harrison held firm**   WHH to Secretary of War Henry Dearborn, May 19, 1808, in WHH, *Messages and Letters*, 1:290-91.

124 **"Father—I hope what I now say"**   The Prophet to WHH, June 24, 1808, in WHH, *Messages and Letters*, 1:291-92.

125 **Harrison softened his stance**   WHH to the Prophet, Summer 1808, in WHH, *Messages and Letters*, 1:292-94.

126 **Messengers had arrived**   Edmunds, *Shawnee Prophet*, 70-71, and Sugden, *Life*, 170-71.

127 **If British forces and allied nations**   Sugden, *Life*, 171-74. See also "William Claus," *Dictionary of Canadian Biography*, http://www.biographi.ca/en /bio/claus_william_6E.html, accessed June 7, 2020.

129 **"A very shrewd intelligent man"**   Edmunds, *Tecumseh*, 115.

CHAPTER 10: THE GOVERNOR'S NEW BOSS

130 **"Never did a prisoner"**   From "Thomas Jefferson to Pierre Samuel Du Pont de Nemours, 2 March 1809," Founders Online, National Archives, https:// founders.archives.gov/documents/Jefferson/99-01-02-9936, accessed May 4, 2021.

130 **In March 1809, James Madison**   Madison's biographical details come from James Madison's Montpelier website: https://www.montpelier.org/learn/ the-life-of-james-madison.

131 **"This is the first request"**   "Journal of the Proceedings of the Indian Treaties at Fort Wayne and Vincennes September 1 to October 27, 1809," in WHH, *Messages and Letters*, 1:368.

132 **This had thwarted**   Owens, *Hammer*, 199.

133 **He had first written**   WHH to Eustis, May 16, 1809, in WHH, *Messages and Letters*, 1:346-47.

133 **These three million acres, he argued**   Sugden, *Life*, 183; Owens, *Hammer*, 199.

133 **The president did, however**   Eustis to WHH, July 15, 1809, in WHH, *Messages and Letters*, 356-57.

133 **"Your Excellency [Governor Harrison] will be satisfied"**   Eustis to WHH, June 5, 1809, in WHH, *Messages and Letters*, 347-48.

133 **"Permit me to assure you Sir"**   WHH to Eustis, July 5, 1809, in WHH, *Messages and Letters*, 349-55.

134 **Napoleon's armies had upended**   Owens, *Hammer*, 200. See also "Journal of the Proceedings at the Indian Treaty at Fort Wayne and Vincennes, September 1 to October 27, 1809," in WHH, *Messages and Letters*. In a speech to the Native people to sell their lands, WHH refers to the falling prices of furs due to the troubles in Europe, 365.

134 **"With astonishing abandon"**   Sugden, *Life*, 178.

135 **He would dispense 7,000 gills or 218 gallons**   Owens, *Hammer*, 200-1.

135 **Eastern Potawatomi, who lived near the south**   Ibid., 200, refers to those Potawatomis around Fort Dearborn (Chicago) and the St. Joseph River in contrast to the Western Potawatomis, which he describes as "fiercely anti-American." Sugden, *Life*, 183, also discusses the desperation of the Eastern Potawatomis on 183-84.

135 **"The poverty and wretchedness"**   WHH to Eustis, November 3, 1809, in WHH, *Messages and Letters*, 1:387-91.

135 **An Eastern Potawatomi "government chief"**   See Owens, *Hammer*, especially 204. Winamac is only one chief among the Eastern Potawatomi, and he was friendly toward the United States.

136 **In the run-up to the conference, Harrison had admitted**   See WHH to Eustis, July 5, 1809, in WHH, *Messages and Letters*, 349-55.

137 **"Look at their Woman & Children"**   "Journal of the Proceedings," in WHH, *Messages and Letters*, 367.

137 **slam previous Miami associations with the British**   Ibid., 371-72.

137 **This meant that they would not receive**   Owens, *Hammer*, 202.

138 **"[Harrison] invited the Potawatomis and Delawares"**   Ibid., 204-5.

138 **Cleverly using other tribes**   See Tanner, *Atlas of Great Lakes Indian History*, for geographic areas occupied by various tribes, and map "Indian Villages and Tribal Distribution, c. 1768," 58-59.

139 **"These and almost all the other"**   Edmunds, *Shawnee Prophet*, 81.

139 **"I have the honor to inform you"**   WHH to Eustis, October 1, 1809, in WHH, *Messages and Letters*, 1:358.

139 **"As it is the arrangement which has been made is just"**   WHH to Eustis, November 3, 1809, in WHH, *Messages and Letters*, 1:387-91.

140 **If any "ill blood"**   Ibid., 388.

140 **Harrison displayed "ruthless pragmatism"**   Owens, *Hammer*, 204-6.

CHAPTER 11: IN THE WALNUT GROVE

141 **He first traveled first west**   Edmunds, *Tecumseh*, 120.

141 **"The white devil with his mouth"**   Sugden, *Life*, 134.

142 **Also listening to Tecumseh's impassioned speech**   Ibid., 180–81. Details of the event are also found in Drake, *Tecumseh*, 115–16.

142 *If Governor Harrison were there*   Drake, *Tecumseh*, 115, and John Johnston to Harrison, June 24, 1810, in WHH, *Messages and Letters*, 1:430–32.

143 **Winamac of the Eastern Potawatomi**   Sugden, *Life*, 183–84.

143 **A warning emanated from Prophetstown**   Edmunds, *Shawnee Prophet*, 82.

143 **The result of Harrison's**   Edmunds, *Tecumseh*, 124–25.

144 **He had heard of the threats**   WHH to Eustis, November 3, 1809, in WHH, *Messages and Letters*, 1:387–91.

144 **It declared that the governor believed**   WHH to the Prophet (translated from the French), July 19, 1810, in WHH, *Messages and Letters*, 1:447–49.

144 **"There is your grave"**   Ibid., n1, quoting Dillon, *History of Indiana.*

145 **Barron reported their conversation in detail**   WHH to Eustis, August 6, 1810, in WHH, *Messages and Letters*, 1:456–59.

145 **It was a "middle ground"**   Edmunds, *Tecumseh*, 108–9.

147 **"One of the finest looking men I ever saw"**   See Drake, *Tecumseh*, 125, and Cleaves, *Old Tippecanoe*, 72.

147 **About forty warriors**   Drake, *Tecumseh*, 125. Dillon, *History of Indiana*, 442, says seventy-five. Sugden, *Life*, 198, says perhaps seventy-five warriors camped with Tecumseh about a mile above town. Lieutenant Jesse Jennings, of Kentucky, who headed WHH's security detail, was killed the following summer in a duel against a fellow officer, Captain Thorton Posey, from Fort Knox at Vincennes. See WHH, *Messages and Letters*, 1:461n1.

148 **Harrison sat down in his armchair**   Dawson, *Historical Narrative of WHH*, 156, makes note of WHH's armchair. Sugden, *Life*, 242, notes that Tecumseh carried a tomahawk pipe on his southern tour.

149 **"You are continually driving the red people"**   "Tecumseh's Speech," August 20, 1810, in WHH, *Messages and Letters*, 1:463–67.

149 *Ne-kat-a-cush-e Ka-top-o-lin-to*   The image and the translation that Tecumseh used in his speech that day is cited in Law, *Colonial History of Vincennes*, 86. A number of accounts exist about this confrontation between Tecumseh and Harrison, some more detailed than others. For the most part, the author has relied on Law's *Colonial History of Vincennes*, as it contains considerable detail, and Law took up residence in Vincennes only a few years after the confrontation. He spent many years in the early 1800s researching and compiling his *Colonial History*, and he clearly spoke with eyewitnesses to the confrontation. He appears to have possessed written statements from some. *Colonial History of Vincennes* was first presented as an address given to the Vincennes Historical and Antiquarian Society on February 22, 1839. Drake,

Tecumseh, also gives a detailed account of this confrontation and the manner in which both sides jumped to their feet. Dawson, *Historical Narrative of WHH*, written in the early 1800s, gives detailed accounts of this incident as well. Drake draws from Dawson's account, which may have come from WHH himself.

150 **At this moment, that village chief, Winamac** Drake, *Tecumseh*, 127.

151 **William Henry Harrison was taken aback** Law, *Colonial History of Vincennes*, 87.

151 **But most of all he impressed with his defiance** See ibid. and Sugden, *Life*, for interpretations of how impressively Tecumseh came across to Harrison in this meeting.

152 **"There was 'no foundation in fact'"** Law, *Colonial History of Vincennes*, 87–88.

153 **Taking a legalistic approach** Dawson, *Historical Narrative of WHH*, 156. This was a contemporary biography of WHH written in 1824 by Cincinnati newspaper editor Moses Dawson, who says in the introduction it was written in part to defend WHH against calumny from his enemies. Dawson states that he had WHH's cooperation.

153 **Governor Harrison jumped up from his armchair** Drake, *Tecumseh*, 127. See Dawson, *Historical Narrative of WHH*, 156, for a description of WHH disengaging himself from his armchair, Captain Floyd drawing his dirk, and Reverend Winans running for the house.

155 **White men had recently visited** WHH, *Messages and Letters*, August 21, 1810, 1:468-69. See also Law, *Colonial History of Vincennes*, 90-91, and Dawson, *Historical Narrative of WHH*, 158.

156 **"I am authorized to say"** WHH, *Messages and Letters*, August 21, 1810, 1:469.

156 **"The President would never admit"** Dawson, *Historical Narrative of WHH*, 158. See also accounts in other sources, above, such as Drake, *Tecumseh*, 128-29, citing Dawson.

157 **Tecumseh received the two hospitably** Dawson, *Historical Narrative of WHH*, 158-59.

158 **"Well," said Tecumseh, "as the great chief"** Ibid., 159. See also Dillon, *History of Indiana*, 446, for this statement.

CHAPTER 12: THE GOVERNOR'S DARK THOUGHTS

161 **Harrison and the Shawnee brothers** Edmunds, *Tecumseh*, 144.

161 **Traveling on a fast black pony** Sugden, *Life*, 206-12.

162 **"If you do not join"** Ibid., 207.

162 **"You, Father, have nourished us"** Ibid., 213, quoting "Speech of Tecumseh" enclosed in letter Elliott to Clause, November 16-18, 1810.

163 **The British officials tried to remain** Edmunds, *Tecumseh*, 136-37.

163 **"The time is drawing nigh"** William Clark to Eustis, May 24, 1811, in WHH, *Messages and Letters*, 1:520-21.

163 **"On the 2nd of May General William Clarke"** WHH to Eustis, June 6, 1811, WHH, *Messages and Letters*, 1:512-17.

166 **This, although Madison himself had repeatedly** See Eustis to WHH, October 26, 1810, in WHH, *Messages and Letters*, 1:482-83. Wrote Eustis: "But at this time more particularly it is desirable that peace with all the Indian tribes should be preserved, and I am instructed by the President to express to your Excellency his expectation and confidence, that in all your arrangements this may be considered (as I am confident it ever has been) a primary object."

    Also, see Eustis to WHH, July 20, 1811: "Since my letter of the 17th instant, I have been particularly instructed by the President, to communicate to your excellency his earnest desire that peace may, if possible, be preserved with the Indians, and that to this end every proper means may be adopted."

166 **"The President's injunction with regard"** WHH to Eustis, December 24, 1810, in WHH, *Messages and Letters*, 1:496-500.

167 **The population of the Indiana Territory** Cayton, *Frontier Indiana*, 185.

167 **"Is one of the fairest portions"** "Annual Message to Indiana Territorial Legislature," November 12, 1810, in WHH, *Messages and Letters*, 1:487-96.

168 **In the Shawnee awareness** Sugden, *Life*, 16-17. See also Howard, *Shawnee!*, 162-64, and Alford, *Civilization*, 18-19. Trowbridge, in *Shawnese Traditions*, also goes into detail of Shawnee spiritual life based on material from informants in the early 1800s.

168 **"It is my opinion that Government"** Sugden, *Life*, 185.

168 **Native women who grew corn** Sleeper-Smith, *Indigenous Prosperity*. See Indigenous Women of the Ohio Valley.

169 **"With the Indian tribes, also, the peace"** "President's Annual Message," December 5, 1810, Annals of Congress, Senate, 11th Cong., 3rd Sess., 13.

169 **"Having received no orders"** WHH to Eustis, April 23, 1811, in WHH, *Messages and Letters*, 1:506-10.

170 **He reported that agent William Clark** WHH to Eustis, July 2, 1811, in WHH, *Messages and Letters*, 1:526-28.

170 **"His determination is"** WHH to Eustis, June 19, 1811, in WHH, *Messages and Letters*, 1:518-19.

170 **"You shall not surprise us"** WHH to Tecumseh, June 24, 1811, in WHH, *Messages and Letters*, 1:522-24.

171 **"These events, Sir, require no comment"** WHH to Eustis, July 2, 1811, in WHH, *Messages and Letters*, 1:526-27.

171 **He quickly replied by canoe messenger** Tecumseh to WHH, July 4, 1811, in WHH, *Messages and Letters*, 1:529.

172 **Tecumseh's reply did little to quell** WHH to Eustis, July 10, 1811, in WHH, *Messages and Letters*, 1:532-35.

173 **"It is impossible to doubt"** Petition to James Madison, President of the United States, from citizens of Vincennes, July 31, 1811, in WHH, *Messages and Correspondence*, 1:540-42.

173 **In early August 1811** Eustis to WHH, July 17, 1811, in WHH, *Letters and Correspondence*, 1:535-36.

173 **Eustis sounded a note of alarm** Eustis to WHH, July 20, 1811, in WHH, *Letters and Correspondence*, 1:536-37.

174 **This meeting at Grouseland, however** Edmunds, *Tecumseh*, 144-46.

174 **On Tecumseh's arrival** Sugden, *Life*, 221.

175 **"I believe Sir that . . . the combination"** WHH to Eustis, August 7, 1811, in WHH, *Messages and Letters*, 1:548-51.

CHAPTER 13: TENSKWATAWA MAKES A GAMBLE

177 **Embedded in the Great Bear** See "The Great Bear," *Woodland Ways Bushcraft Blog*, www.woodland-ways.co.uk/blog/natural-navigation-tips/the-great-bear/, accessed December 12, 2022.

178 **The four hundred regulars of the Fourth Regiment** Cleaves, *Old Tippecanoe*, 84-88.

178 **A phalanx of these dandified regulars** See Winkler, *Tippecanoe*, 49, for a schematic layout of the marching order.

178 **Governor Harrison's idea** Ibid., 52, quoting WHH to Eustis. For Harrison's marching orders to his troops, see also "General Orders, September 27, 1811," WHH, *Messages and Letters*, 1:592-94.

179 **He had calculated** Sugden, *Life*, 229.

179 **That night, a sentry** See Bingham's statement, in WHH, *Messages and Letters*, 1:704.

179 **Governor Harrison and the tempestuous Colonel John Boyd** Cleaves, *Old Tippecanoe*, 86.

180 **A little over a decade later** For details on Congress's ban on slavery and

"involuntary servitude" in the Northwest Territory, see http://www.loc.gov /rr/program//bib/ourdocs/northwest.html, accessed May 14, 2020. See also the Northwest Ordinance of 1787 document, Article 6: https://www.loc.gov /resource/bdsdcc.22501/?sp=2, accessed May 14, 2020.

181 **Opponents dubbed it "A Law"**   Owens, *Hammer*, 112.

182 **This only added to the dawning reality**   Sugden, *Life*, 229.

182 **Harrison sent out expert trackers**   Cleaves, *Old Tippecanoe*, 95.

182 **He summoned an Indiana militia officer**   Burr and Burr, *Life and Times of WHH*, 135–36.

182 **According to a biography of Harrison published**   Ibid.

183 **Harrison gave him an opening**   Edmunds, *Shawnee Prophet*, 107–8.

183 **Tenskwatawa sent a return message**   Winkler, *Tippecanoe*, 57–58.

184 **On the afternoon of November 6**   WHH to Eustis, November 18, 1811, WHH, *Messages and Letters*, 1:618–31.

185 **By all accounts it was a chill**   Lossing, *Pictorial Field-Book*, 203, describes the weather as "dark" and in n5, states that two Winnebago Indians were chosen for assassination attempt on WHH: "There was a slight drizzle of rain at intervals, and the darkness was intense, except occasionally when the clouds parted and faint moonlight came through."

185 **The utter blackness**   Winkler, *Tippecanoe*, 62.

185 **At four forty-five A.M., with dawn's light**   Various accounts give the time of the attack as 4:45 A.M. or 5:45 A.M. The timepieces of Harrison's officers read 4:45 A.M., an hour earlier than watches on the East Coast. In modern times the region that includes the Tippecanoe Battlefield has been designated part of the Eastern Time Zone, which means the battle started at 5:45 A.M. as time is calculated there today. See explanation in Winkler, *Tippecanoe*, photo caption of Simon Kenton timepiece, 70.

185 **"'Brigham, let us fire and run in'"**   Winkler, *Tippecanoe*, 67.

187 **At nearly the same moment**   Ibid., 67. See also Cleaves, *Old Tippecanoe*, 99.

188 **Harrison had called to his servant George**   WHH to Dr. John Scott, December 1811, in WHH, *Messages and Letters*, 1:689–92.

189 **For the Indians looking in from the darkness**   Winkler, *Tippecanoe*, 74.

189 **Surrounded by "the yells"**   "Funk Narrative," from Draper Collection, in WHH, *Messages and Letters*, 1:717–23.

189 **"Will you permit me to dislodge"**   Ibid., 721–22.

190 **"I am a dead man"**   "Statement of William Brigham," in WHH, *Messages and Letters*, 1:703–10.

190 **The Fourth Regiment and mounted dragoons**   "Walker's Journal" in WHH, *Messages and Letters*, 1:702.

190 **"Huzza! Huzza! Huzza!"**   Winkler, *Tippecanoe*, 87.

190 **That day Harrison's army buried**   Ibid., 88.

191 **William Henry, however, called it a "glorious victory"**   WHH to Secretary of War, December 28, 1811, in WHH, *Messages and Letters*, 1:686-87. WHH complains bitterly in this letter that many of the papers are calling it "a most distressing disaster" and "a horrible massacre." He complains particularly about the newspaper *The Baltimore Whig*. Also, see toasts and cheers for men, for WHH, etc., at dinner in Kentucky, December 27, 1811, in WHH, *Messages and Letters*, 1:681-82. "May the 7th of Nov. prove to our enemies that the spark of '76 is not yet extinguished.— 9 cheers."

CHAPTER 14: A LAMP IN THE WEST

193 **After concentrating his earlier recruiting**   For detailed description of Tecumseh's southern tour, see Sugden, *Life*, 238-51.

194 **"In each of the tribes"**   Ibid., 238-39.

195 **As Tecumseh and his fellow chiefs traveled**   Ibid., 242-43. See also Edmunds, *Tecumseh*, 146-48.

195 **"Halt! Tecumseh, listen to me"**   This is the speech that has been preserved in oral history, although its word-for-word accuracy is difficult to judge. "Choctaw Chief Pushmataha Response to Chief Tecumseh on War Against the American," *Great American Indian Speeches*, vol. 1 (New York: Caedmon, 1976), American Rhetoric Online Speech Bank, https://www.americanrhetoric.com/, accessed August 4, 2020.

195 **The Choctaws gave up four million acres**   "Treaty with the Choctaws, 1805," Mississippi Band of Choctaw Indians, www.choctaw.org/aboutMBCI/history/treaties1805.html, accessed July 30, 2022.

195-96 **Tecumseh had relatives here**   Sugden, *Life*, 15.

196 **"Col. Hawkins, at length"**   Ibid., 245.

197 **It climaxed with all the chiefs**   This description of a Shawnee war dance is based on the passage in Denny, *Military Journal*, 71-72, cited in Sugden, *Life*, 440n7.

197 **Insofar as this speech to the Creeks**   For a summary of Tecumseh's speech to the Creeks, as best as Edmunds could reconstruct it from various partial accounts, see Edmunds, *Tecumseh*, 150.

197 **Tecumseh's message resonated**   Versions of the origins of Red Sticks are from Sugden, *Life*, 246, about red clubs, and Drake, *Tecumseh*, 143-45.

198 **"It is certain that an Indian"**   Letter from Francis McHenry in *The Georgia*

Journal, as quoted in *The Halcyon Luminary, and Theological Repository* 1, no. 6 (June 1812): 275–77.

199 **Originally an Ohio Valley tribe**   See Andrea A. Hunter, "Ancestral Osage Geography," Osage Nation, www.osagenation-nsn.gov/who-we-are/historic -preservation/osage-cultural-history, accessed July 30, 2022.

199 **"I wish it was in my power"**   Hunter, *Memoirs of a Captivity*, 43–48. Also see Sugden, *Life*, 254–56.

200 **Just two years earlier, Osage leaders**   Sugden, *Life*, 252–53.

202 **At Grouseland, hundreds of miles**   Account on guided tour of Grouseland by Lisa Ice-Jones, August 2019.

203 **Still out in the Mississippi River country**   Sugden, *Life*, 256–57.

203 **Santee Dakota Sioux**   "History of the Santee Sioux Tribe of Nebraska," http://www.santeedakota.org/santee_history_ii.htm, accessed August 12, 2020.

203 **It was a scene of "great destruction"**   Sudgen, *Life*, 257.

CHAPTER 15: A CASE OF NERVES

206 **The outspoken "War Hawks" in Congress**   See "War Hawks Urge Military Confrontation with Britain," National Park Service, https://www.nps.gov/ articles/war-hawks.htm, accessed August 2, 2022.

206 **"It was foreseen that our Atlantick cities"**   Brackenridge, *History of the Late War*, 27.

207 **"Thousands of American citizens"**   "Special Message to Congress on the Foreign Policy Crisis—War Message," June 1, 1812, Miller Center, University of Virginia, millercenter.org/the-presidency/presidential-speeches/ june-1–1812-special-message-congress-foreign-policy-crisis-war, accessed July 31, 2022.

208 **"It was a war," wrote historian**   Hildreth, *History of the United States*, 2nd ser., 3:352, cited in Lossing, *Pictorial Field-Book*, 248.

208 **Although the United States declared**   See Lossing, *Pictorial Field-Book*, 258–59, for a detailed account of how letters and word of war reached various British and U.S. outposts.

208 **By July 15, news had reached**   Richardson, *War of 1812*, 22n2.

208 **About a month after President Madison**   For a detailed account of the invasion of Mackinac Island from St. Joseph Island, see Lossing, *Pictorial Field-Book*, 269–71. See also Brackenridge, *History of the Late War*, 32–33.

209 **"The situation completely commands"**   Brackenridge, *History of the Late War*, 33.

210 "**It was a fortunate circumstance**"   John Askin, Jr., as quoted in Lossing, *Pictorial Field-Book*, 271.

210 **had laid the groundwork for tribes**   Sugden, *Life*, 287.

210 **they had captured what some strategists**   Brackenridge, *History of the Late War*, 33, refers to it as "the American Gibraltar."

212 **Hull was old enough**   See Sugden, *Life*, 286-87, for a physical description of Hull and a portrait of Hull by Stuart, mentioned by Lossing, along with other Hull bio details, in 296n1.

213 **Why didn't he keep going to Canada**   Lossing, *Pictorial Field-Book*, 263. Lossing refers to a "mutinous spirit" among some of the Ohio volunteers for not immediately invading Canada as the British built fortifications across the river at Sandwich.

213 **"After thirty years of peace and prosperity"**   Ibid., 262-63.

214 **"No," he said indignantly**   Drake, *Life of Tecumseh*, 163.

215 **"I can scarcely restrain my indignation"**   Robert B. M'Afee, in *History of the Late War in the Western Country*, quoted in Lossing, *Pictorial Field-Book*, 265.

216 **"His appearance was venerable"**   Lossing, *Pictorial Field-Book*, 282n1.

217 **"As the soldiers fled"**   Sugden, *Life*, 288-89.

217 **Occurring on July 25, 1812, and orchestrated by Tecumseh**   Lossing, *Pictorial Field-Book*, 267. See Edmunds, *Tecumseh*, 172, on Tecumseh's role in these first skirmishes.

CHAPTER 16: WARRIOR FROM THE EAST

219 **"No other sound"**   Richardson, *War of 1812*, 34.

220 **"Had I been at home"**   Tecumseh to Elliott, June 8, 1812, in WHH, *Messages and Letters*, 2:60-61.

220 **Secretary of War Eustis ordered Harrison**   Edmunds, *Tecumseh*, 163.

220 **But Harrison went further**   Sugden, *Life*, 265-66. See also Drake, *Tecumseh*, 157.

220 **But with the thaws of March**   Sugden, *Life*, 260.

221 **"We defy a living creature to say"**   "Speeches of the Indians at Massassinway by the Wyandots," May 15, 1812, in WHH, *Messages and Letters*, 2:50-53.

221 **"Father & Brothers! We will now"**   Tecumseh to Elliott, June 8, 1812, in WHH, *Messages and Letters*, 2:60-61.

222 **Working with fellow chiefs**   Sugden, *Life*, 271-75, 284-85, details these wampum belts and other messages sent to distant tribes. He points out that it is unclear from the existing historical record exactly what Tecumseh and other

chiefs were asking of these tribes. Some anecdotes indicate that Tecumseh planned a unified uprising against the Americans across this large span of continent.

222 **He arrived on July 1**   Edmunds, *Tecumseh*, 169. Sugden, *Life*, 275, has Tecumseh leaving Fort Wayne and meeting with Indian agents there on June 21.

222 **He instructed Tenskwatawa**   Wells to Harrison, July 22, 1812, in WHH, *Messages and Letters*, 2:76–78.

223 **He had just received an intelligence report**   Lossing, *Pictorial Field-Book*, 278.

224 **"Soldiers," Colonel Miller called out**   Ibid.

224 **"On the morning of Sunday, the 9th"**   Richardson, *War of 1812*, 33–34. For a Richardson biography, see the biographical introduction to his *War of 1812*, as well as his entry in *Dictionary of Canadian Biography*, http://www .biographi.ca/en/bio/richardson_john_1796_1852_8E.html, accessed August 30, 2020. Richardson had grown up into his teen years at Amherstburg, where his father was based.

224 **Just a few days earlier**   Lossing, *Pictorial Field-Book*, 272.

225 **The combined force**   Sugden, *Life*, 295, and Lossing, *Pictorial Field-Book*, 279.

225 **A single musket shot rang**   Lossing, *Pictorial Field-Book*, 279–82.

226 **"Charge! boys, charge"**   Ibid., 280. Many of the details on the U.S. side of this battle come from Judge Witherell, cited by Lossing.

227 **The U.S. officers declared a victory**   For the perspective of a U.S. officer on the battle, see "Major Dalliba's Account," in Richardson, *War of 1812*, 37–45.

227 **Colonel Miller's forces suffered**   Sugden, *Life*, 297.

227 **Both Tecumseh and Muir received wounds**   Drake, *Life of Tecumseh*, 165.

227 **"Ultimately, then, Tecumseh and Muir had suffered"**   Sugden, *Life*, 297.

228 **"A great part of the banks"**   Brock's orders from August 12, 1812, in Brock, *Life and Correspondence*, 225–26.

228 **Isaac Brock had hungered**   For a Brock biography, see "Brock, Sir Isaac" in *Dictionary of Canadian Biography*, http://www.biographi.ca/en/bio/brock _isaac_5E.html, accessed August 26, 2020.

229 **Before it erupted**   Ibid.

229 **When the threat at Fort Malden**   Lossing, *Pictorial Field-Book*, 273–74.

230 **"Do, pray, Elliott, fully explain"**   Brock, *Life and Correspondence*, 227.

230 **At General Brock's side that night**   "John Baskerville Glegg," *The Canadian Encyclopedia*, https://www.thecanadianencyclopedia.ca/en/article/john -baskerville-glegg, accessed September 1, 2020.

230 "Tecumseh's appearance was very prepossessing" Brock, *Life and Correspondence*, 227–28.

230 Aide-de-camp Glegg descended "John Baskerville Glegg," *The Canadian Encyclopedia*, https://www.thecanadianencyclopedia.ca/en/article/john-baskerville-glegg, accessed September 1, 2020.

231 General Brock called out Glegg, in Brock, *Life and Correspondence*, 228–29.

231 Warriors had come from far away Sugden, *Life*, 281, lists various tribes of warriors gathered at Bois Blanc Island as of mid-July, about 350 total. This increased as word spread of the Indian and British victories over the Americans.

232 Tecumseh gave "expressions of joy" Glegg in Brock, *Life and Correspondence*, 228–29.

232 "Ho-yo-o-e!" he exclaimed James FitzGibbon to Ferdinand Brock Tupper, September 27, 1845, in Ferdinand Brock Tupper papers, cited in Sugden, *Life*, 300 and 446n10. Sudgen observes that FitzGibbon, who provided this remark years later to Brock's biographer, Ferdinand Brock Tupper, was not actually present at this meeting, but said he heard it from an eyewitness.

232 On August 15 McAfee, *History of the Late War*, 98–99. Also see Hatch, *Chapter of the History*, 43–44, for a detailed description of a rowboat, rowed by two men, with two men sitting aft, that appeared in the darkness. The men then went up to General Hull's headquarters for three hours, this on the night of August 13–14. It is Hatch's contention that a secret surrender was arranged between Hull and Brock at that time.

233 "Sir—The force at my disposal" Brock, *Life and Correspondence*, 230–31.

233 At the same time Richardson, *War of 1812*, 59–62, reproduces General Brock's thanks to his officers after the fort's surrender, including Captain Dixon of the Royal Engineers for the placement of the batteries.

234 "Sir—I have received your letter" Brock, *Life and Correspondence*, 100.

234 The American troops at the fort Lossing, *Pictorial Field-Book*, 286.

235 One British shell, the story was later told Ibid., 287n2, quoting Judge Witherell. This main street later became known as Jefferson Avenue.

235 In the disconcerting midnight silence Sugden, *Life*, 301.

235 "Tecumseh, taking a roll of elm bark" Drake, *Tecumseh*, 166.

236 The craft landed on the riverbank For terrain, see the map in Lossing, *Pictorial Field-Book*, 266.

236 Loading the guns with massive charges Richardson, *War of 1812*, 52–55.

236 "Nothing but the boldness of the enterprize" Ibid., 52–53.

237 General Brock gave the order Ibid., 54.

237 **There were so many uncertainties**   For General Hull's thoughts at this
moment, see his defense of his own actions in his letter to Secretary of War
Eustis, August 26, 1812, quoted in Lossing, *Pictorial Field-Book*, 289n4, and
also in Brock, *Life and Correspondence*, his numerous items of defense of his
actions. Hull gives his thoughts about his difficult situation in this moment in
his *Memoirs of the Campaign*, 166–67.

237 **He had about 1,500 men**   This rough count is from Sugden, *Life*, 301–4.
Sugden says Hull had 1,060 men fit for duty, plus 300 to 400 Michigan militiamen (many of whom defected) and that he ultimately surrendered 2,188 men,
consisting of 582 regulars and 1,606 militia. The surrendered total includes the
350 men out on the mission to rescue the Ohio supply train at the time of the
attack.

238 **"I killed your husband"**   See the graphic example in John Dunn Hunter's
Memoirs of a Captivity, 25–26.

239 **The room in the house where Hull's daughter**   Lossing, *Pictorial Field-
Book*, 288. See also Hatch, *Chapter of the History*, 41–42. "The same ball
passed on and mortally wounded Surgeon Reynolds of the third regiment volunteers, by taking off both legs above the knee."

239 **He stepped into a room of the barracks**   Lossing, *Pictorial Field-Book*,
289 and 289n1.

CHAPTER 17: A SECRET PASSAGE OUT

240 **Several months earlier, William Henry**   Cleaves, *Old Tippecanoe*,
110–11.

240 **When alarming reports**   Ibid.

242 **A pause—an ominous one**   WHH to Eustis, January 7, 1812, in WHH,
Messages and Letters, 2:3–5.

242 **They greeted Governor Harrison**   Cleaves, *Old Tippecanoe*, 113.

242 **"Each member of the company"**   Ibid., quoting *The Frankfort (Ky.) Argus*,
July 1, 1812.

244 **"The American Backwoodsman"**   Cleaves, *Old Tippecanoe*, 143, quoting
Cincinnati *Gazette*, August 3, 1812, reporting dinner held on July 9, 1812.

245 **In a letter to the secretary of war**   WHH to Eustis, August 12, 1812, in
WHH, *Messages and Letters*, 2:84–88.

245 **But then urgent mounted messengers**   Cleaves, *Old Tippecanoe*, 115.

246 **The post amounted to a new**   For an illustration of Fort Dearborn, see
Lossing, *Pictorial Field-Book*, 303.

246 **The traders living next** Ibid., 305–13, gives a detailed account of the fall of Chicago, based on eyewitness reports. Many of the details here are taken from Lossing's account.

246 **"The white chiefs' wives are amusing"** Ibid., 304, citing Mrs. John H. Kinzie, *Wau-Bun*, chap. 18. Kinzie's father-in-law was one of the post's traders.

247 **Some of the women, eyewitnesses later** Ibid., 310.

248 **The Ohio Valley and Upper Midwest** McAfee, *History of the Late War*, 129, and Lossing, *Pictorial Field-Book*, 313, state that Indians and British could drive the border back to the Ohio River.

248 **The eating of William Wells's heart** Ibid., 313n1.

249 **Settlers began to flee** Governor Shelby to Eustis, September 5, 1812, in McAfee, *History of the Late War*, 133.

249 **One homesteader who stayed** Lossing, *Pictorial Field-Book*, 314n4, quoting Zebulon Collings.

249 **They had captured 2,188 men** Sugden, *Life*, 304.

249 **took over a pleasant white house** Ibid., 305–6 and 446–47n14 describes the house.

249 **"When he could perceive no alternative"** Lossing, *Pictorial Field-Book*, 294–95.

249 **"A more sagacious or more gallant warrior"** Ibid., 310–11, citing Brock to Liverpool, August 29, 1812.

250 **"Well," Tecumseh told Wallace** Ibid., 305–6, citing Wallace interview with John D. Shane.

251 **Adding still more momentum** Ibid., 325n2.

251 **"Difficulty, argument, and intimidation"** Sugden, *Life*, 312.

252 **Kentucky's outgoing governor, Charles Scott** Cleaves, *Old Tippecanoe*, 115–16.

252 **"The backwoodsmen are a singular people"** WHH to Eustis, September 3, 1812, in WHH, *Messages and Letters*, 2:108–10.

253 **"In an army but one can rule"** Cleaves, *Old Tippecanoe*, 126.

253 **The Potawatomis had waited** Edmunds, *Tecumseh*, 182.

254 **Tenskwatawa's followers from Prophetstown** See Sugden, *Life*, 315–16, for an account of the attack on Fort Harrison.

256 **But he recognized that none** WHH to Eustis, December 12, 1812, in WHH, *Messages and Letters*, 2:240–43.

257 **As one participant, Squire Reynolds** Coffin, *1812*, 203.

257 **"No sight could be more beautiful"** Richardson, *War of 1812*, 134.

258 **Three days later**   Lossing, *Pictorial Field-Book*, 354.

258 **Only thirty of the Americans**   See Sugden, *Life*, 322–23, for numbers on casualties.

258 **"The appearance of the American prisoners captured"**   Richardson, *War of 1812*, 140.

259 **"Never, dear mother"**   Lossing, *Pictorial Field-Book*, 355n1.

259 **"Remember the River Raisin!"**   Ibid., 360.

CHAPTER 18: GENERAL JANUARY

260 **While General Hull invaded**   The invasion of the main body of troops into Canada occurred on July 12, 1812; see Lossing, *Pictorial Field-Book*, 262.

261 **By November 14, the temperature**   See Charles Minard graph of Napoleon's Russian Campaign (compiled 1869) in "Napoleonic Wars—The Retreat from Moscow," *Encyclopedia Britannica*, www.britannica.com/event/Napoleonic-Wars/The-retreat-from-Moscow, accessed October 13, 2020.

264 **Whatever it was, he slowly gained**   Sugden, *Life*, 323.

264 **Tecumseh's revolt had spread south**   Ibid., 320–21, discusses the Seminole-Black uprising in Florida.

268 **"The fire of the 24-pounder battery"**   Richardson, *War of 1812*, 149.

268 **The pedestal for the Statue of Liberty**   Benjamin Levine and Isabelle F. Story, Statue of Liberty: Early History of the Island, National Park Service, 1961, http://www.libertystatepark.org/statueofliberty/sol14a.shtml, accessed January 3, 2023.

270 **"painted almost every color"**   Sugden, *Life*, 332–33, quoting the unpublished journal of George Carter Dale, in Wisconsin Historical Society collections.

271 **Harrison's forces suffered**   Sugden, *Life*, 338–39.

271 **Tecumseh arrived in the midst of this**   Richardson, *War of 1812*, 154.

CHAPTER 19: THE FLEET IN THE WILDERNESS

273 *Frolic*, **18 guns, Broadside**   From Coffin, *1812*, 77n.

274 **"I believe I have as perfect a knowledge"**   Dobbins to Elliot, quoted in Denys W. Knoll, "Battle of Lake Erie: Building the Fleet in the Wilderness." Naval Historical Foundation. https://www.navyhistory.org/battle-of-lake-erie-building-the-fleet-in-the-wilderness/. Other details of the ships' construction also come from this pamphlet, published in 1979.

276 **By now, huge numbers** Sugden, *Life*, 342–45.

276 **Procter, recently promoted** Coffin, *1812*, 198, quoting Squire Reynolds, born at Fort Detroit in 1781 and an eyewitness to many of these events. Coffin interviewed Reynolds at age eighty-three.

277 **In order to keep their villages** Sugden, *Life*, 242–43.

278 **Tecumseh called Commodore Barclay** See "Robert Heriot Barclay," *The Canadian Encyclopedia*, www.thecanadianencyclopedia.ca/en/article/robert-heriot-barclay, accessed October 15, 2020.

278 **A British witness to this council** Robert Reynolds recollection, in Coffin, *1812*, 210–11. Other sources suggest that Reynolds might have recalled a different meeting where this conflict between Elliott and Procter erupted.

279 **Tecumseh and Roundhead had hatched** Sugden, *Life*, 346–49, gives an account of the second assault on Fort Meigs in spring 1813.

279 **General Harrison had left the fort** Cleaves, *Old Tippecanoe*, 172–73.

280 **"When the fort shall be taken"** Lossing, *Pictorial Field-Book*, 501.

280 **The watching Native warriors thought** Edmunds, *Tecumseh*, 199.

281 **Anticipating just such a charge** Lossing, *Pictorial Field-Book*, 502–3.

281 **The toll came to** Sugden, *Life*, 348.

281 **"impressed with a high sense"** Lossing, *Pictorial Field-Book*, 504n3.

282 **The Wyandots, suggested Harrison** Edmunds, *Tecumseh*, 200.

282 **privately relayed to the messengers** Sugden, *Life*, 355–56.

283 **But Captain Dobbins had that figured** Knoll, "Battle of Lake Erie."

283 **Taking command of the U.S. fleet** See "Oliver Hazard Perry," Naval History and Heritage Command, https://www.history.navy.mil/browse-by-topic/people/historical-figures/oliver-hazard-perry.html, accessed October 16, 2020.

284 **"From Tecumseh's perspective"** Edmunds, *Tecumseh*, 202.

285 **Early on the brilliant blue day** Lossing, *Pictorial Field-Book*, 519–20, gives a detailed account of the weather, commands, etc., as the battle begins. Coffin and Richardson also give vivid details of this naval battle on Lake Erie.

285 **He ordered the decks sprinkled** Ibid., 521.

CHAPTER 20: IN THE HANDS OF THE GREAT SPIRIT

288 **Sister Tecumpease was there** Sugden, *Life*, 362. Sugden also speculates on what the situation might have looked like to her at this moment, when they have to move again and the men in her life have to go off to battle.

288 **At Chillicothe, she had helped**   For a description of the Bread Dance and the I-la-ni-wag-a-way, the male dance for warriors, see Alford, *Civilization*, 62.

289 **It was not until four days after**   Ibid., 357.

289 **Through whistling balls and shot**   See Coffin, *1812*, 217. See also Lossing, *Pictorial Field-Book*, 521–27, for a detailed description of the action, and see Perry's first-person report of the action, in Richardson, *War of 1812*, 200.

291 **An hour later, Perry scribbled out**   Lossing, *Pictorial Field-Book*, 530.

291 **When the messengers**   Edmunds, *Tecumseh*, 203, and Sugden, *Life*, 360–62.

293 **Lean, wiry, strong**   Richardson, *War of 1812*, 204–7, gives an intimate description of Tecumseh's bearing and dress in this moment and a complete transcription of his speech.

295 **"[Laughter erupted]"**   Edmunds, *Tecumseh*, 205.

295 **Tecumseh gazed into the bed**   Ibid., 210–11, gives detail of Tecumseh's actions and mood around the campfire the night before the Battle of the Thames.

296 **One writer of the period**   See "William Foster Coffin," *Dictionary of Canadian Biography*, www.biographi.ca/en/bio/coffin_william_foster_10E.html, accessed October 23, 2020. His family moved from England to Quebec in 1813 when he was five years old, so he had an understanding of Canadian wilderness traveling conditions in this era.

296 **"Whether for advance or for retreat"**   Coffin, *1812*, 219–20.

297 **880 British regulars**   Sugden, *Life*, 365. Sugden lists the different nations of Indian warriors on page 362.

298 **"The landing of our army"**   Winkler, *Thames*, 52–53.

298 **Fifty miles into the Canadian interior**   The designated spot to make a stand, known as the Forks of the Thames, is located near present-day Chatham, Ontario.

299 **Tecumseh erupted in rage**   Sugden, *Life*, 264–65.

299 **Harrison was riding at the head**   Winkler, *Thames*, 56.

299 **"Gen. Harrison soon came up"**   Ibid., 60, quoting McAfee's journal.

300 **"Father, tell your men"**   Sugden, *Life*, 371.

300 **Tecumseh arrayed his eight hundred Native warriors**   Edmunds, *Tecumseh*, 208–14. For a description of the cedar swamp, see Richardson, *War of 1812*.

301 **Tecumseh unbelted his sword**   Sugden, *Life*, 370–71, citing Anthony Shane's account.

301 **General Harrison's 3,500-man army**   Ibid., 372.

302 **General Procter turned his horse's tail to the action**   Ibid., 372–73.

302 **Believing it to be Harrison**   Winkler, *Thames*, 77.

302 **Tecumseh took the ball squarely**   Sugden, *Life*, 379.

303 **It appeared that an Indian barrier state**   Sugden, *Life*, 385. British authorities earlier had promised Tecumseh that if they won the war against the United
States, Britain would return to the tribes all lands north of the Ohio claimed by
the United States. In peace talks at the war's conclusion, Britain asked for an
Indian barrier state beginning at the Greenville Line.

SELECTED BIBLIOGRAPHY

JOURNALS, DIARIES, LETTERS, AND MEMOIRS

Alford, Thomas Wildcat. *Civilization: And the Story of the Absentee Shawnees*. Norman: University of Oklahoma Press, 1936.

Andrews, Edward Deming. "The Shaker Mission to the Shawnee Indians." *Winterthur Portfolio* 7 (January 1972): 113–28. https://doi.org/10.1086/495806.

Bradbury, John. *Travels in the Interior of North America in the Years 1809, 1810, and 1811*. London: Sherwood, Neely & Jones, 1817.

Collot, Victor, and Joseph Warin. "A Journey in North America, Containing a Survey of the Countries Watered by the Mississippi, Ohio, Missouri and Other Affluing Rivers . . . Illustrated by 36 Maps, Plans, Views and Divers Cuts." Gallica, 1826. https://gallica.bnf.fr/ark:/12148/bpt6k399999j.

Denny, Ebenezer. *Military Journal of Major Ebenezer Denny, an Officer in the Revolutionary and Indian Wars*. Philadelphia: Historical Society of Pennsylvania, 1859.

Harrison, William Henry. *Messages and Letters of William Henry Harrison*. Vol. 1, *1800–1811*. Vol. 2, *1812–1816*. Governors Messages and Letters. Indianapolis: Indiana Historical Commission, 1922.

———. Papers. Library of Congress. Digital Collections, Library of Congress. https://www.loc.gov/collections/william-henry-harrison-papers/about-this-collection/.

Hull, William. *Memoirs of the Campaign of the North Western Army of the United States, A.D. 1812: In a Series of Letters Addressed to the Citizens of the United States, with an Appendix, Containing a Brief Sketch of the Revolutionary Services of the Author*. Boston: True & Greene, 1824.

Hunter, John Dunn. *Memoirs of a Captivity Among the Indians of North America: From Childhood to the Age of Nineteen: With Anecdotes Descriptive of Their Manners and Customs*. London: Longman, Hurst, Rees, Orme, Brown, and Green, 1824.

Jay, Sarah Livingston. Correspondence with Susan Livingston Symmes. Jay Papers, Columbia Digital Library Collections. https://dlc.library.columbia.edu/jay/ldpd:80968.

Naylor, Judge Isaac. "The Battle of Tippecanoe as Described by Judge Isaac Naylor, a Participant—A Recently Discovered Account." *The Indiana Quarterly Magazine of History* 2, no. 4 (Dec. 1906). http://archive.org/details/jstor -27785458.

Richardson, John, and Alexander Clark Casselman. *Richardson's War of 1812: With Notes and a Life of the Author.* Toronto: Historical Publishing Company, 1902.

Ruddell, Stephen. "Reminiscences of Tecumseh's Youth." Handwritten manuscript. Draper Collection, Wisconsin Historical Society Digital Library and Archives, Document No. AJ-155. http://content.wisconsinhistory.org/cdm/ref /collection/aj/id/17916.

Rush, Richard. *Washington in Domestic Life: From Original Letters and Manuscripts.* Philadelphia: Lippincott, 1857.

Sargent, Winthrop. Papers, 1771–1948. https://www.masshist.org/collection-guides/view/fa0261.

———. "Winthrop Sargent's Diary While with General Arthur S. Clair's Expedition Against the Indians." *Ohio History Journal* 33, no. 1 (1924): 237–73. http:// resources.ohiohistory.org/ohj/browse/displaypages.php?display[]=0033& display[]=237&display[]=273.

Short-Harrison-Symmes Families Papers, 1760–1878. Mixed material. http://hdl .loc.gov/loc.mss/eadmss.ms010259.

Smith, James. *An Account of the Remarkable Occurrences in the Life and Travels of Col. James Smith.* Lexington, Ky.: John Bradford, 1799.

Spencer, O. M. *The Indian Captivity of O. M. Spencer.* Edited by Milo Milton Quaife. Chicago: Lakeside Press, 1918.

Symmes, John Cleves. *The Correspondence of John Cleves Symmes: Founder of the Miami Purchase.* Edited by Beverley W. Bond, Jr. Published for the Historical and Philosophical Society of Ohio. New York: Macmillan, 1926.

———. *The Intimate Letters of John Cleves Symmes and His Family, Including Those of His Daughter, Mrs. William Henry Harrison, Wife of the Ninth President of the United States.* Edited by Beverley W. Bond, Jr. Cincinnati: Historical and Philosophical Society of Ohio, 1956. http://archive.org/details/intimate letterso00symm.

OFFICIAL PROCEEDINGS, TREATIES, AND SPEECHES

"A Century of Lawmaking for a New Nation: U.S. Congressional Documents and Debates, 1774–1875." https://memory.loc.gov/cgi-bin/ampage?collId=llsp& fileName=007/llsp007.db&recNum=289.

Annals of Congress Links: U.S. Congressional Documents. https://memory.loc.gov
/ammem/amlaw/lwaclink.html#anchor6.

Founders Online: "I. Address of Black Hoof, [5 February 1802]." http://founders
.archives.gov/documents/Jefferson/01-36-02-0331-0002.

Online Speech Bank: "Chief Pushmataha—Response to Tecumseh." https://www
.americanrhetoric.com/speeches/nativeamericans/chiefpushmataha.htm.

"Treaty with the Wyandot Etc—1795." (Treaty of Greenville.) https://www.first
people.us/FP-Html-Treaties/TreatyWithTheWyandotetc1795.html.

United States Congress. *American State Papers: Documents, Legislative and Executive, of the Congress of the United States.* Washington: Gales and Seaton, 1832.
http://archive.org/details/americanstatepap_c01unit.

ARTICLES

"Brock, Sir Isaac." *Dictionary of Canadian Biography.* http://www.biographi.ca/en
/bio/brock_isaac_5E.html.

Cave, Alfred A. "The Shawnee Prophet, Tecumseh, and Tippecanoe: A Case Study
of Historical Myth-Making." *Journal of the Early Republic* 22, no. 4 (2002):
637. https://doi.org/10.2307/3124761.

Gilbert, Bil. "The Dying Tecumseh and the Birth of a Legend." *Smithsonian
Magazine,* July 1995. https://www.smithsonianmag.com/history/the-dying-
tecumseh-97830806/.

"Glegg, John Baskerville." *The Canadian Encyclopedia.* https://www.thecanadian
encyclopedia.ca/en/article/john-baskerville-glegg.

"Gore, Francis." *The Canadian Encyclopedia.* https://www.thecanadianencyclo
pedia.ca/en/article/francis-gore.

"Harrison, Anna Tuthill Symmes." The White House. https://www.whitehouse.gov
/about-the-white-house/first-ladies/anna-tuthill-symmes-harrison/.

"Hull, William." *The Canadian Encyclopedia.* https://www.thecanadianencyclo
pedia.ca/en/article/william-hull.

Johnson, Geoffrey. "The True Story of the Deadly Encounter at Fort Dearborn."
Chicago, January 4, 2010. http://www.chicagomag.com/Chicago-Magazine
/December-2009/The-True-Story-of-the-Deadly-Encounter-at-Fort-Dearborn/.

Knoll, Denys W. "Battle of Lake Erie: Building the Fleet in the Wilderness."
Naval Historical Foundation. https://www.navyhistory.org/battle-of-lake-erie-
building-the-fleet-in-the-wilderness/.

Lankford, George E. "Losing the Past: Draper and the Ruddell Indian Captivity."
The Arkansas Historical Quarterly 49, no. 3 (1990): 214–39. https://doi.org
/10.2307/40030798.

"The Life of General Harrison." *The Port Folio.* April 1815. https://babel.hathitrust
.org/cgi/pt?id=nyp.33433081659413;view=1up;seq=342.

"Life of John Cleves Symmes." New Jersey Historical Society. http://archive.org
/details/2nd5t8proceedings05newjuoft.

"Mississippi Band of Choctaw Indians." https://www.choctaw.org/aboutMBCI
/history/index.html.

"Procter, Henry." *Dictionary of Canadian Biography.* http://www.biographi.ca/en
/bio/procter_henry_6E.html.

Randall, E. O. "Tecumseh, The Shawnee Chief." *Ohio Historical and Archaeological Publications,* 1906.

"Richardson, John (1796-1852)." *Dictionary of Canadian Biography.* http://www
.biographi.ca/en/bio/richardson_john_1796_1852_8E.html.

"The Ruddell Family." *The Virginia Genealogist* 27, no. 4. https://www.frontierfolk
.net/ramsha_research/ruddell.html.

Siebert, Frank T. "*Shawnese Traditions.* C. C. Trowbridge, Edited by Vernon Ki-
nietz and Erminie W. Voegelin." *American Anthropologist* 42, no. 1 (1940):
145-47. https://doi.org/10.1525/aa.1940.42.1.02a00160.

"St. Clair's Campaign of 1791: A Defeat in the Wilderness That Helped
Forge Today's U.S. Army." https://www.army.mil/article/65594/st_clairs_
campaign_of_1791_a_defeat_in_the_wilderness_that_helped_forge_todays_
us_army.

"Thayendanegea (Joseph Brant)." *Dictionary of Canadian Biography.* http://www.
biographi.ca/en/bio/thayendanegea_5E.html.

Voegelin, C. F., and E. W. Voegelin. "The Shawnee Female Deity in Historical Perspective." *American Anthropologist* 46, no. 3 (1944): 370-75. https://doi.org
/10.1525/aa.1944.46.3.02a00080.

BOOKS

Alford, Thomas Wildcat. *Civilization: And the Story of the Absentee Shawnees.* Norman: University of Oklahoma Press, 1936.

Barnhart, John D. *Valley of Democracy: The Frontier Versus the Plantation in the
Ohio Valley, 1775-1818.* Bloomington: Indiana University Press, 1953.

Beard, Reed. *The Battle of Tippecanoe: Historical Sketches of Famous Field Upon
Which William Henry Harrison Won Renown That Aided Him in Reaching the
Presidency.* Fourth Edition. Chicago: W. B. Conkey company, 1911.

Bird, Harrison. *War for the West 1790-1813.* New York: Oxford University Press,
1971.

Bond, Beverley W., Jr. *The Civilization of the Old Northwest: A Study of Political, Social, and Economic Development, 1788-1812.* New York: AMS Press, 1969. Reprinted from 1934 edition.

Booraem, Hendrick V. *A Child of the Revolution: William Henry Harrison and His World, 1773-1798.* Kent, Ohio: Kent State University Press, 2012.

Bottiger, Patrick. *The Borderland of Fear: Vincennes, Prophetstown, and the Invasion of the Miami Homeland.* Lincoln: University of Nebraska Press, 2016.

Brackenridge, Henry Marie. *History of the Late War, Between the United States and Great Britain: Containing a Minute Account of the Various Military and Naval Operations; Illustrated with Plates.* Baltimore: Cushing & Jewett, 1818.

Brock, Sir Isaac. *The Life and Correspondence of Major-General Sir Isaac Brock, K. B.* London: Simpkin, Marshall, 1845.

Brown, Dee. *Bury My Heart at Wounded Knee: An Indian History of the American West.* New York: Holt, Rinehart & Winston, 1970.

Burnet, Jacob. *Notes on the Early Settlement of the North-Western Territory.* New York: D. Appleton & Co., 1847. http://hdl.handle.net/2027/pst.000007073014.

Burr, S. J., and Samuel Jones Burr. *The Life and Times of William Henry Harrison.* Philadelphia: L. W. Ransom, 1840.

Calloway, Colin G. *The Indian World of George Washington.* New York: Oxford University Press, 2018.

———. *The Shawnees and the War for America.* New York: Penguin, 2007.

———. *The Victory with No Name: The Native American Defeat of the First American Army.* New York: Oxford University Press, 2015.

Campbell, William J. *Speculators in Empire: Iroquoia and the 1768 Treaty of Fort Stanwix.* Norman: University of Oklahoma Press, 2012.

Cayton, Andrew R.L. *Frontier Indiana.* Bloomington: Indiana University Press, 1996.

Cleaves, Freeman. *Old Tippecanoe: William Henry Harrison and His Time.* Newtown, Conn: American Political Biography Press, 2015. Originally published in 1939 by Charles Scribner's Sons.

Coffin, William F. *1812: The War and Its Moral: A Canadian Chronicle.* Montreal: John Lovell, 1864.

Collins, Gail. *William Henry Harrison.* The American Presidents Series. New York: Times Books, Henry Holt, 2012.

Cozzens, Peter. *Tecumseh and the Prophet: The Heroic Struggle for America's Heartland.* New York: Vintage, 2021.

Dawson, Moses H. *Historical Narrative of the Civil and Military Service of Major-General William H. Harrison.* Cincinnati: Self-published, 1824.

Dillon, John B. *History of Indiana, From the Earliest Exploration by Europeans to the Close of Territorial Government in 1816.* Indianapolis: Bingham and Doughty, 1859.

Drake, Benjamin. *Life of Tecumseh and His Brother the Prophet; with a Historical Sketch of the Shawanoe Indians.* Cincinnati: Anderson, Gates and Wright, 1841.

Drake, Daniel. *Natural and Statistical View; or Picture of Cincinnati and the Miami Country, Illustrated by Maps. With an Appendix, Containing Observations on the Late Earthquakes, the Aurora Borealis, and the South-West Wind.* Cincinnati: Looker and Wallace, 1815. http://hdl.handle.net/2027/loc.ark:/13960/t0zp4cq39.

Drake, Richard B. *A History of Appalachia.* Lexington: University Press of Kentucky, 2001, Paperback edition 2003.

Drake, Samuel Gardner. *The Book of the Indians of North America.* Boston: Antiquarian Bookstore, 1833. http://hdl.handle.net/2027/nyp.33433081681557.

Dubois, Ellen Carol, and Vicki L. Ruiz, eds. *Unequal Sisters.* New York: Routledge, 1990.

Eames-Sheavly, Marcia. *The Three Sisters: Exploring an Iroquois Garden.* Ithaca, N.Y.: Cornell Cooperative Extension, 1993.

Eckert, Allan W. *The Frontiersmen: A Narrative.* New York: Bantam Books, 1967. (Historical novel.) Follows the opening of the Old Northwest through re-created person of Simon Kenton. Highlights the great Indian leader Tecumseh, as well as William Henry Harrison.

Edmunds, R. David. *The Shawnee Prophet.* Lincoln: University of Nebraska Press, 1983.

———. *Tecumseh and the Quest for Indian Leadership.* New York: Longman, 1984.

Eggleston, Edward, and Elizabeth Eggleston Seelye. *Tecumseh and the Shawnee Prophet: Including Sketches of George Rogers Clark, Simon Kenton, William Henry Harrison, Cornstalk, Blackhoof, Bluejacket, the Shawnee Logan, and Others Famous in the Frontier Wars of Tecumseh's Time.* New York: Dodd, Mead & Co., 1878.

Fitzgerald, Michael Oren, ed. *The Essential Charles Eastman (Ohiyesa): Light on the Indian World.* Bloomington, Ind.: World Wisdom, 2007.

Frech, Harrison. *Anthony Shane: Metis Interpreter: A Bridge Between Two Cultures, Scout, Interpreter, Town Founder, Witness to History.* Self-published, 2003.

Freeman, Douglas Southall. *George Washington: A Biography.* 7 vols. New York: Scribner's, 1948.

Galloway, William Albert. *Old Chillicothe: Shawnee and Pioneer History, Conflicts and Romances in the Northwest Territory.* Xenia, Ohio: Buckeye Press, 1934.

Gilbert, Bil. *God Gave Us This Country: Tekamthi and the First American Civil War.* New York: Atheneum Books, 1989.

Goebel, Dorothy Burne. *William Henry Harrison: A Political Biography.* Indianapolis: Indiana Library and Historical Department, 1926. http://hdl.handle.net /2027/uva.x001039269.

Hall, James. *A Memoir of the Public Services of William Henry Harrison, of Ohio.* Philadelphia: Key & Biddle, 1836.

Hartley, Cecil B. *The Life and Times of Colonel Daniel Boone, Comprising History of the Early Settlement of Kentucky, to Which Is Added Colonel Boone's Autobiography, Complete.* New York: Derby and Jackson, 1860.

Harvey, Henry. *History of the Shawnee Indians, from the Year 1681 to 1854, Inclusive.* Cincinnati: Ephraim Morgan & Sons, 1855.

Hatch, William Stanley. *A Chapter of the History of the War of 1812 in the Northwest: Embracing the Surrender of the Northwestern Army and Fort, at Detroit, August 16, 1812: With a Description and Biographical Sketch of the Celebrated Indian Chief Tecumseh.* Miami Printing and Publishing Company, 1872.

Hawke, David Freeman, and Judith Hawke. *Everyday Life in Early America.* New York: Harper & Row, 1988.

Hinderaker, Eric. *Elusive Empires: Constructing Colonialism in the Ohio Valley, 1673-1800.* Cambridge, UK: Cambridge University Press, 1997.

Hook, Jason, with plates by Richard Hook. *American Indian Warrior Chiefs: Tecumseh, Crazy Horse, Chief Joseph, Geronimo.* London: Brockhampton Press, 1998. Originally published by Firebird Books, 1989.

Howard, James H. *Shawnee! The Ceremonialism of a Native American Tribe and Its Cultural Background.* Athens, Ohio: University of Ohio Press, 1981.

Howe, Henry. *Historical Collections of Ohio: Containing a Collection of the Most Interesting Facts, Traditions, Biographical Sketches, Anecdotes, Etc. Related to Its General and Local History with Descriptions of Its Counties, Principal Towns, and Villages.* Printed for the author, 1848.

James, William. *A Full and Correct Account of the Military Occurrences of the Late War Between Great Britain and the United States of America: With an Appendix, and Plates.* Printed for the author, 1818.

Jones, Rev. David. *A Journal of Two Visits Made to Some Nations of Indians on the West Side of the River Ohio, in the Years 1772 and 1773.* New York: J. Sabin, 1865. Reprint, Fairfield, Wash.: Ye Galleon Press, 1973.

Jortner, Adam. *The Gods of Prophetstown: The Battle of Tippecanoe and the Holy War for the American Frontier.* London: Oxford University Press, 2011.

Kinzie, Mrs. John H. "Wau-Bun: The Early Day in the Northwest." New York: Derby, 1856. http://www.gutenberg.org/cache/epub/12183/pg12183-images.html.

Lakomaki, Sami. *Gathering Together: The Shawnee People Through Diaspora and Nationhood, 1600-1870.* New Haven, Conn.: Yale University Press, 2014.

Law, John. *The Colonial History of Vincennes, Being an Address Delivered by Judge Law, Before the Vincennes Historical and Antiquarian Society, February 22d, 1839.* Vincennes, Ind., 1858. http://hdl.handle.net/2027/aeu.ark:/13960/t9d51787z.

Lossing, Benson J. *Pictorial Field-Book of the War of 1812.* New York: Harper & Brothers, 1868.

Macleod, William Christie. *The American Indian Frontier.* New York: Alfred A. Knopf, 1928.

McAfee, Robert Breckinridge. *History of the Late War in the Western Country.* Historical Publications Company, 1919.

McKenney, Thomas Loraine, James Hall, Hatherly B. Todd, and Joseph Z. Todd. *History of the Indian Tribes of North America : With Biographical Sketches and Anecdotes of the Principal Chiefs. Embellished with One Hundred Portraits from the Indian Gallery in the War Department at Washington.* Philadelphia: D. Rice, 1872. http://archive.org/details/historyofindiant01mckerich.

Moffat, Mary Maxwell. *Queen Louisa of Prussia.* New York: Dutton, 1907.

Morgan, Lewis H. *League of the Ho-De'-No-Sau-Nee or Iroquois.* New York: Dodd, Mead, 1904.

Ostler Jeffrey. *Surviving Genocide: Native Nations and the United States from the American Revolution to Bleeding Kansas.* New Haven, Conn.: Yale University Press, 2019.

Owens, Robert M. *Mr. Jefferson's Hammer: William Henry Harrison and the Origins of American Indian Policy.* Norman: University of Oklahoma Press, 2007.

Paxton, James. *Joseph Brant and His World: 18th Century Mohawk Warrior and Statesmen.* Toronto: James Lormier, 2008.

Shaffer, Lynda Norene. *Native Americans Before 1492: The Moundbuilding Centers of the Eastern Woodlands.* Armonk, N.Y.: M. E. Sharpe, 1992.

Silver, Peter Rhoads. *Our Savage Neighbors: How Indian War Transformed Early America.* New York: W. W. Norton, 2008.

Skaggs, David Curtis, and Larry L. Nelson, ed. *The Sixty Years' War for the Great Lakes, 1754-1814.* East Lansing: Michigan State University Press, 2001.

———. *William Henry Harrison and the Conquest of the Ohio Country: Frontier Fighting in the War of 1812.* Baltimore: Johns Hopkins University Press, 2014.

Sleeper-Smith, Susan. *Indigenous Prosperity and American Conquest: Indian Women of the Ohio River Valley, 1690-1792.* Omohundro Institute of Early American History, and University of North Carolina Press, n.d.

Stone, William L. *Life of Joseph Brant—Thayendanegea: Including the Border Wars of the American Revolution and Sketches of the Indian Campaigns of Generals Harmar, St. Clair, and Wayne, and Other Matters Connected with the Indian Relations of the United States and Great Britain, from the Peace of 1783 to the Indian Peace of 1795.* Cooperstown: H. & E. Phinney, 1845.

Sugden, John. *Tecumseh: A Life.* New York: Henry Holt, 1997.

Tanner, Helen Hornbeck. *Atlas of Great Lakes Indian History.* Vol. 174 of *Civilization of the American Indian.* Norman: University of Oklahoma Press, 1987.

Thompson, Christine K. *The Battle of the Wabash and the Battle of Fort Recovery: Mapping the Battlefield Landscape and Present Day Fort Recovery, Ohio.* Muncie, Ind.: Department of Anthropology, Ball State University, 2016. https://www.bsu.edu/-/media/www/departmentalcontent/aal/aalpdfs/abpp%20composite%20map%20document%20final.pdf?la=en.

Thomson, John Lewis. *Historical Sketches of the Late War, Between the United States and Great Britain.* Philadelphia: Thomas Desilver, 1817.

Todd, Colonel Charles S., and Benjamin Drake. *Sketches of the Civil and Military Service of William Henry Harrison.* Cincinnati: J. A. and U. P. James, 1847.

Tracy, Nicholas, ed. *The Naval Chronicle 1799-1804: The Contemporary Record of the Royal Navy at War.* London: Stackpole Books, 1998.

Treat, Payson Jackson. *The National Land System, 1785-1820.* New York: E. B. Treat, 1910. http://archive.org/details/nationallandsys00treagoog.

Victor, O. J. *The Life, Times and Services of Anthony Wayne.* New York: Beadle and Adams, 1861.

Wallace, Anthony F. C. *Jefferson and the Indians: The Tragic Fate of the First Americans.* Cambridge, Mass.: Belknap Press of Harvard University Press, 1999.

Warren, Stephen. *The Shawnees and Their Neighbors, 1795-1870.* Urbana: University of Illinois Press, 2005.

———. *The Worlds the Shawnees Made: Migration and Violence in Early America.* Chapel Hill: University of North Carolina Press, 2014.

Weeks, Stephen Beauregard. *Southern Quakers and Slavery: A Study in Institutional History.* Johns Hopkins Press, 1896.

Winkler, John F. *The Thames 1813: The War of 1812 on the Northwest Frontier.* Oxford: Osprey Publishing, 2016.

———. *Tippecanoe 1811: The Prophet's Battle.* Oxford: Osprey Publishing, 2015.

———. *Wabash 1791: St. Clair's Defeat.* Oxford: Osprey Publishing, 2011.

Winter, Nevin Otto. *A History of Northwest Ohio: A Narrative Account of Its Historical Progress and Development from the First European Exploration of the Maumee and Sandusky Valleys and the Adjacent Shores of Lake Erie, Down to*

the Present Time. Chicago: Lewis, 1917. http://archive.org/details/historyof
northwe00wintuoft.

Wrong, George McKinnon, and Hugh Hornby Langton. *Chronicles of Canada: Tecumseh, the Last Great Leader of His People.* Glasgow, 1915.

Young, Nancy Beck. "Anna Tuthill Symmes Harrison." In *American First Ladies: Their Lives and Their Legacy.* Second Edition. Edited by Lewis L. Gould. New York: Routledge, 2001.

INDEX

Page numbers of illustrations appear in italics.

Lalawethika (Tecumseh's brother), the
    Prophet, 40, 50, 76, 110, 327n40
appearance, 95
Battle of Tippecanoe, 182–92, 184n,
    342n189
British overtures and, 126
Changing Feathers and, 87
deterioration of, alcohol and, 76, 78
evening prayer ritual, 96–97
faith in his prophesies shattered, 204
Fort Wayne Treaty (1809) and, 140
Harrison and, 89, 97, 104–5,
    116–17, 124–25, 143–46, 170,
    335n116
Harrison plans to attack, 170, 173–74
on Jefferson, 119, 120
new name: Tenskwatawa "The
    Open Door," 87
Ohio governor's delegation, 110–12
opponents, 99, 119, 162
peace promised by, 113, 115
pilgrimages to, 99–100
preaches return to traditional ways,
    tribal unity, xvii, 88, 98, 100, 119,
    120
preaching and spread of message,
    95–100
predicts solar eclipse, 89–90
rejects "medicine bags," 88, 99
response to Little Turtle, 119–20
settlement at Tippecanoe
    (Prophetstown), 117–18, 120–24
settlement near Fort Greenfield,
    92–97, 110, 115, 116, 117
spiritual beliefs, syncretism, 98,
    333n98
stories of supernatural powers, 90
Tecumseh's anger after the Battle of
    Tippecanoe and, 204, 264
Tecumseh's role with, 101–2,
    113–14, 222
transformative experience of, 87, 95
tribes following, 245

tribes gathered at settlement, 110–12
tribes making pilgrimages to, 97–98
U.S. fears about, 100–101, 110, 111,
    124
visions of, 187
winter of 1812–13, 264

Lame Hand, chief, 225
Law, John, 150, 151, 152, 338–39n149
Law of Nations (Vattel), 81
Lear, Tobias, 14
Lee, Henry "Light Horse," 10
Leopold II of Austria, 17
Lewis, Meriwether, 80
Lewis and Clark Expedition, 4–5n,
    21n, 60n, 80
Little Bighorn, Battle of, 14
Little Turtle, Miami war chief, 11, 13,
    17, 20, 22, 101, 244
    advocates negotiation, 22
    alliance with Indian agent Wells, 119
    Battle of a Thousand Slain, 44, 111
    Battle of Fallen Timbers, 23
    death of, 251
    Fort Wayne Treaty and, 136, 138,
        139, 143
    as a "government chief," 118–19
    Greenville Treaty and speech, 26,
        27, 101
    opposes the Prophet, 119
    rejects Brant's line of settlement, 46
Louisa, Queen of Prussia, 106
Louis XVI of France, 17

Mackenzie, Alexander, 65
Mackinac Island, 205, 208–9, 210,
    229, 344n208
Madison, Dolley Todd, 130
Madison, James, 130–34
    appoints Harrison general, Kentucky
        militia, 253
    appoints Hull to lead U.S. Army of
        the Northwest, 213

ABOUT THE AUTHOR

PETER STARK is an adventure and exploration writer and historian. Born in Wisconsin, he studied English and anthropology at Dartmouth College and earned a master's degree in journalism from the University of Wisconsin. A longtime correspondent for *Outside* magazine, Stark has also been published in *Smithsonian*, *The New Yorker*, *The New York Times Magazine*, and *Men's Journal*. His book *Astoria* was a *New York Times* bestseller, received a PEN America Literary Award nomination, and was adapted into an epic two-part play. His book *Young Washington: How Wilderness and War Forged America's Founding Father* was a finalist for the George Washington Book Prize.